THE
CALIFORNIA
NATIVE
LANDSCAPE

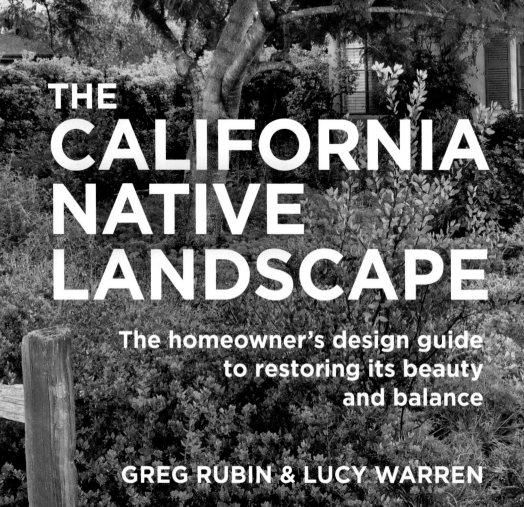

THE
CALIFORNIA
NATIVE
LANDSCAPE

The homeowner's design guide to restoring its beauty and balance

GREG RUBIN & LUCY WARREN

TIMBER PRESS
Portland, Oregon

Frontispiece: An inviting California native landscape opens a window onto nature.

Photographs by the authors, except frontispiece, and those on pages 8, 16, 28, 42, 58, 94, 112, 222, 262, 290, 308, 326, and 348 by Saxon Holt; 225, 238, 239 (both), 246 (top), and 256 (top) by Nicolas M. Reveles; 47 and 49 by Mycorrhizal Applications; 331 (bottom) and 338 by Richard W. Halsey; 214 (right) by Tracy Blake Murray; 324 by Gabi McLean; and 354 by Kristen M. D'Angelo.

Acrylic illustrations on pp. 96, 98, 100, 102, and 104 by Edmond Piffard.

Published in 2013 by Timber Press, Inc.

The Haseltine Building
133 S.W. Second Avenue, Suite 450
Portland, Oregon 97204-3527
timberpress.com

Book design by Susan Applegate
Printed in China
Third printing 2015

Library of Congress Cataloging-in-Publication Data

Rubin, Greg, horticulturalist.
    The California native landscape: the homeowner's design guide to restoring its beauty and balance/Greg Rubin and Lucy Warren.—1st ed.
        p. cm.
    Includes index.
    ISBN 978-1-60469-232-7
    1. Native plant gardening—California. 2. Landscape gardening—California. 3. Native plants for cultivation—California. 4. Plants, Ornamental—California. I. Warren, Lucy. II. Title.
    SB439.24.C2R83 2013
    712.09794dc23   2012025839

A catalog record for this book is also available from the British Library.

Acknowledgments

This book is the result of 26 years of passion. Along the way, many people have provided influence and support. William Entz, along with my brother Ed, encouraged me to landscape my parents' Chatsworth house in native plants, despite vehement protestations on my part. Their passionate advocacy changed my life forever. Thanks to my dear friend Valerie Phillips, a brilliant native plantsperson, for unwavering encouragement and dazzling ideas along the way.

Early influence came from the late Ray Walsh, who owned Wildwood Nursery in Upland, and left us much too early. Ray patiently let me hang out and ask questions all those years ago.

Thanks to friends and colleagues for their kindness and help along the way: Rick Halsey, Bart O'Brien, Mike Evans, the late Jeanine DeHart, the late Kevin Connelly, the late Ed Petersen, Kelly and Laura Tierney, Melanie Keeley, Jane Carpenter, Ed Piffard, Kim Kamrath, Hank and Su Kraus, Tracy Blake Murray, and all those at the Theodore Payne Foundation. My deepest appreciation for all of my employees at California's Own Native Landscape Design, including Leo Hernandez (my amazing foreman for 17 years). And thanks to Timber Press and Tom Fischer for giving us the opportunity to create this book, to Mike Dempsey for all of his help in making it happen, and Susan Applegate for her brilliant design.

To co-author Lucy Warren for her horticultural acumen and unwavering ability to take my mash of words and translate it into readable English full of flair and fun, all the while providing steadfast support and prodding when required (too frequently).

Special applause to my greatest mentor, Bert Wilson, owner of Las Pilitas Nursery. I met Bert in the early 90s and was captivated by his ecological approach to native landscaping, something glaringly absent from much contemporary thinking. Putting his observations to the test made me a true believer. I have built my career on these principles, which now infuse this text from cover to cover.

Lucy thanks her parents Raymond W. and Lucy G. Warren for early exposure to all things of nature, the opportunity to grow up in and appreciate the garden and the countryside with curiosity and wonder. She so appreciates the encouragement of the late garden writer Carol Greentree, who mentored her through a complete career change, urging her to follow her passion for plants and writing. To Vincent Lazaneo, UCCE Home Farm Advisor, who has always been generously available with answers from his encyclopedic knowledge and UC research. And thanks to Karen Stauffer, who patiently read several iterations of this book with a keen eye for errors. Putting this book together has been an amazing journey full of fantastic, quirky, dedicated, incredible writers, editors, and plant-crazed people such as the late Jeanine de Hart, Pat Hammer, Pat Welsh, Karen Wilson, and so many more, all of whom she holds dear.

Contents

INTRODUCTION
A new horticulture

Welcome to a new world of horticulture in California. This book will give you an in-depth look into the exciting world of successful landscaping with California native plants. It challenges conventional wisdom about California natives by dispelling myths with practical information and instruction for success. It focuses on the horticulture that works for native plants by tossing traditional gardening methods out the window. Here you will find useful advice, including many plant suggestions, on how to easily emulate natural ecology in the landscape, rather than trying to force native plants to survive in an alien environment. The design principles go beyond plant color and texture to illustrate how to create a fundamental structural framework for the landscape. Using appropriate techniques and principles as described, you will be able to create native gardens that are beautiful year-round with low mortality and easy maintenance.

Take a seat and relax as you begin your journey to your beautiful, easy-care, native landscape.

O UR EXPERIENCE and focus is in southern California, but the principles hold true throughout the state. If the practices we describe work well in *our* plant-stressing rainfall and climate conditions, they will only work better in the more forgiving climates of our northern counterparts. If the plant examples we cite are not appropriate for your area, you will find plants with similar characteristics that work. Think and buy local as much as you can—we would love to have native plant nurseries expand and thrive, giving us ever more wonderful selections.

Why use native plants?

People are often shocked to find that none of the plants in their landscape are native to California (not even the weeds). Furthermore, non-native plants also dominate much of the landscape they are accustomed to seeing beyond the cities. In the past it was difficult to find even a single California native plant in most nurseries—so many different plants from all over the world seem to thrive so easily in our mild climate (with artificial life support) that people ask, "What's the big deal? Why should I use natives?" Here are some things to consider.

Beauty and color

A well-designed native landscape looks attractive throughout the year. Hundreds of varieties of evergreen native plants with foliar contrast, color, and texture are available to provide backbone and year-round interest. Many of these species possess beautiful flowers and berries. Additionally, many native perennials are torches of color and bloom at different times of the year. Achieving year-round color in a native landscape is easy. Just ask the British. That's right, the British have been growing California natives for over 150 years. And no one would dispute that they know a thing or two about gardening.

Creating this strong, evergreen backbone is the key to minimizing native garden maintenance; 75 percent of the landscape should be made up of these plants. The perennial color spots, conversely, are positioned right out front where people can see them, with easy access for deadheading. The impression of masses of color belies the limited amount of input required. Mixing perennials with different bloom cycles promotes year-round color.

If you have come across landscapes of native plants that look dry and forlorn during the late summer and autumn months, it is a result of poor design or ignorance about the tremendous palette of available native plants.

Sense of place

Few know how California used to look; within historical memory, it was definitely a lot greener. John Muir spoke of being able to walk from the City of Los Angeles to the northwest San Fernando Valley without ever leaving the shade of an oak tree. California is the most ecologically diverse state in the continental United States. There is literally a plant for every situation imaginable. Why not celebrate this richness and embrace it as part of our true identity? We don't go to places like Big Sur, Yosemite, Big Bear, Death Valley, or Julian to see palms and red apple ice plant. As development pushes farther and farther out into what is left of our natural areas, the natural envelopes should be part of a seamless approach to integrating neighborhoods into the surrounding beauty, not creating tropical islands devoid of habitat value and local context.

Minimal maintenance expense

A landscape filled with native plants requires far fewer resources than non-native landscapes. There is no need for the weekly mow-and-blow crew, just a quarterly freshening up that you may want to do yourself. And you can forget about fertilizers, as these plants thrive in our lean native soils. You'll probably put most of your yard-maintenance power equipment on Craigslist.

Low water requirement

Most native landscape plants are quite drought and heat tolerant, especially those from the southern portion of the state. Water cost savings over a conventional landscape tend to be in the 60–90 percent range, and this still includes light levels of plant irrigation through the summer months for dusting off and fire resistance. A typical monthly summer water bill in San Diego for a large (1-acre) yard conventionally landscaped might run upward of $900 per month, whereas a client with a native landscape on the same size property might pay around $125. These kinds of water savings are significant and could potentially ameliorate critical water shortages without having to resort to more dams, reservoirs, and infrastructure.

Erosion control: Soil stabilization

The non-native grasses and weeds now covering most hillsides are terrible soil stabilizers. Many groundcovers from other areas of the world, such as ice plant, have shallow root systems that slough off entire embankments under heavy rain conditions. Seeding fast-growing, non-native weeds in the backcountry after fires, under the mistaken belief that non-native seeds will provide quick coverage and prevent erosion, has actually made erosion worse, especially after two or three years.

In contrast, native plant communities like chaparral are supported by a massive network of soil fungi, collectively termed *mycorrhizae*. This fungal network provides nutrition and moisture in an environment largely devoid of these elements. It forms a tremendous volume of interconnecting, stabilizing biomass in our soils, much like the glass filaments in fiberglass, cementing soil particles together while also allowing aeration and moisture infiltration. Stabilization is lost through ecosystem destruction and replacement with largely non-mycorrhizal plants like weeds, resulting, in part, in mudslides. Worldwide, as native forests are replaced with weeds and crops, thousands of people are buried alive when converted slopes fail. Few landslides occur in healthy native chaparral.

Fire safety

Despite conventional wisdom, a native planted next to a house will not somehow spontaneously combust and burn it down. In fact, the opposite might be true. Dozens of homes in the path of the great fires in San Diego did not burn, even though they were surrounded by native gardens. In many cases neighboring houses on both sides burned to the ground.

Most of these native landscapes returned to health in a few months, despite being singed, scorched, and appearing as if dead. The ability of these plants to achieve hydration on very low levels of moisture was critical to their resistance to fire. This does not guarantee that a home landscaped with natives will always survive a firestorm, but the results are encouraging.

Habitat preservation

Where have all the horned lizards gone? Many Californians remember playing with them as kids; they were all over the place. Now they are on the endangered species list. The reason? Horned lizards have a very specialized diet—they only eat harvester ants. These ants require dry conditions in order to survive. As lawns and tropical clichés have replaced our natural plant communities, conditions are too wet for the harvesters to survive. Lacking this important food source, the lizards are disappearing. Creating a native buffer between the house and wild lands increases available habitat. Just imagine the joy of seeing horned lizards in your yard again. As more and more enlightened homeowners provide habitat, it is beginning to happen.

Attracting wildlife

Nothing attracts native birds and butterflies like a native landscape—these are the plants that they evolved with. Your native yard will be an oasis for wildlife in a desert of exotics. Unneeded bird feeders may end up in the trash. A properly designed native landscape has the appropriate forage for native birds and butterflies (not the feral types often attracted to feeders). The mess of seeds and rodent problems will disappear. A toyon (*Heteromeles arbutifolia*) covered in brilliant red berries is California's most important food source for wintering birds. Better to spend your limited time and energy providing a moisture source for these creatures (e.g., a birdbath) that will definitely bring in wildlife. Select plants to provide year-round benefits. Fortunately, many of the most attractive plants do double duty as wildlife support.

A note on geographical boundaries

By conscious choice all the plants described in this book are found within the borders of the state of California, including the Channel Islands. Borders are a human political construct, so many of these species cross into Mexico and our surrounding states. Species are included that represent much of our ecologically diverse state with some emphasis on southern California. We have included some plants that are not utilized widely, but should be. The principles and techniques for installation, maintenance, and care apply throughout the region.

UNFORTUNATELY, no one has a living memory of the original beauty and diversity of the California landscape prior to European settlement, save for the occasional preserved remnant that the cows couldn't reach. Adding to the challenge, thousands of exotics have been introduced through agriculture and as ornamentals. Population pressure has only exacerbated the deterioration, adding to the disturbance and increased fire cycles that the native ecosystem has difficulty tolerating (but that the weeds love). As California loses its identity, it is becoming a dried-out, burnt-up hulk of its former self. The good news is that all is not lost—it can be brought back one habitat restoration, one landscape plant at a time. As that occurs we will undoubtedly discover many more plants with landscape potential and spur incredible regional native-plant nurseries to fill the demand.

Our work is ongoing; there is always more to learn. Many protocols in this book are working theories that have demonstrated repeatable results based on observation. Further research may modify them and will undoubtedly yield more discoveries.

Opuntia welcomes you to a new ecology.

THE CALIFORNIA ENVIRONMENT
A study in diversity

1

Any discussion of California's native plants must begin with a look at the state's physical environment. California's relative isolation, diversity, and complex geological history have encouraged the development of plants exclusively adapted to thrive in their habitats. In fact, the California Floristic Province is one of 25 designated "hot spots" in the world for both the rich endemic variety of plants and the extent to which they are endangered by human activity. Because of the state's unique environmental conditions, there are not just hundreds, but thousands of species that are native to California alone. In 2000, after years of detailed taxonomic research, 4426 native plant species were recorded, making California one of the richest areas of biodiversity on the planet.

The beauty of early California was often described as park-like with an abundance of wildflowers.

YET WHILE nature has spent millions of years providing a lush, varied, and exciting native plant palette, most landscapers and homeowners are unfamiliar with the potential of this rich resource, relying instead on plants that are familiar from their own childhood experiences or easily available from chain stores and nurseries. To understand the landscaping potential of these marvelous plants, it helps to know how they evolved and what factors contribute to their adaptation and diversity. Elements in this rich tapestry include geological history, weather, climate, and soil.

California is a land apart. Although it is firmly attached to the rest of the North American continent, its geography separates it from the rest of the country. Within a few hours anyone can drive the width of California and experience everything from sparkling coastal beaches and inspiring bluffs to breathtaking mountains and life-threatening deserts. Beneath the surface are rich mineral resources, such as the precious metals that lured the forty-niners. Above ground are thousands of fascinating plants adapted to their unique environments. Beaches host salt-tolerant plants; mesas burst forth in vernal pools; deserts support a flora that can survive blistering heat; and alpine meadows above the timber line erupt in summer wildflowers. The environment of one of the longest-lived plants, the alpine bristlecone pine (*Pinus longaeva*), is marked by brutal climactic conditions and barren soil.

Geological history

The complex geography that we see in California today is the result of eons of tectonic plate activity. About 165 million years ago, the Farallon Plate, adjacent to the North American Plate, began to slip under North America. Gradually, nearly all of this massive section of the earth's crust moved farther and farther eastward, pushing up the Rocky Mountains and other terrain, thereby creating the rough topography in the western third of the continent.

Adjacent to the Farallon Plate, the immense Pacific Plate pressed up against the western shore of the North American Plate. At the leading edge, successive waves of islands buckled up, forming in the sea and pushing eastward, smashing into the coast. These ripples in the earth's mantle became coastal ranges, with some remaining in the sea as our Channel Islands. Simultaneously, the Pacific Plate began slipping under the North American Plate, crushing and compressing the mass and thrusting it upward. Islands and debris rose above sea level, thereby extending the continent. For many thousands of years, the entire Central Valley of California remained under the sea. At the leading edge of this upheaval, the Sierra Nevada rose up as the newest mountains on the continent. The ocean floor was lifted high into the newly formed mountains. Tectonic pressure continued in a rippling effect, forming a nearly parallel series of coastal ranges and valleys.

The debris field of this clash of titans juxtaposed rock masses from completely diverse geologic origins. These masses became intermixed with molten rock. Thus California is uniquely composed of a complex geological milieu: sedimentary, metamorphic, and igneous rock, all layered and jumbled together.

While tectonic plates still struggle for supremacy—thrashing and pounding, erupting and cooling—shaping the continent from beneath and pushing it upward into hills, mesas, and mountains, erosive forces tear it all down and disburse the source material. Mountains forced upward over the eons are also constantly torn down by wind, water, weathering, glacial grinding, and decomposition. Water rains down gently in drops, gathering energy in flowing streams and rivers, sometimes forcefully in flash floods, ripping away at the rock and soil, then dropping silt when the land levels and the flowing water slows.

Climate history

Weather and climate change have also had a profound effect on the development of California flora. California began as a warm, humid, tropical paradise, lush with primitive plants such as ferns and other primitive plant forms. Around 60 million years ago temperatures began to cool. Over the next 20 million years, tropical plants gave way to temperate forests full of conifers and broadleaf trees, particularly throughout the northern areas. Many of these trees are those that blanketed the northern realms of the rest of the continent, such as alder, ash, beech, maple, and oak. As the climate cooled, tropical and semitropical plants had to adapt or perish. Some found sheltered nooks, some retreated to warmer areas, while others mutated into forms that could survive the environmental change. Many disappeared completely.

California's Ice Age—which was actually a succession of alternating heating and cooling periods—did not cover the entire state, but mountain-valley glaciers left U-shaped valleys, horn-shaped peaks, saw-toothed ridges, and eroded basins in the alpine regions. At their extreme, the glaciers extended to the peaks of the San Bernardino Mountains. Glaciers from the Ice Age persisted until about 10,000 to 12,000 years ago when temperatures again warmed, melting the final remains. Mammoth ice floes slowly broke off vast quantities of rock and gravel, some of which

The rare Torrey pine (*Pinus torreyana*) in nature.

was carried away by melting streams; more was left in moraines as the ice melted and retreated. A familiar example of the effects of glacial erosion and deposit is the magnificent Yosemite Valley.

The next major change, which began 4 million years ago, initiated a different wave of plant development. As the California climate warmed, cold-hardy plants retreated northward or to higher altitudes. (Temperatures fall about 3 degrees for every 1000-foot rise in elevation.) Because the higher-elevation tops of hills and mountains are separated like islands, the plants there developed unique adaptations to their own isolated communities.

Amid these major temperature swings there have been many shorter cycles of heating and cooling, with more and less precipitation, which also have affected the development of the plant community. Each of these periods encouraged some species and limited others.

From about 8000 to 5000 years ago the temperature heated up even more, hotter than our current temperatures, and desert plants populated much of California. Many of the desert-adapted or xerophytic plants migrated northward to the United States from the Sonoran Desert. The cool-weather plants climbed even higher into the hills and mountains.

Since then the weather pattern has been persistently warm and dry, though not to such an extreme. Coastal areas are moistened by fog from the cool ocean currents, but inland areas receive only limited, seasonal precipitation. Now fully developed, the mountain peaks capture the higher clouds and receive the most rain, creating dry areas or rain shadows on the leeward side.

These climate changes have required an entirely different adaptation from the plant community. Now plants had to survive with both less water and less dependable water.

California's Mediterranean climate

Today, much of California has a Mediterranean climate, characterized by cool wet winters and warm to hot, dry summers. Temperatures are influenced by cold ocean currents and remain moderate despite seasonal variation. Large subtropical high-pressure areas, influenced by inland deserts, suppress summer cloud development and precipitation. During the winter, when the temperature of the land mass cools, the high-pressure system weakens, allowing the moist ocean air to bring rain to the region.

Only five regions in the world share this climate: California, the Mediterranean basin, western Chile, the South African Cape region, and southwestern Australia. These exceptional and limited climate areas share similar geography and occur at approximately 30 to 40 degrees latitude north and south.

They also share similar types and forms of vegetation specifically adapted to the precipitation pattern. Every Mediterranean climate includes plant communities comprising coastal scrub, chaparral, foothill woodland, and montane evergreen forest. Plants are most lush and green from winter to early summer and then slow their growth to conserve water through the hot, dry season. Regular, deep irrigation of these plants during the summer can actually reduce their lifespan. Southern California is the most dramatic of the world's Mediterranean climate zones; it receives less water and has more extreme temperatures, particularly inland,

Ferns such as California polypody, *Polypodium californica*, were some of the earliest plant forms.

where ocean currents do not afford their cooling temperature and coastal moisture.

In California, the Pacific Ocean's Alaska Current cools the coastal region to an even lower temperature, varying only modestly from day to night or summer to winter. Early summer fog banks moderate the temperature and reduce the available sunlight along the coastline. Farther inland, the maritime influence diminishes and the temperature range expands both daily and seasonally.

Other essential environmental conditions also vary throughout the state. Northern California receives more rainfall. Average rainfall in Crescent City is 72 inches a year, San Francisco receives 25 inches, and San Diego averages only 10 inches a year. Although California has a lengthy coastline and is relatively narrow, the mean elevation is roughly half a mile (2887 feet). The land rises quickly from the coast and undulates upward through coastal mountain ranges as high as the top of Mount Whitney at 14,505 feet and descends through vast valleys as low as Death Valley, 282 feet below sea leavel. These vast differences in elevation greatly affect local plant populations throughout the state.

Plant climate and hardiness zones

Most gardeners and landscapers in the United States rely on the United States Department of Agriculture (USDA) climate zones to determine what to plant in their area. This system of categorizing areas by the minimum winter temperature in 10-degree increments provides a useful index for plant hardiness—that is, the ability of the plant to withstand frost and low temperatures. Thousands of plants in the landscaping trade have been tested and designated for cold hardiness. It is the most used method for plant selection for a region. Continental United States includes 11 temperature zones measured from coldest, lowest temperature (Zone 1) to completely frost-free tropical zones (Zones 10 and 11). Residents throughout the country can review a map of the United States and quickly determine their general climate zone. An updated version of the map was released in January 2012 reflecting data collected from 1975 to 2005.

While much of the country can rely on the USDA map, this becomes much more difficult in California's complex environment. As an example, for anyone who has taken a ride on the aerial tramway from the desert floor of Palm Springs up to the top of San Jacinto Peak, the course of that ride alone passes through 8 of the 11 major hardiness zones. As you ascend it is easy to see different plants living at various altitudes. Climate zone maps are far too general to account for this degree of local variability.

Realizing that gardening practices on the West Coast required different resources, in 1939 Sunset Publishing produced their first gardening manual (originally titled *Sunset's Complete Gardening Book*) directed specifically to western gardeners. Subsequently the same organization developed a more elaborate and specific set of climate zones for the West, based on the following variables:

LATITUDE Recognizes the differences in day length by distance from the equator and poles

ELEVATION Temperature decreases with altitude thus intensifying length of winter and cold temperatures; at higher altitudes night temperatures are generally cooler year-round

MARITIME INFLUENCE Pacific Ocean's Alaska Current moderates coastal temperatures year-round with winter seasonal precipitation and coastal fog

CONTINENTAL AIR INFLUENCE Seasonal heating and cooling of the North American continent creates greater temperature ranges; this influence increases at greater distances from the coast; persistent wind also affects open interior climates

MOUNTAINS AND VALLEYS Increase or reduce maritime or coastal air influence by holding or blocking the air flow

GROWING SEASON Average number of days between the last frost in spring and the first frost in fall

MICROCLIMATES The influence of the local terrain on the general climate zone: cooler north-facing slopes, warmer south facing slopes, thermal belts, cold air basins due to warm air rising while cold air sinks; each garden has its own internal micro habitats—as for example, plants grown on the north side of the home have more shade and cooler temperatures than those grown to the south or west

For traditional horticulturists the current edition of the *Sunset Western Garden Book* is a great tool, and includes many of the more common California native plants (for example, it describes more than 30 manzanitas). Yet even this region-specific resource with its more comprehensive analysis fails to come close to explaining the breadth and diversity of habitats of California native plants.

Seaside daisy (*Erigeron glaucus*) and dudleya hanging out on a cliff together. Who said California natives were difficult to grow?

Soil

Landscapers and gardeners typically classify soil type by the size of the soil particles, with the smallest comprising clay; the middle-size, loam or silt; and the largest, sand. Savvier horticulturists have their soil tested before investing in permanent landscaping, for there is a great deal more to soil than just the size of the particles.

Soil, by definition, is a mixture of ground-up rocks and organic matter. The ground-up rocks provide the principal mineral content and micronutrients that plants use to grow. The rock may be microscopically fine or in large granules, like sand. The rock components of California soils come from multiple sources and exist in many forms. California has a greater number of minerals and a wider variety of rock types than any other state. Road cuts reveal layers from up to three different tectonic plates, complex mineralogical materials from lava flows, stable compressed metamorphic layers, glacial moraine, sediment from lifted ancient sea beds, and silt carried along and deposited by streams and rivers. These materials have been weathered, heated, cooled, squeezed, buried, smashed, ground, erupted, torn, drowned, and lifted over the eons.

The United States Department of Agriculture has worked for decades defining and mapping over 20,000 soil-series descriptions by location. Begun as a national project nearly half a century ago and now almost finished, the resulting data is available online (websoilsurvey.nrcs.usda.gov). From coastal sand to cooled magma, there are over 2000 soil descriptions in California, more than any other single state.

One rare soil type that has affected plant adaptation is commonly known as serpentine. In 1965, serpentine became the official California state stone. This shiny, blue-green igneous stone from early lava flows has outcroppings covering more than 1100 acres through the middle to northern portions of California. Although varied in specific mineral content, serpentine soils are generally low in the normal essential nutrients for plant growth; high in magnesium, iron, and toxic, heavy metals nickel and chromium; and low in nitrogen. This combination is toxic to most plants. Nevertheless, some plants have adapted specifically to grow in this soil base and quickly decline if transplanted into what are considered more plant-friendly soils. A number of serpentine endemic plant groups have become rare and endangered as human populations and alien species overrun their habitat.

The beauty of California's natural landscapes is in this incredible complexity, and in the way native plants are so finely adapted to their environments. By utilizing the amazing and beautiful array of California native plants, gardeners can reduce their costs in precious water, materials, time, and energy. The benefits reach far beyond just the plants in attracting native birds and protecting endangered species in the environment where they developed and in connecting people to a truly beautiful and inspiring region.

Field of native California wildflowers recreated by Greg Rubin.

HUMAN IMPACT ON THE LANDSCAPE
Deterioration of the California environment

2

Imagine, for a moment, the California encountered by the first peoples to arrive in western North America, 12,000 to 15,000 years ago or perhaps earlier. Most hills were covered in a velvet tapestry of textural greens that appeared almost smooth from a distance. This mantle was broken only by billowy fingers of taller trees winding up every draw and ravine. The valley bottoms were covered in oak woodland. Streams running through these valleys found their terminus in marshy wetlands as they exited to the sea.

A glimpse of true native gold in a wetlands meadow full of Bigelow's sneezeweed (*Helenium bigelovii*) in El Dorado National Forest.

EXPANSIVE sandy beaches followed the coastline, the deposition of sand uncompromised by dams. Salmon made their way upstream all along the length of California in these same unobstructed waterways. The spouts of migrating gray and blue whales were visible from shore, as well as pods of dolphins dancing in the waves. During migrations, great clouds of birds darkened the sky.

A dense blanket of chaparral—the predominant plant community in the state—blocked most passage inland. Access through this elfin forest was typically limited to animal trails later widened to paths by indigenous people. Occasional meadows of native grasses, sedges, and forbs (nongrass herbaceous plants, including wildflowers) broke the low forest.

There were no weeds. No mustard, fennel, filaree, dandelion, or non-native grasses. Long after their initial encounter with this Eden, the Indians described being able to walk barefoot for hundreds of miles. Between shrubs, clean soil was covered in well-consolidated duff and/or crypto-gamic crust—a fragile layer of lichen, mosses, algae, and bacteria forming a protective layer over bare soil and intimately tied into the biology of the plant community.

Further inland, the magnificent California grizzly bear foraged, leaving huge prints like pock marks in the landscape. This largest of all grizzlies was an omnivore. Its diet included berries, large herbivores, and occasional beasts of prey, at times a human or two. Its habitat was strictly the chaparral. California's abundant wilds easily supported these grand animals.

The California condor soared over the foothills, another creature of the chaparral nearly lost. The remaining few pairs were all captured in 1987 to be bred and reintroduced in the wild in 1992. The wild population of condors at the time of this writing is approximately 127, but the grizzly is lost forever.

Chaparral merged seamlessly with oak woodland. Beneath the majestic, old-growth oaks was a fairy woodland of delicate, shade-loving companions including meadow rue, ferns, currants, redberries, monkey flowers, and canyon sunflower.

The low valleys captured moisture from runoff, forming hundreds of acres of ecologically rich and fertile wetlands and marshes along the coast and through vast Central Valley areas. Seaside and bayside marshes hosted plants and animals adapted to the brackish interface. Migratory birds by the hundreds of thousands came to rest and feed in the wetlands.

Higher elevations saw chaparral converging with pine forest. Rich green stands of mixed conifers abounded, unravaged by the scourges of invasive bark beetles and air pollution. Beneath the trees was a rich under-story of snowberry, gooseberry, currants, strawberry, ferns, false indigo, and other shade-loving plants.

Montane chaparral turned abruptly into desert further inland. The dividing line was distinct (no oaks grow with Joshua trees and vice versa). The ecologies were and are starkly different. California's Mediterranean zones receive nearly all of their moisture in winter with dry summers. However, California deserts receive as much of their limited precipitation in the summer as they do in winter due to thunderstorm activity. Desert plants are more widely spaced and less thickly foliated, forming little organic mulch. Instead, desert mulches are primarily inorganic rock or

Cryptogamic crust is composed of lichen, mosses, algae. This fragile crust takes years to develop and can be destroyed with a single footstep.

sand, protecting the roots of the plants. Prior to large-scale human disturbance, deserts were clean and could have been navigated in bare feet, as
long as you were careful to avoid spines. Each plant claimed its perimeter
according to its water needs, and after wet winters the desert floor came
alive with wildflowers.

Wild lilac and Torrey pine, Torrey Pines State Reserve.

Native American influence

With no written record, theories abound on the early migration and habitation of North America. It is generally accepted that the earliest settlements occurred 12,000 to 15,000 years ago. Successive waves of peoples found their homeland in California throughout the entire diversity of the region from coastal beaches, to mountains, valleys, forests, and deserts. These peoples brought only what they could carry and introduced no alien species of flora or fauna. Estimates of early Indian populations in California vary greatly, but we know that, prior to the arrival of the Europeans, it was, north of Mexico, the most highly populated area of North America. Native tribes inhabited not only our current urban sites, but also areas generally considered wilderness to us and uninhabited today. Estimated figures range from 300,000 to possibly 325,000 Indians throughout the state. Unlike southern populations such as the Aztecs, Mayans, or Incans, they did not form cities or a dominating central society, nor did they develop a written language. Communities typically were small villages and groups of villages comprising from 100 to 400 people, with the location and size of groups determined by availability of food and water.

Prior to European contact, the human impact on the California landscape was minimal and localized. In coastal areas there is evidence that limited areas around settlements were burned to clear and open up the dense, impenetrable chaparral; the mineral-rich ash from these fires promoted new plant growth. Occasional burning, once every 10 to 20 years, was sufficient to keep the meadows cleared of encroaching shrub. The cleared areas encouraged establishment of diverse native grasses and forbs providing broad-based and nutritious food sources, including as many as 100 to 200 plant species. Open meadows attracted grazing animals such as deer, antelope, bison, elk, rabbits, quail, and seed-eating birds. Abundant natural food sources obviated the need to practice agriculture on a large scale or to centralize and transport foodstuffs.

Alterations to the natural order included planting trees and shrubs useful as food sources, medicine, or materials. Abundance of these plants at a site is often evidence of an earlier community. The area now called

California had attained a balance of humans and nature; the Indians lived well and carefully tended their resources.

The arrival of Europeans

The West Coast of the United States came late in the timeline of European colonization and settlement. California was the farthest away and least accessible region by land or by sea. The Jesuit fathers had their hands full in Mexico, the Southwest, and Baja California. There was not enough interest or resources to colonize the northern portion of the region, Alta California, especially when early reports did not promise immediate financial gain.

European exploration of California began a half-century after Columbus discovered America, with Juan Rodriguez Cabrillo. On 28 September 1542, his flotilla of ships encountered "a closed and very good port," which they called San Miguel, later renamed San Diego Bay. The expedition continued northward as far as the Russian River for nearly a year. Cabrillo

Mission-style cactus fence.

died before the party returned. Although viewed as somewhat unsuccessful at the time, the expedition proved the feasibility and viability of exploitation. The process of discovery and change had begun.

Over two centuries later, little was known of the interior of Alta California beyond sailors' mentions of snowcapped mountains visible from the shore and general descriptions of the coastline. On 15 February 1769, the first inland expedition—including Don Gaspar de Portola, governor of Baja California, his soldiers, Father Junipero Serra, and other friars—set out northward to explore possible sites for a series of missions to secure dominion under Spanish authority. The ultimate journey covered over 2000 miles.

The vivid and detailed written account of the journey by Father Juan Crespi became the original first-hand description of Alta California. Father Crespi was an expert observer and amateur botanist, relating plant names from his own experience.

The Spanish Mission Era

The Mission Era took root with outposts at San Diego and San Luis Rey, then quickly jumped up the coast to Monterey Bay and filled in with missions approximately a day's journey apart up the coast. Initially, these primitive outposts were small and had limited supplies, surviving on the local resources with occasional contact from supply ships. Too arrogant and ignorant to learn from the local populace, the fathers of the church relied on familiar plants, animals, and agricultural practices imported from Europe. And, in the beginning, the land was able to accommodate newly introduced practices.

Limited water supplies forced the padres to practice hydrozoning, grouping plants with similar water needs together. Vegetables and flowers were grown together in limited plots near the settlement with compost from domestic animals. Trees had to survive on their own, and until well into the 20th century, dry farming of fruit trees was a very successful practice in many parts of the state. Franciscans introduced food, decorative, and medicinal plants from Spain grown close to and within mission complexes.

Most devastating to the California landscape were the weeds accompanying the colonists. Silently and insidiously, seeds clung to priests' robes and were held in the coats and forage of domesticated livestock. European weeds also arrived in the holds of ships, escaping in ballast offloaded to allow ships' entry into shallower draft harbors. These plants had no natural enemies in the new continent to contain or suppress their expansion as they overran and displaced the native plants that had evolved for eons in a natural balance appropriate for the delicate ecosystem.

Domesticated animals—cattle, horses, mules, swine, and sheep—previously unknown in California, soon required altering the native landscape to provide pasturage, which overwhelmed native grasses and sedges. Fairly quickly, cattle became a primary source of income for the missions, principally for tallow and hides. Eventually, as many as 11,000 head of cattle grazed on the western side of the San Francisco peninsula—a very profitable venture for the padres and a devastation to the native ecology. The colonists were soon confronted by a lack of pasture for their grazing animals, so they turned to a centuries-old European technique, slash and burn. This technique successfully converted Europe to agriculture long before, explaining why so much of the land in Spain, Italy, and other Mediterranean countries is now covered in annual grasses.

Since it is far more economical to burn than to hand-clear large acreage, settlers lit fires and let them burn themselves out, sometimes a million acres or more at a time. Overgrazing the new growth quickly robbed the vigor of perennial native grasses and thwarted reestablishment of native chaparral.

European forage crop seed was spread by the animals themselves in open grazing, either in their fur or in their manure. It has been estimated that the process of transformation from native ecology to European-like pastures was largely completed within 75 years of initial colonization. The process has been documented in samples of historic adobe bricks from different periods. Even as late as the 1930s, naturalist Lester Rowntree observed the reduction of native wildflowers year after year due to loose and forgiving grazing policies, as livestock were permitted to graze California's backcountry throughout public lands.

The list that follows summarizes the European colonization and subsequent impact of the California landscape.

Historic events affecting the development of California from wilderness to urban sprawl

15,000 TO 12,000 YEARS AGO "NATIVE" AMERICANS
Minimal impact on landscape, local land management practices. Most populated area of North America and northern Mexico.

1542 JUAN RODRIGUEZ CABRILLO Sailed coast to Mendocino

1579 SIR FRANCES DRAKE Sailed coast, repaired boats in San Diego harbor.

1602–03 SEBASTIAN VIZCAINO Sailed coast from Baja looking for pearls, developed first map of coastline.

1768 RUSSIANS Invaded northwest coast. European interest in California increases.

1769 PORTOLA EXPEDITION First land expedition of California, covering 2000 miles. A recorded journey of flora and fauna including earthquakes.

1769–1821 MISSION ERA Local settlements to establish missions. Introduced plants: food, medicinal, floral. Grew crops. Introduced cattle in limited open range. Dispersed limited land grants. Conscripted native Americans. Introduced weeds. Began repurposing the land. Native American population declined.

1775–76 DE ANZA EXPEDITION Brought 200 cattle overland. Increased herds promoted slash-and-burn techniques to clear land for grazing and growing hay.

1796 TRADERS AND TRAPPERS First captured sea otters, profited from natural resources.

1796 MEXICAN INDEPENDENCE WON

1821–47 MEXICAN RULE Mexican government took over missions and distributed over 500 land grants. Explosion of cattle range for hides and tallow.

1826   **JEDEDIAH STRONG SMITH "PATHFINDER"** Led first
        overland settlers opening the path to general settlement.

1846   **MEXICAN–AMERICAN WAR**

1848   **CALIFORNIA CEDED TO THE UNITED STATES OF
        AMERICA** Mexican land claims disputed, creating a free-for-all
        land grab. Land opened to agriculture, forestry, mining, ranching,
        and development.

1849   **GOLD DISCOVERED AT SUTTERS MILL** Gold rush
        devastated the backcountry of California. The destruction of the
        landscape is still evident. Population soared, Native American
        population declined further.

1850   **FEDERAL GOVERNMENT GIVES CALIFORNIA LAND**
        Eight million acres given to the state of California.

1869   **TRANSCONTINENTAL RAILROAD** Completion led to easy
        transportation for new citizens to move to the state. Railroads,
        grabbing 11 percent of California land, opened and controlled
        agriculture in the Central Valley.

1869+   **URBAN HORTICULTURE** Trial and introduction of thousands
        of non-native plants for commercial and residential landscaping.

1950+   **INTERSTATE HIGHWAY SYSTEM** Post–World War II
        population explosion. With readily available transportation,
        suburbia takes over ever-increasing huge tracts for development.

Recent history

In the 1950s, the interstate highway system opened vast areas of land for
private development. Since World War II California has seen a population explosion with all the attendant alternative land uses in urbanization, freeways, shopping centers, corporate facilities, and housing developments. As an example, San Diego alone currently includes 144 square
miles of impermeable hardscape, including the footprints of buildings,
sidewalks, roads, and parking lots.

Ornamental landscaping took precedence over native landscaping.

Many marvelous plants from all over the world will grow in one or more of California's climate zones. Palm trees, bright geraniums, exotic orchids, temperate fruit trees, citrus, European vegetables—the list includes thousands of plants. Home gardeners and commercial landscapers face a cornucopia of plants available and capable of thriving. Many of these plants, particularly from exotic or temperate zones, require copious amounts of water; others have escaped gardens only to displace California natives. Most of all, urban and suburban households, educational facilities, corporate parks, recreational facilities, and shopping centers alike worship the green lawn—the anathema of sustainability and conservation of resources in the California landscape. This monotypic, thirsty, resource-intensive culture has overtaken millions of acres in California.

The common, seemingly mandatory, lawn for every home, park, and corporate campus is the least sustainable horticultural ravage in our region. It is a relatively recent feature, representing the furthest possible deviation from California ecology.

Iconic California landscape denuded by cattle.

With the advent of the first lawn mowing equipment in the 1830s and the proliferation of suburban housing with private yards, lawns became a popular status symbol in the United States in the late 19th century. However, they only became common in California when sprinkler technology was developed for irrigation in the 20th century. By the 1960s, virtually every home with a yard was surrounded by its own thirsty green sponge.

Increased development and decreased water supply are now calling this paradigm into question. Landscape irrigation is one of the greatest uses of water in the state. A lawn consumes about 30 gallons of water per square foot annually. Compare this to the 3 to 5 gallons per square foot needed annually for a drought-tolerant native landscape. People are beginning to recognize that maintaining our communities as moist pastureland is not sustainable. Rather, we are coming full circle and looking at what nature had to offer all along.

Where do we go from here?

In the process of growth, urbanization, and suburbanization, native plants, unfamiliar to those who immigrated to the state, languished or were destroyed. Even with their own special beauty, they remained unconsidered and unappreciated in the typical California landscape. After all, they represented wilderness, not the brilliance of plants hybridized and tamed by centuries of cultivation in temperate, rain-filled climates. The native plants' careful utilization of resources for survival in the natural ecosystem and weather patterns has been largely ignored.

Immense quantities of water are necessary to support agriculture and urban development, particularly in the southern portion of the state. Dams and canals capture the water from northern California mountain snowmelt and transport it to the fertile valleys and populous cities at great expense, utilizing enormous amounts of energy. According to the Natural Resources Defense Council, in 2004 the amount of energy used to deliver water to residential customers in southern California was equivalent to approximately a third of the total average household electric use in the region.

And this all worked—for a while.

Global warming and the realization that we have reached the limits of our natural resources are wake-up calls. They afford us an opportunity to work with what nature has given, to create beautiful landscapes based on a more realistic and healthful protocol. Instead of streets where house after house is fronted by swaths of emerald-green lawns needing to be mowed, fertilized, plugged, doused with insecticides, and watered to a fare-thee-well several times a week, imagine a much more interesting future neighborhood, one where beautiful native oak, sycamore, and ash trees provide shade and strong branches from which to hang a swing. Under those trees, native shrubs provide textural color and seasonal bloom. Some even offer edible fruits. There are rocks for kids to climb on and places for them to play hide-and-seek. The leaves drop in place to enhance the soil—soil rich with microbial life constantly breaking down organic matter to sustain new life. Seasonal wildflowers splash the neighborhood in spring—flowers that children can pick and give to family and friends. In the dry season, California's summer puts sensible plants into dormancy, and evergreen shrubs are placeholders; the scents of herbal oils from the leaves enhance the air, and the hydrated, summer-spritzed natives protect homes from wildfire damage.

Millions of gallons of water once used to maintain front-yard urban marshes—also known as lawns—are diverted to quench the thirst and maintain the health of the large population. The millions of gallons of gasoline formerly burned to mow the lawns and blow the trimmings are powering fuel-efficient vehicles. The thousands of pounds of fertilizers and insecticides no longer run down the sewers to poison sea life.

California landscapes reflect the native abundance and beauty. The plants are selected with foresight and purpose. This is a vision worth striving for.

SOIL
The world down under

3

Landscaping with California native plants differs from typical ornamental horticulture. Nonetheless, people approach all landscaping with the same broad brush. The dictates of general horticulture are held up as incontrovertible truths. If you want beautiful plants these are the rules: Till the soil; add amendments to enrich the earth—the richer the better; water plants regularly, making certain they never dry out; fertilize plants on a regular basis; if a plant is suffering or wilting, add water; when in doubt, add more fertilizer and water. All these practices affect the medium in which plants grow—the organic and inorganic components of the soil—in dramatic and unnatural ways.

Allowing leaves to mulch the soil encourages essential soil microorganisms.

Sustainable practice

Think about California native ecology. Where in the state do these enhanced conditions of disturbance, fertility, and moisture naturally occur? The chaparral? Coastal sage scrub? Obviously not. So why try to grow native plants with an alien protocol? Upland, drought-tolerant habitats are stable and undisturbed with low water and low fertility. The only California habitats analogous to traditional ornamental horticultural dictates are wet meadows, marshes, and streamside woodlands. Even those have no paradigm equivalent to annual hoeing or tilling.

The origin and wisdom of standard gardening rules and practices came from Old World agriculture. Many ancestors of our most popular garden vegetables and flowers originated in temperate European wetlands. When brought into cultivation, these plants benefited from supplemental nutrition and water. Isolated from competitors and selected for admirable characteristics, these flowers and vegetables thrived in tended gardens, growing larger, sweeter, and more attractive over the centuries. These same plants accompanied the first European explorers. In water-scarce California, the plants required copious amounts of supplemental water and fertility to survive. Some didn't survive at all. By trial and error, a culture of artificial life support became the cornerstone of ornamental horticulture in the region. The increased availability of a reliable source of water from the California aqueducts and development of modern irrigation systems seemed to support everything. Now, it is becoming abundantly clear that we have been living in an era of dreams. Our resources are not unlimited—particularly water, the life-sustaining fluid.

Shifting to a water-thrifty lifestyle comes with the need for a better understanding of all the components of our native ecology and how they work together. One of the most important and least understood factors is soil.

Partners in the soil

There is far more growing within the soil than all the plants and animals that could ever grow above it. Certainly, roots are a part of that. Lesser known is the amazing array of partners that support our native ecology and enable our plants to survive in the harshest of conditions. Fungi, bacteria, lichens, mosses, and many other actors combine in a complex web of life that thrives in some of the driest and most infertile conditions on earth. It is ironic that the very practices we have been taught to support and enhance plant life are exactly the actions that will doom natives in this ecology.

Synergistic bio-relationship

The term *mycorrhizae* is derived from "mykes," which is Greek for fungus, and "rhizae," meaning roots. The fungus connects to the root system of the plant, multiplying the effective capacity of the root mass many times. Branched tubular filaments, known as hyphae, have much finer diameters than the roots themselves, and are able to extend into the smallest spaces between soil particles. By utilizing the fungi to exploit a greater volume of soil, the plants are able to function with real root systems that appear impossibly small relative to their ability to tolerate environmental stress. Neither plant nor animal, fungi are in their own biological kingdom, one that surpasses the others in numbers, yet is the least understood or explored.

More than 90 percent of the world's plants are mycorrhizal to one degree or another. The symbiotic, mutually beneficial relationship between the soil fungi and roots has existed for hundreds of millions of years, and may have enabled aquatic plants to become terrestrial. Minutely detailed, 400 million–year-old sedimentary fossils from Scotland clearly show mycorrhizal fungi connected to rootless terrestrial plants, providing them with nutrients from inorganic "soil" of the time. Non-mycorrhizal plants, like mustard, are relatively recent biological developments.

In California plants, this ancient, codependent relationship evolved, enabling plants to obtain nutrients from inorganic soil and optimizing moisture storage in the fungal biomass. The fungi also protect plants from soil pathogens and heavy metals. In return, the fungi are fed 20 percent of the carbohydrates produced by the plants.

The rhizosphere

Different types of soil bacteria are also part of this complex equation. The rhizosphere is the zone where the fungi, bacteria, and roots meet. It is an amazing web of interconnected partners. In this zone, growth inhibitors that hinder the development of *all* plant roots are produced, favoring mycorrhizal plants supported by the fungal network. This is how native plants outcompete and exclude non-mycorrhizal weeds, or ruderals. Mycorrhizae in the rhizosphere secrete plant hormones (auxins) that stimulate plant growth into their hosts' roots. The mycorrhizae send a biochemical signal announcing to the plant that they are attached and it is okay to grow. The plant roots in turn emit a chemical that tells the fungi to grow. This vigorous system also supports healthy bacteria that give off chemicals telling the fungi to grow and reproduce. The energetic symbiotic relationship between plants and the rhizosphere promotes vital, sustainable growth in an ecology scarce in moisture and fertility.

When abnormal supplemental levels of nutrients and moisture are provided to native plants, this delicate balance is completely disrupted. Beneficial bacteria and fungi in the rhizosphere are replaced by pathogens. The plants sever their ties with the mycorrhizae, which are now treated as parasites stealing 20 percent of their carbohydrates. Unprotected by the mycorrhizae, the plant roots are left completely exposed to pathogenic infection, and the plant community collapses rapidly, sometimes overnight.

One qualitative way to check whether a native nursery plant is mycorrhizal is to look at the root ball. The roots should not be bright white in color. Native mycorrhizal roots are yellow, orange, brown, or black, with, at most, white root tips. You can distinguish non-mycorrhizal weeds (ruderals) in the pot because their white roots will stand out. Also, the root ball will have a neutral to sweet fragrance, even smelling like the plant community to which the plant belongs. A sour or musty odor indicates anaerobic bacterial activity—that plant will not be long for this world.

There are three major categories of mycorrhizae: endo-, ecto-, and ericoid. Not only does each type have a different physiology, but their function explains how plants are adapted to different site conditions.

Endomycorrhizae

Endomycorrhizae penetrate root cell membranes. They form structures that increase surface area within the cell to promote the exchange of minerals and moisture. These structures are either balloon-like (known as vesicles) or multi-branched clusters (known as arbuscules). They are referred to as vesicular-arbuscular mycorrhizae, or VAM (an acronym now often shortened to AM). Endomycorrhizae are the most common form of symbiotic root fungi, inhabiting about 80 percent of the world's plants. In California, they predominate in our coastal sage scrub, grassland, and desert communities, although always in conjunction with other types of mycorrhizae. In nature, the more the merrier—having many different types of fungi helps keep the plant community stable under different conditions and seasons. Endomycorrhizae are present in most root systems except for mustard family plants (Brassicaceae).

Endomycorrhizae are particularly efficient at extracting phosphorus out of mineralized soil. This is especially true in alkaline (high pH) soil where the phosphate ions cannot be taken up by the roots alone. They function well with both rock mulches and organic mulches as they retain moisture for the overall plant community. AM is generalized and can usually tolerate higher levels of nitrogen, moisture, and disturbance than other types of root fungi. Desert forms are the exception, as they do not like high levels of nitrogen. The ability to withstand higher fertility makes endomycorrhizae quite popular as agricultural inoculants. Other than phosphorus, however, AM is not as efficient at pulling nutrients or water from bad soils. If nitrates, water, or particularly phosphorus are added in any great quantity, the plants will drop the AM, which die off quickly, being unable to survive for long when detached from their root partners. The plants are then left susceptible to infection by pathogens, and death is usually assured.

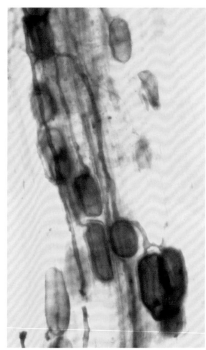

Vesicles of endomycorrhizae embedded within the cellular structure of a root hair where the exchange of nutrients and moisture occurs. The finely branched structures are hyphae, which pull nutrients from the soil.

One important function of AM is the production of a glycoprotein known as glomalin. This combination of protein and sugar coats the hyphae of endomycorrhizae, sealing the microscopic tubules so water and phosphorous can pass through them. Glomalin is a sticky substance sloughed off into the soil as older hyphae far up the root begin to die off naturally. Accumulated glomalin cements soil particles together, creating clumps that increase the moisture capacity and aeration of soils. It lends stability to the dirt, allowing it to resist water and wind erosion. On a larger scale, soil structure and stability can prevent slope failure. You typically do not see landslides in the chaparral, but instead on disturbed, graded slopes, covered in non-mycorrhizal groundcovers such as ice plant.

Studies have shown that glomalin accounts for 27 percent of all the carbon stored in soils. Since endomycorrhizae are the only known producers of this glycoprotein, restoring AM-based ecosystems has real value for offsetting the world's carbon dioxide pollution. In fact, some private markets have already started selling carbon credits for endomycorrhizae-rich land.

Ectomycorrhizae

In contrast to AM, ectomycorrhizae (EcM) form a sheath known as a "mantle" around root hairs. Their hyphae surround the cortical root cells, rather than penetrating the cell membranes. This is where moisture and nutrition exchange occurs. EcM inhabit about 10 percent of the world's plants. In California, they are associated with woodland trees and shrubs in areas with wet winters and dry summers. Examples of ectomycorrhizal plants include pines (*Pinus* spp.), oaks (*Quercus* spp.), firs (*Abies* spp.), and manzanita (*Arctostaphylos* spp.).

Organic mulches are essential to EcM plants, as bacteria slowly break down the leaf litter during the rainy months providing small amounts of nutrients that the mycorrhizae can then process. Therefore, EcM is most active during winter and spring. The fungal hyphae extend into the litter layer, where they can easily access the nutrition provided by the mulch bacteria. Because the EcM soil distribution is so shallow, less than a foot deep, it is highly vulnerable to disturbance. Research has shown that certain types of EcM actually lure and poison tiny insects in the soil, deriving nitrogen from their dead bodies.

Scientists used radioactive carbon isotopes to track movement of nutrients among different plants attached to the ectomycorrhizal grid. They show nutrition movement from areas of abundance to areas of deficiency. This reveals EcM as critical to the control of nutritional distribution in the plant community, helping to regulate and/or promote growth despite localized differences in soils and exposure. Once again, we recognize that most California plants, within their communities, are not sole actors, but are part of a mutualistic system. The symbiosis between native plants and mycorrhizae is one of the most important survival strategies for the native plants of California.

As plants in the forest grow, the mycorrhizae that support them often develop and become more refined. Young woodland trees may start their lives dependent on a generalized form of endomycorrhiza, which is tolerant of higher levels of nutrition and moisture—conditions that led to

The ectomycorrhizal sheath around root hairs does not penetrate individual cells but forms a mantle around the top of the root hair. Hyphae extend in all directions from the ectomycorrhizal sheath like nets between the outer cells, where the nutritional exchange occurs.

the initial germination of the seedlings. As the trees mature, they evolve to higher forms of AM and ectomycorrhizae. It can take as long as several months for EcM to establish on new plants. They initially direct the plants to support root and fungal growth rather than top growth. That is why some trees you plant appear to just sit there for an extended period of time, apparently doing nothing, sometimes for a year or longer. What you don't see is what is going on underground—their root/mycorrhizal systems are another story. Bert Wilson, owner of Las Pilitas Native Nursery, reported that a manzanita (an EcM plant), dug up after 10 days because it was planted in the wrong spot, already had roots grown out an inch.

In another instance, some native plants that had been in the ground for a year didn't appear to be growing and needed to be moved for practical reasons. Although there was little growth above ground, these plants had grown root and mycorrhizal connections forming a root ball extending at least 3 feet. Roots only take in nutrients and moisture near the tips. Digging the plants for transplanting cut through the elongated root system, severely limiting their ability to access nutrients and water. The plants went into shock and died. Had they been left in place, they were probably on the verge of explosive top growth.

Ectomycorrhizae are visible to the naked eye, unlike endomycorrhizae, which are microscopic and must be stained and viewed with a scanning electron microscope. A close look at EcM root systems with a magnifying glass reveals the fungal mantle that sheaths the root hairs. Fungal hyphae extend out in all directions, as if they were miniature roots. A cross section shows the mantle covering the outside of the root hair like bark, as well as the fungus extending in between individual root cells, forming structures known as Hartig nets. The exchange of minerals, moisture, and carbohydrates occurs at this interface.

Specific seasonal mushrooms are obvious indicators of EcM. Whereas endomycorrhizae (AM) do not have external spore cases, EcM fruiting bodies are mushrooms. Not all mushrooms are mycorrhizal. In fact, most are saprotrophic—that is, they break down and digest organic matter in the soil. EcM mushrooms, however, include some of our most edible forms, such as truffles, morels, and chanterelles. Commercially cultivated chanterelles, for instance, are grown on the roots of pine trees. Having aboveground spore cases allows for effective and far-reaching distribution of EcM fungi.

EcM and AM are both present on oak trees. Ectomycorrhizae, with their external mushroom spore cases and dependence on mulch, inhabit the upper layers of soil, even extending into the leaf litter to pull out nutrients provided by bacterial decomposition. EcM presence is usually less than a foot deep. Endomycorrhizae occur deeper, below the EcM, the ideal location for providing nutrients from the mineralized soil. Ectomycorrhizae are extremely vulnerable to soil compaction and disturbance. That is why removing the mulch layer or compressing the soil is so detrimental to the health of oak trees.

Ericoid mycorrhizae

A third general type of mycorrhizae inhabits plants in the heather family (Ericaceae). Plants colonized by ericoid fungi include: rhododendron (*Rhododendron* spp.), many species of manzanita (*Arctostaphylos* spp.), salal (*Gaultheria shallon*), and huckleberry (*Vaccinium ovatum*). Ericoid plants are almost always colonized by EcM, as well. Ericoid mycorrhizae are distinct from other mycorrhiza but are not well understood.

The plant communities occur in wet or boggy soils with high levels of organic matter, like peat moss. Site conditions are typically acidic and the organic soil component is low in nitrogen and phosphorous. As such, ericoid mycorrhizae are less common in California, especially in the southern part of the state. Ericoids have strong saprotrophic tendencies, and supply nitrogen and phosphorus to the associated plants. This is different from ectomycorrhizae, which rely on bacteria in the leaf litter to slowly digest the organic matter. Ericoids form hyphal coils in the outer layer of root cells, thus increasing the surface area available for nutritional exchange. They can promote some drought resistance, but this is not a primary function, as they mostly occur in plant communities located near areas of high moisture.

All types of mycorrhizal fungi can and do occur at the same time in plant communities. Typical combinations are AM only, EcM only, AM and EcM together, or EcM and ericoid together. There are tens of thousands of species of fungi, and hundreds may occur on just one plant. The more species present, the more stable the plant community, as the fungi perform specific beneficial tasks during different seasons, ensuring year-round plant protection.

Endomycorrhizae excel at pulling phosphorous out of inorganic soils, especially in highly alkaline soils where phosphate ions cannot be accessed by roots alone. They like inorganic mulches (such as occur in the desert), but can tolerate leaf litter if it helps retain moisture for the system. They do best in soils with limited nitrogen, and are probably more tolerant of site nutrition than other mycorrhizae. However, adding too much nitrogen and any amount of phosphorous can cause the plants to drop these fungi. These fungi inhabit the deeper regions of the plant root zone.

Ectomycorrhizae, on the other hand, are positioned at the surface of the root zone and are completely dependent on organic mulches and seasonal moisture. As such, they occur in woodland plant communities, often in conjunction with AM or ericoid mycorrhizae.

Finally, ericoid mycorrhizae occur where the conditions are acidic, boggy, and rich in low-nitrogen organic matter.

Plants that exhibit varying combinations of mycorrhizae can serve as bridges between different site conditions and plant communities. Bert Wilson noted that plants like oaks (*Quercus* spp.), willows (*Salix* spp.), cottonwoods (*Populus* spp.), currants (*Ribes* spp.), and coffeeberry/redberry (*Rhamnus* spp.) are important energy shunts in an ecosystem with varying soil moisture, nutrition levels, and plant strategies.

Other soil partners

Although mycorrhizal fungi are important symbiotic partners in plant communities, they are far from the only actors in this complex ecological web. Beneficial bacteria are also important to the survival of California's native plants. Some are essential to the health of the rhizosphere, others are associated with specific plants. As an example, plants in the legume family (Fabaceae) capture nitrogen from the atmosphere through the plants' symbiotic relationship with nitrogen-fixing bacteria known as rhizobia.

Signaled by the release of flavanoids from the legume's roots, the bacteria secrete a substance known as a nodule factor. This "nod factor" causes root hairs to form nodules incorporating the rhizobia. The bacteria take atmospheric nitrogen and supply it to the plant in a useable form, as ammonium (NH_4^+). In return, the rhizobia receive carbohydrates, protein, and oxygen from the host legume. Since several independent strains of rhizobia can infect a single plant, some might be able to "cheat" and steal nutrition from the plant without providing nitrogen. Research is showing that plants like native lupine (*Lupinus* spp.) can detect less productive nodules and limit resource allocation to those specific strains. Other native genera in the family Fabaceae that form a symbiotic relationship with rhizobia include: *Cercis, Lotus, Acacia, Lathyrus*, and *Prosopis*.

While plant enthusiasts know that legumes fix nitrogen with their rhizobia partners, few are aware that other California native genera also fix nitrogen through symbiotic relationships with another bacterial colonizer known as frankia. *Ceanothus, Alnus, Cercocarpos, Myrica, Cowania*, and *Sheperdia*, as well as many other genera, benefit from the filamentous nodules that form on their root systems. The relationship is complex, since frankia partners with mycorrhizae and other beneficial fungi and bacteria. Frankia provide nitrogen support, while associated partners provide other benefits to the web of participants. Contributions include production of root hormones, pest control (including root nematodes), exclusion of pathogens, new paths for roots' colonization, water storage, enhanced metabolization of minerals, and nutrient sharing.

Frankia are the major source of nitrogen fixation in some plant communities. They provide all the nitrogen their plant partners require, so they enable the associated plants to thrive in nitrogen-poor environments. Their plant partners gain a significant competitive edge over alien species requiring more site nutrition. Frankia-infected plants often have the darkest green leaves. The nitrogen-rich nodules are surprisingly large and hard, sometimes greater than an inch across. Those unfamiliar with their appearance may be alarmed to find them growing on the roots of an infected plant, such as a ceanothus, when they are removed from the pot for planting.

There is an anecdote about a landscape contractor who contracted with a native nursery to grow a large quantity of ceanothus for an installation. While planting, employees noticed very large, white nodules on the root systems. Unfamiliar with these curious forms, they took the plants to a local agricultural extension office. Unfortunately, an equally unaware agent advised erroneously that the plants were infected with some type of pathogen. The contractor returned all the plants to the nursery and demanded his money back. The nursery, correctly suspecting that the nodes were indeed frankia, sent samples to a university specializing in their study. The researchers confirmed these frankia were some of the largest examples they had ever seen. In fact, they had never seen frankia growing on potted plants before. The contractor never knew the gift he gave back. Fortunately, the nursery sold all the ceanothus later. The irony is that something so vital to the long-term health of the plants was viewed as an extreme negative because it was outside the realm of typical horticulture. In fact, one reason ceanothus has a reputation for being short-lived may be the inability of nurseries and horticultural practice to promote and sustain this vital ecological relationship.

Another nitrogen-fixing partner grows on the surface of the soil but is

Nitrogen-fixing Frankia attached to ceanothus root.

intimately connected to the rhizosphere. As you've been out hiking, have you ever noticed that the soil is occasionally covered in a dark-colored, sometimes billowy crust? This is known as cryptogamic crust. It consists of spore-producing lichens, algae, mosses, and fungi. Cryptogamia refers to an old primary division of plants that reproduce without true flowers and seeds. This primordial layer is an important soil stabilizer throughout drought-adapted plant communities in the West. It is one reason why our deserts do not resemble the Sahara, at least not yet.

The presence of these crusts is an indicator of a healthy, undisturbed plant community. They often bridge the gap between rock lichens and soil microorganisms. Cryptogamic crust is also a mighty foe of alien species, as long as it remains undisturbed. Unfortunately, it is incredibly fragile and requires 7 to 14 years to recolonize a disturbed site. It is heavily damaged by footsteps and completely destroyed by cattle. Because these crusts require long-term undisturbed conditions to regenerate, grazing and fire easily destroy them and their ability to withstand conversion to weeds. No greater evidence exists than the free-range grazing of our deserts over the last century. The crusts are gone in many areas, now being replaced by noxious invaders like Sahara mustard (*Brassica tournefortii*) and cheat grass (*Bromus tectorum*). Worse still, these areas are now burning. The desert was never meant to burn. Most of the native vegetation is destroyed in just one fire, further promoting spread of the noxious weeds. Before long, our deserts really will resemble the Sahara.

Science has only begun to explore soil complexity. We have included just a few recognized relationships; countless more are still to be discovered. Many more actors are still to be identified, yet these relationships are completely interdependent on multiple levels. The systems are impossibly complex and poorly understood. We'd be fooling ourselves to even think we could know and predict the behavior of plants dependent on such complex ecology. Outcomes of our interventions are often counter-productive. We know that increasing soil fertility and moisture far beyond natural conditions for these plant communities ends in plant failure. This despite the admonitions of ornamental horticulture that we need to amend and water to ensure the health of the plants.

The best approach is to emulate natural ecological conditions to the best of our knowledge. This includes high-quality mulch that is slow to break down and is composed of organic material that occurs in these environments. In the absence of ground-up chaparral, the best is shredded redwood bark, followed by cedar bark or ground pine and oak chips. Some plant communities, like desert, coastal strand, or grassland, do not have natural organic mulch and prefer inorganic sand and rock. The soil and mulch need to be in direct contact in order to allow unimpeded access by the soil microorganisms.

Watering should mimic natural rainfall, supplying even moisture to the entire rhizosphere within the tolerance limits of the plant community. Low-volume overhead sprinklers do a good job of this. Drip emitters, on the other hand, often recommended for low-volume watering, provide intensely localized and highly saturated delivery, inconsistent with most native plant communities' ecology. Drip grids provide greater moisture distribution but do not allow for trans-mulch permeation, and still saturate the soil. This may be tolerated by marsh-type ecology, but not by upland drought-tolerant communities. Exceptions may occur where the soil has perfect drainage and the garden location is more moderate, such as near the coast. We do not recommend drip irrigation.

Fertilizers, and more recently, mycorrhizal inoculums, are often added to enhance the health of landscapes. In general, commercial fertilizers containing high levels of nitrogen and phosphorous are not appropriate for native plant landscapes. While California soils are low in these nutrients, partners in the native rhizosphere are especially adept at providing them. Adding these fertilizers to the native landscape only causes the plants to drop the beneficial partners (which give them a competitive edge over weeds), only to be replaced by pathogens.

The introduction of exotic earthworms has also had significant impact on the rhizosphere. Populations of introduced nightcrawlers or red wigglers have been exploding as gardeners are sold on their benefits for ornamental horticulture. Far from the benign, beneficial partners they are portrayed to be, these earthworms have a real appetite for fungal hyphae, consuming the mycorrhizal grid, as well as breaking the links between the network and the plants. Worms also encourage mixing between the mulch and underlying soil, which increases the nutrient loading of the dirt. As has been discussed, increased soil nutrition causes the plant community to break the essential bonds with their mycorrhizal partners. This is yet another example of the unintentional consequences of soil manipulation leading to negative impacts.

The jury is still out on mycorrhizal inoculums. They may be beneficial for ornamental or agricultural plants grown in a non-mycorrhizal medium, or where the soil is so completely degraded that there are no available mycorrhizae left to colonize the new natives. However, these are specific, theoretical situations. We don't know the consequences of introducing non-native myccorhizae into the very complicated native rhizosphere. Better to use properly grown native plants. That is, vigorous plants grown with appropriate ecology in the pot to serve as the inoculum for the site, not those on artificial life support.

The ecology that supports our delicate California native ecosystems is incredibly complex and poorly understood. Most variables still have not been identified, yet they are all interdependent. We don't understand these systems well enough to predict the consequences of alien inputs. It is a chaotic equation where the smallest disturbance can cause the whole system to destabilize and spin out of control. We do not know when our actions will create a "butterfly effect," where the beating wings of a butterfly can cause a ripple effect that leads to a hurricane on the other side of the world. We prefer to stay as close to nature as we can.

DESIGN
Start with the bones

4

Good planning and design are essential to your ultimate joy and satisfaction with your landscape. These issues cannot be overemphasized. Do not shortcut this process in your garden. Many landscape design books cover the basic principles and mechanics of the process. This chapter will talk about the principles of good design for native landscapes, including plant considerations as well as hardscape and decorative elements. Take your time with the design process. Each landscape is unique, and the more you know before you start, the happier you will be with the end results.

From naturalistic to modern, native landscape design can cover the continuum of stylistic choices with panache and drama, as evidenced by red twig dogwood (*Cornus sericea*) and white bark poplars (*Populus tremuloides*).

W HEN DEVELOPING a landscape, many of us become so focused on plant choices that we easily overlook the basic elements of good garden design, especially for landscapes using California native plants. Our errors are basic: no backbone, over-reliance on herbaceous perennials, poor size selection, really bad mixing, too many species (we'll admit to that one occasionally), and all the other things they warn you about in Garden Design 101.

If you are replacing or refurbishing a landscape, carefully consider the existing plants and whether they will work with a native landscape. Assess each plant's compatibility with native plants to decide how much of the old landscape to keep. Most people start from scratch, but if you have a beautiful, mature, drought-tolerant tree that you love, in just the right spot, it might make sense to keep it.

Different parts of every property vary in shade, temperature, wind, or rain pattern. These considerations will affect your plant choices. Think about your property strategically, so you can make good decisions in selecting just the right plants to create your new landscape.

Consider all the different ways you can enjoy your yard. Think about the paths, views, and style of landscape you would like. Get pictures and start a list of native plants you like with notes about their mature size. Think about how the plants look together. Pay attention to which ones need shade or full sunlight. Although most natives are drought tolerant, some have higher water needs, such as those that grow near streambeds or in bogs.

It is extremely hard to visualize a tiny 1- or 5-gallon plant as a full size tree or shrub. Even professionals overplant, but you don't have to. Make your design drawing with the mature size of the plants and plant the 1-gallons on the center where the mature plant will grow. You will be amazed at how many fewer plants you actually install than if you just eyeball the space and start poking things in. You will also save time and energy by not planting, maintaining, and ultimately removing the excess plants.

Draw your plants during different seasons to visualize their bloom, seasonal color, and dormancy. You may need more evergreens when many of your original choices go dormant. Great! Just choose some different plants.

Conceptualizing the completed landscape before digging in will help you achieve more satisfying results. Take a look at native landscapes that have matured. Pay attention to what you like and what you don't, what works and what doesn't. More professionals who design and install landscapes for a living should watch their projects grow in over time to spot mistakes and improve on current and future projects; they would learn a great deal. Landscapes are not static; it is important to see how they hold up over time.

Planting design

Different plants have different functions in the landscape. A field of grasses, even native grasses, is just a field. You bring your vision of your landscape to life by manipulating and carefully placing combinations of trees, shrubs, and perennial plants around your home and hardscape (the permanent structural and non-plant elements of your landscape). Add seasonal color for accent. The following guidelines provide the basics for good native garden design.

Structure

Structure is everything in creating a native landscape. The key to long-lasting beauty is a solid backbone of evergreen plants with foliar color that complements the building and hardscape. This is why we are not huge fans of grass gardens. Although they may look dramatic and stunning in their prime, grasses look ragged during the later part of the year. Grasses, even low-water natives, require a lot of care to keep them looking healthy.

Think of landscape design as a study in proportion and mass. Use features of the existing home or yard to scale landscape features and plantings in multiples or fractions of the baseline. Create a sketch showing simple masses and voids—balanced, and in proportion to your house. The positive features are massed areas of plants, boulders, or large structures; the voids are open areas of groundcover or flatwork like paths and patios. This sketch will help you to visualize the physical positive and negative layout of the yard. Next, add the hardpoints like paths, patios, sitting areas, and

The curving branches of the sycamore and soft rounding mounds of artemisia are mirrored in the hardscape, capturing line in the landscape.

mulched or gravel areas—everything that will create the framework and context for your plant design.

Once you have determined the basic proportions and balance of positive to negative massing and have laid out the structural framework of the garden, then you can look at plant design. Place the lowest-growing plants and perennials in front, increasing in height as you progress back—you want to be able to see it all. You gain a sense of depth with this visual stacking; by planting the taller plants near the house tapering down to the smaller plants, you create an optical illusion of a larger yard when you look out a window.

If a path or access runs all the way around a planting group, place the tallest plant at or near the center. Trees and large shrubs used singly as specimens form central focal points from which the planting group radiates.

Always, always, always keep in mind the mature size of your plants. Fight the urge to overplant to achieve quick fill. A common mistake, overplanting leads to congested, out-of-control chaos, requiring constant care and editing. This is particularly important with trees—be aware of their final size, the shade they will cast, and their proximity to buildings. Untold numbers of trees have met premature demise because they were planted too close to structures, or too close together. Double plant with colorful perennials to help fill your need for instant gratification (and also help jumpstart the ecology), but know that these plants will be culled out to optimize the final structure of the landscape.

One technique to create garden interest is to change soil levels. Homeowners are building and planting more mounds. Be aware, however, that mounding often creates problems. Plants on the mound struggle to get enough water, while those at the base drown from the runoff. The line between too little and too much moisture can become impossibly thin. If you must have mounds, be sure the slopes are gradual and well compacted. A better alternative is to use the plants to create apparent changes in level. Planting shorter and taller species of the same genus is quite effective. Accent groups of large boulders can also help enhance verticality. Native landscapes are well adapted to using native boulders. Remember, our clash of tectonic plates gave California a lot of beautiful rock.

Island oak, ceanothus, and manzanita define the garden perimeter, with perennial shrubs and grasses at the leading edge of this young garden.

A cottage with a fence and gate define the hardscape edges of this garden room.

Incorporate boulder outcrops to help support the plantings and create a realistic reason for their existence.

Another garden structure technique is to create "garden rooms," which may be literal or implied. These small distinctive sections of a garden incorporate a focal point or usage area. Boundaries can be real or implied. A room may be as simple as a bench surrounded by some boulders and shrubs. Or it could include an elaborate overhead structure with flooring, a barbeque, firepit, or even walls. Hedging plants make great visual screens for defining spaces. Outdoor rooms entice people out into the garden, creating waypoints and depth, slowing them down, and increasing the illusion of garden size. Well planned to human scale, garden rooms enhance the garden experience.

Use your skills to proportion these areas so they are integral to the garden experience and have purpose. Well-conceived garden rooms can create useful destinations, intriguing pathways, and surprising nooks. When misapplied, the garden becomes a disjointed scramble of unrelated spaces, more jarring than restful; more worry than wonder.

Foundation

A typical garden design mistake is to bypass or ignore foundational plants. So often we neglect them in favor of herbaceous (summer-dormant) perennials, shrubs, and grasses. The "instant gratification" landscape may be a riot of color in spring, only to disintegrate into tumbleweeds in fall. This also happens with seasoned landscape professionals. Unfortunately, native landscapes get a bad rap because of this error, when, in fact, they have every potential to be beautiful year-round.

Why is this tendency so prevalent? It is probably the result of poor plant knowledge. Designers often stick with a few basic, easily obtainable California natives: Cleveland or white sage (*Salvia clevelandii* or *S. apiana*), deer grass (*Muhlenbergia rigens*), *Ceanothus* 'Yankee Point' or 'Concha', woolly blue curls (*Trichostema lanatum*), and maybe something weird like redberries (*Rhamnus crocea*).

Do not mix in completely foreign non-native plants, such as Indian hawthorn, plumbago, rosemary, cistus, lavender, etc., which require more water and different watering seasons than the natives. In trying to keep the alien plants alive with supplemental water, the woolly blue curls are usually dead in a few months, followed by ceanothus in a few years. Mass plantings of grasses are not maintainable. Without proper maintenance the grasses soon resemble an abandoned cornfield and, inevitably, weeds take hold. The summer-dormant sages are full of spent blossoms, and, well, you get the picture. Not much wonder people hesitate to install a native landscape.

The remedy requires greater understanding of native plant design and characteristics, and an expanded native plant palette—there are so many more to choose from. The basic structure of a native landscape should be proportioned as follows: 60 to 70 percent of the plants should be a handful of evergreen species with nice foliar color, texture, size, and habit. Next, 20 to 30 percent should be colorful, small-scale perennials that bloom at different times of the year, sited mostly along the edges. The remaining 10 to 20 percent can be specimen plants and trees, employed as accents, and larger-scale feature plants.

The evergreen foundation is absolutely critical to the structure of the landscape. If your signature tree or trees are deciduous, they support the foundational structure with their height and visual weight even when bare, providing seasonal variation in the landscape. The rest of the plants are the window dressing of the design.

Massing and repetition

Massing is grouping the same species of plants together to create swaths of color and texture. This ties the design together, creating flow and drama. Plant collectors really struggle with this. We want one of every plant that grows in California in our yards. However, this aesthetic does not work for most people.

Going hand in hand with massing is repetition, using the same plant in multiple places in the landscape. Just as nature seeds the same plants in multiple areas, repeated use of a plant creates visual consistency. The rule of thumb is to group odd-number multiples, but it is also possible to have a large mass in one area with smaller repetitions in other places, creating

Natural branches are used to create this whimsical garden stage.

Massing and layering manzanita, non-native santolina, ceanothus, and eriogonum in the garden creates drama and flow.

Repetition of baccharis, coffeeberry, spike rush, and 'Sunset' manzanita draws the viewer into the garden.

Layering 'Pozo Blue' salvia, 'Montara' artemisia, Santa Cruz Island buckwheat, and tree mallow lends a sense of dimension and depth.

visual flow and balance. Repetition is useful for establishing pattern and rhythm.

The more disciplined approach to counter the "onesies" is to plant odd-numbered groupings of species—say five, seven, or more. The textural consistency of massing and repetition creates a comforting feel that helps draw the visitor in, rather than the jolting effect of a busy assortment of colors and textures. Nature works the same way. One of the most enticing natural gardens we have ever seen was just outside Idyllwild. Imagine a soft grouping of medium green red shanks (*Adenostoma sparsifolium*) in the background, a mass of forest green *Ceanothus greggii* in 3-foot mounds forward of them, and lower-growing grey buckwheat (*Eriogonum fasciculatum* var. *polifolium*) at the front—simple, beautiful, and completely natural. Just a three-plant palette, it was exquisite.

Color, contrast, and texture

People usually think of flowers as the color element in the garden, but color in the native landscape can and should be achieved in several ways. California has no shortage of flowering plants. Spring can be overwhelming with all the blossoms. Designers rely so heavily on spring-blooming plants that the landscape often looks drab or unkempt by fall. Fortunately, when we talk about evergreens in California we're not limited to conifers. Evergreen foliar color is so important, as is the use of lesser-known species of flowering shrubs and perennials that bloom at different times of the year. Definitely consider the ephemeral flowers. However, for year-round interest, also remember to include color that lasts longer, as in stems, leaves, and berries.

Leaves are the most visually prominent and lasting color form of a plant. Using plants all with the same size leaves is like creating a painting entirely in the same shade of gray. Even if the color varies, the effect looks flat. Create a mix of larger- and smaller-leaved species, including interesting leaf shapes. The magnificent toyon (*Heteromeles arbutifolia*), with its large dark leaves, is in complete contrast to the smaller, smaller-leaved, medium green coyote brush (*Baccharis pilularis* var. *consaguinea*). This contrast and texture variation creates subtle interest, variation, and complexity.

Manzanitas (*Arctostaphylos* spp.) are incredibly useful for achieving foliar color. They are so important, yet so underutilized. Their leaves demonstrate nearly every color in the spectrum: orange, red, pink, bronze, chartreuse, blue, grey, yellow, and, of course, green. The bark is universally red, often dark and satiny. A healthy *A.* 'Sunset' or 'John Dourley' exudes warm tones of yellow, red, and orange throughout the year. 'Ghostly', on the other hand, an upright pillar of near white blushed in pink, stands out like an apparition floating against a dark backdrop. The aptly named *A. rainbowensis* is a rarely used mounding species, full of color, even purples and pinks, while new growth stands in bright green contrast to the mature leaves. *Arctostaphylos pajaroensis* 'Paradise' has orange, bronze, and red tips that contrast with gunmetal grey foliage; *A. uva-ursi* 'Radiant' is a floor-hugging species displaying warm color as it coats the ground only a few inches high.

Many evergreen natives display foliar color. The wonderfully fire-resistant, low-growing, medium green *Baccharis pilularis* 'Pigeon Point' contrasts nicely with the darker foliage of ceanothus and manzanita. The year-round blooming island bush poppy (*Dendromecon harfordii*) has large, steel blue leaves that contrast with sulfur-yellow flowers with orange stamens. *Leymus condensatus* 'Canyon Prince' is a wonderful clumping grass, about 3 feet tall, blue-leaved with lovely upright white flowers. Several artemisias, like *Artemisia californica* 'Montara' and *A. pycnocephala* 'David's Choice', as well as the salvias, like *Salvia* 'Point Sal' and 'Bee's Bliss', present low-growing, silver-white mounds that are nearly evergreen when given light supplemental watering.

White berries, in particular, make a special contribution. Snowberry (*Symphoricarpos* spp.) creates highlights in any woodland garden. Highly symbiotic with oak and pine, these shrubs produce bunches of porcelain white berries that are dramatic in autumn, brightening up any shady area. Similarly, brown twig dogwood's (*Cornus glabrata*) attractive layered clusters of small white flowers are superseded by equally attractive clusters of white berries. Don't blink, however, as these delicious morsels are relished by nearly every berry-eating bird around.

Coffeeberry (*Rhamnus californica*) is a formal plant so elegant and

Using foliage to create color in the garden: dark leaves of ceanothus contrast the bright color of 'Paradise' manzanita and blue tones of 'Canyon Prince' rye grass.

New leaves of 'Sunset' manzanita brighten the landscape.

colorful that we often use it in Japanese gardens. Its rich green foliage, neat leaves, and red branches recommend it as a fantastic foundational plant, but when the large, multicolored berries come into season the plant visually pops. The drupes are produced over a long period, coming into maturity at different times, yielding a Christmas-tree effect of green, yellow, red, and dark purple fruit, simultaneously. Many native bird species fight for the berries. A close relative of coffeeberry, holly-leaved redberry (*Rhamnus crocea* ssp. *ilicifolia*) has nearly translucent, crimson fruit reminiscent of salmon eggs. The foliage is neat, bright green, and serrated.

Finally, the king of the California berry plants is toyon, or California Christmas berry (*Heteromeles arbutifolia*). This shrub/tree lights up with brilliant red berries just as winter holidays approach. Legend (in some dispute) has it that Hollywood was named for this plant. An aviary on a stick, it is the most important winter food source for birds in California. Up to 10 different species of birds can be found on it at one time. Most years it rivals bougainvillea for color. Usually, toyon is a 10 to 15 foot shrub. However, an old adobe in Long Beach has a huge specimen, approximately 80 to 100 feet tall, attesting to the natural magnificence of mature native plants that we have lost, and which we hope to one day regain.

East Coast residents instinctively understand that plants need a resting period. They accept autumn leaf drop and naked trees in winter. Bare branches and evergreen spires laden with snow define the holidays. However, most of California has no white blanket to cover summer's slumber. In summer heat and drought, plants like artemisia, encelia, and salvias often shrivel and lose their leaves as protection against moisture loss. Nowadays, whole hillsides turn brown and bleak, as too-frequent fires have shifted the balance of native chaparral vegetation toward summer deciduous native shrubs and non-native annuals. Understandably, most observers might think this is what their native landscape will look like.

Native landscapes can yield year-round beauty, not only with the aforementioned huge variety of foliar color, but with year-round flowers and berries as well.

Winter is surprisingly rich with native color. Manzanitas begin blooming late fall to early winter. *Arctostaphylos refugionensis* is often covered in flowers by early December. Most manzanitas continue to bloom into February or March.

Numerous ceanothus species are also winter bloomers. *Ceanothus verrucosus* and *C. cuneatus* are covered in white flowers by late January. *Ceanothus arboreus*, *C. maritimus*, *C.* 'Tassajara Blue', 'Blue Jeans', and 'Snowball' are all reliable early bloomers.

Currants and gooseberries are winter-flowering shrubs. *Ribes sanguineum* var. *glutinosum* and *R. indecorum* are usually covered in candelabra clusters by February. *Ribes speciosum*'s well-armed arching branches are laden with hanging fuchsia-like flowers by March.

Anyone who has seen a western redbud (*Cercis occidentalis*) in bloom will never forget the brilliant magenta fountain of flowers this small tree creates by February. Combined with the heart-shaped leaves that follow, this is an essential specimen tree in all but the most coastal areas.

Surprisingly, some sages start blooming in winter. One of the most prominent is black sage (*Salvia mellifera*). An especially useful variety, lavender-blue-flowered *Salvia mellifera* var. *repens* is a wonderful slope groundcover with a long bloom cycle and nearly evergreen character.

Epilobiums (Zauschnerias) of summer may bloom well into December. The same holds true for *Erigeron glaucus* and *E. mimulus*. *Iris douglasiana* often starts blooming in February.

Otherwise, everything seems to bloom in spring. Ceanothus often defines the season, with many of the perennials, and manzanitas often continue blooming into spring. Wildflowers abound.

Summer is the domain of Cleveland sages and their cultivars. Plants like *Salvia* 'Pozo Blue' and *S. clevelandii* 'Whirly Blue' and 'Aromas' begin blooming in late May and continue through September. Monardellas are reliable summer bloomers. Lakeside ceanothus (*Ceanothus cyaneus*) is a spectacular wild lilac that usually starts blooming in May and can continue through June, with huge, deep purple flower clusters hanging like wisteria blossoms.

Autumn is akin to winter in other parts of the country—a season of transition. Summer-blooming perennials may span the autumn. Berries ripen. Grasses achieve their seasonal golden hues. Many native deciduous

A green palette of contrasting leaf size, form, and hue using 'Canyon Prince' rye grass, St. Catherine's lace, bishop pine, 'Ray Hartman' ceanothus, and 'Paradise' manzanita to create texture in the garden.

Brilliant redbud blossoms brighten winter landscapes.

plants display fall color. Sycamores (*Platanus racemosa*) turn bright yellow if fall has been chilly. Buttonwillow (*Cephalanthus occidentalis*) leaves turn orange and red as the weather cools. Redbud (*Cercis occidentalis*) and western crabapple (*Malus fusca*) may turn crimson in fall, though they do so more reliably in north or central California or at higher elevation. And, finally, there is little to compare to the fall color of 'Roger's Red' wild grape (*Vitis* 'Roger's Red'), which turns brilliant red no matter where it's growing, including southern California.

Non-plant features

Creating a successful landscape involves more than just the green stuff. Landscape features create focal points, whimsy, and practical amenities to support and encourage participation in this important outdoor living space.

Paths in the garden

Pathways give the observer access to the garden. Paths set up the structure of the garden, define planting areas, and create visual flow, enticing the viewer around bends to see what lies just beyond. They direct and control traffic in the garden.

Select practical path materials sympathetic to the overall design. The simplest path is just plain dirt. This is the stuff of trails. Make a dirt path by not applying mulch in that area. While this may seem the easiest and most natural, it is fraught with problems. Clay soil paths turn into a mucky mess with every watering or rain. Undoubtedly, the area has already been disturbed, so bare earth quickly becomes a magnet for every weed seed, creating a maintenance nightmare. Dirt pathways create dust in dry weather and mud when wet, both easily tracked into the house.

The best naturalistic pathway or trail choice is decomposed granite, or DG. DG is granite that has oxidized and weathered to the point of crumbling. It flakes away in a plate-like structure resembling sand but in scales not grains. This material compacts beautifully to form a surface nearly as hard as concrete. DG is a warm, neutral, naturalistic path material when used correctly. However, the small, grainy material pits hardwood floors when it is tracked inside on shoes, so it is also important to add hard points for the last steps of the walkway and/or a way to clean off your feet before going inside.

DG is available in a wide range of colors. Choose earthtones of buff, gold, red, cream, or gray to match existing features or hardscape. Edge paths with wood, composite, or even metal, although we often prefer no edging at all, as it can channel runoff along the sides of the path accelerating erosion.

Stepping stones also make good paths. There are many choices, including pre-cast concrete and flagstone. Some people opt for "mixed-media" combinations of rock, concrete steppers, and wood to create whimsy. Regardless of the material, anchor what is being stepped upon. The most secure method is to create a pedestal of concrete under the individual stepper to support and anchor it. Sand works best for large surfaces that are innately stable. Too often smaller pieces of rock or flagstone set on sand end up tipping, becoming unsightly and dangerous to walk on. Another dramatic, although more complex, treatment is planting low groundcovers like creeping thyme (not native), woodland strawberry (*Fragaria californica*), yarrow (*Achillea millefolium* var. *californica*), or even *Horkelia* spp. between the stones. These groundcovers require dedicated irrigation support.

Whatever you use, it is important that it is set in for safety and stability. A recently popular material is recycled broken-up concrete fragments, commonly called urbanite. Obviously, the only limit for pathway form or materials is your imagination.

Furniture

Providing places to sit in the landscape further slows observers, inviting them to rest and enjoy the beauty. Benches are often focal points in their own right. Select a style compatible with the garden, from a simple knee-high boulder to a complex dimensional object. They are commercially available in many styles and price ranges.

A decomposed granite pathway.

Every yard needs a place to sit and enjoy the garden.

Ideas for benches are limitless. They may exhibit great complexity and craftsmanship. Many are rustic yet charming. Simply mounting a board or large piece of stone on top of rock or cement makes an excellent place to sit. Mount a bench into a retaining wall or onto a natural boulder.

While benches provide resting places in the garden, tables invite activity. What is better than dinner "al fresco" in the open air of a beautiful garden? Old fashioned wooden picnic tables with seating attached are perfect for the family—stable, sturdy, strong, and long lasting. It's a great place for kids to do projects while Mom or Dad are relaxing or working in the garden.

Once again, there are a myriad of alternatives for tables from rustic to sophisticated. A leveled stump beside an Adirondack chair provides a resting place for morning coffee. A glass-topped table melts into the landscape and is easily cleaned for guests.

Just be certain that the feet of the table are sturdy and the ground surface is stable so dishes or projects don't go flying. This is where a patio slab may be appropriate. You'll also want a table surface that is resistant to moisture.

If you are eating in the garden, you may also want to cook there. The simplest solution is a small firepit for roasting marshmallows but you can also create a full-on kitchen with a barbeque, possibly a wood-fired pizza oven, and maybe even counter space for food preparation.

Maybe you'd like a place to truly relax and take a snooze—a hammock for easy summer days. Sweet dreams!

Utilizing rocks and boulders

Nothing provides an anchor, nor adds a sense of permanence, like well-placed boulders. They can be used singly, in groups, or to create large outcroppings. We incorporate them into features like walls, birdbaths, and dry creek beds. Rock setting is a discipline developed over centuries with one goal in mind: to create something that looks a part of the natural environment and not just a pile of rocks. Few but the most formal landscapes are complete without some form of rockwork.

In selecting boulders, try to match any existing rockwork or the natural stone in the area. There should be a reason for the boulders' existence. At the very least, they should all be of one type, not a mishmash of colors and

Flagstone integrates this bench into the landscape.

Create a place to enjoy your garden with a table and chairs.

Ceanothus 'Heart's Desire' surrounds boulders integrating them into the landscape.

geology. Create boulder groupings with good-sized rocks (larger than 18 inches, in most cases) so they will not be covered in vegetation. If the rocks are stratified, line up the strata, so the group looks like an exposed outcrop. Arrange boulders in odd-numbered groupings, fairly close together, in roughly triangular forms. A very dramatic grouping might include a flat rock, a medium-sized rock, and a large or tall rock, viewed together like a spiral staircase.

On steep slopes, you may be lucky enough to have natural stone outcrops. Only when it is safe and practical may you consider exposing some of the underlying geology. Planting in-between outcroppings creates a dramatic "rock wall" effect. Dudleyas, bulbs, buckwheats, ferns, and monkey flowers are excellent for this. Lit up at night, these slopes can be stunning.

Boulders give a sense of solidity and place to this Mediterranean garden.

Dry streams or bioswales

The typical traditional response to excess water in the landscape is installing subterranean drainpipes with catch basins to carry the excess water off-site into storm drains. Why not turn this underground liability into an attractive and interesting aboveground landscape feature? Using runoff is a good sustainable solution. Keep as much water as possible on-site to benefit the landscape, meanwhile enjoying the flowing water of a seasonal creek when it rains. Dry streams, also known as bioswales, should be both ornamental and functional. Route downspouts and runoff into these features. Well-designed streambeds vector water away from structures, slowing down the flow and allowing the moisture to percolate and filter into the landscape before reaching the storm drain.

A dry streambed must be designed like a real stream. We have all been jarred and dismayed by ill-conceived and executed straight gravel ditches with large rocks along the edges. These are drainage ditches, not dry streams. Curves are very important. Water does not typically run in a straight line. It creates sweeping bends as it bounces back and forth flowing downstream, jostling around existing groups of boulders. As water flows around curves, unless there is something to stop it, the flow becomes shallower and widens. Terrain is often gouged out on the outside of the curve; the hard points and boulders are on the inside. Streams narrow and deepen in the straights. Sections will back up to create pools behind little cascades and island rocks, only to flow over as small waterfalls. Stones along a creek bed come in many sizes: sand, gravel, pebble, rock, and boulder.

A properly designed bioswale emulates all these characteristics. Use good-sized boulders (at least 18 inches) at strategic points, especially on inside curves and in the middle of the stream. Real streams have island boulders in the center. Large rocks can also be placed on the side, like steps, to create cascades. It is better to grade the stream as a series of stairs rather than a straight decline, slowing the water and creating eddy pools as the water drains. The stream should terminate in an enlarged pool that allows the remainder of the water to collect prior to being discharged into the storm drain. The stream slows the water, distributes it, and allows it to percolate into the soil, staying on-site as much as possible.

A natural-looking dry streambed is made with mixed sizes of rocks and curving course.

This bioswale retains water through the use of large gravel-filled sumps.

The stream skeleton is established with larger boulders and rocks. For filler, use a random mixture of different-sized stones and pebbles. Just tossing these smaller rocks into the stream approximates natural deposition. Deliberately placing each stone looks completely unnatural. Finally, add coarse sand. The sand fills in around the pebbles adding detail, completing the effect.

Special situations

Every property is unique. Challenges may arise in a landscape situation that require special attention. Two of the most common are slopes and wet areas, especially if lawn is included.

Slopes

Slopes are a natural for native landscapes. They fit the criteria beautifully: good drainage, lean soils, and the need for stability. Native plants require no soil amendments (hard to apply on a steep slope). Very little irrigation is required, so the slope is not undermined by excess moisture. The presence of the mycorrhizal fungal biomass in the upper 3 feet of soil helps bind soil particles together while creating porosity for aeration and moisture capacity, and, by definition, the drainage is perfect.

Select plants for slopes as for any other part of the yard, though ground-covers predominate, with larger shrubs at the top and sides. Neighbors directly at the top of the slope will appreciate shrubs that do not block their view, preserving good relationships. For access, cut switchback trails into the slope. Use lots of plants on both the upper and lower sides of the path to help maintain stability. Place boulders or rocks along the edges of the paths to help retain soil. Steeper slopes may require a more elaborate system of retaining walls. This can get expensive very quickly.

Use the low-volume overhead rotaries recommended for irrigating other parts of the native landscape. If the soil or slope make it impossible to trench, use UV-resistant (brown) PVC pipe on top of the soil. Mount irrigation heads on risers supported with stakes. Set sprinklers or risers perpendicular to the slope. For aesthetic purposes, cover all exposed piping with mulch.

Design and install irrigation so it does not directly hit the paths. This requires particular attention to design. If using general area coverage instead, stabilize the paths with stabilized decomposed granite or concrete, or else install a system of chevrons to direct drainage off the path. An alternative is to simply mulch the paths with the same shredded redwood bark used for the rest of the landscape. As the paths are used, the mulch will compact and the pathways will be distinguishable. The compacted mulch will still provide erosion protection.

Shredded redwood bark adheres to 1.5:1 slopes as long as it is matted down with water. It is an excellent all-around erosion control. On especially steep or unstable slopes, first install jute netting over the soil and anchor it with U-shaped staples. Cut holes in the jute to accommodate plants. Lay redwood mulch directly over the jute (which will disintegrate over a few seasons).

Native groundcovers stabilize steep slopes.

Shredded redwood bark adheres to newly planted steep slopes.

Poorly draining areas and freshwater marshes (i.e.,lawns)

You may have an area that does not drain well. Or, you may decide to retain or install a lawn. Perhaps you have children or a dog and feel that a lawn is an appropriate feature for them to play on. As a general rule, we allocate about 300 square feet of lawn per child or pet.

Ecologically, lawns are freshwater marshes. They represent an area of high moisture, fertility, and disturbance, much like a marsh or stream-side woodland. In fact, it could be interesting to create your own wetland. Use natives that naturally grow in wet environments. A myriad of plants are available. Pacific wax myrtle (*Myrica californica*) is a beautiful, ever-green, foundational, large shrub or small tree. Marsh elder (*Iva hayesiana*)

A slope planting after only one year.

is a fairly neat, evergreen, mounding groundcover. Alkali heath (*Frankenia salina*) is a surprisingly handsome small sub-shrub with lovely pink flowers capable of growing in the wettest and saltiest clay soils. Color plants include yellow or cardinal monkey flower (*Mimulus guttatus* or *M. cardinalis*), scarlet lobelia (*Lobelia cardinalis*), white-flowered yerba manza (*Anemopsis californica*), and marsh fleabane (*Pluchea odorata*). Provide spiky accents with sedges (*Carex* spp.) or rushes (*Juncus* spp.). Use additional native grasses at the edges, like deer grass (*Muhlenbergia rigens*), alkali sacaton (*Sporobolus airoides*), or bent grass (*Agrostis pallens*). Wetlands are highly attractive to many birds and insects. If you have an expanse that is too wet to walk on, build a boardwalk to traverse it, like in a nature preserve. Rather than a single-species, monocarpic expanse like a lawn, imitate nature with multiple species and intrigue. Use your imagination.

Putting it all together: Creating the landscape design

Once your base drawing is complete, make several copies for working and editing purposes. Professionals use separate sheets to designate different elements, one for irrigation, one for electrical, etc. Decide on your landscape style, as this will drive the types of features you create, and also the plant selection and usage. Your creative tissue copies, sketching out ideas, can provide inspiration and concepts for your final plan.

Proportion is a very important consideration. John Brooke, in his excellent book *Garden Design*, emphasizes the need to select some prominent feature on the house and use it as a scaling factor. Using that basic dimension, use an overlay and draw a grid over the design, sometimes at angles to the house, to create flow. Follow this basic grid as you add in features, thus assuring that the entire landscape will be in appropriate proportion to the house.

Using your bubble drawing and grid guides you can now begin to compose your landscape. Start by drawing the paths and flatwork. This creates the framework of the landscape. Add your desired features—boulders, dry streams, bridges, benches, walls, fencing, decking, and so on. Use your scaling grid in sizing these features, as well.

The planting plan

The basic framework for the landscape has been established, all the features have been defined and located, and now it is time to add the icing to your cake: plants. Begin by determining the types of plants and numbers you will need: trees, shrubs, perennials, groundcovers, etc.

Use your planting plan to establish the location of each. Use a circle template to represent plants in your drawing. While there is no magic formula for selecting your specific plants, use the information in this book's plant section to guide you. It will assist you in plant selection and usage, as well as aid you in determining plant communities and compatibility.

Have a purpose for each plant. This is important. Use trees to create shade, define spaces, and channel or block views. Larger shrubs can break up expansive planting areas, screen views, create garden rooms, and establish a leafy backdrop along the perimeter. Medium shrubs create the backbone of the garden. Groundcovers help tie everything together and set up the foreground for everything else in the design. The perennials are used along the edges and in combination with features to create bright color accents that change seasonally.

Of course, you are designing to the elements of your selected garden style. But, to review, it is important to mass most of the plantings that form the backbone of your landscape. Massing creates flow and drama. As mentioned, most of the plantings (about 70 percent) should be evergreen. As enticing as all the individual plants seem, resist the urge to have one of everything in your landscape. Create a well-integrated landscape instead of a specimen garden. Plant to the mature size of the plant, not its size in the nursery container. Patience pays great dividends in landscaping. Following these principles will assure that the basic design will give you low-maintenance satisfaction over time.

Woodland nativescape behind pool with deer grass and alder.

GARDEN STYLE
It's your party

5

Used creatively, California native plants can be designed to produce any landscape style. Naturalistic landscapes are certainly the most common, limiting perceptions of just how flexible the plant palette can be. Creating a garden style is about knowing how to use the plants and accessories. Virtually any style of landscape is possible with the wide variety of native plants available. This includes formal, contemporary, Mediterranean, Southwestern, and even Asian. The trick is in knowing the plants and selecting the right forms and shapes with the right placement and maintenance.

Vine maple (*Acer circinatum*) is an excellent native substitute for Japanese maple in the Asian-style garden.

Formal style
Geometry, balance, symmetry

The formal style is one of the legacies of old Europe. The phrase brings to mind the glorious gardens of Versailles, the disciplined gardens of Rome, castles, hedges, and ornately designed colorful carpet beds. For the most part they are not of nature. They are a celebration of human mastery over the environment, conveying a sense of opulence, discipline, and attention to detail. These gardens are highly controlled and are, therefore, maintenance intensive. Most California homeowners find the style more intimidating than inviting. Yet, these are landscapes that have withstood the test of time, and there are those whose idea of a perfect landscape embodies this style. Others find it just plain fun to play with people's preconceptions.

It is realistic to create a formal garden entirely composed of California native plants. The rules of proportion, geometry, balance, and symmetry inherent in formal gardens are achieved in the garden layout. Ornamentation, pathways, and statuary are all elective and can be taken from any era. There are native evergreen plants that can be shaped and maintained as hedges, columns, and regular forms, as well as grasses that take low watering for formal lawns.

It is important to use evergreen plants that can be closely clipped into formal shapes in creating a formal garden. Massing is also key. Formal gardens utilize architectural forms like box hedges, screening hedges, spheres, and even topiary. These are set along basic geometric lines accented with flourishes. The hardscape includes well-defined pathways, benches, fountains, and even statuary, which may be classical to quite ornate. Paths are usually gravel or decomposed granite.

Plants like lemonadeberry (*Rhus integrifolia*) or sugar bush (*Rhus ovata*) are great for tall, long hedges. *Arctostaphylos densiflora* 'Howard McMinn' makes a great medium hedge. Consider plants like redberry (*Rhamnus crocea*) and *Arctostaphylos hookeri* for clipped box hedges. Several native cypresses can substitute for Italian cypress—Gowen cypress (*Cupressus goveniana*), Tecate cypress (*C. forbesii*), and San Pedro Matir cypress (*C. montana)* come readily to mind. Incense cedar (*Libocedrus decurrens*) forms a large-scale conical feature. Massed seaside daisy (*Erigeron glaucus*) or perennial buckwheats (*Eriogonum* spp.) are excellent for color monoliths as is the attractive *Arctostaphylos* 'John Dourley'. A formal garden may not be your first choice for a landscape, but it can be fun to bust a paradigm if you have the interest.

In this garden note the four columns with balls in the center and the statue fountain along the northeast side, which is surrounded by evergreen currant trained up a trellis to form a solid backdrop. The 'Sunset' manzanita in the center is pruned into a four-foot pyramid. The Catalina cherries are pruned as single-trunk lollipops. Other plants are pruned into hedges. Beach strawberry is used as a groundcover.

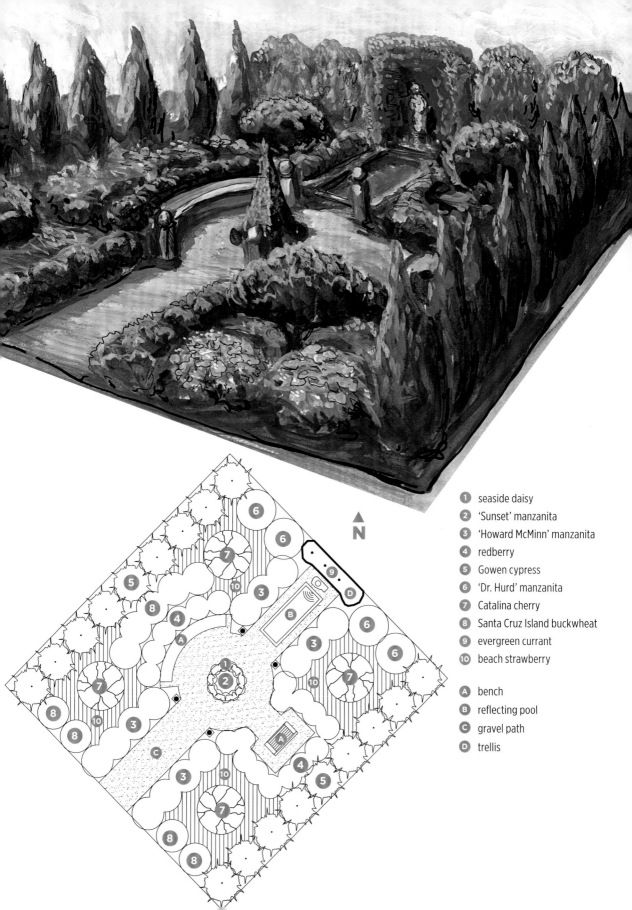

1 seaside daisy
2 'Sunset' manzanita
3 'Howard McMinn' manzanita
4 redberry
5 Gowen cypress
6 'Dr. Hurd' manzanita
7 Catalina cherry
8 Santa Cruz Island buckwheat
9 evergreen currant
10 beach strawberry

A bench
B reflecting pool
C gravel path
D trellis

N

Contemporary or modern style
Linear shapes, perspective, minimalist

Like the formal landscape, a modern garden emphasizes massing and control. However, the setting is minimalistic and contemporary, with clean lines framed by hardscape. The plants themselves become part of the architecture. They may be used singly or in geometric grids. Vertical and horizontal linear accents are very important. So is strong contrast, both in shape and color.

Spiky native plants are ideal for modern-style gardens. Yuccas, nolinas, and agaves are highly architectural in appearance. So are deer grass (*Muhlenbergia rigens*) and dune grass (*Leymus condesatus* 'Canyon Prince'). Be careful with grasses, however, as they can require a lot of maintenance, at least yearly or bi-yearly trimming back, and over time the individual bunches usually spread. Regardless, the plants should be spaced far enough apart so that the grid pattern is still evident. Conversely, they can be placed close enough together so that the overall effect is contiguous and monolithic, almost a single element.

Contrast is also important. Spiky vertical accents should be contrasted with low, horizontal elements. *Arctostaphylos cruzensis, A. edmundsii* 'Carmel Sur', or *A.* 'John Dourley' work well. Their green color contrasts nicely with the blues of foothill yucca (*Yucca whipplei*) or *Leymus condensatus* 'Canyon Prince'. Upright *Ceanothus* 'Anchor Bay' and *C. maritimus* have small, regular, dark green leaves, so they are architecturally dramatic, though on a larger scale. The silver-blue color of *Arctostaphylos* 'Pacific Mist' combines nicely with the spiky dark green *Agave shawii* or deer grass (*Muhlenbergia rigens*). The flat native dwarf juniper (*Juniperus communis*) is another gray-green, low ground-cover with a beautiful, feathery texture. Pair it up with field sedge (*Carex praegracilis*) as a dark green, but none-too-tall, spiky accent. They both like a bit more moisture. Finally, sulfur buckwheat (*Eriogonum umbellatum*) planted in a distinctive grid is neat and clean enough to create a dramatic, colorful effect.

Native plants are rarely considered for use in a contemporary garden. The preconception that they are "wild" belies the fact that many architectural species are available. Vertical and horizontal forms are contrasted throughout. Gravel is used as clean top-dressing complementing the orthogonal structure of the concrete flat work. Rectangular planters, benches, and fountains mirror one another and create horizontal changes in level. Plants are massed in neat, geometric rows. La Cruz manzanita is maintained in neat mounds with Shaw's agave in cylindrical pots. 'Dr. Hurd' manzanita is underplanted with purple three awn grass. The field sedge is surrounded by dwarf juniper.

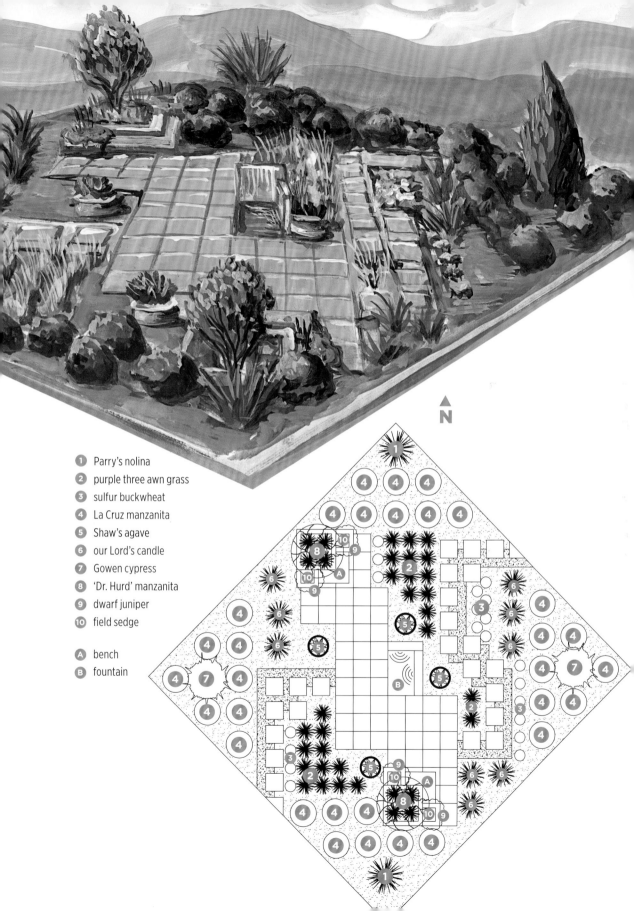

1 Parry's nolina
2 purple three awn grass
3 sulfur buckwheat
4 La Cruz manzanita
5 Shaw's agave
6 our Lord's candle
7 Gowen cypress
8 'Dr. Hurd' manzanita
9 dwarf juniper
10 field sedge

A bench
B fountain

Mediterranean style
Warmth, softness, color

The Mediterranean style is characterized by bright colors, soft forms, vertical accents, and less rigid formality. There is some leeway in the Mediterranean style as befits its ancestry—think Spain, Italy, Southern France, Greece, North Africa, Turkey. The Mediterranean region was the birthplace of the sultans' gardens with limited water resources but prominent water features.

California native plants are ideal for this style of landscape. Our plants evolved in similar climates, and this landscape approach evolved in response to comparable lifestyles. It reflects a sun-saturated, easygoing, naturalistic living environment. Yet these gardens still retain defined form and structure. The hardscape also reflects these attributes. Masonry is accented with stucco and colorful tiles. Decomposed granite, gravel, flagstone, or paver stepping stones are used for paths. Tile, paver, or flagstone patios, fountains of various styles, and birdbaths complete the composition.

Sages readily come to mind for this setting. Carefree color, strong fragrance, and billowy texture feature prominently. Individual shrubs of ceanothus, manzanita, and buckwheat may also add to the effect. Structural massing is not as critical in this form—individual specimens make distinctive accents. Native cypress can be effective as a vertical accent. Even native wild roses are reminiscent of Mediterranean ambiance.

Although we are designing primarily with native plants, subtropical fruits of the Mediterranean region are compatible and appropriate for this garden style. Mediterranean gardens are as practical as they are beautiful. Dwarf citrus are both ornamental and edible. They are extremely compatible with native plants. Pomegranates are also appropriate. In a tribute to the viticulture of the region, why not add the native grape *Vitis* 'Roger's Red' on a trellis, overhead, or on a fence to create a beautiful burgundy accent in fall? These native grapes are edible and make a great juice if crushed and filtered.

In this garden Mexican tile pavers are the main flat surface, with square pavers along the southwest side and in the north and east corners. Woodland strawberry is used between the square pavers as groundcover. A perennial mix of 'Margarita BOP' foothill penstemon, California fuchsia, cut yarrow, and seaside daisy is used as a groundcover in the east and south corners. Shredded redwood bark is used as mulch in other parts of the garden. The wild grapes are trained to the trellis and the cypress are maintained columnar.

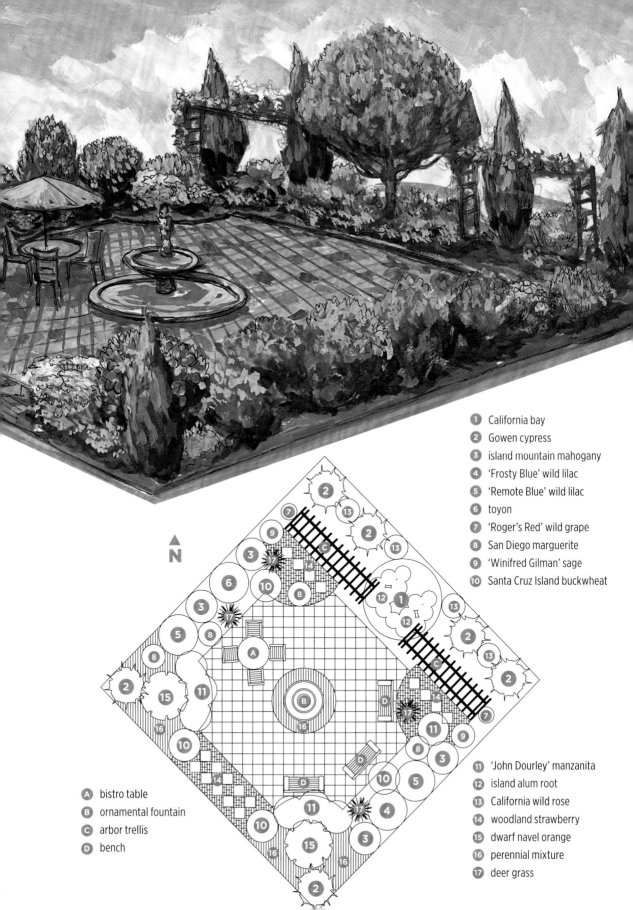

1 California bay
2 Gowen cypress
3 island mountain mahogany
4 'Frosty Blue' wild lilac
5 'Remote Blue' wild lilac
6 toyon
7 'Roger's Red' wild grape
8 San Diego marguerite
9 'Winifred Gilman' sage
10 Santa Cruz Island buckwheat

N

A bistro table
B ornamental fountain
C arbor trellis
D bench

11 'John Dourley' manzanita
12 island alum root
13 California wild rose
14 woodland strawberry
15 dwarf navel orange
16 perennial mixture
17 deer grass

Desert or southwestern style

Architectural, sparse, inorganic

Although little of California is actual desert, Southwestern-style landscapes are possible throughout most of the state. Again, it is all about using layout, setting, and supporting materials to create the effect. Desert gardens are characterized by low planting density, inorganic mulches (especially a mix of sand, pebbles, and rocks), and boulders. Stylized forms of this approach may use gravel as a uniform mulch; however, using a sand or rock mixture is much more authentic and visually appealing.

Desert plants are so good at conserving and maximizing their resources that they do not intrude on each other's territory. Desert vegetation is widely spaced, almost as though each plant is a specimen, in and of itself. Most desert shrubs have an open structure and smaller leaves with less surface area to minimize transpiration of vital moisture. Many of our native desert plants are adaptable to other locations; however, an irrigation schedule is critical. Unlike chaparral plant communities, the Southwest receives most of its moisture in summer, in the form of monsoons. Think of a summer thunderstorm when the water comes down hard and fast; it doesn't linger, but drains away in a flash flood. Good drainage is essential. The plants soak up the moisture and hang onto it to utilize until the next storm. Therefore, a desert garden must be set up with a separate irrigation system for summer supplementation. Most Southwestern landscapes are left completely unirrigated during the wet winter months.

Some highly adaptable desert trees include desert willow (*Chilopsis linearis*) and palo verde (*Cercidium floridum*). Despite its name and slender leaves, desert willow is not a willow at all. It has beautiful trumpet-shaped fragrant flowers in a variety of pink-based colors with a very long bloom cycle, often from May through September. *Cercidium* 'Desert Museum' is a more recent palo verde introduction. This three-way hybrid of two cercidium and one parkinsonia species has beautiful structure, large yellow and red flowers over a long period, and, best of all, is thornless.

Shrubs for the Southwestern-style landscape include brittlebush (*Encelia farinosa*), desert or apricot mallow (*Sphaeralcea ambigua*), Apache plume (*Fallugia paradoxa*), pink fairy duster (*Calliandra eriophylla*), desert sage (*Salvia dorrii*), and jojoba (*Simmondsia chinensis*). Remember, space these shrubs out individually, although odd-numbered groupings of up to five shrubs will still preserve the effect. Also include spiky plants like *Yucca* spp., *Agave* spp., ocotillo (*Fouquieria splendens*), and *Nolina* spp. These plants are best used singly, as specimen accents. Finally, a smattering of cacti will add significantly to the drama. Native cactus species are important, as well, including *Opuntia* (beavertail and cholla), *Ferrocactus* (barrel cacti), and *Mammilliaria* (fishhook and pincushion). We use cacti sparingly to more accurately reflect the nature of our California deserts. Dense use of cacti starts to move the style more toward a succulent garden, and has the practical effect of being prickly to maintain.

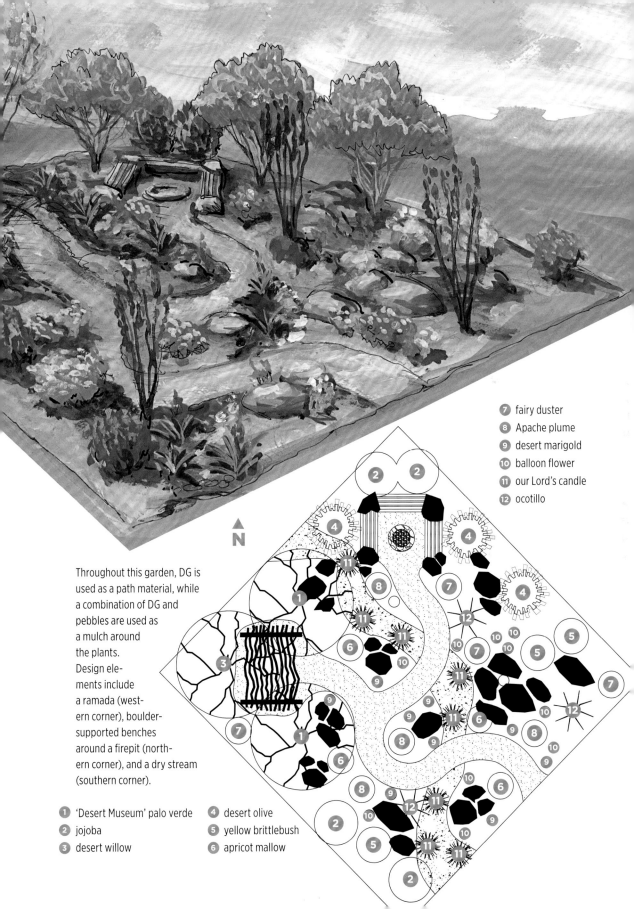

7 fairy duster
8 Apache plume
9 desert marigold
10 balloon flower
11 our Lord's candle
12 ocotillo

Throughout this garden, DG is used as a path material, while a combination of DG and pebbles are used as a mulch around the plants. Design elements include a ramada (western corner), boulder-supported benches around a firepit (northern corner), and a dry stream (southern corner).

1 'Desert Museum' palo verde
2 jojoba
3 desert willow
4 desert olive
5 yellow brittlebush
6 apricot mallow

Asian or Japanese style
Evergreen, flowing, stylized nature

At first glance, creating an Asian-style garden from California native plants is completely counterintuitive. Afterall, this style developed halfway around the world, in a completely different climate. However, it is not nearly the stretch you might think. There are many native plants that lend themselves beautifully to an Asian garden, creating an effect that is authentic to the style, yet very native.

A well-designed Japanese garden requires a lot of staging. The philosophy of stylized nature is more controlled than may be first apparent. Every element has a purpose and a metaphor. Mountains and trees surrounding the garden area are "borrowed," or brought into the landscape to make it appear expansive. Mounds and boulders within the landscape reflect surrounding hills and terrain. The calming, contemplative effect of water is highly important, represented by everything from a large pond and waterfall to a suggestion of a waterway consisting of pebbles and boulders. A zen garden uses smooth gravel carefully raked around boulders to create a sense of fluidity and movement. Paths and bridges leading to and connecting the observer with the water features are also critical.

Carved rock (or molded concrete) lanterns lend or imply lighting along the pathways. They beckon the wanderer to explore further through the "forest," and suggest the restrained hand of humankind. These lanterns may include votives or low-voltage lighting to complete the effect at night.

Structures in an Asian garden may include fences, railings, arbors, benches, and even a tea house, should you be so inclined. Asian garden structures are generally built of regionally inexpensive and abundant bamboo. Large willow limbs, straight and extremely fast growing, can be used to simulate the bamboo form. Another interesting bamboo-like building substitute could be *Arundo donax*, a noxious Mediterranean reed now destroying native riparian wetlands. Be careful that the reed is fully cured, or you may get more *Arundo donax* than you bargained for. This plant loves to sprout and multiply.

Most plants in the Asian garden are evergreen. Subtle foliar color and texture are much more important than gaudy splashes of flower color. Trees and shrubs, especially small pines, are carefully maintained to appear contorted, suggesting windswept age (like large bonsai). Lodgepole pine (*Pinus contorta*) is an excellent substitute for Japanese black pine, and much more drought tolerant.

Coffeeberry (*Rhamnus californica*) is an elegant evergreen shrub with red stems, dark green oval leaves, and large colorful berries. It comes in a number of varieties ranging in form from low mounds to large shrubs.

Manzanitas (*Arctostaphylos* spp.), with mahogany red bark and dramatic branching structure, are perfect subjects for the Japanese garden. Use tall species to display their impressive sculptural scaffolding. Medium shrubs create near-perfect evergreen mounds with dense flowers and brilliant berries. Low-growing varieties

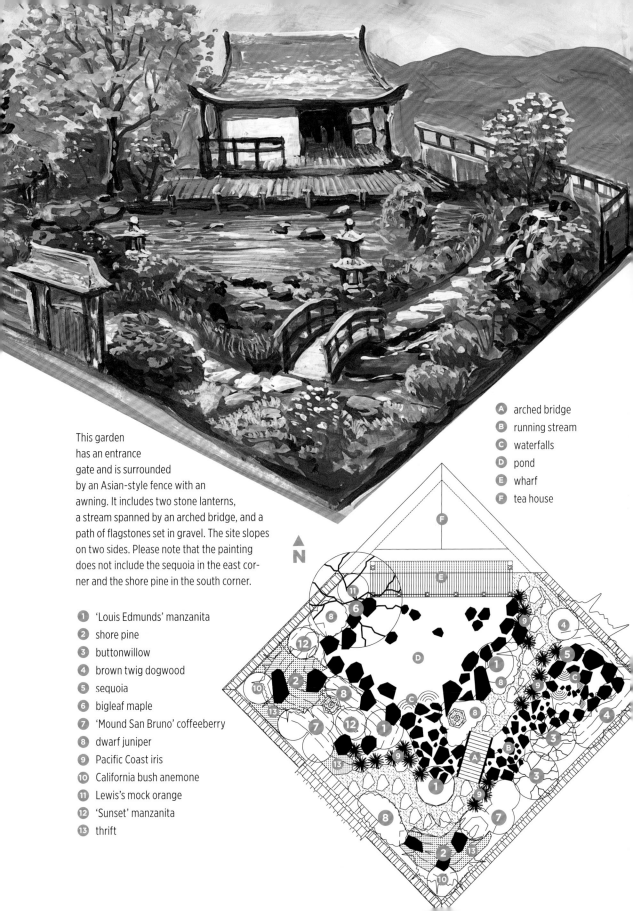

This garden has an entrance gate and is surrounded by an Asian-style fence with an awning. It includes two stone lanterns, a stream spanned by an arched bridge, and a path of flagstones set in gravel. The site slopes on two sides. Please note that the painting does not include the sequoia in the east corner and the shore pine in the south corner.

N

- A arched bridge
- B running stream
- C waterfalls
- D pond
- E wharf
- F tea house

1. 'Louis Edmunds' manzanita
2. shore pine
3. buttonwillow
4. brown twig dogwood
5. sequoia
6. bigleaf maple
7. 'Mound San Bruno' coffeeberry
8. dwarf juniper
9. Pacific Coast iris
10. California bush anemone
11. Lewis's mock orange
12. 'Sunset' manzanita
13. thrift

with high-density, evenly spaced leaves form lush carpets. Use varieties with different leaf coloration for interest and contrast.

Many other native species are ideal for Japanese gardens. Our native azalea (*Rhododendron occidentale*), with fragrant white flowers with yellow highlights, holds its own with any exotic variety. Pacific Coast iris *(Iris douglasiana)* creates the spiky texture of mondo grass. Many of our grass-like sedge and spike rush species are highly reminiscent of Asian varieties—some are even circumboreal, surviving more northern climates. *Juniperus communis* is a beautiful, very low-growing silver juniper, ideal in this type of landscape.

Considering color for the Japanese garden, appropriate plants include thrift (*Armeria maritima*), another circumboreal native with low grass-like leaves and bright pink pompon flowers. California bush anemone (*Carpenteria californica*) can be used like an upright gardenia, with its lovely fragrance and evergreen character. *Mahonia nervosa* strongly resembles the Japanese forms of barberry. Mock orange (*Philadelphus* spp.), California redbud (*Cercis occidentalis*), and snowdrop bush (*Styrax officinalis* var. *californica*) are striking for both their beautiful flowers and delicate deciduous nature. Our native birch (*Betula occidentalis*) has lovely fall color and beautiful bark. Buttonwillow (*Cephalanthus occidentalis* var. *californicus*) and native dogwoods (*Cornus californica, C. labrata, C. nuttallii, C. occidentalis, C. sessilis, C. stolonifera*) are also attractive deciduous shrubs. And finally, vine

maple (*Acer circinatum*) can be used to emulate the color and form of the Japanese maple (*Acer palamatum*).

Large trees for an Asian-style garden include white alder (*Alnus rhombifolia*), bigleaf maple (*Acer macrophyllum*), and redwoods (*Sequoia sempervirens* and *Sequoiadendron giganteum*). These are used primarily in the background or to define large garden spaces. Appropriate native understory plants include: native sedges, *Iris douglasiana*, evergreen currant (*Ribes viburnifolium*), creeping mahonia (*Mahonia repens*), snowberry (*Symphoricarpos* spp.), and woodland strawberry (*Fragaria californica*). Plants like the enormous giant chain fern (*Woodwardia fimbriata*), western sword fern (*Polystichum munitum*), and wood fern (*Dryopteris arguta*) complete the look of the Japanese shade woodland.

Natural stone is a basic and critical element in the composition of Asian gardens. Large boulders are a significant feature, carefully selected for volume, form, type, and color. One of the most popular types of stone is gneiss, a beautiful metamorphosed sedimentary rock. It is full of striations, often contorted, and has lots of color. Gravel is an appropriate stone mulch—not our typical roadway gravel, but a more refined, smaller size, colored to blend and contrast with path materials. Pathways are often flat stones and may also consist of an eclectic mix of materials. Native mosses can soften stone edges and planters, lending a sense of permanence and age. Again, it is important to create the illusion that the garden is as old as the ages.

Modern landscapes emphasize spiky, clean, geometric forms.

Spare architectural lines are enhanced by monkey flower, sage, artemisia, ceanothus, and manzanita.

Mediterranean landscapes include soft forms and less rigid formality.

Vegetable bed in native garden.

Low-density desert mallow and non-native prickly pear cactus with inorganic mulch and boulders.

Asian or Japanese style

Silhouette windswept pine on slope of native grasses and ceanothus in Japanese style.

Blooming ceanothus and pink-flowering currant in intimate garden setting.

PLANT SELECTION
A plant for every purpose
6

Landscaping your yard with California natives takes foresight, patience, an eye for beauty, an appreciation for nature, and the ability to look beyond popular myths and misconceptions. You may have heard the rhetoric—native plants look dead half the year, they are difficult to keep alive, they don't have any color, etc. Fortunately, this opinion is based on limited knowledge of native horticulture and plant choices. This chapter will show you a wide array of terrific plants available to the native landscape designer for any landscape situation, and the underlying ecology that supports their successful use. It will hopefully leave you excited for the potential of the rich California native plant palette. We have grouped the plants in the ways that we use them in the landscape, starting with the signature plants and working from the largest plants to the smallest—for example, large deciduous trees, then evergreens; followed by small deciduous trees, and again evergreens; before moving on to the backbone of shrubs, again by size. If your lot is too small for the largest plants, just skip them and look at the ones that are scaled to your property.

Due to proper plant selection, this rainbow of seasonal flower color only enhances the year-round combination of 'Concha' ceanothus and western redbud. Annual native wildflowers clarkia and California poppy bloom brightly in front.

California native plants adapted to survive in harsh environments. The principal systemic adaptation is the cooperative plant community. Rather than competing for limited resources, the plants in compatible plant communities work in synergy for mutual benefit. Compatible groups of different species of plants evolved to share resources in common soil, hydrologic, geographic, and climate conditions. The plant groups are repeatable for each occurrence of the same conditions. The plants utilize soil organisms to extract meager nutrients from poor soils and to store water. These same organisms transport and distribute moisture and minerals to best benefit the plant community. These specifically adapted, mutualistic, repeatable plant groups are known as plant communities.

To take advantage of the natural symbiosis of these plants and to help your landscape to thrive, group plants according to their plant communities. Biodiversity for a stable planting can be established with as few as five species from the same plant community. So long as the plants from the same communities are grouped together, you can create several communities in your landscape. Pay attention to three major divergent geographical regions: immediate coastal, inland, and desert, as it is best to stick to plant communities from only one of these regions for consistency in your garden.

Many plant communities are incredibly specific while others are more widespread. Some plants are adapted to more than one plant community. The table that follows describes the principal plant communities.

In a garden setting, one of the principal defining characteristics of a plant community is the nature of the mulch. Therefore we have grouped these descriptions by the type of mulch that best suits each community. For more in-depth descriptions of plant communities, see www.laspilitas.com/nature-of-california/communities.

Communities that require inorganic mulches (boulders, gravel, sand)

COASTAL STRAND Communities immediately adjacent to the sea, within reach of the salt spray. In this context beach sand, coastal bluffs, coastal prairie, and coastal salt marsh can be included. These areas become very salty as they dry out in late summer or early fall. Soils are shallow, often sand on hardpan. Wetter areas of fresh water support grasses and forbs (prairie), or where there is tidal influx, salt marsh plants.

GRASSLAND Inland from the sea are many spots characterized by shallow soils (usually less than a foot deep) on hardpan or bedrock (they correlate nicely with soil depth). Inundated with water in winter, bone dry in summer. Typically a small clearing in the midst of another plant community, they support perennial grasses and forbs. Often the perennials and annuals (wildflowers) are more abundant than the grasses.

RIPARIAN Areas of flowing water that cross many different plant communities. Usually the moisture nucleus for the surrounding community, with the trees acting as the moisture shunts. Supports an amazing array of plant and animal species. Fast-growing deciduous trees abound. Abundant softer plants like rushes used by birds for nesting. Lots of moisture, fertility (organic matter), and disturbance. Therefore, highly susceptible to invasion by exotics.

DESERT Regions generally east of the mountains including: alkali sink, Joshua tree woodland, creosote bush scrub, shadscale scrub, and sagebrush scrub. Usually receives less water than coastal areas, and rainfall is more evenly distributed throughout the year due to summer thunderstorms. Soil often contains high levels of sodium and boron, is highly inorganic, and pH is usually high. Summer temperatures often exceed 100 degrees for months on end. Our deserts are under extreme threat because of the proliferation of annual exotic weeds, which are promoting fire and destroying non-fire-adapted desert natives.

PINYON-JUNIPER WOODLAND
Pinyon-juniper woodland occurs in well-draining, principally inorganic soils above 1000 feet, often as a transitional community between desert and chaparral. It is diverse and often contains a mix of species from the surrounding communities. The pinyon pines (*Pinus monophylla, P. edulis,* and *P. quadrifolia*) occur where there is slightly more moisture than the areas inhabited by the junipers (*Juniperus californica*), with a tremendous number of associated shrubs and perennials. Some organic mulch will form under the pines and junipers.

Communities that like organic mulch with rocks at the base of the plants if possible

COASTAL SAGE SCRUB The predominant plant community just inland from the coastal strand. Occupies the California coast from San Francisco south. Under serious threat due to fires, development, and grazing. Often referred to as soft chaparral, with which it commonly intergrades. Plants are lower growing and more pliable than chaparral, often summer deciduous. Large range of soil types, from sand to clay, acid to alkaline. The clay areas easily type-convert to non-native grassland. Receives most of its moisture in winter, with some fog drip other times of the year. Thunderstorms are rare.

CHAPARRAL This is (or was) the predominant plant community in California. Often referred to as "Elfin Forest," made up of hard evergreen shrubs with hard leaves. It shares much in common with coastal sage scrub, although it usually occurs in areas with less fog drip. Can be a precursor to oak or pine forest, given enough time (hundreds of years?) and sufficient moisture. Doesn't usually make it that long. Helps increase local humidity levels by releasing moisture slowly over time. There is virtually no runoff or erosion in pristine chaparral ecosystems. Frequent fires (less than every 40 years) usually doom this plant community, type converting it to non-native weeds and grasses.

OAK WOODLAND Oak woodland is composed of southern, central, and northern representatives. Typically occurring in deeper soil (greater than 3 feet deep), pH ranges from slightly acidic up north to alkaline in the south. Can intergrade with coastal sage scrub, chaparral, or pine forest, depending on location. Heavily dependent on plant community partners. Historically, grasses were not a large component; most of the "savannah" now seen is actually weeds. Oaks are under extreme habitat threat from these invaders, which also create especially hot fires that destroy oaks.

REDWOOD FOREST California's version of the rain forest—up to 100 or more inches of rain per year, with heavy fog drip in summer. Occurs within the fog belt—very dark and wet. Acidic soils and a deep layer of organic mulch. Redwood (*Sequoia sempervirens*), the tallest tree in the world, can live over a thousand years. Grows back from cut stumps and fallen trees and can tolerate soil burial.

Communities that require deep organic mulch

MIXED EVERGREEN FOREST
Exists primarily in central and northern California but also limited spots in southern California. Comprised of mostly evergreen (with a few deciduous) leafy trees and shrubs, and some conifers. Soil pH is neutral to acidic. Relative humidity is usually less than 50 percent. Heavy understory of companion plants. Where soil depth drops to a foot or less, meadows of grasses and forbs exist. Can often occur as a transition community between redwood forest and pine forest.

PINE FOREST A generalized term for a group of communities including: yellow, lodgepole, and closed-cone pine forest, as well as the Douglas fir, red fir, and subalpine forest. All are characterized by coniferous trees growing in areas that receive 30 to 65 inches or more of precipitation, usually in well-drained, often inorganic soils. Most are found in the mountains, although Douglas fir and closed-cone pine can occur along our northern coast. Yellow pine forest is the most heat and drought tolerant of the group.

PLANT SELECTION
Native Trees

A popular perception is that few native trees in California are appropriate for residential landscapes. Nothing could be further from the truth. Native trees are available in all sizes and configurations: small or large, deciduous or evergreen, small or large leaved—you name it.

Specimen trees define the landscape.

California has many large native winter-dormant trees, some growing to heights greater than 100 feet. Residential lots may be too small to accommodate these behemoths, but where space permits, these trees are unparalleled in lending beauty, shade, and cooling comfort over a wide area.

LARGE MAPLES

Acer spp.

Bigleaf maple (*Acer macrophyllum*) and California box elder (*A. negundo* ssp. *californicum*) are beautiful large trees. The bigleaf maple can grow to an enormous size in the northwestern states, but generally stays in the 30- to 40-foot range in landscapes. With winter chill the leaves create a colorful autumn display. It creates far less litter than trees like the European ash (*Fraxinus excelsior*). In spring, new double-winged seeds (samara) are reddish hued, spinning as they fall. Once established, bigleaf maple is surprisingly drought and heat tolerant in its native range; however, it resents interior heat and low humidity.

California box elder has compound leaves, atypical of the maple family. Each leaf is composed of three or more individual leaflets. Although box elders are often viewed as "weed" trees in the Midwest, the California form is well behaved, maintaining a nice woodsy look. A rapidly growing shade tree, it tops out at about 50 feet—not overwhelming for residential landscapes—and becomes drought tolerant with age. California box elder has interesting filamentous flowers and the leaves often turn bright yellow in fall. Trees are either male or female (dioecious).

PLANT COMMUNITIES riparian, mixed evergreen forest, pine forest

LANDSCAPE USAGE Bigleaf maple and box elder are small enough to fit into most residential yards. Of the two, box elder has a greater tolerance of varying conditions. It is heat tolerant and becomes quite drought tolerant. Bigleaf maple has the feel and look of a stereotypical maple tree but is much better suited for California landscapes. It will tolerate heat and some drought in areas with higher humidity. It is susceptible to powdery mildew in dry heat.

California box elder (*Acer negundo* ssp. *californicum*) has compound leaves and filamentous flowers.

Use white alder near water sources.

WHITE ALDER

Alnus rhombifolia

This is a large (over 50-foot) extremely fast-growing tree that is not at all drought tolerant but solves the question "What native tree can I plant where the soil doesn't drain?" in native landscapes. This tree thrives in the middle or edge of a lawn. It often grows with its feet in a stream (do not plant white alder over sewer lines or septic systems, or you'll regret it). It is in the birch family (Betulaceae) and creates a nice large grove effect when planted in clusters. Alders have distinctive "eyes" that form at old branch collars, accenting the silver bark. Many love the deep green foliage. Indians used the bright orange sap as an important dye. Briefly deciduous, it drops last year's leaves as new ones emerge. Cone and leaf drop can be messy.

PLANT COMMUNITY riparian (up to 8000 feet)

LANDSCAPE USAGE This large, water-loving tree has aggressive roots. No more than one tree should be used in a small yard, out of reach of septic or sewer lines. Place it at a poorly draining spot or next to a large feature like a dry streambed. If the area is not naturally moist, you must provide supplemental irrigation. As reward, it can grow 10 to 12 feet per year to become an effective shade tree in just a few years. We plant this one and then get out of the way!

WESTERN SYCAMORE
Platanus racemosa

Western sycamore is a defining tree for California. Sinewy stretches of riparian forest are often filled with sycamores and their oak woodland companions. It is majestic in scale (over 75 feet) with a mottled white trunk that glows in the winter sunset. Its huge, maple-like leaves turn tawny yellow in fall. It is a "tree of life," supporting species of birds and butterflies, especially swallowtails. Sycamores are often multi-trunked, cloning themselves from side shoots. An old specimen (potentially exceeding 500 years) usually consists of a ring of huge trunks surrounding a central void from which the original tree has long since vanished. Western sycamore can become drought tolerant with time. Sycamores suffer from anthracnose, especially after a moist, cool spring, causing the first flush of leaves to drop (see the care and maintenance chapter). Leaves shed in the autumn are large and do not break down rapidly. Mulching vacuum blowers help reduce the volume of leaf litter during cleanup.

PLANT COMMUNITY riparian (to 6000 feet)

LANDSCAPE USAGE This enormous tree fits only the largest yards. Its breadth may exceed 50 feet. Do not plant sycamores under power lines. Robust, shade-tolerant plants are a must for understory plantings. Few plants grow under sycamores in the wild.

Western sycamore attracts native wildlife.

WESTERN COTTONWOOD
Populus fremontii

Western cottonwood is another enormous tree (over 100 feet tall and wide) inhabiting riparian zones in nearly all communities. Cottonwoods grow unbelievably fast—30 feet in a single year has been reported. The tree is extremely heat tolerant once it taps into a ground-moisture source, even a deep water table. Cottonwoods help provide moisture for the rest of the plant community by utilizing their strong taproot to access deep moisture sources, and then share water with the rest of the associated plants through mycorrhizal fungi. The root systems are deep and extremely aggressive. Do not plant this tree anywhere near a septic system or under power lines. Distinctive flat-stemmed leaves quake in the breeze, apparently helping with cooling. They turn a warm yellow color in fall. Cottonwood bark, deep-furrowed with age, adds character. All kinds of birds and insects inhabit these trees. Range tolerant and fast growing, they are often the first trees to grow in a disturbed site, allowing great numbers of wildlife to reestablish quickly. Cottonwoods transpire so rapidly that they create a cooling shade temperature difference of up to 30 degrees.

PLANT COMMUNITY riparian (to 6600 feet)

LANDSCAPE USAGE This is a tree for a large yard; plant it away from sewer lines, septic systems, and flatwork. It may grow as wide as it is tall. Use cottonwoods in hot summer areas. They love heat and serve as wonderful air conditioners in the desert. Be sure to use male clones when possible; the female plants produce copious amounts of cottony fiber.

DECIDUOUS OAK TREES

Quercus spp.

California's magnificent deciduous oaks exhibit dramatic form, color, and, in some cases, great size. Some have ovoid leaves, while others have deeply lobed leaves that people classically associate with oaks. Oaks are highly plant-community oriented. Never allow weeds to infest the understory. Deciduous oaks are especially susceptible to weed encroachment, since they do not accumulate a massive litter layer like their evergreen counterparts. Plant appropriate companion plants around oaks—it helps the oak and it just looks right.

Valley oak (*Quercus lobata*) is one of California's largest, most stately, and fastest-growing oak trees. It is found from Los Angeles to Sonoma. Many old movie ranches were located in valley oak woodland areas. They prefer rich, deep soils, as are often found in valley bottoms. They tolerate heat and drought once established; however, they require a deep source of water. Valley oaks like stability in whatever situation they occur. Many old valley oaks have died after wells depleted water tables in their natural growing grounds. As landscape plants, they are adaptable to a wide range of conditions, as long as the soil is deep. They may grow 3 to 4 feet per year when happy. The leaves turn yellow or light orange prior to dropping. Acorn production is heavier in alternating years.

Blue oak (*Q. douglasii*) occurs only within the borders of California. As the name suggests, the leaves are lightly lobed with a rich blue-green color that turns yellow-orange in the fall. Unlike valley oak, these trees are truly drought

The stately Engelman oak (*Quercus engelmannii*).

Valley oak (*Quercus lobata*) needs deep soil.

tolerant and are able to survive in poor, thin soils. The bark has attractive linear furrows. Blue oak grows very slowly, which may challenge the patience of some gardeners. This lovely tree rewards those who wait.

California's rarest oak is the Engelmann oak (*Q. engelmannii*), native from the base of the San Gabriel Mountains south into Riverside and San Diego counties. This beautiful tree is under-utilized in native landscaping. Striking blue-green leaf color dramatizes the distinctive branching structure and furrowed bark. Color-blend it with plants in the blue spectrum of garden color. Engelmann oak grows in shallow soils

and is drought tolerant. It can easily grow 2 feet per year, starting to form a nice small tree in 5 to 10 years. It withstands heat and smog, as well. Engelmann oak is semi-deciduous in winter-moist years, hanging onto the previous year's leaves. The color is stunning, as the bronzy newer leaves contrast against the older blue leaves when the tree is covered in yellow blossoms in spring. The small acorns (about 1 inch) are easily manageable. However, this tree does not defend itself well against weeds; eliminate exotic weeds out to about 1½ times the diameter of the canopy. Surround it with companion plants like currants (*Ribes* spp.), honeysuckle

(*Lonicera* spp.), and redberry (*Rhamnus crocea*).

Elegant, colorful, black oak (*Q. kelloggii*), with deeply lobed leaves, grows in the mountains from Oregon to Baja California. It has year-round appeal, bursting forth with rose pink new leaves in spring, followed by rich greens in summer and warm yellows, oranges, and reds in fall. It is not completely drought tolerant, requiring some summer moisture in lower-elevation southern California gardens. Black oak prefers afternoon shade, as well. The large acorns, a preferred food choice by indigenous populations, take two years to develop. This tree grows quite large with age; however, unless it is located under perfect acidic, well-draining soil conditions, it can be used in landscapes as a smaller specimen tree due to its extremely slow growth rate.

PLANT COMMUNITIES oak woodland, chaparral, coastal sage scrub, mixed evergreen forest, riparian

LANDSCAPE USAGE The deciduous oaks of California are useful and dramatic in a native landscape. All but the Engelmann oak produce some litter, so they are better located away from pavement. Engelmann oaks, however, are nice trees for courtyards, sidewalks, or patios as they have small acorns, do not overwhelm their spaces, and create only a manageable amount of litter. On the other hand, valley oaks grow large quickly and should be used in the middle or outer reaches of the garden.

Large evergreen trees

California has a variety of large evergreen trees. Many are conifers, though there are leafy species, as well. Most leafy evergreens are slower growing than the large deciduous trees. Use them where they will be allowed time to reach the full potential of their majestic beauty.

MADRONE
Arbutus menziesii

Madrone is unique and truly stunning, with its large, dark green leaves and peeling red bark. People compare it to an avocado crossed with a manzanita. It grows in the coastal range from British Columbia to Baja California. A moisture lover, madrone grows in areas receiving over 40 inches of precipitation per year. It performs well in northern California gardens. In southern California it may be finicky, requiring both good drainage and supplemental irrigation. Afternoon shade, such as found in a canyon, is beneficial. Provide madrone with an ample layer of good quality organic mulch. In optimal conditions this tree can grow more than 5 feet per year, but it usually grows more slowly. Clusters of white urn-shaped flowers are followed by bright red, edible fruits. Birds love this tree.

PLANT COMMUNITIES chaparral, mixed evergreen forest, oak woodland

LANDSCAPE USAGE Use madrone to create a strong focal point in the landscape. Consider it where you want year-round shade. It is easier to use in coastal northern California, but it can

also be used in the south, as long as there is sufficient moisture and drainage. It will even tolerate clay under those conditions. This is not a good street tree because it drops litter. Madrone can be difficult to establish, needing some shade and mulch when getting started. Like manzanita, it can suffer from branch dieback for which there is no cure (see the care and maintenance chapter).

SANTA CRUZ ISLAND IRONWOOD

Lyonothamnus floribundus var. *asplenifolius*

Santa Cruz Island ironwood is a beautiful, slender upright tree with ferny

Large, glossy leaves are characteristic of madrone.

compound leaves, large flat clusters of white flowers, red ribbony bark, and a wonderful woodsy fragrance. Primordial ironwood covered much of the western United States until the first Ice Age. Thereafter, cyclical climate changes reduced its range, pushing it ever westward, until remnant groves hang on only in the Channel Islands. From a distance these marvelous fossil trees resemble weeping redwood (*Sequoia sempervirens*).

PLANT COMMUNITIES chaparral, coastal sage scrub

LANDSCAPE USAGE Use ironwood to create a woodland feel. It is magnificent planted in a copse, like a grove of small redwoods. This tree is best grown

Fossil tree, Santa Cruz Island ironwood.

near the coast, where it grows to 35 feet. Inland it should be given afternoon shade. It grows well on interior, north-facing slopes or behind north-facing buildings. Its slender growth habit accommodates narrow spaces. For dramatic effect, feature an ironwood in a woodland atrium paired with appropriate shade-tolerant understory shrubs.

LARGE PINE TREES
Pinus spp.

Pinus is the largest genus of trees in California including many large forms. Different species occur from the coast to the highest mountains. Pines have clustered needles for leaves and pine cones that range from 2 to 18 inches or more in length.

Torrey pine (*Pinus torreyana*) is one of the rarest species in the United States, growing in sandstone deposits in the Del Mar area north of San Diego and on Santa Rosa Island. These pines grow fast with long, gray, five-needle bundles. Despite their restricted natural range, they are highly adaptable landscape trees. On the coast, salt-laden winds contort and twist their form into beautiful shapes; in the interior they can rapidly grow to 70 feet or more with straight trunks. Their pine cones hold large, edible bean-sized seeds, which were relished by local Indians.

Coulter pine (*P. coulteri*) is fairly common in the mountains of southern California. It is fast growing (2 feet per year) to over 80 feet and highly adaptable. Inland forms have rich blue-green 12-inch-long needles in bundles of three. This robust tree is drought and heat tolerant once established. Coulter pine's distinctive massive pine cone, up to 14 inches long, is covered in sharp scales. The largest pine cone in the world, it can weigh up to 10 pounds. Never plant this tree near a traffic or pedestrian area. Just hearing a Coulter pine cone crash to the ground from 70 feet is unforgettable!

Gray pine (*P. sabiniana*) is a useful landscape tree with an unusual airy appearance; it casts very light shade, contrasting well with dark, evergreen trees. Gray pine can exceed 100 feet in height and is drought tolerant. It can also abide some air pollution. Because of its light shadows, it is an easier pine to garden under. The people native to its range used the needles (three to a bundle) and roots to make baskets. The nutritious pine nuts are held in very large cones. Like Coulter pine, gray pine should be kept well back from traveled areas, due to its large cones.

Jeffrey pine (*P. jeffreyi*) is a slow-growing, truly beautiful pine with a grayish cast. It can handle drought, heat, and some pollution. Its slightly orange-red bark smells of vanilla. Jeffrey pine grows very slowly up to over 125 feet tall. Better to plant this one with oak trees or other pines when possible, as it benefits from strong plant-community

Five-needled Torrey pine (*Pinus torreyana*) can grow to 70 feet.

associations. Jeffrey pine needle bundles are in threes.

PLANT COMMUNITIES coastal sage scrub, chaparral, oak woodland, pine forest

LANDSCAPE USAGE Large pines are background trees, most appropriate for large spaces and estates. Dry needles are especially flammable, so plant these trees away from structures where dropping needles can collect on a roof. Many also have dangerously large pine cones (some potentially deadly, as with Coulter pines) requiring placement away from paths and sitting areas. Unfortunately, many are susceptible to blue stain fungus, which is transmitted by bark beetles. This fungus plugs up sapwood allowing beetles to persist as they girdle and kill the tree. Having said this, healthy trees are rarely attacked. Given enough room, they create a stately, dramatic focal point in the landscape. In the wild, trees growing in intact, weed-free ecological communities are somewhat less susceptible to beetle attack, although none are immune.

CATALINA CHERRY
Prunus ilicifolia ssp. *lyonii*

Catalina cherry is the native answer to ardent *Ficus benjamina* fans. It has rich green, smooth-margined leaves and beautiful light bark. Far more

Coulter pine (*Pinus coulteri*) in bloom.

Catalina cherry has edible fruit but large pits.

drought tolerant than its prosaic looka-like, the roots are non-aggressive and non-destructive. It grows about 3 feet per year after establishment, topping at 25 to 40 feet. You can also plant bulbs or groundcovers beneath it. It is called "cherry" for its sweet, Bing cherry–flavored fruit. Indians fermented the thin flesh for a beverage, and ground up the pits for delicious cherry marzipan. The abundant fruit attracts many berry-eating birds.

PLANT COMMUNITIES chaparral, coastal sage scrub

LANDSCAPE USAGE Catalina cherry is a handsome, easy-to-grow tree appropriate for formal and modern landscapes. It becomes fairly drought tolerant once established. Because its abundant fruit production can stain and litter concrete, it is better used away from flatwork. It's a true star in native landscapes.

EVERGREEN OAK TREES

Quercus spp.

Majestic evergreen oak trees are iconic "California." These gentle giants, dramatic and timeless, bridge back to when California looked like California. Maintain weed-free zones under the canopies of these oaks—better yet, plant native companion plants. These highly mutual-istic, plant-community-based trees per-form much better when grown among

community-compatible California native plants. If the environment beneath a mature oak has degraded to non-native weeds, then the oak is in imminent dan-ger. Judicious weeding benefits these oaks greatly and will allow them to attain their beautiful long-life potential.

One of the most common, signature oak trees is the coast live oak (*Quercus agrifolia*), found from Mendocino County south to Baja California. Its leaves are oval shaped, cupped, and ser-rated. Leaf form may vary considerably, even on the same tree. Coast live oak produces abundant acorns, all ripen-ing in a single season; this makes them an easy, though not always favorite, food source for numerous Indian tribes. Coast live oaks host an incredible array

Island oak (*Quercus tomentella*) is like coast live oak on steroids, with gorgeous glossy leaves.

of wildlife, including birds like oak titmouse, scrub jay, oriole, and acorn woodpecker, as well as the California sister butterfly. Coast live oaks are surprisingly fast growing when young, up to 3 feet a year when they are really happy. Use as a shade or background tree. Plan for a nice small tree of less than 30 feet. It does not usually lift pavement, although its continuous, ever-dropping, leaf litter may pose a maintenance issue.

Handsome, but underutilized, canyon live oak (*Q. chrysolepis*) is native to the mountains above 1000 feet, and is adaptable to nearly all landscape conditions. Canyon live oak can be found growing side by side with coast live oak. The leaves, dark green on top and fuzzy gold below, can be either toothed or smooth margined, often on the same tree. This tree is often multi-trunked with a broad canopy, growing to a height of 50 feet or more. It can tolerate one watering per week once established. The large, turban-shaped acorns, once a favorite of local Indian tribes, take two years to develop. Pioneers roasted the acorns to use as a coffee substitute. The only drawback to this magnificent tree is its slow growth rate, usually no more than a foot per year.

Island oak (*Q. tomentella*) is another evergreen oak with fine landscaping potential. Native to the Channel Islands, it was once prevalent on the mainland. Fossils of *Q. tomentella* found in the Mojave Desert date back 60 million years.

Coast live oak (*Quercus agrifolia*) hosts an abundance of wildlife.

It is like a coast live oak on steroids, with huge, luscious, dark green leaves and large acorns. Island oak is one of the few fast-growing evergreen oaks, up to 3 to 4 feet per year. It is more upright than most oaks, enabling use as a tall, narrow, stately accent in landscapes. Ideal in a formal garden setting, it can tolerate garden conditions. Use it in a transition planting about 1 to 15 feet from a lawn. Island oak is a real gem with much potential for savvy native landscapers.

PLANT COMMUNITIES oak woodland, chaparral, coastal sage scrub, mixed evergreen forest, riparian

LANDSCAPE USAGE The evergreen oak trees of California are useful as backdrop trees in creating a wooded theme. Their thick foliage creates deep shade, making them valuable interior shade trees. These oaks are adaptable to different soils and conditions. They are usually drought tolerant once established. The island oak works well in formal and modern gardens due to its dark green color and columnar shape.

COAST REDWOOD
Sequoia sempervirens

This plant demands superlatives. The state tree of California, redwood is the largest tree on earth. It is also one of the longest living—one specimen is known to exceed 2200 years of age. Use this tree for a large yard where you want to make a statement. Better yet, if you

have the room, plant this tree in a grove with a winding path and lots of native understory plants like wild strawberry (*Fragaria californica*), wild ginger (*Asarum caudatum*), huckleberry (*Vaccinium ovatum*), and Douglas iris (*Iris douglasiana*). In a grove, pruning redwoods vertically will give the illusion of much greater size and age. Coast redwood grows rapidly, up to 8 feet per year. This tree is not drought tolerant—it needs to be watered at least once per week in summer when planted south or inland from its native range. In southern California, larger trees grow best planted directly in a lawn or with misters mounted up in the canopy to simulate fog drip.

Coast redwood needs moisture.

PLANT COMMUNITY redwood forest

LANDSCAPE USAGE Use this tree singly or in groves to make a statement. Do not plant it in a small yard or near structures. The roots are widespread and aggressive (there is no taproot). They easily heave pavement or foundations. This is a great tree to use beside or within a lawn. Plant it on the north side of a tall structure in hot interior areas or mist its upper canopy.

CALIFORNIA BAY
Umbellularia californica

California bay is a highly aromatic, very handsome, and refined tree, appropriate for even formal or modern gardens. It grows slowly but can get quite large (over 100 feet tall). Slow growth makes it useful as a potted patio tree, somewhat like an ornamental ficus (without the nasty roots). It is shade tolerant and grows as an understory plant in the redwood forest. Nearly all parts of this tree have ethnobotanical value. The powerfully aromatic leaves are used as seasoning, usually at less than half concentration. Teas and infusions are used to treat various ailments. The fruit has an edible period, similar to avocado, after its volatility has settled down, but before it becomes overripe. The nut can be roasted, tasting somewhat like spicy unsweetened chocolate. The California bay's finely grained hardwood is excellent for woodworking.

PLANT COMMUNITIES chaparral, mixed evergreen forest, redwood forest, pine forest, oak woodland

LANDSCAPE USAGE Although California bay is ultimately a very large tree, its slow growth rate encourages use as a patio tree, especially in a large container, so long as the fruit is cleaned up or suppressed. The bay appreciates moisture, thriving under the same conditions as redwoods (*Sequoia sempervirens*). It tolerates many soil conditions and may be grown in sun or shade, growing more slowly and shrubby in full sun. This handsome, adaptable evergreen tree is usually pavement friendly.

California bay is appropriate for formal gardens and is highly aromatic.

Native patio and street trees less than 30 feet tall are ideal for a typical residential space. Most have non-invasive roots, so they work well around flatwork and structures. We begin with deciduous trees, which lose their leaves for part of the year, usually winter. Deciduous trees are nature's air conditioners, because they allow sunny exposure during winter, and humidified shade during summer.

SMALL MAPLES
Acer spp.

Few people know there are small maples native to California. These are particularly useful in creating a Japanese-style garden with California native plants. Vine maple (*Acer circinatum*), with reddish bark and beautiful white flowers with red sepals, is native to northern California. It requires cool, moist shade, and often displays yellow, orange, or red fall color. The small mountain maple (*A. glabrum*) is native to the mountains of California. It likes part shade and garden moisture. Planting near an eastern wall would be ideal. Mountain maple can have nice fall color, though the vine maple is much more reliable.

PLANT COMMUNITIES riparian, pine forest

LANDSCAPE USAGE Both of these small trees are excellent substitutes for Japanese maple, will thrive under the same conditions, and need regular water. Both grow to about 12 feet. Vine maple looks more delicate than mountain maple, but is a little touchier to grow.

'DESERT MUSEUM' PALO VERDE
Cercidium 'Desert Museum'

'Desert Museum' palo verde is an exceptional, free-flowering landscape tree that grows rapidly in well-drained soils. It is another intergeneric hybrid, developed in Arizona. This palo verde is thornless, with larger and more copious flowers than either parkinsonia or cercidium. Spring finds it covered in large, yellow flowers for several months. Hardy to about 60 degrees, it is adaptable in landscapes. Although technically deciduous, all palo verde stems and branches possess chlorophyll, so trees grow year-long. Leaf drop for palo verde is a drought adaptation that cuts down transpiration during the hottest weather.

PLANT COMMUNITIES desert, riparian washes

LANDSCAPE USAGE Because 'Desert Museum' palo verde is smaller and thornless, it is excellent as a tree for patios, streets, or parking lots. It tolerates a wide range of soil and moisture conditions provided there is good drainage.

REDBUD
Cercis occidentalis

This extraordinarily beautiful and useful multi-trunked tree has numerous virtues. Vase shaped, the silver sawtooth-patterned branches create a beautiful silhouette in winter. *Cercis* is covered in luscious heart-shaped leaves most of the year. Native redbud has lots of variability in localized populations, including a form with reddish purple leaves throughout the year. It bursts into flower in late winter or early spring before leafing out. The attractive silver branches host beautiful garlands of tightly packed pea-shaped flowers varying from white to deep magenta and purple. The flowers are edible, so use them to decorate a salad. Later, pea-shaped magenta seedpods hang like ornaments as the tree leafs out.

An excellent patio tree, 'Desert Museum' palo verde is thornless.

Redbud bursts into flower in late winter.

PLANT COMMUNITIES chaparral, desert, pine forest, oak woodland

LANDSCAPE USAGE This incredibly tough, easily grown tree is highly adaptable from the coast to the desert (with adequate moisture in the desert). Like many stone fruits, winter chill stimulates heavier bloom. It typically grows less than 15 feet tall, a perfect size for small yards and patios. Pruned into a single trunk, it can be used in parking strips, though it is ideally a multi-trunked specimen tree. Although deciduous, it is rarely messy, making it ideal around patios.

DESERT WILLOW
Chilopsis linearis

Desert willow's popularity is increasing, especially in hot-summer areas. It grows easily, fairly fast, and is disease resistant. Recent variety introductions have large and colorful flowers in a wide range of shades. Although desert willow's narrow leaves and multi-trunked form are reminiscent of a willow, this tree is in the trumpet vine family (Bignoniaceae) with frilly, fragrant, large, orchid-like flowers. It tolerates a wide range of soils and locations, even areas with occasional snow, as long as the temperature stays above freezing.

Another popular small tree, ×*Chitalpa tashkentensis* (developed in Tashkent, Ukraine), is an intergeneric cross between *Chilopsis linearis* and the

midwestern tree *Catalpa bignonioides*. Two forms have either white or pink flowers. ×*Chitalpa tashkentensis* leaves are wider than the straight desert willow. It enjoys heat and is prone to mildew near the coast. Single-trunk forms create a beautiful 20-foot lollipop tree.

PLANT COMMUNITIES desert, riparian

LANDSCAPE USAGE Heat-tolerant, single-trunk forms of *Chilopsis linearis* are popular trees for parking lots and strips. With manageable seasonal leaf drop it is a great tree for patios or to shade small courtyard areas. The

Desert willow sports large and vibrant flowers.

dramatic branching structure has attractive silver bark. It holds onto the fibrous seedpods in winter, but seedless forms like 'Art's Seedless' and 'Monhew's' are tidier. This is a rising star among native small trees.

DESERT OLIVE
Forestiera neomexicana

Desert olive is a very small, multi-trunked relative of the edible olive with satiny smooth white bark and small, deciduous leaves. It produces a dark-colored fruit relished by birds. The olive-like leaves turn bright yellow in fall. The bark is brilliant white. Desert olive grows to full size, about 15 feet, in just a few years. Desert olive cohabits a wide range of plant communities, a testament to its adaptability. This is an underutilized tree in California gardens.

PLANT COMMUNITIES desert, chaparral, coastal sage scrub, oak woodland, riparian

LANDSCAPE USAGE Desert olive is equally appropriate in a desert landscape as in a woodland garden. Select male plants for patio and street trees because they do not set fruit. Female plants are great bird attractors. Use against a rock wall, for a Santa Fe–type home, or in a modern garden with its stunning white branches exposed. This is a versatile plant deserving wider use in California landscapes.

FLOWERING ASH
Fraxinus dipetala
OREGON ASH
Fraxinus latifolia
VELVET ASH
Fraxinus velutina

Native ash trees are better behaved and better scaled for most gardens than their huge, messy European cousin, *Fraxinus excelsior.* Unlike the weedy versions, native ashes are smaller, less messy, and have less aggressive root systems. Flowering ash (*F. dipetala*) is a smaller form with white, fragrant flowers. It resembles a delicate elm with small, compound leaves. It thrives in shade, such as the north side of a large building or in the shadows of larger trees. Slower-growing Oregon ash (*F. latifolia*) has larger leaves than its flowering cousin. Velvet ash (*F. velutina*) resembles the larger-leaved *F. latifolia* but grows much faster and larger. These latter two hybridize readily, creating a small, fast-growing, large, compound-leaved tree. All are quite handsome, becoming drought tolerant with age.

PLANT COMMUNITIES chaparral, oak woodland, riparian, pine forest

LANDSCAPE USAGE All three ash species are excellent small shade trees for residential gardens. Although they have some leaf and seed (samara) drop, they are far cleaner and better behaved than the European ash. The flowering ash is the most delicate, lending a forest or woodland feel to the landscape. It

The native flowering ash (*Fraxinus dipetala*) is a good tree for shady areas.

Velvet ash (*Fraxinus velutina*) is a fast-growing tree with attractive compound leaves.

is best used in filtered shade. All three are good patio and street trees, provided they are located at least 5 feet away from pavement. The hybrid *Fraxinus latifolia* × *velutina* is showing much promise in the landscape.

ELDERBERRY

Sambucus mexicana
Sambucus caerulea

These similar, closely related large shrubs form nice, small trees when pruned up. *Sambucus mexicana* typically grows at lower elevations or closer to the coast, whereas *S. caerulea* grows at high elevations. The coastal form has large panicles of yellowish flowers in spring, whereas the mountain form exhibits bright white flowers. The clustered berries are nearly black, their waxy coating lending a bluish sheen, and are an important summer food source for birds in California. Cook the edible fruit before eating it in any quantity. Elderberry can grow amazingly fast—easily 8 to 10 feet per year. In time, the shredding bark lends a gnarled, rancho feel. Prune this large, rapidly growing shrub to establish and maintain tree-like form. In just a few seasons, with its speedy growth and shred-textured bark, it will look and function as an established small tree. Elderberry is rather messy and has strong roots, so it is better kept away from patios or similar structures. Since it can be twiggy, plan on regular pruning.

The showy flowers and fruit of elderberry (*Sambucus mexicana*) attract native birds.

Higher-elevation mountain elderberry (*Sambucus caerulea*) has bright white flowers.

PLANT COMMUNITIES chaparral, coastal sage scrub, riparian, oak woodland (*S. mexicana*); pine forest (*S. caerulea*)

LANDSCAPE USAGE Use it as a great little shade tree in the middle of the yard, or a large screening shrub at the perimeter. Showy flowers and fruit attract an amazing variety of birds and butterflies, making elderberry ideal for a habitat garden. It becomes drought tolerant once established.

Small Evergreen Trees

Small evergreen trees provide shade all year long. Many are also classified as large shrubs, but they possess strong branching character, making them suitable as small trees. Because they do not drop leaves seasonally, most are viable as patio and street trees, although berry drop may be an issue.

RED SHANKS
Adenostoma sparsifolium

The beautiful, small tree red shanks deserves more attention. Possibly shunned for its reputation as being fire prone, when it receives light yet dependable watering its flammability is significantly diminished. Use red shanks as a single specimen tree and consistently prune to remove dead wood; with these safeguards, it is a unique accent with its fine bright green leaves and red, shredded bark. It is highly drought and heat tolerant, grows well in very poor soil, and is a highly dramatic, almost alien-looking tree.

PLANT COMMUNITIES chaparral, coastal sage scrub, pinyon-juniper woodland

LANDSCAPE USAGE This unusual, dramatic small tree deserves more widespread use in landscapes. It is a nice patio tree so long as it is well maintained.

TREE MANZANITA
Arctostaphylos spp.

Most people consider manzanitas to be shrubs. However, there are a couple hybrid selections derived from Parry's manzanita (*Arctostaphylos manzanita*) large enough to be considered small trees. An amazing specimen plant, *A. manzanita* 'Dr. Hurd' grows to about 15 to 18 feet tall. It has large, glossy green leaves with satiny, maroon-colored bark. It can easily grow 3 to 4 feet per year, which is quite fast for a manzanita. It has beautiful white flowers and red, edible berries relished by birds. The large leaves are reminiscent of madrone.

The large, relatively fast-growing 'Austin Griffiths' manzanita (*A. manzanita* × *densiflora* 'Austin Griffiths') can easily be pruned into a small tree. Like 'Dr. Hurd', 'Austin Griffiths' has beautiful,

smooth, red bark, but smaller green leaves and bright pink flowers. Like all manzanita, it has red apple–like edible fruit in early spring.

Bigberry manzanita (*A. glauca*) also grows large enough to form a small tree. This plant has striking steel blue leaves that contrast beautifully with any green-leaved plant in the vicinity. Bigberry's new growth changes color as it emerges, from red-glazed to bronze to light green and finally blue. The bright white flowers, about twice the size of any other form, give way to dazzling large berries up to a half-inch in diameter. This spectacular plant is very slow

Arctostaphylos manzanita 'Dr. Hurd' grows to 18 feet with glossy green leaves.

Bright new growth of bigberry manzanita (*Arctostaphylos glauca*) will eventually change to blue green.

growing, usually not much more than a foot per year. If you have the time and patience, however, you will be amply rewarded.

PLANT COMMUNITIES chaparral, oak woodland, pine forest

LANDSCAPE USAGE Most manzanitas are surprisingly tolerant of a wide range of soil conditions as long as they have good drainage (in other words, do not put them in a lawn). Forget mixing organic matter in the soil; rather, use high-quality organic mulch on top, maybe with some 6- to 12-inch boulders at the base of their trunks. These manzanita tree forms are majestic showstoppers. 'Dr. Hurd' and 'Austin Griffiths' are fast, reliable, and adaptable to most landscape conditions. Slower-growing bigberry manzanita wants conditions like its native habitat. If this is practical, *Arctostaphylos glauca* is worth the trouble. If using any of these manzanitas as small street trees, use flat rocks to protect their base.

Arctostaphylos manzanita × *densiflora* 'Austin Griffiths' has smaller green leaves.

TREE WILD LILACS

Ceanothus spp.

Few native plants have been more maligned than ceanothus. They are rumored to be short-lived and difficult, with published life spans of less than 10 years. Yet, in the wild, most live long—50 to 100 years or more—and completely carefree lives. It is traditional ornamental horticulture that is deadly to ceanothus.

The largest wild lilacs are the straight species and hybrids of *Ceanothus arboreus*— *arboreus* meaning "tree" in Latin. This wild lilac is native only to the Channel Islands. It has large, luscious, tropical-looking leaves and pale blue, almost white flowers. Naturally bright blue forms include 'Cliff Schmidt' and 'Owlswood Blue'. The beautiful *C. arboreus* can grow to over 20 feet tall in multi-trunked form or pruned up into a single trunk.

Probably the best-known large ceanothus is 'Ray Hartman', a hybrid between *C. arboreus* and *C. griseus* introduced in the 1940s. This old, very reliable variety tolerates a large range of soils, and can be grown near the coast or inland. Its glossy green leaves are slightly smaller than its island parent. Like *C. arboreus*, however, it can grow to 20 feet. Spring finds it covered in brilliant blue flowers with pink buds, inherited from its *C. griseus* parent. It grows extremely rapidly, often 6 to 8 feet per year, attaining mature size in just three to five years. Many gorgeous, single-trunk tree specimens of 'Ray Hartman' can be seen at the Old City Cemetery in Sacramento.

Lakeside lilac (*C. cyaneus*) is a more obscure species, large enough to be pruned into a small tree. One of the most beautiful ceanothuses in the world, it has yet to find recognition in California landscapes. Lakeside lilac has amazing, huge (over 8-inch-long), purple flower clusters that hang down like wisteria. Its mirror-like leaves are brilliant green. The trunk is greenish blue—hence its name. It grows extremely fast, easily 6 feet a year. The delicate appearance belies a tough constitution, as it grows in some of the hottest, driest areas in California. Its only drawback is that it does not tolerate much summer water. Once established, water in summer

Fast-growing Lakeside lilac (*Ceanothus cyaneus*) is spectacular in bloom.

Ceanothus arboreus has beautiful near-white flowers and large, glossy green leaves.

The beautiful blue *Ceanothus* 'Ray Hartman' is a time-tested variety.

only enough to wet the leaves. Lakeside lilac's hybrid offspring, *C.* 'Sierra Blue' (*C. griseus* apparently the other parent), is much more popular in the trade, possibly because the hybrid displays slightly better garden tolerance; however, under appropriate landscape conditions, 'Sierra Blue' has shown little or no improvement over its parent.

PLANT COMMUNITIES chaparral, coastal sage scrub

LANDSCAPE USAGE These large ceanothus species all make good evergreen specimen trees. Nothing compares to a ceanothus in bloom—they are simply jaw dropping. Add redbud (*Cercis occidentalis*) and flannel bush (*Fremontodendron* spp.) to the landscape and you have a spectacle. As single-trunked trees the ceanothuses may require occasional pruning during the first few years to maintain clean form and prevent top heaviness. *Ceanothus* 'Ray Hartman' is one of the most commonly available standard forms. *Ceanothus arboreus* should be utilized more frequently as a standard, as well. *Ceanothus cyaneus* is vertical in habit and prefers to be multi-trunked. Ceanothuses all make great patio and street trees. As with manzanita, when using ceanothus as a street tree, place some flat rocks at the base to help prevent trunk damage and soil compaction caused by pedestrians. These really large ceanothuses are also great perimeter screening plants if left as large shrubs.

TOYON (California holly, California Christmas berry)
Heteromeles arbutifolia

Toyon is one of the best-known native shrubs in California. Unsubstantiated legend has it that Hollywood was named for this red-berried wonder. It is the most important winter food source for berry-eating birds in California. This outstanding, easy-to-grow plant can be used as a large screening shrub, small tree, or even topiary. It is covered in white flowers during spring, then bursting into brilliance with red, holly-like berries during the winter holidays. Bougainvilleas have nothing on this plant. Most garden toyons grow to 12 to 20 feet, but they can grow larger with age. One growing at an old adobe in Long Beach is approximately 80 feet tall with a 6-foot-diameter trunk. Imagine it completely covered in bright red berries (and birds) in winter—this is the magnitude of California natives we have lost, but hope to regain one day. Ironically, Asian photinia (*Photinia ×fraseri*) has been popularly planted in California when toyon has been growing under our noses the whole time. The former Latin name for toyon was *Photinia arbutifolia*.

PLANT COMMUNITIES chaparral, oak woodland, coastal sage scrub

LANDSCAPE USAGE Toyons are typically used as multi-trunked, densely foliated screening trees. Recently they

Toyon is covered with white blossoms in spring and red berries in winter.

are gaining popularity as single-trunk standard trees, rarely exceeding 20 feet in height. Proper location is important—their intense berry production and attraction to birds lead to high-maintenance, messy sidewalks.

SMALL PINES

Pinus spp.

California hosts a number of small native pines, excellent for smaller gardens and well scaled for residential lots. Knobcone pine (*Pinus attenuata*) is handsome and moderately fast growing, to about 25 feet in a landscape setting.

The numerous small cones resemble tree ornaments. This pine tolerates garden conditions and does well if watered weekly.

Shore pine (*P. contorta* var. *contorta*) occurs on the coast from northern California to Alaska, usually growing to less than 15 feet. An excellent substitute for Japanese black pine (*P. thunbergii*), it is somewhat more drought tolerant. In its natural, windswept environment it may resemble a shrub. This pine is best used in coastal sites since it grows naturally along coastal bluffs in northern California. For inland use, give it afternoon shade. Shore pine has great bonsai potential.

Bishop pine (*Pinus muricata*) will tolerate poor soils and may grow to 40 feet.

Bishop pine (*P. muricata*) is native to coastal California and the Channel Islands. It is a fast-growing, small tree, rarely exceeding 40 feet. It tolerates poor soils and is a good substitute for the native Monterey pine (*P. radiata*) because it resists pest and disease problems. Bishop pine is highly adaptable and has done well as far inland as Bakersfield. It also tolerates some boron in the soil. Bishop pine benefits significantly from a thick layer of good mulch.

The pinyon pines (*P. edulis*, *P. monophylla*, *P. quadrifolia*) are a group of very slow-growing small pines that are highly tolerant of heat and poor soil. They usually grow less than a foot per year. They are well suited for a miniature garden setting or for bonsai. The small cones contain edible nuts, though they take up to 20 years to start producing.

PLANT COMMUNITIES chaparral, oak woodland, pine forest, pinyon-juniper woodland

LANDSCAPE USAGE These small pines are all well suited to the residential landscape. Bishop and knobcone pines are valuable as street trees, despite their needle drop. They are superior to the commonly used Canary Island pine (*Pinus canariensis*). The pinyon pines are great for an outdoor railroad or in a very small yard. They are neat in appearance but unbelievably slow growing.

Native Shrubs

Evergreen shrubs should comprise over half of the landscape.

Climbing down the size ladder brings us to California's rich diversity of shrubs. These plants are less than 20 feet high and normally have multiple branches from the base with leaves to the ground. The distinction gets blurred when considering small trees, many of which are large shrubs pruned vertically to expose one or several trunks, topped with a canopy. Native shrubs abound since chaparral—often referred to as scrubland—is (or was) the most prevalent plant community in California.

Large Screening Shrubs

Utilizing large shrubs around the perimeter of a landscape obscures boundaries and creates a feeling of endless landscape, shifting distance focus to borrowed visual elements like mountains and large neighboring trees. Dense shrubbery provides less costly privacy than constructed barriers. Shrubs can also be used as featured elements within the landscape, and, if pruned up, can sometimes be converted to small trees.

MANZANITA
Arctostaphylos spp.

Manzanitas are an important, large, and diverse group of plants within California. Most are easy to grow, extremely neat in appearance, and fill a wide range of needs. They form the perfect backbone of native landscapes. Yet they appear so infrequently, probably because they are killed by standard ornamental horticultural methodology. These landscape workhorses need to be used more, in all forms.

Arctostaphylos manzanita × *densiflora* 'Austin Griffiths' and *A. glauca* have been described for their suitability as small, evergreen trees, but their natural, untrimmed habit is more shrubby. Pinkbract manzanita (*A. pringlei*), an impressive and large 10-foot shrub, shows good adaptability for landscaping. In spring bloom, the pink flower clusters and showy reddish bracts with emerging pinkish new foliage give this shrub a lot of color value.

Mexican manzanita (*A. pungens*) has narrow, dark green to gray leaves in most cases, but can be highly variable. It tops out at about 8 feet. This is one tough manzanita, tolerating soils from clay to gravel. It is widely distributed from San Francisco to Baja, Montana to Texas. It is a good choice for a specimen or as a background shrub with showy, light pink flowers, deep red bark, and somewhat narrow, upright habit. It produces copious amounts of berries relished by birds. This plant is gravely underutilized.

Island manzanita (*A. insularis*) is another large species from the Channel Islands. Its oval, glossy green foliage is especially handsome in landscape settings. New growth is lighter and often ringed in red. It sports numerous large clusters of light pink flowers in spring.

Island manzanita (*Arctostaphylos insularis*) has glossy oval leaves that sparkle in the sunlight.

This upright manzanita (*Arctostaphylos glauca*) has grayish leaves and colorful new growth in the spring.

The narrow leaves of pointleaf manzanita (*Arctostaphylos pungens*) can be gray to dark green.

Island manzanita looks appropriate in highly ornamental landscapes. It tolerates a wide range of soils, but needs good drainage. 'Canyon Sparkles' is an especially colorful, smaller form.

Numerous named manzanita varieties are exemplary as screening shrubs. 'Louis Edmunds' is an upright form similar to *A. pungens* that performs well in landscapes. However, it is a bit faster growing, with gray leaves, deep pink flowers, and purple bark. It has a remarkable tolerance for clay soil, although it does fine in mineralized soil as well. 'Louis Edmunds' is beautiful against a rock wall, pruned up to show the dark purple bark.

'Mama Bear' is a fine adaptable and stable 8-foot introduction from Las Pilitas. It is distinguished by large, oval, gray-green leaves and burgundy bark. 'Mama Bear' has light pink flowers and beautiful branching structure. The flower clusters cover the plant in spring. This is an easy, fast-growing, large shrub for most native landscapes.

PLANT COMMUNITIES chaparral, oak woodland, pine forest

LANDSCAPE USAGE Manzanitas are some of the critical backbone plants for the native landscape. The large, upright forms can be used as individual specimen plants or massed along the perimeter to create tidy, colorful backdrops. If used as individual specimens, some vertical pruning will expose the beautiful branching color and structure. These plants are not used enough, even in native landscapes, for the unfounded fear that they are difficult. They are not, as long as they are given lean soils, good mulches, and reasonable watering.

'Mama Bear' manzanita (*Arctostaphylos* 'Mama Bear') has large, oval, gray-green leaves and burgundy bark.

WILD LILACS
Ceanothus spp.

The other principal group of large screening shrubs in California is the wild lilacs (*Ceanothus* spp.). Most are fast growing and evergreen. Their flowers vary in color from white to deep purple to indigo. The genus includes many forms, from towering to groundcovers. The following are useful shrubs.

Lakeside wild lilac (*C. cyaneus*) is one

of the largest, fastest-growing shrubs in California. It has been mentioned as a small, multi-trunked tree candidate, but deserves another reference here for its rapid growth, showy flowers, and beautiful glossy foliage. The same goes for C. 'Ray Hartman', another rapid grower with beautiful flowers and dense evergreen foliage.

Another truly great ceanothus is C. 'Frosty Blue'. It is time tested and one of the most garden tolerant of all wild lilacs. It derives its name from deep blue flowers with touches of white. It just sparkles. 'Frosty Blue' is fast growing and can achieve mature height in less than two years. It is also fairly long lived as long as it's not abused. Its rich green, dense foliage makes it an excellent screening plant.

C. 'Julia Phelps' is darker flowered and small leaved. This old garden staple has proven its worth over the years. It can grow to 12 feet tall, resembling a dark blue ball in spring. Flowers may completely obscure the foliage. Pink buds give this plant sparkle. It is adaptable to a wide range of garden conditions. It seems more stable and longer lived than a similar variety known as 'Dark Star'.

C. 'Mountain Haze' is a lighter blue than 'Frosty Blue', but grows faster and does better in sandy or loamy soils. Bert Wilson of Las Pilitas Nursery relates how one of his was attacked by a gopher, fell over, and still made 8 feet in three years, albeit a little crooked. If using this ceanothus in heavier soil, do not overwater. In lighter, well-draining soils, it can tolerate one watering per week. It is a fantastic informal hedge plant.

C. 'Remote Blue', another introduction from Las Pilitas Nursery, is performing mightily in native landscapes. Its unique leaves are oval and mirror like. Sky-blue flowers contrast beautifully with more common darker blues in this 8- to 10-foot size range. It is highly adaptable to a wide range of exposures and garden conditions. This is one of the most handsome and easiest ceanothuses around. It is great for screening or as a stand-alone specimen.

C. 'Snow Flurry' is a long-favored, white-flowered wild lilac. Growing to over 10 feet in height, its foliage is very smooth and glossy. This one tolerates most landscape conditions, but does not take hard frosts. 'Snow Flurry' grows better near the coast where winter temperatures are moderated. It is useful as a contrast to the blue flowers of most ceanothuses.

A new introduction, 'South Coast Blue' (C. 'South Coast Blue'), with deep blue flowers, shows promise in native landscapes. It has a nice, upright stature and can achieve 10 feet in just a few years. The foliage is smooth, triangular, and slightly cupped. 'South Coast Blue' has shown good garden tolerance and its upright habit is excellent for creating a narrow screen. It was discovered by Greg Rubin and introduced through Moosa Creek Nursery in 2009.

PLANT COMMUNITIES chaparral, oak woodland, coastal sage scrub

Ceanothus 'Frosty Blue' sparkles in the landscape.

Ceanothus 'Julia Phelps' is darker blue than 'Frosty Blue' with pink buds.

LANDSCAPE USAGE These larger, upright, evergreen wild lilacs are excellent for background plantings, screening, and informal hedges. They are extremely fast growing. Massing ceanothuses of different colors creates the effect of a "Monet painting" when in bloom. They also can be paired up with large shrubs or small trees like flannel bush (*Fremontodendron* spp.) and redbud (*Cercis occidentalis*) to create truly stunning groupings. Interestingly, ceanothuses are able to fix nitrogen (despite not being a legume) through their close root association with the microbial frankia. Ceanothuses' unfortunate reputation for being short lived stems from subjecting the plants to ornamental horticultural conditions of too much water and fertility. Most live upward of 75 years in the wild.

Ceanothus 'South Coast Blue' is a tall, narrow, upright shrub with deep blue flowers and glossy green leaves.

The striking white blossoms of *Ceanothus* 'Snow Flurry'.

MOUNTAIN MAHOGANY
Cercocarpos betuloides

Mountain mahogany is an elegant, drought-tolerant, upright plant with birch-like, evergreen leaves and beautiful gray bark. It grows much taller than wide, making it a great narrow screen. Backlit by the rising or setting sun in late summer or fall, the feathery fruits light up the whole plant. Mountain mahoganies usually reach a mature height of 12 to 14 feet; however, very old specimens may grow to 25 feet and resemble a multi-trunked tree. There is an island variety (*Cercocarpos betuloides* var. *blancheae*, syn. *C. alnifolius*) that has much larger 3- to 4-inch leaves, giving it a more lush appearance.

PLANT COMMUNITIES chaparral, coastal sage scrub, oak woodland, pinyon-juniper woodland, pine forest

LANDSCAPE USAGE Cercocarpos is the ultimate screening shrub for very narrow confines. Use this where you would consider bamboo. Use it against rock or adobe walls. It looks at home against a Santa Fe–type structure. Although not a legume, cercocarpos is one of many species that are nitrogen fixing through their association with frankia. Deer like browsing this plant, so it may require some protection in deer areas. This is a great native plant waiting to be discovered.

SUMMER HOLLY
Comarostaphylis diversifolia

This is a handsome, large, evergreen shrub that is almost unknown to horticulture. It looks like a cross between a manzanita and a toyon. It is also sometimes confused with mission manzanita (*Xylococcus bicolor*). Unlike mission manzanita, however, it has rough bark, flowers in spring, and sets red, edible berries in summer. The foliage is fairly dense.

PLANT COMMUNITY chaparral

LANDSCAPE USAGE This shrub can reach 20 feet in height and can be pruned into a small tree. The white

Summer holly blooms profusely but grows slowly.

flower show in spring can be dazzling, and the linear bunches of berries are equally attractive. Berry-eating birds love this shrub. It is very drought tolerant and easy to maintain. Its only drawback is that it tends to grow slowly, no more than a foot or two per year. However, if you have the time to indulge it, your patience will be amply rewarded.

NATIVE CYPRESS

Cupressus spp.

Native cypresses are wonderful screening plants. The ones discussed here are narrow and have a soft woodsiness, adding beautifully to the native landscape. They are useful in creating whimsical, even "Tuscan" vertical contrasts in the garden.

Tecate cypress (*Cupressus forbesii*) is native to the mountains of San Diego. It is a fast-growing, grayish-green-leaved plant that tolerates a wide range of soil conditions. It is extremely drought tolerant and withstands high temperatures. Watering may boost its growth rate to over 5 feet per year; however, overwatering may cause the plant to topple over when the upper growth overwhelms the support capability of the root system. This is a fine screening plant.

Gowen's cypress (*C. goveniana*) is a lovely, upright plant (to 15 feet) with bright, medium green foliage and a lemony scent. It matures quickly, growing several feet per year, and can tolerate a wide range of soils, from decomposed granite to clay. Gowen's cypress is not phased by nasty, sandstone-type soils near Pebble Beach, where it tolerates salt wind and spray. It usually becomes extremely drought tolerant once established. It can be susceptible to borers.

PLANT COMMUNITIES chaparral, pine forest

LANDSCAPE USAGE The native cypresses are excellent screening plants due to their rapid growth, evergreen leaves, and narrow habit. They provide dramatic accents used singly on slopes and flat areas to create whimsical, columnar accents. Take care to not overwater them, as they can topple over or become susceptible to disease and pests.

Upright Gowen's cypress (*Cupressus goveniana*) with bright green foliage.

FLANNEL BUSH

Fremontodendron spp.

The unique, primitive-looking flannel bushes are another of California's plant treasures. Popular in native landscapes and around the world, particularly in the United Kingdom, they become huge balls of yellow flowers in spring, as they burst forth with rows of large, saucer-shaped flowers, with nectar pooling at the base of each petal. The thick leaves are maple shaped. Tiny hairs cover this plant, so beware—they can be extremely irritating. Flannel bush is definitely a show-stopping plant when in bloom, especially paired with ceanothus and cercis.

The most popular landscape varieties of large flannel bush are 'California Glory', 'Pacific Sunset', and 'San Gabriel'. All are hybrids of *Fremontodendron mexicanum* and *F. californicum*. 'California Glory' is a 50-year veteran, proven reliable in flower color and longevity in the native landscape. The other two varieties look similar. All can grow to 20 feet high and wide—use these only where you have plenty of room. They make very effective specimen plants as well as privacy screens.

The straight species *F. californicum* var. *napense* is smaller in stature and rather tolerant of clay soils, as long as they are not kept moist.

PLANT COMMUNITIES chaparral, coastal sage scrub, pine forest

LANDSCAPE USAGE With few exceptions, fremontodendrons require well-draining, mineralized substrates. Many grow in rocky or gravelly soil, often in alluvial areas inundated with moisture in winter but bone-dry in summer, with only a little moisture available at the tips of the lower roots. If you have clay soil, consider planting flannel bush in a raised bed to ensure good drainage. These plants are extremely impressive in bloom and mix beautifully with wild lilacs and redbud.

Flannel bush (*Fremontodendron* 'California Glory') living up to its name.

SILK TASSEL BUSH
Garrya spp.

At first glance, silk tassel bush resembles a large-leaved manzanita. It is distinguished by the display of long, gray-white tasseled flowers that burst forth in spring. These catkins make the entire plant look as if it is covered in icicles. The tassels mature into strings of purplish fruits. Silk tassel bushes range in size from 6 to 15 feet tall. They are densely foliated and make excellent screening plants.

PLANT COMMUNITIES chaparral, mixed-evergreen forest, pine forest

LANDSCAPE USAGE *Garrya elliptica* 'James Roof' is one of the showiest selections with catkins to over a foot in length. This species does well in full sun near the coast, preferring shade inland. It grows well in either clay or decomposed granite. It can tolerate considerable moisture if it has good drainage. Those in the southern, inland regions of California should consider using *G. flavescens* or *G. veatchii* instead. They are very tolerant of heat and sun and are quite showy in their own right. *Garrya flavescens* is better for clay; *G. veatchii* does well in mineral soils.

COFFEEBERRY
Rhamnus californica

An elegant evergreen shrub, coffeeberry can grow to 10 feet tall. This plant is appropriate for Japanese gardens. It has

Garrya elliptica displays foot-long white tassels in spring.

The dark foliage of 'Eve Case' coffeeberry provides nice contrast to the lighter, medium green baccharis in the foreground.

lovely green elliptical leaves, red bark, clusters of small white flowers, and large showy berries that can simultaneously exhibit shades of green, yellow, red, and black. It tolerates clay or mineralized soils. Beautiful as a background shrub, coffeeberry grows well as understory to large oak trees, and can be planted within 10 feet of a lawn.

PLANT COMMUNITIES chaparral, coastal sage scrub, mixed evergreen forest, redwood forest, oak woodland

LANDSCAPE USAGE The selection *Rhamnus californica* 'Eve Case' has impressive, large leaves and fruit. Use coffeeberry in moister areas, provided there is good drainage. After it is

established, hot, wet soil can kill this plant. This is an exceptional, large-scale foundation plant that also shines as a singular specimen or accent plant.

SUGAR BUSH
Rhus ovata
LEMONADEBERRY
Rhus integrifolia

These large, evergreen shrubs are densely foliated with leathery leaves, making them great screening shrubs on the periphery of the native landscape. Lemonadeberry grows along the coast, while sugar bush grows inland, even into the desert transition. Sugar bush is highly

Lemonadeberry (*Rhus integrifolia*) grows along the coast.

Sugar bush (*Rhus ovata*) has impressive blossoms in the spring.

tolerant of frost and snow. These handsome shrubs can be pruned into formal hedges, sculpted into trees, or left to grow as large, rambling natural mounds. The flowers are pink to red, followed by small, edible pink- to salmon-colored fruits. Soaking (or steeping) the lemonadeberry fruits in water makes a refreshing lemonade-like drink. Add sugar to taste, just like you would with regular lemonade; it is delicious.

PLANT COMMUNITIES coastal sage scrub, chaparral

LANDSCAPE USAGE These shrubs grow to be large, dense screens. They can be easily trimmed into formal shapes, if desired. They tolerate most soil types and become very drought tolerant once established. Both are easy to grow in most situations—basically, just plant them and forget them (once established). Use sugar bush in areas with frequent frost.

Medium shrubs

Medium-size shrubs are used most often for foundational shrubs. They grow to about 6 feet in height. Use native shrubs instead of common exotic landscape materials like India hawthorn (*Rhaphiolepis indica*), escallonia (*Escallonia* spp.), Australian mock orange (*Pittosporum* spp.), and many others. Most of these natives are evergreen, although some are deciduous. Use medium shrubs for structure and massing.

MEDIUM-SIZE MANZANITAS
Arctostaphylos spp.

The numerous, attractive, and easy-to-grow medium-size manzanitas exhibit classic evergreen leaves, reddish bark, urn-shaped flowers, and apple-shaped edible fruits. Many have strong foliar hues adding color to the landscape without added maintenance typical of seasonal flowers. In addition to straight species, there are many horticultural selections and hybrids selected for garden worthiness.

Rainbow manzanita (*Arctostaphylos rainbowensis*) appears to be a natural hybrid of *A. glandulosa* and *A. glauca*.

Arctostaphylos densiflora 'Howard McMinn' is garden tolerant.

Rainbow manzanita (*Arctostaphylos rainbowensis*) has large, medium green leaves.

Arctostaphylos 'Sunset' has new growth in setting sun colors.

This showy, garden-adapted species has large, medium green leaves, and pink flower stalks. Another gorgeous species is Otay manzanita (*A. otayensis*). The lovely gray leaves and white flowers create a strong foliar contrast to greener shrubs.

One of the great manzanita selections of all times is *A. densiflora* 'Howard McMinn', a 4- to 5-foot shrub that grows relatively fast and is tolerant of most standard garden conditions. In early spring, it blooms with masses of pink flowers. Another outstanding medium-size evergreen manzanita is 'Sunset', with new growth in every color of the setting sun. For most of the year, the tip foliage holds a striking red-orange hue,

creating a powerful contrast to the green foliage of other foundation plants. *Arctostaphylos pajaroensis* 'Paradise', another intensely foliar-colored manzanita, has gray and bronze leaves tipped in brilliant red. It is larger than 'Sunset' (up to 6 feet) and can be used as a stand-alone specimen plant.

Easy to grow, *A.* 'Baby Bear' has green leaves and brilliant pink flowers. It grows 1 to 2 feet per year to a maximum height of about 5 feet. With burgundy-colored bark it pairs nicely with groundcover ceanothuses, such as 'Joyce Coulter'. Another nice upright medium-size manzanita is *A.* 'Ian Bush', which displays good branching structure on a 5-foot-tall mini-shrub. The scaled-down

Arctostaphylos pajaroensis 'Paradise' has gray and bronze leaves tipped in red.

Arctostaphylos 'Ian Bush' is upright with good structure and is well scaled to residential landscapes.

open lattice nicely frames walkways or fronting low walls.

PLANT COMMUNITIES coastal sage scrub, chaparral, oak woodland, pine forest

LANDSCAPE USAGE All of the medium-size manzanitas are perfect foundation plants that obviate the use of non-native, thirsty shrubs. Shrub manzanitas are great around the base of a house or for creating backbone elements. Use masses of various foliage colors to create flow and drama.

BARBERRIES

Berberis spp.
syn. *Mahonia* spp.

Native barberries are beautiful, colorful, often shiny-leaved evergreen shrubs especially appropriate for woodland gardens. Think shade—afternoon shade as a minimum, but full shade works well, too. Sharp spiny leaves make barberries suitable to grow beneath bathroom and bedroom windows for protection. Clusters of bright yellow fragrant blooms produce edible blue berries when fully ripe. Native species are true barberries, similar to those found in Persian food. While these shrubs can take conventional watering, they are also quite drought tolerant. Barberries grow slowly but are worth the wait.

PLANT COMMUNITIES chaparral, mixed evergreen forest, redwood forest

California barberry (*Berberis pinnata*) grows to 4–5 feet.

New growth of compact barberry (*Berberis aquifolium* var. *compacta*).

Nevin's barberry (*Berberis nevinii*) is a gray-green-leaved species.

Berberis 'Golden Abundance' has glossy foliage and magnificent yellow flowers.

LANDSCAPE USAGE California barberry (*Berberis pinnata*) is especially useful as it is adapted to a wide range of temperatures and soils and grows 4 to 5 feet in height. 'Golden Abundance' is a long-popular, larger (8- to 10-feet) version. The compact barberry (*B. aquifolium* var. *compacta*) is less than 2 feet high and creeps along to form a beautiful thicket along the north side of a house or in deep shade.

SAN DIEGO MARGUERITE

Bahiopsis laciniata

This marvelous little shrub deserves more widespread usage. San Diego marguerite is only about 2 feet tall, has dark green foliage, and blooms profusely with small yellow daisies several times throughout the year. Its small size makes it perfect for even postage-stamp residential gardens. It tolerates every soil type from clay to sand, but is not very frost tolerant (it grows from San Diego south into Baja California). In frost-free areas, it really shines. It is even tolerant of part shade.

PLANT COMMUNITIES coastal sage scrub, chaparral

LANDSCAPE USAGE This adaptable plant is useful as a massed element in large gardens or used singly in tiny gardens. It is a dependable accent plant, covered with bright yellow daisies most of the year, and is beautiful paired with sages, apricot mallow, or woolly blue curls.

San Diego marguerite blooms several times a year.

The pink powder puff of fairy duster.

FAIRY DUSTER

Calliandra eriophylla

Fairy duster is a small lacy shrub with delicate compound leaves and pink puffs of flowers. It is somewhat inconspicuous until it blooms with bright pink blossoms in spring. It likes sandy soil, inorganic mulches, and inland conditions.

PLANT COMMUNITY desert

LANDSCAPE USAGE Use this 1- to 3-foot plant as a color accent in a desert garden. It prefers good drainage, mineralized soil, and rocky mulch—do not use organic mulch with this one.

MEDIUM-SIZE WILD LILACS

Ceanothus spp.

There are a variety of useful medium-size ceanothuses for the native landscape. *Ceanothus* 'Celestial Blue' is a 6-foot (sometimes larger) shrub with deep purple-blue flowers. Its small (under 1-inch) leaves are often completely covered by flowers in spring. Use 'Celestial Blue' in sand or decomposed granite. With good drainage it can tolerate moderate watering, though it can become extremely drought tolerant.

Ceanothus 'Concha' is a medium, reliable, time-tested ceanothus with intense, indigo-blue flowers. It has been specified as 4 feet in size, but can easily grow to 6 feet or larger, so leave some room. For smaller scale, consider using *C.*

'Wheeler Canyon', an umbrella-shaped 4-foot plant, which has the same indigo-blue flowers with lovely pink buds. Both can tolerate sand or clay.

'Skylark' is hard to beat. This medium blue, highly adaptable form of *C. thyrsiflorus* is one of the smallest wild lilacs, growing to only 4 feet or less. Neat, almost formal looking, 'Skylark' has dark green leaves and is well scaled for foundational planting. A similar-sized, equally useful, white-flowered form is *C.* 'Snowball', a selection of *C. rigidus*. This tough little plant blooms brilliant white in spring and is highly drought tolerant on most sites. Both 'Skylark' and 'Snowball' tolerate a wide range of soil conditions.

PLANT COMMUNITIES coastal sage scrub, chaparral, mixed evergreen forest, redwood forest

Ceanothus 'Celestial Blue' has small leaves and deep blue flowers.

Ceanothus 'Concha'

Ceanothus 'Wheeler Canyon' is similar to, but smaller than *C.* 'Concha'.

LANDSCAPE USAGE The medium-size ceanothuses are all excellent foundation and specimen plants. They pair up nicely with similar-size manzanitas. Most ceanothuses do not like warm saturated soils in summer after establishment, but don't mind having their leaves washed off and mulch wet once every couple of weeks or so. With lean soils and light watering, they far outlive more pampered specimens.

ISLAND BUSH POPPY

Dendromecon harfordii

Island bush poppy is an "I gotta have it!" plant that can be difficult for the beginner because it thrives on neglect. Sulfur yellow poppies with orange centers bloom year-round on a fast-growing shrub with large blue leaves. It is very drought tolerant once established and grows well in either shade or sun, preferring a little afternoon protection inland. Closely related, *Dendromecon rigida* grows on the mainland and is a better choice for hot, inland, full-sun locations. Its narrower leaves may look a bit scruffier than the island form. Both plants draw people in with their amazing bloom cycle.

PLANT COMMUNITY chaparral

LANDSCAPE USAGE Great as either a specimen or mixed with chaparral

Island bush poppy has rich yellow flowers nearly year-round.

plants, especially ceanothus. This shrub makes a lovely screen and grows well in the shade of an oak tree. Bush poppies need excellent drainage. Island bush poppy is a little more moisture tolerant than its mainland cousin. If the plant's health suddenly declines, it may be infested with mites; promptly cut it back to its large, basal burl and you may save the plant. It will recover as if it were in a burn—one reason *D. rigida* is often abundant after large chaparral fires.

COAST SUNFLOWER
Encelia californica

Fast growing to about 3 feet, coast sunflower is covered in bright yellow daisies from spring into summer. Since it goes dormant in summer heat, use this plant for quick fill and color with the foundational, evergreen species filling in behind it. The flowers make great cut flowers. Rabbits generally avoid this one.

PLANT COMMUNITIES coastal sage scrub, chaparral

LANDSCAPE USAGE Use coast sunflower for fast-growing color, especially on a slope. It can grow to 3 feet in one year and help jumpstart the soil ecology for the manzanita and ceanothus backbone plants. Use gray-leaved, desert-adapted *Encelia farinosa* for more inland locations. Another nice form with orange-centered daisies is the somewhat smaller *E. actonii*.

Coast sunflower provides quick fill and color.

Eriogonum fasciculatum with blue-gray foliage and white flowers.

SHRUBBY BUCKWHEAT

Eriogonum spp.

Largely ignored, buckwheats are wonderful garden plants only beginning to be appreciated by native landscape enthusiasts. Colorful, highly drought tolerant, and adaptable, buckwheats are magnificent butterfly attractors. The ones mentioned here all have dramatic structure and flowers.

The largest shrubby buckwheat is Saint Catherine's lace (*Eriogonum giganteum*). Native to the Channel Islands, it has large gray leaves and enormous, flat clusters of pinkish-white flowers that fade to rust in autumn. These clusters are held high above the foliage and make wonderful dried flower arrangements.

Another Channel Island native is Santa Cruz Island buckwheat (*E. arborescens*). This blue-green, narrow-leaved shrub has lovely pink flowers that fade to rust, then brown, holding different colors at the same time. A neat, trim, 3-foot hemisphere, it is ideal for a formal or modern setting. Butterflies and seed-eating birds love the flowers.

Other highly useful shrubby buckwheats include ashyleaf buckwheat (*E. cinereum*) and a gray form of flattop buckwheat called *E. fasciculatum* var. *polifolium*. The first is native to the Santa Monica Mountains with gray triangular ¾-inch leaves and light pink pompon flowers. The second grows from the chaparral to the desert, a blue-gray compact form of *E. fasciculatum* with bright

Santa Cruz Island buckwheat (*Eriogonum arborescens*) forms a 3-foot ball.

white flowers. Both are neat, about 3 feet in size, and create wonderful blue-gray accents in the backbone planting. Both are tolerant of sand or clay soils.

PLANT COMMUNITIES coastal sage scrub, chaparral, desert

LANDSCAPE USAGE Buckwheats need to be planted in areas with good drainage, although most are tolerant of either sand or clay. Wash off the leaves but do not create wet, warm soils once established. Place 6- to 12-inch boulders right on the root ball when planting. They make wonderful accents or can be massed.

SMALLER FLANNEL BUSHES
Fremontodendron spp.

Not all flannel bushes grow to enormous sizes. The Napa Valley flannel bush (*Fremontodendron californicum* var. *napense*) grows to about 6 feet in height. It has some tolerance for clay soils, as long as it drains well. Pine Hill flannel bush (*F. californicum* var. *decumbens*) is about 4 feet tall with bright apricot flowers. Hybrids between this plant and either *F. mexicanum* or *F. californicum* have produced wonderful mounding varieties with good garden tolerance, larger flowers, and scaled-down size. Consider: 'Ken Taylor', 'West Hills', and 'El Dorado Gold'.

PLANT COMMUNITIES chaparral, pine forest

LANDSCAPE USAGE Use the smaller flannel bushes in native gardens for smaller properties where the larger *Fremontodendron mexicanum* or *F. californicum* species will not fit, or as color accents in larger spaces. They have good garden tolerance, long bloom cycles, and are show stoppers when paired with wild lilacs, redbud, and manzanitas.

BUSH MALLOWS
Malacothamnus spp.

Bush mallows in bloom look like firework displays. Bert Wilson of Las Pilitas Nursery refers to them as "party plants" because they are often covered in birds and butterflies. The flowers are either pink or lavender (rarely white), enveloping the plant from spring through summer. They tolerate well-drained clay or sand, and grow rapidly to about 5 feet.

PLANT COMMUNITIES coastal sage scrub, chaparral

LANDSCAPE USAGE The chaparral mallow (*Malacothamnus fasciculatus*) has a light green leaf and lavender to pink flowers; the many-flowered bush mallow (*M. densiflorus*) has darker green leaves and rose-pink flowers. These plants are easy to grow, suitable to a large range of conditions, and become drought tolerant once established.

Fremontodendron 'Ken Taylor' is one of the smallest hybrids.

Fremontodendron 'El Dorado Gold' has golden yellow flowers.

Chaparral mallow (*Malacothamnus fasciculatus*) has lavender to pink flowers.

Bush mallow (*Malacothamnus densiflorus*) blossoms.

BLADDERPOD
(burrofat, California cleome)

Peritoma arborea
syn. *Isomeris arborea*
syn. *Cleome isomeris*

Unique and distinctive, no one seems to be settled on what to call this plant in either the common or Latin nomenclature. Recently recategorized as *Peritoma arborea*, it may also be found in nurseries under the botanical names of *Isomeris arborea* or *Cleome isomeris*. In various regions it is called bladderpod, burrofat, or California cleome. For all this it is a tough, largely overlooked plant for the landscape with distinctive yellow flowers nearly year-round, but especially winter to spring. Bladderpod deserves much wider usage. This gray-green evergreen shrub grows to a neat 4-foot ball in all soil types, especially thriving in harsh coastal conditions, providing a nice color contrast to greener shrubs. Heat and drought tolerant, when established, and highly fire resistant, hummingbirds and butterflies love it while deer avoid it. Be sure soil drains well. The seeds are edible and can be prepared like capers.

PLANT COMMUNITIES coastal sage scrub, desert

LANDSCAPE USAGE A beautiful, reliable shrub from coast to desert, bladderpod is a neat foundational plant that needs little care and provides color variation in a native landscape. Its size and foliage color makes a nice transition midway from larger background landscape plants.

Bladderpod (*Peritoma arborea*) has gray-green foliage and yellow flowers.

MEDIUM-SIZE COFFEEBERRY
Rhamnus californica

Selected varieties of coffeeberry are appropriate to the medium-size shrub category. These elegant shrubs have beautifully sculpted evergreen leaves, red stems, and large colorful berries ranging from green to yellow to red to black, all at once. Many larger berry-eating birds like scrub jays love this plant. This is great to use in Japanese gardens.

PLANT COMMUNITIES chaparral, coastal sage scrub

LANDSCAPE USAGE These gorgeous plants are wonderful foundational shrubs with lots of year-round interest. 'Mound San Bruno' has smaller leaves and grows 4 to 6 feet. It is an excellent choice around homes and can be integrated into conventional landscapes. 'Leatherleaf', another handsome variety with dark, rounded leaves, is great as a background plant. 'Tranquil Margarita' has a slightly more open structure, while 'Seaview' is the lowest, tightest-growing selection at only 2 to 3 feet high. Avoid warm, wet soil in summer—coffeeberries can tolerate moist soil as long as it is well draining. They appreciate afternoon shade and can accept hedging.

BASKETBUSH
Rhus trilobata

This plant deserves more widespread usage. It resembles poison oak, without the toxicity. The tri-lobed deciduous leaves turn yellow, orange, and red in the fall. Indians coveted the long stems to use in baskets. They made a tea-like pink lemonade with the berries (those with poison oak sensitivity should be careful about imbibing and may not want to expose delicate internal organs). Tidy in appearance, basketbush is great for the shade woodland garden, although it grows well in full sun. The berries are relished by wildlife. In cold-winter areas, this plant has dependable fall color.

PLANT COMMUNITIES chaparral, coastal sage scrub, oak woodland

LANDSCAPE USAGE Often found in the oak woodland community, basketbush is a great plant to use in the shade of oaks. As a deciduous hedge, its branches are dense, growing to about 4 feet. Basketbush is easy and graceful in the landscape.

CURRANTS and GOOSEBERRIES
Ribes spp.

Currants and gooseberries are gifts to gardeners. They are easy to grow, have magnificent flower displays, and produce edible berries favored by humans and birds alike. They are usually

Basketbush has long stems and three-part leaves that resemble those of poison oak.

Golden currant (*Ribes aureum* ssp. *gracillimum*) has yellow flowers and delicious berries.

White-flowering currant (*Ribes indecorum*) grows in dry shade.

Pink-flowering currant (*Ribes sanguineum* var. *glutinosum*) puts on a beautiful display.

Fuchsia-flowering gooseberry (*Ribes speciosum*) is spiny.

deciduous shrubs under 6 feet tall that grow in afternoon shade. Gooseberries are similar but have sharp spines; currants do not. Our best edible currant is the golden currant (*Ribes aureum* ssp. *gracillimum*) with yellow flowers followed by delicious fruits that change color in maturity from green to orange to black. It is one of the few currants that can be grown in full sun. Three similar species sport pendulous flower clusters on upright plants. White-flowering currant (*R. indecorum*) has clusters of white flowers, chaparral currant (*R. malvaceum*) has reddish flowers, and pink-flowering currant (*R. sanguineum* var. *glutinosum*) has the largest flower bunches beginning white at the tip and fading to deep pink at the top—truly magnificent! Finally, one of the best and easiest gooseberries is fuchsia-flowering gooseberry (*R. speciosum*) with tubular red flowers hanging vertically beneath arched stems. In full flower it is breathtaking. Look but don't touch—with vicious spines it must be planted away from traffic areas. Locate this plant where you do not want a living soul to enter.

PLANT COMMUNITIES coastal sage scrub, chaparral, oak woodland, pine forest

LANDSCAPE USAGE These are all great oak companion plants. Locate golden currant at the edge of the oak canopy where it gets more sun, or in a chaparral planting. White and chaparral currant only need afternoon shade, as does fuchsia-flowering gooseberry. Pink currant should be sited in full shade except immediately along the coast.

MATILIJA POPPY
Romneya coulteri

Drama is Matilija poppy's first, last, and middle name. This garden diva, with large smooth-lobed, gray-green leaves, boasts fragrant 8-inch flowers with crinkly white, crepe-paper petals and brilliant golden stamens. It's is a knockout from spring to summer. It is our largest native flower. Also called fried-egg plant and tree poppy, it grows to 6 feet tall in a season and spreads like gangbusters, only to disappear completely in the late summer. That said, if its not happy, particularly in clay soils and inland, nothing can persuade it to grow. This plant

Matilija poppy is also called fried-egg plant.

likes loose well-drained soil—sandy soils or slopes are best. Do not let the water sit on the roots. When healthy, be prepared to practice control methods, digging it out where it has overstepped its bounds.

PLANT COMMUNITIES chaparral, coastal sage scrub

LANDSCAPE USAGE Not appropriate for small properties unless constrained by a root barrier. Plant Matilija poppy in the background. Don't worry, it will show itself above medium-size evergreen foliage before it disappears for the season. Give it room to spread unless contained. On large properties, it is spectacular on a distant slope, or perhaps as a massed informal seasonal screen.

SAGES
Salvia spp.

California has wonderful medium-size perennial sages. As sensory nerve centers of the garden, sages bring color, fragrance, birds, and butterflies. Sages are fragrant, colorful, and magnetic to wildlife. All sages are culinary; it just depends on your flavor preference. Most people like to cook with either black or Cleveland sage. White sage is sacred to western Indians for blessing and cleansing ceremonies. Summer dormancy means that sages are best used as accent plants rather than massed foundation plants. They can be mixed to achieve

color in different seasons. Black sage (*Salvia mellifera*) has white to blue blooms on dark green foliage in winter and early spring. Purple sage (*S. leucophylla*) blooms pink on silver leaves in spring. White sage (*S. apiana*) blooms white to lavender on large-leaved pungent white stems. Cleveland sage (*S. clevelandii*) has deep purple flowers on sweetly scented small shrubs starting in late spring through most of the summer.

PLANT COMMUNITIES coastal sage scrub, chaparral, oak woodland, pine forest

LANDSCAPE USAGE Dot sages here and there in the garden—especially near intersections of paths and next to sitting areas—to create delightfully fragrant accents throughout the landscape. Most Cleveland sages on the market are

White sage (*Salvia apiana*) is sacred in native cultures.

Cleveland sage (*Salvia clevelandii*) is usually hybrid 'Winnifred Gilman'; the species is more compact and darker flowered than common hybrids.

Salvia 'Pozo Blue' is a floriferous popular hybrid suitable for most gardens.

Small, purple-flowered Munz's sage (*Salvia munzii*).

actually hybrids of *Salvia clevelandii* and *S. leucophylla*, larger crosses more tolerant of heavier soils. 'Pozo Blue', 'Whirly Blue', and 'Aromas' are popular examples. Island black sage (*S. brandegei*) is a beautiful, blue-flowered salvia with dark nearly evergreen leaves, and deserving of more popularity. So is the fairly small, purplish-flowered Munz's sage (*S. munzii*), native to San Diego County. 'Emerald Cascade' is an especially compact small-leaved form that tolerates clay soils.

APRICOT MALLOW
Sphaeralcea ambigua

In flower, apricot mallow is a traffic-stopping small shrub. The blooms are

Apricot mallow brightens desert gardens.

brilliant orange on gray to green leaves. It makes a wonderful cut flower. Despite it being a desert plant, this mallow is highly adaptable in most garden situations, as long as it has good drainage and is allowed to dry out between waterings. The orange flowers are stunning against blue and purple sages, and yellow brittlebush (*Encelia farinosa*) or San Diego marguerite (*Viguiera laciniata*). This plant blooms on and off throughout the year attracting the attention of people and butterflies.

PLANT COMMUNITY desert

LANDSCAPE USAGE Apricot mallow is a must-have plant for any native landscape with full, warm sun and good drainage. It is surprisingly tolerant of clay soils. Pair it with sages and native daisies.

BLUE CURLS
Trichostema spp.

Everyone loves woolly blue curls (*Trichostema lanatum*) for its amazing beauty and drama. And, nearly everyone kills it. This popular plant feeds the rumor that native plants are difficult to grow because it does not tolerate conventional horticulture. Yet, when its undemanding but particular needs are met, it can be quite easy, and will grow even in asphalt cracks. The narrow, rosemary-like leaves are brilliant green with an unforgettable sweet, sage-like fragrance. The flowers have lavender buds and purple petals with blue pollen that turns bees' pollen sacks bright blue. Called "romero" by the native Indians, who made a delicious and important medicinal tea from its leaves.

Trichostema does not tolerate poorly draining soils; it requires excellent drainage. If the drainage is good, it can tolerate clay and loam soils. Keep the roots as cool as possible. This one loves to have a 12-inch or larger boulder placed on its root ball, especially on the south side. You can plant it into a mound of soil less than an inch high to help ensure good drainage. It is native to areas that receive up to 40 inches of rainfall, so it can take some moisture as long as it is not in standing water.

PLANT COMMUNITIES coastal sage scrub, chaparral, desert

LANDSCAPE USAGE Woolly blue curls is so beautiful it is worth growing for the fragrance and flowers alone, even if it takes a few tries to get it to take. Mountain blue curls (*Trichostema parishii*) is less finicky and grows in the chaparral–desert interface. It is smaller in stature and surprisingly easy to grow. It prefers granitic soils and good drainage, but has shown tolerance for clay soil. It is rarely propagated, so grab one if you find it. Either form is striking.

Grow woolly blue curls (*Trichostema lanatum*) for flowers and fragrance.

PLANT SELECTION
Native Groundcovers

Groundcover is an important landscape element so often shortchanged. Most people think only of lawn grass and have no idea that there are many beautiful native groundcovers ready to serve as the base for the rest of the landscape. Groundcovers are low growing (typically under 2 feet in height), dense, and cover a large area of the surface of the soil, spreading from a central source. Some even tip root on their journey. A mixed bag of plants, they include some shrubby plants, some vines, and other bushy-type perennial plants.

A stunning, dense, evergreen ground-cover, *Ceanothus thyrsiflorus* var. *repens* has shiny dark green leaves, blue flowers in spring, and grows to 7 feet across.

MANZANITAS

Arctostaphylos **spp.**

The variety in form, color, and size of manzanitas is amazing. Generally considered medium to large shrubs, quite a few are less than 18 inches high and much wider across. These evergreen beauties comprise some of the prettiest groundcovers ever used in landscaping.

Arctostaphylos 'John Dourley' is a brightly colored mounding form, introduced by Tree of Life Nursery. It makes a wonderful evergreen 5-foot-wide low mound in the landscape with brightly hued red and orange new growth. It is adaptable to a wide range of soils, as is Franciscan manzanita (*A. franciscana*), which has been grown successfully from the coast to the inland valleys. Franciscan manzanita was thought to be extinct in the wild until a single specimen was found in the Golden Gate region of San Francisco. Fortunately, it has been propagated by native landscapers since the early 1940s. With bright green and reddish highlights, it grows about 5 feet across, 2 feet or less in height. A recent introduction by Las Pilitas Nursery, Del Mar manzanita (*A. glandulosa* ssp. *crassifolia*), is about 18 inches high and up to 6 feet across, with gray-colored foliage and pinkish highlights.

Very low-growing manzanitas (under 6 inches high) create beautiful evergreen mats. 'Emerald Carpet' is one of the most popular forms of *A. uva-ursi*. It has small leaves, but requires a fair amount of

Bright new growth on *Arctostaphylos* 'John Dourley'.

Low-mounding Franciscan manzanita (*Arctostaphylos franciscana*) is adapted to a wide range of soils.

water and can be grown directly around a lawn. Forms of *A. uva-ursi* occurring throughout the northern hemisphere may be called kinnikinnick or bearberry. More colorful and drought-resistant forms include: 'Radiant', 'Point Reyes', and 'Wood's Compact'. A form of A. *edmundsii* known as 'Carmel Sur' has superlative, dense foliage. 'Danville' has a little more leaf and flower color.

PLANT COMMUNITIES coastal sage scrub, chaparral, oak woodland, pine forest

LANDSCAPE USAGE These manzanitas are superlative landscaping groundcovers. They are evergreen with neat foliage, colorful flowers, and bird-attracting bright red berries. Most are adaptable to different soils. The *Arctostaphylos edmundsii* selections do well in full sun, while the *A. uva-ursi* selections appreciate some afternoon shade away from the coast. Other species mentioned do well in full sun in most locations. All are attractive spilling over walls.

CALIFORNIA SAGEBRUSH
Artemisia californica

Artemisia smells like California. There are two low-growing forms: 'Canyon Gray', from the Channel Islands, and 'Montara', from the Bay Area. 'Canyon Gray' is considered a species of *Artemisia californica* adapted to growing

Groundcover form Del Mar manzanita (*Arctostaphylos glandulosa* ssp. *crassifolia*) has gray-colored foliage and pinkish highlights.

Arctostaphylos edmundsii 'Carmel Sur' has superlative, dense foliage.

very low. It flows over retaining walls like soft gray rivulets. 'Montara' is more robust and may be a hybrid between *A. californica* and sandhill sage (*A. pycnocephala*). Of the two, 'Montara' is more evergreen while 'Canyon Gray' goes summer dormant.

PLANT COMMUNITIES coastal sage scrub, chaparral, oak woodland

LANDSCAPE USAGE This excellent groundcover with light gray foliage contrasts beautifully with the greens of most other plants. 'Montara' is less dormant in summer but not as low growing. Both are adaptable to sand to clay soils.

DWARF COYOTE BRUSH
Baccharis pilularis 'Pigeon Point'

Coyote brush is a superlative slope stabilizer. This beautiful, foot-high groundcover grows up to 10 feet across. Evergreen by habit and bright green in color, its flowers are inconspicuous, slightly fragrant yellow discs. This foliar plant is one of the best slope groundcovers. Given some supplemental irrigation in summer, it becomes extremely fire resistant. It also attracts a wide variety of insects. *Baccharis pilularis* 'Pigeon Point' is one of the best forms of dwarf coyote brush since it does not get woody in the middle.

Artemisia californica 'Montara' is a fragrant, soft silver California sagebrush.

PLANT COMMUNITIES coastal strand, coastal sage scrub

LANDSCAPE USAGE Plant dwarf coyote brush as a groundcover for large areas and on slopes. A good separation distance is 6 feet on center. Closer planting (as many specifications unfortunately require) leads to overcrowding and woody chaos as plants pile over each other. Given room to spread, they form a beautiful, undulating low groundcover.

WILD LILACS

Ceanothus spp.

Wild lilacs provide the other large group of evergreen groundcovers. As with manzanitas, most people consider ceanothuses medium to large shrubs; however, there are many superb low-growing varieties for groundcovers. Most popular is 'Yankee Point' (*Ceanothus thyrsiflorus* var. *griseus*), about 2 feet tall, spreading to 20 feet across. It has shiny, evergreen leaves and blue flowers in spring. One reason for its popularity is its high moisture tolerance. 'Yankee Point' provides color contrast to other groundcovers like 'Pigeon Point' coyote brush. Also popular, C. 'Joyce Coulter' is more floriferous, more drought tolerant, and better able to tolerate inland exposures. And, it is less attractive to deer. *Ceanothus*

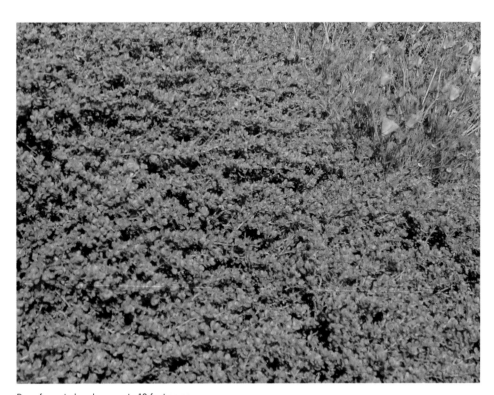

Dwarf coyote brush grows to 10 feet across.

'Anchor Bay' is a form of *C. gloriosus* with very dark green, crinkly leaves and deep lavender-blue flowers. Its serrated leaves are less attractive to herbivores. It tolerates moisture and likes afternoon shade in inland locations. Bluff California lilac (*C. maritimus*) is another very low-growing wild lilac with serrated leaves. This plant grows about a foot high, up to 5 feet across, and loves clay. It does very well in inland locations, as long as it gets some afternoon shade. Very salt and boron tolerant, it is perfect along the coast.

Little-known *C. thyrsiflorus* var. *repens* has smooth leaves and prostrate blue blossoms. This plant looks and functions like a scale model of 'Yankee

Ceanothus 'Joyce Coulter' has shiny leaves and bright blue blossoms.

Ceanothus thyrsiflorus var. *griseus* 'Yankee Point' is popular for its moisture tolerance.

Point'. It grows up to 9 feet across, tolerating a wide range of soils and exposure. This is a nice one to use near oak trees, on slopes, and as a groundcover that will spill over retaining walls.

PLANT COMMUNITIES coastal sage scrub, chaparral, mixed evergreen forest, redwood forest

LANDSCAPE USAGE Low-growing wild lilacs make fantastic groundcovers that are densely foliated, fast growing, and covered in blue flowers in spring. They make great slope covers and provide nice contrast to other shades of green. Most are drought tolerant, but some coastal species may require supplemental moisture and light shade inland. The flowers attract pollinators like native bees. Smooth-leaved ceanothuses are attractive to rabbits and deer, especially in inland locations. Better to use serrated-leaved varieties if herbivores are a problem.

Bluff California lilac (*Ceanothus maritimus*) has small leaves and tolerates clay.

WILD STRAWBERRY
Fragaria spp.

Wild strawberries are excellent, underused groundcovers. They make a wonderful lawn substitute. Beach strawberry (*Fragaria chiloensis*) has dark green leaves and spreads by runners. It grows in full sun with regular water. Occasionally bearing fruit, it may be one of the parents of domesticated strawberries. In shady locations, nothing compares to the woodland strawberry (*F. californica*),

Little-known prostrate *Ceanothus thyrsiflorus* var. *repens* grows to 7 feet across.

Woodland strawberry (*Fragaria californica*) prefers shade.

with emerald green leaves and delicious half-inch berries (said to rival European field strawberries for flavor). Beach strawberry does better in sand, while woodland strawberry doesn't care, as long as it has shade.

PLANT COMMUNITIES coastal strand, coastal sage scrub, oak woodland, mixed evergreen forest, pine forest

LANDSCAPE USAGE Both plants make outstanding, evergreen groundcovers. Beach strawberry rarely fruits, while woodland strawberry always fruits. Use *Fragaria chiloensis* in especially sandy locations, and give it some shade inland. *Fragaria californica* is not finicky, as long as it gets at least

Beach strawberry (*Fragaria chiloensis*) likes full sun and regular water.

afternoon shade (it can handle full sun next to the coast).

PROSTRATE GUM PLANT

Grindelia stricta **var.** *platyphylla*

Prostrate gum plant is a very low-growing perennial that is somewhat evergreen and blooms with bright yellow, daisy-like flowers in summer through fall. An excellent slope stabilizer, its form is tight and neat, as long as it is maintained with deadheading. This gum plant will tip root as it spreads, although it is not aggressive.

PLANT COMMUNITIES coastal strand, coastal sage scrub

LANDSCAPE USAGE Use grindelia for stabilizing coastal slopes, along with dwarf coyote brush and seaside daisy. It is lovely combined with erigeron, contrasting masses of lavender and yellow daisies. Prostrate gum plant is quite salt tolerant.

HONEYSUCKLES

Lonicera **spp.**

Some honeysuckles create attractive evergreen groundcovers beneath oaks and pines, while others form a clean-looking shrub in full sun. California honeysuckle (*Lonicera hispidula*) has large blue-green opposite leaves with bright pink flowers and large clusters of

Prostrate gum plant tip roots as it spreads.

California honeysuckle (*Lonicera hispidula*) has bright pink flowers.

Southern honeysuckle (*Lonicera subspicata*) has creamy, light yellow flowers.

L. subspicata var. *denudata* is the smallest native honeysuckle.

red berries. Given some supplemental moisture, this plant becomes evergreen. Entwining an oak, it adorns the tree with bright pink flowers, and later, red berries. Another groundcover form, southern honeysuckle (*L. subspicata*) has bright evergreen leaves and creamy yellow flowers yielding to orange to black berries. This honeysuckle forms a small shrub in full sun. The subspecies *L. subspicata* var. *denudata* is probably the smallest, lowest, and neatest form. Honeysuckle berries attract wildlife.

PLANT COMMUNITIES coastal sage scrub, chaparral, oak woodland, pine forest

LANDSCAPE USAGE Honeysuckles are highly symbiotic with oaks and pines. They are neat and colorful. They can look very formal, especially if they are pruned occasionally.

CATALINA PERFUME CURRANT
Ribes viburnifolium

Catalina perfume currant is an underutilized groundcover for shade, especially under oaks, with which it forms a nice partnership. It grows about 18 inches high and up to 8 feet across. This ground-hugging currant is evergreen with a nice fragrance and shiny leaves. Its red flower clusters are inconspicuous. The red stems peak out from

Catalina perfume currant is excellent under oaks.

beneath leaves. In shade this plant can be quite drought tolerant.

PLANT COMMUNITIES coastal sage scrub, chaparral

LANDSCAPE USAGE Use Catalina perfume currant as a shade ground-cover. If given support, it can also form an evergreen vine. It is easy to grow and can be trimmed to fit small planters.

GROUNDCOVER SAGES
Salvia spp.

The salvia family includes beautiful groundcovers. *Salvia sonomensis* is parent to numerous groundcover sages. *Salvia* 'Dara's Choice' is an attractive shiny green-leaved, blue-flowered hybrid with black sage (*S. mellifera*) heritage. It spreads up to 6 feet across by about a foot a month. For a gray contrast, *S.* 'Bee's Bliss' hybrid (with either *S. clevelandii* or *S. leucophylla*) has prolific blue flowers in spring and is often confused with 'Gracias'. *Salvia sonomensis* straight species is extremely low growing (less than 6 inches) with deep blue flowers. It spreads by tip rooting along the ground.

The challenge with all *S. sonomensis* varieties is their susceptibility to verticillium wilt. The following varieties are showing disease resistance: 'Mrs. Beard', a green-leaved variety; 'Rubin's Baby', which looks like a miniature; 'Dara's Choice', which is showing promise; as

are straight species of *S. sonomensis* growing in San Diego County.

Other low-growing salvias are related to *S. mellifera*, including subspecies *S. mellifera* var. *repens*, a tough, fast, enormous (up to 15 feet across), blue-flowered, disease-resistant groundcover under 2 feet tall. It is an excellent slope groundcover. *Salvia* 'Terra Seca' is lower growing, wider leaved, and white flowering, spreading to about 7 feet across.

A low-growing version of purple sage (*S. leucophylla*) has white leaves, pink flowers, and a nice mounding form. This disease resistant, clay soil–tolerant variety is 'Point Sal'. Its only drawback is possible late-summer dormancy, though light and infrequent overhead watering

Salvia sonomensis, the straight species, has deep blue flowers.

Salvia sonomensis 'Bee's Bliss' is low growing with gray foliage.

Salvia sonomensis 'Dara's Choice' has shiny green leaves.

Pink-flowered *Salvia leucophylla* 'Point Sal' has white leaves.

Salvia mellifera var. *repens* has blue flowers and can grow to 15 feet across.

(like fog drip) staves off withering leaves.

PLANT COMMUNITIES coastal strand, coastal sage scrub, chaparral, oak woodland, pine forest

LANDSCAPE USAGE The low-growing sages contrast shiny evergreen groundcovers and are amazingly floriferous. Most are drought tolerant, though they appreciate some light overhead watering two to three times per month, which is consistent with their coastal nature. Many *Salvia sonomensis* varieties are sensitive to verticillium wilt, which is disfiguring though rarely fatal. Consider using *S. mellifera* or *S. leucophylla* varieties where wilt is a problem.

CREEPING SNOWBERRY
Symphoricarpos spp.

Snowberries, with small pink flowers, are beautiful mounding groundcovers that form thickets under oaks and pines. Related to honeysuckle (*Lonicera* spp.), they associate closely as understory partners to these trees. Fall finds snowberries covered in brilliant, porcelain-white berries, attracting berry-eating birds and mammals. Common snowberry (*Symphoricarpos albus*) has large fruit and grows up to 4 feet tall. Stunning when its branches are laden with fruit—it glows in the shade. Creeping

snowberry (*S. mollis*) is similar but grows less than 2 feet tall and spreads by rhizomes.

PLANT COMMUNITIES chaparral, oak woodland, mixed evergreen forest, pine forest

LANDSCAPE USAGE Use snowberries as a groundcover under pines and oaks. Their lustrous white berries light up the shadiest spots during fall, which can be a slow time for color. Use *Symphoricarpos albus* for inland locations, and *S. mollis* for coastal gardens.

Common snowberry (*Symphoricarpos albus*) grows to 4 feet while creeping snowberry (*S. mollis*) is similar but grows to only 2 feet.

PLANT SELECTION
Native Perennials, Vines, and Monocots

Color plants are gardens' accessories, bright highlights but ephemeral.

Once you have determined the structure of your landscape with the trees, shrubs, and groundcovers, then you can add details and color with perennials, vines, and grass-like plants. Many people start with these plants and then become disappointed in their native gardens. They may be spectacular in the late winter and spring, and then die back to nothing in the summer heat. Remember, the detail plants add the spice to the recipe. Beautiful as they are, you wouldn't want a front yard entirely full of epilobiums, so sprinkle them in for people to discover as an ephemeral surprise. A mixture of these types of plants will comprise no more than about 25 percent of your landscape.

Perennials

Use native perennials as color spots along the edges of the land-scape. They are typically soft stemmed with lots of seasonal flowers. They often have a dormant period after flowering. Since they require some tidying up after blooming, locating them along the edges of the landscape makes them easier to access and keeps the intense color front and center. These plants are not appropriate for massed foundational planting.

COLUMBINE
Aquilegia spp.

Many people don't realize we have our own native columbines in California. These upright, shade-tolerant perennials have colorful flowers shaped like jesters' hats. Western columbine (*Aquilegia formosa*) has red flowers that node downward with spurs facing upward. Hummingbirds love this plant. Sierra columbine (*A. pubescens*) has large, erect 2- to 3-inch yellow and white flowers. Both plants are wonderful under oaks or in the shade border.

PLANT COMMUNITIES chaparral, mixed evergreen forest, riparian

LANDSCAPE USAGE Columbines require at least afternoon shade. They are great for woodland plantings or along the north side of the house, usually self-sowing freely. Their delicate appearance belies their toughness. They bloom from spring to summer; simply cut them back in late fall before new shoots emerge.

Flowers of western columbine (*Aquilegia formosa*) point down while the spurs point up.

SEA DAHLIA
Coreopsis spp.

These beautiful daisies grow on the Channel Islands, on coastal bluffs and in beach sand. Sea dahlia (*Coreopsis maritima*) is a nice perennial sub-shrub with large orange-centered yellow daisies. It has feathery, deeply lobed leaves. It grows in sandy soil, as does its cousin, the giant sea dahlia (*C. gigantea*). The unusual *C. gigantea* forms an upright shrub with elongated, bare succulent stems, with leaves and flowers forming a large tuft at the top of each trunk. It has an entertaining Dr. Seuss feel. It is said that the stems of *C. gigantea* are edible, with a carrot-like flavor (though we haven't tried it).

PLANT COMMUNITIES coastal strand, coastal sage scrub

LANDSCAPE USAGE Sea dahlias, grown best near the coast, are showy in flower, but not so when dormant. Locate *Coreopsis maritima* in the middle of the border, and *C. gigantea* at the back, where they can be hidden by the evergreen plants when dormant (unless you want to show off *C. gigantea*'s bare contorted elephantine trunks). They prefer soil with excellent drainage and do not tolerate frost. When happy, they will self-sow freely.

LIVEFOREVERS
Dudleya spp.

Dudleyas comprise one of the largest groups of native California succulents. Closely related to popular hens and chicks (*Echeveria* spp.), the liveforevers are similarly varied in shape, size, and flower color. Most are easy to grow and make great accent plants, especially in rock gardens and on rock walls. One of the most common, chalk lettuce (*Dudleya pulverulenta*) is covered with a white chalky coating and is found growing on east- and north-facing cut slopes; it needs afternoon shade. Lady fingers (*D. edulis*) is also common on rocky outcrops and in the shallow soils of grasslands. Its leaves are round and long, somewhat reminiscent of gray ice plant. Creamy yellow flowers bloom in large clusters in late spring. Santa Catalina liveforever (*D. hassei*), from Catalina Island, is blue-green and over time it spreads to cover large areas. It is an excellent groundcover substitute for ice plant and *Senecio mandraliscae*. Both lady finger–type dudleyas tolerate sun.

Lance-leaf dudleya (*D. lanceolata*) has strapping green leaves with orange flowers. It mixes well with chalk lettuce, also liking afternoon shade. Canyon liveforever (*D. cymosa*) is a beautiful broadleaf form with darker colored leaves and bright red-orange flowers. It is one of the few broadleaf varieties that will tolerate full sun. Hummingbirds love this plant.

Santa Catalina liveforever (*Dudleya hassei*) is blue-green and spreads.

Chalk lettuce (*Dudleya pulverulenta*) has a white chalky coating.

Lance-leaf dudleya (*Dudleya lanceolata*) likes afternoon shade.

PLANT COMMUNITIES coastal strand, coastal sage scrub, grassland, chaparral, oak woodland

LANDSCAPE USAGE These succulents are very easy to use as long as they are surrounded with rocks and have good drainage. Do not use organic mulches near them. All tolerate part shade; a few will survive in full sun. Dudleyas are great for creating a succulent-garden look, especially on rock walls or outcroppings. To prevent rotting, always plant them tilted over so their crowns will drain moisture.

HUMMINGBIRD FUCHSIA

Epilobium spp.
syn. *Zauschneria* spp.

Blooming late summer to fall, hummingbird fuchsia is a prominent source of seasonal color in the native garden. It performs reliably and profusely when garden color is scarce. Recently reclassified as *Epilobium*, many native horticulturists still use *Zauschneria*. Using more recent classification, California fuchsia (*E. canum*) has many forms. The straight species is an 8-inch-high, gray-leaved perennial with profuse red flowers in fall. Variants with white and pink flowers make striking varicolored masses in fall. A slightly shrubbier, narrow-leaved version *E. canum* ssp. *angustifolium* has beautiful arching branches up to 2 feet tall. *Epilobium*

canum 'Catalina', introduced by Tree of Life Nursery, grows vertically to 3 feet or more—the tallest in this group. Other robust forms include bush California fuchsia (*E. latifolia* ssp. *johnstonii*), with bright green leaves and red-orange flowers. *Epilobium* 'Uvas Canyon' is shrubby with blue-gray foliage and large flowers. Diminutive Matole River fuchsia (*E. septentrionale*) is less than 6 inches high with wider, shorter white leaves and brilliant scarlet flowers. It is more thirsty than other varieties, but very useful at the front of the landscape.

PLANT COMMUNITIES coastal sage scrub, chaparral, oak woodland, mixed evergreen forest, redwood forest, pine forest, desert

'Catalina' hummingbird fuchsia provides fall color.

LANDSCAPE USAGE Cut these essential fall garden color spots all the way to the ground after blooming. Don't worry, they will return bigger and better next year. If you don't cut them back, they grow rangy with leafless centers. New shoots emerge in late winter. If you are late, cut old foliage back to the new shoots. Plant epilobiums by size, with the lowest growing in front. 'Catalina' can be located at the back of the border, with *Epilobium septentrionale* and *E. canum* in the foreground.

SEASIDE DAISIES
Erigeron glaucus

Seaside daisies are magnificent perennials. Not only do these plants bloom throughout the year, they grow so tight and low that they can be used as a foundational groundcover—as long as they are deadheaded. Removing the old flower stalks will keep the daisies blooming all year long. *Erigeron glaucus* 'Cape Sebastian' and 'Bountiful' are especially floriferous, large-flowered forms. 'Sea Breeze' has bright pink flowers.

There has been confusion between the variety *E. glaucus* 'Wayne Roderick' and a form called *E.* 'WR', both introduced by the great plantsman Wayne Roderick. 'Wayne Roderick' is a selection of the species *E. glaucus* and has electric blue flowers, while 'WR' seems hybridized with some form of aster. It is very low growing, with smaller, aster-like

Seaside daisy (*Erigeron glaucus* 'Cape Sebastian') blooms in cycles throughout the year.

Erigeron 'WR' has aster-like leaves and longer petals than typical seaside daisies.

leaves. It is extremely floriferous, with flowers held on longer stalks. Confusion may have arisen when Wayne distributed plants marked 'WR' and nurseries assumed it was short for 'Wayne Roderick.' Both are marvelous landscape perennials. Control ant populations and use insecticidal soap on sucking insects, as erigerons are susceptible to aphids and mites.

PLANT COMMUNITIES coastal strand, coastal sage scrub

LANDSCAPE USAGE These evergreen perennials are tidy enough to be used as up-front backbone plants. However, they must be deadheaded to maintain neat appearance. Remove the entire stalk, not just the individual flowers; otherwise the yellow, dead stalks look unsightly.

Red buckwheat (*Eriogonum grande* var. *rubescens*) is low growing with bright red flowers.

PERENNIAL BUCKWHEAT

Eriogonum **spp.**

Sub-shrub and perennial buckwheats are extremely useful as reliable color spots and as specimens in the rock garden. Red buckwheat (*Eriogonum grande* var. *rubescens*), from San Miguel Island, has bright red flowers on a low-growing plant. Sulfur buckwheat (*E. umbellatum*) has brilliant yellow flowers on a sub-shrub less than 12 inches high. Coast buckwheat (*E. latifolium*) is similar to red buckwheat but with pinkish-white flowers. Kennedy's buckwheat (*E.*

Sulfur buckwheat (*Eriogonum umbellatum*) sports brilliant yellow flowers.

kennedyi) grows less than 2 inches tall, exhibiting prolific pink pompon flowers in summer. Great for rock gardens, it grows tight to the ground. It is lovely and underused.

PLANT COMMUNITIES coastal sage scrub, chaparral, pine forest

LANDSCAPE USAGE Small, perennial buckwheats are delightful in every way; place them prominently at the leading edge of the native landscape. They bloom for a long period and are uncommonly neat and clean. Most will tolerate a wide range of soils, as long as they receive good drainage and limited moisture once established. They are also useful adorning rock walls or placed between boulders in the rock garden.

GOLDEN YARROW
Eriophyllum confertiflorum

Golden yarrow is a small perennial with brilliant yellow clusters of small daisies. Its common name refers to its resemblance to unrelated yarrow flowers. It grows in little clearings and on exposed slopes, often with monkey flower (*Mimulus* spp.). This easy-to-grow plant, loved by butterflies, provides bright spring color.

PLANT COMMUNITIES coastal sage scrub, chaparral, oak woodland, pine forest

LANDSCAPE USAGE Use this cheerful, bright perennial in the front of the native landscape border. Best used with

Golden yarrow has bright daisy-like flowers.

monkey flowers and around rocks, which can partially hide it after the spent flowers are cut back.

ALUM ROOTS (coral bells)

Heuchera spp.

Heucheras are neat mounding plants that grow in protected areas. Some think they superficially resemble geraniums. Delicate vertical flower spikes bloom in spring/summer—sometimes 100 spikes on a healthy plant. Most grow well in the shade of oaks and pines. Despite their delicate appearance, they are quite tough and tolerate a wide range of soils. Island alum root (*Heuchera maxima*)

Island alum root (*Heuchera maxima*) has delicate white flowers on red stems.

Heuchera 'Wendy' brightens the garden.

is a very large variety that has 36-inch white to pink flower spikes. Pink alum root (*H. rubescens*) has bright pink flowers on a smaller plant with 1-foot flower spikes. The delicately beautiful alum root (*H. micrantha*) produces 24-inch flower stalks with white flowers on red stems. Coral bells are beautiful clustered together in a shady spot. They exude a sense of "fairy woodland."

PLANT COMMUNITIES coastal sage scrub, chaparral, pine forest

LANDSCAPE USAGE These plants are extraordinary in the shade garden. They have neat, evergreen leaves on low mounds. The flower spikes are lofty and lovely. *Heuchera maxima* is very drought tolerant in the shade; the others

Alum root (*Heuchera micrantha*) has delicate white flowers on red stems.

would like water about once per week as long as they have good drainage.

LOBELIAS
Lobelia spp.

Lobelias grow in very wet conditions. Blue lobelia (*Lobelia dunni*) grows next to streams and in seasonal seeps, whereas cardinal flower (*L. cardinalis*) often grows in marshy areas. Blue lobelia has bright-blue tubular flowers on a small perennial that can disappear in droughts, only to reappear with winter rains. The cardinal flower is a hummingbird favorite, a tall spiky perennial with brilliant red tubular flowers.

PLANT COMMUNITY riparian

LANDSCAPE USAGE These plants thrive in moist conditions and can tolerate afternoon shade. Use lobelias for color around wetter areas, especially as a transition from lawn. They are great under dripping birdbaths and effective in dry streams or bioswales.

MONKEY FLOWERS
Mimulus spp.

Monkey flowers group into either dryland type or wetland type. Formerly, the drought-tolerant monkey flowers were placed under the genus *Diplacus*, but in the early 1990s all were reintegrated under *Mimulus*. Some nurseries still use the term *Diplacus*. We will begin with the drought-tolerant species.

Sticky monkey flower (*Mimulus aurantiacus*) has become the great catchall species for most upland monkey flowers. These plants can exceed 4 feet in height and become woody with age. Their tubular flowers resemble the face of a monkey. Natural flower color ranges from creamy white through yellow, orange, and deep brick red. The white stigma (or female pollen receptor) in the flower closes rapidly when touched. In theory, this adaptation discourages self-pollination as a hummingbird pulls its head from the flower throat. Southern monkey flower (*M. longiflorus*) has almost white to yellow and apricot flowers. Red monkey flower (*M. puniceus*)

Red monkey flower (*Mimulus puniceus*) is brilliant red-orange.

Sticky monkey flower (*Mimulus aurantiacus*) has a range of colors.

grows in San Diego with brilliant red flowers.

The wetter lowland species have larger, softer leaves and recurving petals. Scarlet monkey flower (*M. cardinalis*) has bright orange petals, while seep monkey flower (*M. guttatus*) has large, bright yellow flowers with red spots. Lewis's monkey flower (*M. lewisii*) has bright pink flowers and grows best at upper elevations. All these species enjoy wetter conditions, though *M. cardinalis* tolerate as little as once weekly watering.

PLANT COMMUNITIES coastal sage scrub, chaparral, oak woodland, pine forest, riparian

LANDSCAPE USAGE Monkey flowers are important perennials in the native landscape. Given a little supplemental irrigation, the drought-tolerant forms will bloom for many months, but may be shorter lived. While somewhat shrubby, they are best treated as color spots to be cleaned up after flowering. Run your fingers through the bloomed-out branches to effectively remove spent flowers and dead leaves. Cut them back by two-thirds once every few years to renew their leaves and form. Nearly all monkey flowers do well in afternoon shade.

The moisture-loving monkey flowers need to be watered a couple times per week for consistent moisture. This relegates them to dry streams, bioswales, or under dripping birdbaths. They can lend color at lawn edges. Monkey flowers' deep-throated blossoms attract hummingbirds.

FOUR O'CLOCK
Mirabilis spp.

Four o'clocks or wishbone bushes are colorful perennials with pink-, magenta-, or purple-colored tubular flowers. As named, the flowers open in the afternoon, adding brilliant color to the landscape. Often they are low growing, making them ideal for the front of a native border. California four o'clock (*Mirabilis laevis*) has numerous sub-species varying from small sub-shrubs to flat groundcovers. Giant four o'clock (*M. multiflora*) grows 3 feet across and 18 inches high with gray foliage and large magenta flowers.

Bright yellow seep monkey flower (*Mimulus guttatus*) is found near water sources.

California four o'clock (*Mirabilis laevis*) provides magenta accents in the afternoon.

PLANT COMMUNITIES coastal sage scrub, chaparral, oak woodland

LANDSCAPE USAGE California four o'clock is typically lower growing and will spread like a groundcover. However, it goes dormant, so should be placed where it can be hidden by other plants when it dies back. The giant four o'clock is a mounding sub-shrub good for the middle or back of the border where it can be partially hidden during dormancy.

COYOTE MINT

Monardella spp.

Few plants attract butterflies more than the monardellas. These beautiful summer-blooming perennials have large pompon flowers and an unbelievably minty aroma. They make fantastic tea. Hummingbirds particularly love the brilliant blooming red monardella (*Monardella macrantha*). San Diego willowy mint (*M. linoides*) has lavender flowers and blooms well into fall. Mint bush's (*M. subglabra*) large, deep purple flowers can engulf the foliage. Coyote mint (*M. villosa*) blooms with pale purple flowers on grayish leaves. White- to purple-flowered western pennyroyal (*M. odoratissima*) is one of the mintiest in this group, making a fine, flavorful tea used by pioneers to treat sore throats.

PLANT COMMUNITIES coastal sage scrub, chaparral, oak woodland, pine forest

LANDSCAPE USAGE Monardellas are extremely useful as upfront color later in the year, their color often persisting into fall. Their strong minty fragrance is a great sensory experience noticeable at a distance. Remarkably low maintenance, they look neat throughout the year and can be left alone and forgotten until they burst into color.

BEARDTONGUE
Penstemon spp.

Beardtongues, or penstemons, are an amazing group of brightly flowered perennials adding seasonal color and interest to the native landscape. Some, like the electric blue-lavender-flowered 6-foot royal penstemon (*Penstemon spectabilis*), and the bright red, scarlet buglar (*P. centranthifolius*) are upright perennials for the middle or back of a native planting. Other tall forms, like Cleveland penstemon (*P. clevelandii*), have bright pink flowers and gray foliage. The tall, showy balloon flower (*P. palmeri*) is a desert native with fragrant pinkish-white flowers. Firecracker penstemon (*P. eatonii*), with dark green leaves and bright red flowers, is native to the eastern mountain ranges and upper desert.

Plant lower-growing penstemons along edges. Deadhead them after blooming. The low-mounding foothill penstemon (*P. heterophyllus*) displays dozens of flower spikes on each plant, flowering in an electric combination of lavender and blue or pink. *P.*

heterophyllus 'Margarita BOP', a highly popular derivative, was introduced by Las Pilitas Nursery in the early eighties. It is highly adaptable and more garden tolerant than the straight species. Other smaller species include skyblue penstemon (*P. azureus*) and mountain pride (*P. newberryi*), with bright pink flowers and needing perfect soil drainage.

PLANT COMMUNITIES coastal sage scrub, grassland, chaparral, oak woodland, pine forest, desert

LANDSCAPE USAGE There are penstemons for most landscape situations. Generally, penstemon species require good drainage. Some, like *Penstemon newberryi* 'Mountain Pride', can take regular moisture as long as they are in

Royal penstemon (*Penstemon spectabilis*) grows to 6 feet.

Scarlet buglar (*Penstemon centranthifolius*) is a bright red perennial.

perfectly draining granitic soil—they are often seen in the Sierras growing on granite road cuts. Others, like scarlet buglar, can grow in clay soils as long as they do not stay moist in summer. Not demanding other than drainage, most penstemons are incredibly floriferous. They exist to show off.

HUMMINGBIRD SAGE
Salvia spathacea

The only truly perennial sage in California, *Salvia spathacea* has large, soft, aromatic leaves reminiscent of pineapple sage, for which it can be substituted in cooking. It spreads by rhizomes, usually as an understory for chamise (*Adenostoma fasciculatum*) or in colonies under

Penstemon heterophyllus 'Margarita BOP' is popular and dependable in the garden.

oaks (*Quercus* spp.). Spring finds it covered in magenta flower spikes. Some forms, like S. 'Powerline Pink', have flower stalks 6 feet tall. Hummingbirds guard this plant with their lives!

PLANT COMMUNITIES coastal strand, coastal sage scrub, chaparral, oak woodland

LANDSCAPE USAGE If you have the room to let it spread, this plant is fantastic in the shade garden. It is closely symbiotic with oaks and is useful as oak understory, or colonizing as a groundcover over a few years.

INDIAN PINK
Silene laciniata

Plant this delightful perennial among evergreen groundcovers, or peeking out from behind a boulder when it flowers. Its thin, vine-like stems and narrow leaves make it almost invisible, until the brilliant scarlet 1-inch flowers burst forth in late spring. Like other members of the carnation family, the petals are cleanly forked giving it a star-like appearance.

PLANT COMMUNITIES coastal strand, coastal sage scrub, chaparral

LANDSCAPE USAGE Locate this plant behind something else, and let it grow forward to surprise the viewer with its luminous red flowers. Supported by spider-like dark green foliage, flowers seeming to float in mid air, it is a neat perennial deserving of wider use.

Hummers love the hummingbird sage

Indian pink is related to carnations.

Vines are special-situation plants, not for every landscape, but important in the right places. Several species of native vines are appropriate for trellis or shade structures. Some evergreen species were discussed under groundcovers, including: *Lonicera subspicata*, *L. hispidula*, and *Ribes viburnifolium*. Showy deciduous species follow.

DUTCHMAN'S PIPE
Aristolochia californica

The robust Dutchman's vine can cover the ground and grow up trees in full shade when it is happy. It has unusual, pipe-shaped inflated flowers that temporarily trap insects to facilitate pollination as the insects struggle to get out. The showy flowers have an unpleasant odor (not typically apparent) attractive to flies for pollination. The pipevine

Use Dutchman's pipe in a moist shady place.

swallowtail, in eating the plant's leaves, acquires protection from predators from the plant's toxic sap.

PLANT COMMUNITIES chaparral, riparian, mixed evergreen forest, oak woodland

LANDSCAPE USAGE This is a good vine to use in a moist, shady spot. Its flowers are quite unusual, but be aware that it is deciduous in winter. Dutchman's pipe is a great butterfly host plant.

PERENNIAL MORNING GLORY
Calystegia spp.

Perennial morning glories are very showy vines that climb up and cover

Morning glory (*Calystegia purpurata*) goes dormant in drought.

structures. Anacapa pink morning glory (*Calystegia macrostegia*) has large white flowers with pink highlights. Purplish morning glory (*C. purpurata*) has large white flowers with light purple highlights. Both are aggressive spreaders and are stress deciduous, meaning they need supplemental moisture to maintain their leafy good looks. The vines grow from an underground woody base (caudex).

PLANT COMMUNITIES coastal sage scrub, chaparral, oak woodland

LANDSCAPE USAGE These fast-growing plants cover a lot of territory. Each plant can easily swathe 400 square feet in a couple of years. Water them lightly once every week or two so that they retain their leaves; they can look pretty rough when deciduous. These are good plants for covering shade structures.

VIRGIN'S BOWER VINE
Clematis spp.

Wide-ranging virgin bower vines are deciduous. California species are similar in appearance, having creamy white flowers with large stamens. *Clematis lasiantha* and *C. ligusticifolia* are sprawling vines with large showy flower clusters, followed by pinkish plume-like seedheads. *Clematis lasiantha* grows more northerly, while southern *C. ligusticifolia* is more drought and heat tolerant. The smaller-scale *C. pauciflora* can easily be used in most residential landscapes.

Virgin's bower vine has many delicate, creamy flowers.

California grape (*Vitis californica* 'Roger's Red') puts on a spectacular fall display of color.

PLANT COMMUNITIES coastal sage scrub, chaparral, riparian, oak woodland, mixed evergreen forest

LANDSCAPE USAGE Use these plants on fences or to scale background shrubs and trees. They go deciduous, so put them in the back of the border where they can disappear in winter.

HEART-LEAF PENSTEMON (climbing penstemon)
Keckiella cordifolia

Use this beautiful, deciduous plant as a shrub, groundcover, or vine. Sprawling 3 to 6 feet, place it where it can grow through other shrubs, or on a trellis where seasonally bare branches look sculptural. The payoff is a seasonal show of handsome heart-shaped leaves and clusters of long, brilliant, tubular red flowers.

PLANT COMMUNITIES coastal sage scrub, chaparral

LANDSCAPE USAGE When used as a vine, consider mixing it with an evergreen creeper. Or, let the bare branches themselves become part of the trellis.

WILD GRAPE
Vitis spp.

The wild grapes are dramatic vines, growing to be woody ropes and lending a jungle feel to woodland areas. The desert grape (*Vitis girdiana*) grows primarily in southern California, whereas the California grape (*V. californica*) grows in the north. They are similar—both bear small, seedy, edible fruits valuable for wildlife. Hollywood streets Vine and Vineland were inspired by wild grape vines in the canyons. Native Americans used the fruit for raisins, juice, and wine. Edible young leaves have a tangy flavor. *Vitis californica* rootstock is often used by the wine industry for grafting.

PLANT COMMUNITIES riparian, oak woodland, desert

LANDSCAPE USAGE These beautiful, vigorous plants are well suited for creating a "Tuscan" look on trellises and fences. *Vitis californica* 'Roger's Red', a selection by famed horticulturist Roger Raiche, is possibly a hybrid between *V. californica* and *V. vinifera*. Its leaves turn drop dead red in fall. If harvested when fully ripe, the grapes make a delicious, though intense, wild grape juice.

Monocots

The monocots are either true grasses or grass like. They only have one elongated seed leaf when germinating, rather than two opposed seed leaves (known as cotyledons). Monocots include many beautiful flowering plants.

SHAW'S AGAVE

Agave shawii

Shaw's agave is a succulent belonging to the larger group of century plants. This agave has beautiful, dark green leaves with red highlights arranged in a spiny rosette that includes an imprint of the lower leaf on the back of each newer leaf. It grows well in coastal locations, maturing to bloom in 15 to 20 years. While the plant is 2 to 3 feet tall, 4 to 5 feet wide,

Red-tinged leaves of Shaw's agave.

the flower stalk grows to 10 feet, covered in clusters of yellow flowers. The plant dies after going to seed, but usually a large group of pups readily take its place.

PLANT COMMUNITY coastal sage scrub

LANDSCAPE USAGE This bold, architectural plant can be used in most coastal areas. For inland locations, consider using the blue-leaved desert agave (*Agave deserti*).

PURPLE THREE-AWN GRASS

Aristida purpurea

This gorgeous, purple-flowered clumping perennial grass grows to 2 feet tall

Purple three-awn grass provides soft color and movement.

with a beautiful, wispy, soft texture. It becomes quite drought tolerant with age. It spreads slowly by seed over time.

PLANT COMMUNITIES grassland, coastal sage scrub, pine forest, desert

LANDSCAPE USAGE Use purple three-awn grass to replace the overused, invasive non-native weedy Mexican feather grass (*Nassella tenuissima*). Purple three-awn has purple flowers and flows gracefully in the wind. It is lovely massed under sculptures or to highlight other landscape features.

SEDGE

Carex spp.

Native sedges provide beautiful accents in moister areas of native landscape. One of the largest and most dramatic is San Diego sedge (*Carex spissa*). This 4-foot-tall perennial has rigid, strapping blue leaves and yellow flowers. It is similar to rough sedge (*C. senta*), but larger. This plant makes a statement. By contrast, Monterey sedge (*C. subfusca*)—bright green, soft, flowing, and less than 2 feet high—is a nice medium-size sedge. Plant it on the edge of a wet meadow planting or even in a lawn. To create a meadow, consider clustered field sedge (*C. praegracilis*), a lower-growing, soft, grass-like perennial. Unmowed it creates a swirling meadow effect; when mowed it becomes a beautiful, tough lawn substitute mimicking tall fescue

Monterey sedge (*Carex subfusca*) grows to 2 feet.

Field sedge (*Carex praegracilis*), a grass-like perennial.

but using less than half the water and requiring minimal maintenance.

PLANT COMMUNITIES wet areas in all plant communities

LANDSCAPE USAGE Sedges are useful plants for creating spiky accents or meadow areas in the native landscape. San Diego sedge is striking for its large size and blue color, while Monterey sedge is smaller, more green, and softer (great for framing meadow-like areas). Clustered field sedge is finding popularity as an effective lawn substitute.

PACIFIC COAST IRIS
Iris douglasiana

Pacific coast iris is equal parts beautiful and tough. Unlike bearded iris, these strapping, evergreen plants have large, delicately beautiful blue to purple flowers in great numbers on a single plant. This perennial spreads slowly, in time forming a lovely groundcover, especially in light shade or full sun along the coast. Hybridization with other native and non-native species has created a myriad of flower shapes and colors, still retaining the basic strength and evergreen nature of the plant.

PLANT COMMUNITIES coastal sage scrub, pine forest, mixed evergreen forest

LANDSCAPE USAGE Use Pacific coast iris in full sun along the coast and light shade inland. Drought tolerant and

Pacific coast iris is available in a rainbow of cultivars.

Use blue wild rye for striking blue-foliage accent.

spreading with time, Pacific coast iris likes to be divided every few years, as it is a renewing plant. Use in any shade garden—it is highly adaptable and easy to grow.

BLUE WILD RYE
Leymus condensatus 'Canyon Prince'

This amazing, useful accent plant is blue, blue, blue. A well-behaved form of giant wild rye (*Leymus condensatus*), it is only about 2 feet tall but has lovely 5-foot flower stalks allowing 'Canyon Prince' to stand up against any ornamental grass. It is very easy to grow. Overwatering can trigger rapid spreading; otherwise, it stays in a nice 3-foot clump. Finches love the seedheads.

PLANT COMMUNITIES coastal sage scrub, chaparral, oak woodland

LANDSCAPE USAGE This wonderful blue wild rye makes a great contrast to just about any other foliage color. Plant lavender-flowered seaside daisy around its base to create a stunning display.

DEER GRASS
Muhlenbergia rigens

Deer grass is another dramatic native grass that has finally achieved pop-

Deer grass has architectural appeal.

ularity among conventional landscape designers. It is highly adaptable, bold, and fast growing. It can tolerate lots of water or become drought tolerant. The basic clump of deer grass is about 2 feet high, but its rod-like flower stalks can rise to 6 feet. Finches dine on its seed without even bending a flower spike. The most important basketry plant of the California Indians, it is a great plant to use singly or in masses because of its repeatable architectural appeal.

PLANT COMMUNITIES grassland, chaparral, oak woodland, pine forest

LANDSCAPE USAGE Use deer grass to make a bold statement. As with most grasses, it requires maintenance. Cut it down to the base (1 to 2 inches high) every two years or so. Indians would actually burn it to the ground to achieve a similar renewal. Failure to do this results in ratty-looking clumps with indistinct flower spikes that can become a fire hazard. Biennial maintenance precludes using deer grass in massive, monotypic, architectural plantings.

BLUE-EYED GRASS
Sisyrinchium bellum

Perennial blue-eyed grass becomes a ball of deep blue flowers in winter and spring. It has blue, grass-like leaves and may superficially resemble a small

Use blue-eyed grass for seasonal color spots.

YUCCA
Yucca **spp.**

California has amazingly beautiful yuccas. Our Lord's candle (*Yucca* or *Hesperoyucca whipplei*) is a common spiky plant with a 10- to 12-foot flower stalk that creates beautiful white flame-like accents on hillsides in much of California. The stiff leaves have very sharp points—do not accidentally fall on this plant. It blooms dramatically in 5 to 10 years. Yucca die after flowering, but are prolific seeders, and one subspecies (*Y. whipplei* ssp. *percusa*) pups and spreads slowly by rhizomes. Pink-flowering varieties are known to occur. Highly architectural when placed in a row, they can form a neat but impenetrable barrier without appearing overly aggressive. Mojave yucca (*Y. schidigera*), a perennial form, does not die after flowering. It can grow to over 6 feet tall with multiple trunks and flower clusters. Its large, edible banana-like fruits are edible.

PLANT COMMUNITIES coastal sage scrub, chaparral, oak woodland, pine forest, desert

LANDSCAPE USAGE Our Lord's candle is best used as a specimen plant or as an architectural massing element. Do not plant it close to walkways where it could stab pedestrians. Set in the center of a planting, it will create an unforgettable accent when it blooms. Mojave yucca should be used at the back of the border, as its form is more amorphous, and it has multiple (but smaller)

bunchgrass, only to burst forth in spectacular color. It spreads slowly by rhizomes and seed. It is completely drought adapted, although light supplemental watering can extend its flower season.

PLANT COMMUNITIES grassland, coastal sage scrub, chaparral, oak woodland

LANDSCAPE USAGE Use at the edge of the landscape only for color spots. Avoid mass plantings of this iris relative as it completely disappears in summer, leaving little or no trace until it reappears with the winter rains.

Mojave yucca (*Yucca schidigera*) does not die after flowering.

Our Lord's candle (*Yucca* or *Hesperoyucca whipplei*) provides a dramatic garden accent.

individual bloom spikes. Both plants are highly drought tolerant and adaptable. Mojave yucca actually occurs from the desert to the ocean.

S O THERE YOU have it, a small selection of California native plants and how to use them. This teaser should help start you on your journey. It includes some of the best we have found, with enough choices to get you started. Some interesting plants may be more difficult to find, but they are worth the effort. Increased demand for native landscaping should improve availability and encourage local regional nurseries to find and propagate ever more intriguing species native to specific areas.

INSTALLATION
Plant it right

7

Now that you have your design, you are ready to start installing your native landscape. As excited as you may be, before you start putting plants in the ground you need to prepare the site. It's like cooking—it's all in the prep work. These steps are so important. Your preparation work will have a profound effect on the ultimate success of the landscape.

Proper installation techniques encompass much more than just planting when features are incorporated into the native landscape.

Site analysis

The goal in proper site preparation for native plantings is to create a site that is as clean and free of pathogens and weeds as possible. Bare ground is your goal prior to planting. The following sections describe how to get there.

Soil has two components: rock or mineral particles and organic matter. No minerals and it's not soil; likewise, no organic matter and it's not soil. Most native California soils are scant in organic matter. That's the way it is and the plants have adapted to this reality. While traditional horticulture wants you to add nutrients and compost to soils, please resist that temptation if you want your native landscape to thrive. California, with its complex geology, includes nearly 100 distinctive geological soil profiles. The mineral compositions of individual soils make the science increasingly complex.

However, for this analysis we will utilize a simpler categorization. Your soil may be classified by the three basic soils—clay, silt, or sand—based on the sizes of the rock particles in the soil. The sizes of these particles affect how the soil interacts with the roots of the plants, so it is very important information, though relatively easy to determine.

Clay has the smallest particles. Individual particles of clay soils can only be seen with an electron microscope. Clay soil is the densest, holds the most water, and can become hard and compact when it dries out. Clay and heat make ceramics, afterall. Many physical and chemical reactions in soil occur on the surface of the soil particles. Clay soils, with smaller particles, offer far more surface area (mineral or nutrient availability) than soils with larger particles.

On the other hand, clay soil can hold so much water that if the soil is not permitted to dry out, it may not allow enough air to the roots and may drown the plant. This factor is extremely important with California native plants. Pay attention to the books and plant tags that specify, "well-drained soil."

Sand has the largest particles from very fine to very coarse sand. Sand particles are visible and easy to feel. Larger particles mean there is more space between the particles. Sandy soils are loose, open, and drain quickly. With less surface area, minerals are less available than with the smaller particles.

The particles of soil between the sizes of clay and sand are silt, which is also called loam. These particles are visible with a simple magnifying glass. The intermediary sizes can include the best and worst attributes of both the clay and sand. Silt-size particles drain fairly well and retain some nutrients and some water.

In truth, the powers that be never sifted the soil to make certain that the soil particles were all exactly the same size, so most soils contain a combination of all sizes in greater or lesser proportion. Loam is a soil with a combination of particle sizes—ideally equal parts of sand and silt with a smaller portion of clay.

Soil scientists evaluate numerous other soil characteristics principally for the purpose of optimizing conditions for efficient agriculture. Soil characteristics include: texture, bulk, density, soil structure, porosity, color, depth, proportion of organic matter, nutrients, pH, mineral composition, and carbon-to-nitrogen ratio for fertility. All of these factors have

Preparing the site.

some effect on plant adaptation to the specific soil, to a greater or lesser degree, often at the extremes of the measure.

Further, few types of native plants are that critical about soil. They are more sensitive to general plant community, drainage conditions, and elevation. Installing plants that are way off from the local ecosystem usually assures higher mortality (think redwoods in Death Valley). If weeds abound on the site, the soil is capable of supporting life. If nothing has grown there in years—not even weeds—have a soil analysis done.

To collect soil for your soil sample, do not take the stuff from the surface. Dig down a few inches and put a trowel-full in a plastic bag. Take samples this way from several locations on the property and put them in your bag. The analysis usually costs less than a hundred dollars. It is a very wise investment. On large property with visible anomalies, you may want to do more than one.

When you get the analysis back, there are some specific items to review. The pH level is a logarithmic measure of soil acidity or alkalinity. It measures the concentration of hydrogen ions (H^+) versus hydroxide ions (OH^-). A pH of 7 is considered neutral. Being logarithmic, each full point is ten times the acidity or alkalinity of the previous. So a pH of 5 is ten times more acidic than a pH of 6; and a pH of 9 is ten times more alkaline than a pH of 8. Knowing your pH is important in plant selection, as plants that thrive in acid conditions usually don't do well in alkaline soils, and vice versa. In general (and there are always exceptions) plants from woodland areas prefer neutral to acidic soil, whereas inland and desert areas are often quite alkaline. An acid-loving plant in alkaline soil will exhibit burnt leaf margins (black or brown) with a lack of vigor, and will eventually die. An alkaline plant in acidic soil will exhibit yellow leaves, stunted growth, and long-term failure. While rainwater is pure and neutral, much southern California water has traveled long distances, picking up particles and salts along the way, and tends to be alkaline.

Sodium and boron levels are two of the most critical nutrient measures for native plants. Sodium levels above 100 parts per million (ppm) begin to result in leaf burn. Most chaparral species will not tolerate levels above 250 ppm. Levels over 500 ppm support only coastal salt marsh species and/or desert alkaline sink plants (think the bottom of Death Valley). Homes using sodium chloride in water softeners should make certain that the landscape water is drawn off before the household water processed by the softener system. Boron is deadly in the tiniest amounts. Anything over one to two ppm will start killing most native plant communities, but for the two exceptions noted above.

Most native plants are not affected by low levels of nitrogen and phosphorus, nutrients so important in traditional horticulture. In fact, having high levels usually indicates previous soil amending and fertilizing, which may have a negative impact on plant longevity.

Very low potassium levels, however, can be a problem. Acceptable levels are in the 20–40 ppm range. Readings below 10 ppm indicate a need to add potassium sulfate topically (watered in after planting). This is one of the few supplements that may benefit native plants.

Native plant communities correlate strongly to the depth of soil. A clear example is native grasslands. True native grassland usually occurs in shallow soil, less than a foot in depth. Below the surface soil may be a layer of hardpan or bedrock. These areas are inundated with water in winter and bone dry in summer. Many native grass species are active in the wet months and are summer dormant. Many other leafy plants grow alongside the perennial bunch grasses in these communities. According to Bert Wilson, native grassland is actually remarkable for its lack of grass. It is common to find species like *Achillea millefolium* var. *lanulosa*, *Penstemon heterophyllus*, *Solidago* sp., *Sisyrinchium bellum*, *Sidalcea malviflora*, sedges, and annual wildflowers growing in shallow soils. Many species of eriogonum and arctostaphylos can also tolerate thin soils. Coastal sage scrub and chaparral plants usually inhabit soils in the 2- to 3-foot range (or deeper) and oaks will find pockets of yet deeper soil.

Planting history

Try to determine the site history. It's daunting to be told, "Nothing has grown here for 20 years." If that's the case, take several soil samples and have them analyzed. Look for anything out of whack—high salinity and/

Sidalcea is one of the species comprising a native grassland.

or boron are common culprits. For all you know, it could be a superfund site. Or, perhaps, the original builder dumped waste, covering it with a layer of soil to hide the evidence. Occasionally the problem is so bad, it may require total soil replacement. If so, look for a local source of fill dirt, such as a neighbor installing a new pool. Substrate soils are usually fine. If none of these options work, throw a boulder on it and move on. Fortunately, this is a rare situation.

In contrast, the best possible circumstance is a site completely or partially colonized with native plants. It has a functioning ecology, which makes it fairly easy to plug in more natives (compatible with the existing plant community, of course).

Most landscapes are either new construction sites or an existing landscape. With new construction, have the soil analyzed. Be on the alert for washouts in new construction. Ordinances require that all concrete and paint be washed in plastic-lined pits, which are allowed to evaporate prior to removal. Unfortunately, many contractors ignore this and dump directly on the ground. These mini-toxic-waste dumps are often covered with soil for disguise. And they always seem to occur where the plants are going, instead of the driveway or walkway. Additionally, new construction sites often include large amounts of fill soil that could have come from anywhere. If the site has been sitting for a while and has been colonized with vigorous weeds, it will probably support the landscape. Simply remove the weeds and clean to bare mineral soil.

Removing an existing landscape

In reworking an existing landscape you will deal with any problems and pathogens of the previous installation. Smell the soil. Good native soil usually smells neutral to sweet. Bad soil can smell musty or worse. Conventional horticultural practice relies heavily on moisture and fertility, which can promote disease in native plants. If you are removing shrubs and perennials, often the best first step is to just let it all dry out. This helps kill molds and bacterial pathogens. The soil aroma should improve as it dries.

When replacing a lawn, never just cut holes in the turf and plant natives. Always remove the grass. The closest ecological analogue to a lawn is a freshwater marsh, with all its moisture, fertility, and disturbance. Lawn is a highly anaerobic bacterial environment, the direct opposite of a clean fungal-based ecology. It is essential to remove all traces of turf.

The normal procedure for turf conversion for Bermuda grass is to first kill the lawn with herbicides. Other methods such as solarizing with clear plastic or covering with mulch, newspapers, or dirt are not effective for deep-rooted aggressive perennial grasses. Remember that the rhizomes of Bermuda grass can extend down 10 feet. No amount of mechanical removal will do the job. There are stories of people who have dug down 6 feet or more, sifting all the soil, only to have Bermuda return with a vengeance.

If using mechanical removal, be prepared to spot spray for weeds in the new landscape for a long time. Additionally, your post-installation manual weed removal must be *extremely* diligent. Use a large hoe, square shovel, or sod cutter to remove the top 1 to 2 inches of soil along with the grass. This eliminates some of the pathogens, salts, calcium deposits, and

Remove an existing landscape to bare ground. Trees should be removed by the roots, when possible.

fertilizer associated with turf. Lowering the grade in this manner provides room for the new mulch later on.

If you have space, the waste sod can be piled and allowed to compost down. This is an excellent medium for growing vegetables, and raised bed vegetable gardens are a great way to continually use up compost. It certainly is better than filling up landfills. On the other hand, while compost is great for ornamentals, veggies, and roses, it should never touch a native landscape.

The amendments issue

A basic tenet of ornamental horticulture is to amend soils prior to installing new plants. In most cases, this is exactly the wrong thing to do with native plants. Your goal is to emulate natural ecology in the landscape. Adding lots of organic matter to an ecosystem that evolved in the absence of fertility sets up the perfect conditions for anaerobic bacterial development, as opposed to a clean, fungal-based environment. Non-native ornamental plants are free to use all this richness as they wish without requiring the protections afforded by the presence of the fungi. In California, however, this only occurs naturally in a wetland. All the natural biocontrols will try to shift the ecology toward a swamp, killing the drought-tolerant natives in the process. Ironically, indigenous plants are more sensitive to inappropriate conditions than the exotics. This is one reason why natives have an undeserved reputation for being unstable and difficult. We kill them with kindness.

Avoid tilling the soil. Rototilling or hoeing can completely destroy any existing mycorrhizal grid. Additionally, heavy soil disturbance contributes to weed germination. The exception would be in new construction where soil has been imported and/or is highly disturbed already, and is so compacted that it is unworkable. This is especially true for building pads and slopes on decomposed granite. In these specific cases, tilling can help to initially open up the soils and allow the roots and mycorrhizae to penetrate.

While we typically do not add organic amendments to the soil, topical additives are sometimes advisable on top of the soil to be watered in later. For compacted clay soils, adding gypsum (calcium sulfate) to the planting holes and on the soil surface can help open things up. Iron and potassium sulfate can also bring up deficient levels of these elements. Soil sulfur is often used to help bring down pH in alkaline soils. The soil sulfur must be worked into the planting soil to be effective.

Drainage

Drainage is extremely important when installing a native landscape. It can be even more significant than soil type, as many plant communities occur across a spectrum of soils. But you won't see a manzanita growing in a poorly draining marshy area, nor a willow high on a well-draining natural slope.

Drainage can mean a couple of things. It can describe surface features that don't allow water to stand, like sloping topography. Or, it can refer to the capacity of the soil itself to percolate. In the later case, soil types can actually be inferred from the length of time it takes for a shovel-sized hole filled with water to drain out completely. Compacted clay or hardpan can take hours or even days to drain; on the other hand, decomposed granite or sand may only take minutes. Choose plants to fit the soil type, rather than attempt to organically amend soil to try to change its structure. There is far more soil than you could ever amend sufficiently. As the mycorrhizal fungal grid gets established, it opens soils and increases their moisture-holding capacity. In effect, it is the fungi that ultimately lend structure to the soils.

Surface drainage can be manipulated to designate the flow. One method is grading the surface into swales to create appropriate drainage. Swales can be enhanced with boulders and plantings to form dry streams and bioswales. Dry streams utilize well-placed boulders to emulate a natural streambed, which are both functional and a stunning visual focal point, whether wet or dry. Running rain-gutter downspouts into these common drainage features and contouring the landscape into the stream assures adequate flow during rains.

Nowadays, most municipal codes require water to be kept on-site to the greatest degree possible. This is where bioswales come into play. These are dry streams or contoured catchments that provide on-site detention basins. Bioswales hold as much water as possible during normal periods of rain and allow moisture to percolate. Dry streams and bioswales can be designed as streamside or woodland (riparian) zones in your yard. These areas, in turn, serve as moisture nuclei for the rest of the landscape. In a well-established native landscape, mycorrhizal fungi will transport moisture from the riparian area to drier parts of the yard.

Sometimes underground drainage is preferable. A bioswale or dry stream may be impractical where there is a lot of hardscape and the available space is very narrow. First, note whether the grade elevation drops in the right direction to run the drainage. A typical slope for a drainpipe is about three-eighths of an inch per linear foot. Measure for this before digging trenches. The minimum slope is a quarter inch per foot. Anything less and the water will stagnate and/or back up. Use a level line or laser level to maintain the drop.

Ceramic pipe is seldom used anymore and flexible corrugated pipe

Runoff from this relatively steep slope is captured in the bioswale below.

A dry streambed should be both functional and an important visual centerpiece.

is not recommended. The corrugations can trap sediment and the pipe is easily moved by roots and disturbance. Most failed drainage systems involve displaced corrugated pipes. The best systems utilize rigid PVC or polyethylene solid pipe, available in all sizes from 3 inches and larger. Use catch basins with tees for water collection. Secure all joints with specially made drainage tape. Put gravel or cement around each catch basin.

French drains are a further refinement of this concept. They allow water percolation and transportation along the length of an area, and are not dependent on individual catch basins for water collection. In this case, perforated drainage pipe is laid in the bottom of the trench lined with filter cloth, and then gravel is laid on top. The drain may be covered with an inch or two of soil. Some important points to keep in mind: the holes in the pipe must be laid face down, and leave enough cloth to fold over the top of the gravel, which can then be covered with soil.

Irrigation

Irrigating native plants is a controversial subject. Many people assume that natives are not irrigated, or maybe just enough to get them established. This is fine for restoration work, where the plants belong to the local community and can survive on rainfall alone after establishment. However, in a landscape, light supplemental irrigation both enhances appearance by dusting off the plants, and increases fire resistance. In southern California, many native landscape plants come from areas with slightly higher precipitation, so judicious light watering can be essential to maintain vigor. This very light irrigation does not undo the concept of water frugality; the amount of moisture is about 20 percent of that required by a conventional landscape.

Controversy swirls around the delivery system. Philosophically, and practically, the goal is to replicate natural ecology, as best one can in a landscape situation. As Bert Wilson from Las Pilitas Nursery has noted, the idea behind this rationale draws upon the "butterfly effect" of chaos theory. Just as the miniscule beating of butterfly wings on one side of the world could generate a series of cascading events ultimately leading to catastrophic consequences on the other side of the earth, so may the addition of foreign variables to a poorly understood and extremely complex system lead to unintended and unpredictable consequences for the ecology one is trying to establish. In other words, there are countless interdependent variables in an ecosystem, many of which may never be identified but which may have a significant "ripple" effect if altered. Therefore, it is best to try to keep the variables we do control as close to a natural condition as possible.

How does this apply to irrigation? Native ecologies usually receive their moisture from overhead sources—e.g., rainfall, snow, or fog drip. For over 40 million years the native plant communities have adapted to this regime. The only exception is marsh or riparian ecology. Overhead precipitation is best emulated with low-volume sprinklers, misters, or hand watering administered at the right times of year and in the right amounts. This type and volume of application wets the leaves, leaches through the mulch layer, and finely controls moisture depth.

Drip systems, though easy and convenient to install, saturate the soil immediately around the plant. They create a wet zone completely alien to upland, drought-tolerant species. Native plants do not tolerate localized hyper-saturation well. Some newer systems distribute the drip emitters in a grid, leading to hypersaturation. Natives especially hate warm, wet soils. Ironically, the native plants that best tolerate drip are riparian and marsh plants.

There are other issues with drip, as well: Watering at the mulch/soil interface does not allow micronutrients to leach through the mulch. Drip does not address dust buildup on plant leaves in summer. Drip tubing is a great chew toy for most critters. And, the moisture from drip emitters is like X marks the spot for gophers!

If you already have a drip system on your plants, all is not lost. You can easily convert emitters to overhead micro-sprays, which act like a cross between misters and sprinklers. Make this conversion to micro-spray as soon as possible. Unfortunately, you will not eliminate the problems with damage and critters.

The most appropriate irrigation systems for native plants utilize low-

Low-volume rotary irrigation heads apply a fine layer of mist over the landscape, cleaning plant leaves and moistening the mulch without saturating the soil.

volume, rotary-type heads, mounted on 12-inch pop-up sprinkler bodies or risers fed through underground PVC pipe. Hunter Industries offers the MP Rotator system with adjustable rotary nozzles designed to fit virtually any sprinkler body. They offer adjustable patterns and three different radii (10, 20, and 30 feet). Hunter also has strip heads for watering long, narrow areas. Other manufacturers are coming on line with similar products.

Most building codes require sprinkler pipe to be run 12 inches deep. State-of-the-art systems utilize a "swing joint" at each head. It is basically three polyethylene plastic elbows and a length of riser

Twelve-inch pop-up stream rotor sprinkler head assembly attached to the pipe through a swing joint, prior to final placement.

forming an adjustable universal joint that connects to a sideways facing T in the pipe. This allows the head to move in response to kicking without damaging the joint. It also allows adjustment of head position. Sprinkler valves should be automatic and wired in a timer. Include a hose bib where you have a group of valves. A mainline is necessary to feed the valves anyway, so adding a bib on a vertical schedule 80 or galvanized pipe is relatively easy. Include a stake, mounted in a concrete footing for support. Having hose bibs throughout the yard simplifies occasional hand watering, cleaning, spraying, or watering newly installed plants individually.

Over the years, irrigation timers have become more sophisticated, yet easier to use. The newest timers have programmable evapotranspiration coefficients and weather-based systems tied into subterranean moisture sensors. However, the most important feature is the ability to program beyond seven days. Ultimately, the goal is to water lightly during the warm months—once every 10 to 14 days in most areas. This is not possible with a Monday–Sunday only timer.

You can manually water smaller yards with a hose or hose-end sprinklers. In the latter case, it is convenient to incorporate a manual hose timer, so you can walk away while watering and have the water shut off automatically—another good reason for incorporating hose bibs wherever possible.

Installing hardscape features

The site has been prepared, the irrigation installed—it is time to add the hardscape features. These non-plant elements create the framework and character of the garden. Examples of basic features include: rockwork, paths, flatwork, retaining walls, benches, and water features.

Boulders

Rocks and boulders anchor and define a natural landscape. They provide a sense of permanence and stability and create changes in level. However, they are not Easter eggs. Most texts recommend burying a third to half of each rock. Partially bury and arrange boulders in naturalistic groupings to look like they have been there for all eternity. When a boulder sits on flat land, it usually exhibits an "undercut" as the sides curve underneath (unless it is perfectly flat on the bottom). Bury the rock deep enough to at least hide the undercut. Then there is no way to judge the size of the boulder, giving the illusion of larger size.

When setting boulders into an existing slope, it is very important that you take care that this work can be done without destabilizing the slope. If you have *any* questions or doubts, do not attempt it. Again, no more than a third of the rock should be exposed (to be clear: two-thirds of the rock, or more, will be buried). It is only safe to set boulders into stable, cut soil (not fill slope) and the receiving holes need to tilt back into the slope by at least 25 degrees.

It is okay to use large boulders to help support low mounds, less than 3 feet tall. Set them randomly into the mounds, so that the whole hill appears to be naturally formed in conjunction with an outcropping.

Rocks anchor and define a natural landscape.

Upside-down paint is a godsend to the landscaping industry. The spray can functions inverted when marking boulder locations, allowing you to assess alternative layouts prior to bringing in the big boys. Erase the mark, if you need to, by scuffing the soil with a foot. Then dig rough holes or "nests" in which to set the boulders.

Transporting large boulders is challenging. Some people adapt dollies originally intended for moving boxed trees to move boulders up to 4 feet in size. The dollies on double balloon tires are especially useful and stable. Use either a bobcat or mini-excavator to locate and set in even larger boulders. If you are not qualified to operate this equipment, numerous professionals can supply the equipment and operators for a price. Also, many landscape material suppliers who sell boulders offer flatbed delivery with a crane that can set the rock for you, providing there is access within reach of the equipment.

Use upside-down paint to mark rock positions and literally "paint" a landscape.

A delivery crane greatly assists in placing large boulders.

Paths

Paths can be constructed from many types of materials. Some of the most interesting and whimsical treatments utilize an eclectic assortment of items emphasizing contrasting shapes and forms. The simplest is a path created from plain dirt and absence of mulch. Safety and your imagination are the only limits. However, some basic types of paths are easy for most people to create. For instance, decomposed granite, or DG, is a common type of garden path, made popular in English gardens. DG is a sand-like substance compactable into a hard, durable surface. It results from the breakdown of weathered granite. Coloration varies depending on the tint of the original granite. A stabilizer or binder is recommended to enhance the consolidation of the walking surface.

Use upside-down paint to mark curving paths (all paths should meander, unless in a formal or contemporary design). One trick to laying out nice curves is to use garden hose. Even better, pivot a length of PVC pipe around fixed points for large, sweeping curves with smooth even arcs. For stability, following the layout, dig the entire cross section of the path down 2 to 4 inches. Put down a layer of landscape fabric as a liner. Landscape fabric is not recommended for planting areas, but it can really deter worms from destroying your path after heavy rains. It also helps resist rhizomatous plants from growing up through the path. Adding 1 to 2 inches of gravel on top of the liner improves drainage.

Determine whether or not to insert edging. If the path has not been excavated, dig trenches to bury all but the top 2 inches of the edging material. Avoid thin plastic edging, which contracts and expands severely with temperature changes. Plastic edging often heaves out of the trenches, taking the stakes with it. Even if anchored heavily with numerous stakes, plastic edging warps and scallops. Metal or laminated wood edging is the best, especially in commercial applications or high-traffic areas. Set stakes every 3 to 4 feet, nailing or screwing the edging to the stakes.

Not all decomposed granite paths require edging. A simple DG pathway is landscape fabric underneath and a gentle "crown" of compacted DG on top. Mound stabilized DG (with binder added) in 1-inch layers, wetting and compacting between each deposition. Ultimately, the cross section

Laying out paths with landscape fabric as a liner.

Beginning to lay out DG paths. Mound DG in 1-inch layers.

A gravel path provides both texture and crunch.

is 3 to 4 feet wide, about 3 inches high in the middle, feathering down to about 1 inch thick on the edges. Run mulch up to the edges to help contain the path. Crowning assures good drainage. Edged paths channelize runoff, creating ruts right along the edges. This doesn't happen with these simple paths. The result is an easy-to-maintain naturalistic trail. These paths can last for years with occasional light raking to dress them up.

Again, whichever method you choose, it is very important to stabilize the decomposed granite with a commercially available granular or liquid binder. This cements the particles together to maintain firmness and durability.

Many like the sound of crunching gravel underfoot. Construct gravel paths similarly to decomposed granite, but add edging to constrain the more mobile rock chips. Many textures, sizes, and colors of gravel are available.

Flagstone is another beautiful path material that can be used singly as stepping stones, or set en masse to create pavement. Either way, the under-

Stepping stones can create flowing paths that are still geometric.

Flagstone paths are both solid and dramatic.

lying substrate is critical. In order to keep it from cracking, flagstone must be placed on a compliant subsurface that will allow it to be leveled and fully supported. Only large stones, more than 2 feet across, are suitable to place on sand or soil. Anything smaller than that will rock and be unstable on a soft subsurface. Set flagstone steppers on concrete or mortar pedestals to secure them and create stability. Position flagstone stepping stones at the terminus of a DG path to provide a clear hard surface prior to walking indoors. It's a good way to avoid tracking the DG inside, especially on wood floors.

Flatwork

Applied hard surfaces intended for supporting outdoor activities are known as flatwork. Some basic choices include: concrete, flagstone, interlocking pavers, decking, decomposed granite, and gravel. Decomposed granite and gravel are applied as described for paths, only over a larger area. They cost less and are permeable, neutral, and naturalistic in the garden. And, they don't require special skills to apply.

Concrete is the next-least expensive material for flatwork. It is available in many different finishes: natural gray, colored, and stamped to emulate other materials like flagstone, wood decking, or pavers. Sophisticated installations use multiple colors to imitate the natural variability of stone. Adding gravel, pebbles, or even colored glass creates a highly stylish "exposed aggregate" look. Concrete is durable, easy to maintain, and relatively inexpensive. The disadvantages include cracking (most concrete cracks with age), the need for expansion joints, and impermeability. Colored concrete can fade over time, sometimes in splotchy patterns. Concrete can appear monolithic and may easily overwhelm a space if not proportioned correctly.

The popular interlocking pavers are more expensive than concrete. They are available in a variety of shapes, textures, and color. Pavers often are used to create an "old-world" or "Tuscan" feel. They are also permeable. Generally, they are set on compacted layers: first gravel, then road base. Compaction ensures that the pavers will not settle over time. The underlying substrate must be leveled flat before laying out the individual

Concrete is an ideal material for flatwork surfaces.

Patios, like paths, can be made of a variety of materials such as concrete, flagstone, or interlocking pavers.

blocks. Nothing looks more unprofessional than unevenly laid pavers. Edge retention is also important. Specific edging products, both plastic and metal, are designed to be staked around the edge of the pavers to hold them in place. One of the nicest borders, however, is a single course (either end to end or side to side) of pavers set in concrete. It is immobile, permanent, and looks bold. Add *after* all paving has been tightly set to minimize the amount of cutting required.

Flagstone is more expensive. Lay flagstone over a level concrete base. Only set flagstone on a sand base if the individual pieces are at least 2 feet across and are thick. For unbroken flatwork, mortar between the flagstones. For a refined appearance, use colorant in the mortar to accentuate the colors in the stone. If you decide to plant in between the stones with low-growing vegetation, mount each piece of stone on its own individual pedestal. Good native candidates for filling between paving include: *Fragaria californica* or *chiloensis*, *Horkelia parryi*, *Achillea* sp., smaller species of sedge like *Carex praegracilis*, native *Oxalis* sp., and *Ambrosia pumila*. Non-native but effective plants include *Dymondia margaretae* and *Thymus* sp.

Retaining walls

Steep, unstable slopes often require soil retention, especially if you are trying to open up more usable flat space. People typically employ a block or stucco wall, but there are more interesting options. When considering potential materials, it is important to assess the situation. Any retainer over 2 to 3 feet generally requires a permit and professional skill. Many homeowners are capable of building a wall under 2 feet.

Boulders are an impressive low-tech solution for creating changes in level. Large boulders can be set singly, whereas smaller boulders can be stacked to create charming, rustic effects. It is important to stack the stones so that they tilt back into the slope, usually about 2 inches per foot of height. For walls lower than 2 feet, "drystacking" creates a mortarless wall. It's fun to plant creeping species of natives right into a drystack stone wall, like *Eriogonum grande* var. *rubescens*, *E. fasciculatum* 'Dana Point', *Salvia sonomensis* hybrids, *Grindelia stricta* ssp. *venulosa*, *Dudleya* sp., *Fragaria* sp., *Epilobium* sp., and native ferns in shade.

Timber retaining walls during construction.

Retaining walls can be functional and decorative.

crete footings 4 to 6 feet apart, so that their tops are about 16 inches above grade. Attach cross pieces (2×6 in.) front and back to the vertical posts, running the entire length of the bench, including a 1-foot overhang on each end. Then attach a horizontal board (2×12 in.) on top for the seat. Voila, instant bench!

On the other hand, sometimes when we have removed a good-sized tree, we take a 4 to 6 foot length and split the trunk in half. Drill two 2-inch diameter holes under each end and insert straight branches for legs. This creates a functional rustic bench that repurposes and honors the non-native tree we removed to make way for the new native landscape. If you have a little slope, two pieces of 4- to 6-foot-long flagstone, one for the seat and one for the back, make a perfectly stunning functional bench.

Water features

Dry streams and bioswales were discussed in detail in the design section. There are special issues in dealing with the actual liquid. Water features can include ponds, streams, fountains, and birdbaths. You want to prevent them from looking contrived or silly, and make sure that recirculating water elements do not leak. This can be deceptively difficult. Constructing a water feature may be one of the most challenging aspects of landscape construction.

When constructing a recirculating water feature, install waterproof lining throughout the zone, and then do the detailed rock, pebble, and sand work within the overall lining. Trying to follow a stream with all its twists, folds, and changes in level is nearly impossible. If the entire area containing the stream and pond is lined, the job is much easier.

Use liners of either waterproof concrete or butyl rubber. If using a rubber liner, carpet the excavation with sand, old rugs, or fibrous organic material before you put down the liner, making certain there are no sharp edges that could puncture the lining. The pump, filter, and return plumbing should all be held within the lining, and tested to ensure that water does not overflow the edging. Then install the rockwork over the plumbing.

If you choose concrete, construct a shell with cement that has a water-

A beautiful contemporary water feature against the riparian forest
at Rancho Santa Ana Botanical Gardens.

proofing agent added to the mix. Reinforce with fiberglass or steel mesh. Contain all the rockwork within the shell.

The electrical receptacle for the pump must be weatherproof, mounted about 4 feet away from the water feature, and a minimum of 12 inches above grade. The same is true for self-contained fountains. Unlike ponds and streams, fountains are generally pre-cast from concrete or fiberglass. The principal challenge with fountains is to mount them level. Remember, water is heavy. Support fountains on a block of concrete or flagstone to distribute the load, preventing them from settling out of level.

Birdbaths are a simple water feature. There are many pre-cast or manufactured choices. Effective and charming birdbaths are made from rocks or rustic materials that can hold water. Hubcaps, old frying pans, saucers—whatever holds water will work. Since a birdbath needs to be filled with water (which can evaporate in no time at all), we recommend providing a very slow, constant drip of water. Use quarter-inch drip tubing teed

Birdbaths invite nature into your garden.

A simple boulder birdbath.

off a hose bib and run to the edge of the bath. Use a backflow preventer, pressure regulator and an in-line valve to throttle the flow down to the slowest drip possible. Wrap the drip tubing with flexible wire to support it. Plant the base of the birdbath with water-loving natives like *Mimulus cardinalis* or *M. guttatus*, *Lobelia* sp., or *Stachys* sp. They will thrive with the slight overflow of water and help provide cover for birds.

A boulder, set level, with a depression that holds water is a marvelous birdbath. This is true to life, suggesting a small, naturalistic seep—which is probably why they are so popular with birds.

Planting

Once the infrastructure and features have been installed, it is time to plant. (Bet you thought we'd never get here!) For natives, it is about as simple as it comes. Dig a hole and stick them in, green side up. Actually, there are some important things to consider. First, don't get hung up on how the plant appears in a pot. Remember, most native plants are mutualistic and want to be among their companions, not isolated in a sterile container. To become fully mycorrhizal, the plants need to experience a little stress. Often a plant that is a bit scrawny and beat-up looking in a pot will do the best planted out in the landscape, especially with appropriate companion plants.

A beautiful, luscious, and blown-up native plant in the nursery may actually wither and blow away in the wind once it is planted on-site. It has probably been fertilized its entire life and/or grown in a shade house. Do not judge a native plant on first appearance. And, do not be afraid to gently remove it from the pot to look at its roots. If they are all pearly white, they have probably never seen mycorrhizae. Most healthy native root systems are dark in color with only a lighter growing tip. Also, smell the root ball—a dank, sour, or septic smell is an indication of heavy anaerobic bacterial activity. Nicely mycorrhizal root balls often smell neutral to sweet. It is not unusual for the root ball to smell like the plant community it belongs to.

Contrary to popular belief, smaller container plants usually do better than larger sizes. A 1-gallon plant seems ideal. Its above- and below-ground mass is roughly equal. The larger the container, the more shock plants exhibit and the longer it takes them to get established. One- and 15-gallon plants of identical species planted at the same time frequently are the same size within 9 to 12 months. Mortality rates increase with initial pot size, as well. The larger the pot, the more likely the plant will die. Smaller plants are easier to handle and are much less costly. If you are a professional, educate your clients about plant size beforehand. If they can forego the need for instant gratification, their patience will be amply rewarded in little time and at lower cost.

Excavate the planting hole about twice the diameter of the root ball but no deeper. The extra width allows you to get your hands in the hole to plant. Position the root crown about a half to three-quarters of an inch above the surrounding soil to ensure good drainage. If you dig too deep, backfill and compact so that the plant sits about an inch above grade, as it will inevitably settle over time. The worst situation is having plants end up in a hole—most will eventually drown. Planting higher exposes the root crown, which is also not a good situation. Not too high, not too low, but just right!

If your soil is desiccated, you can put water in the hole prior to planting. However, it is extremely important that you don't put the root ball into standing water—the water needs to have fully soaked in prior to planting. Ideally, irrigate to pre-soak the entire site a day or two prior to planting. This is especially helpful during summer installations and it eases digging. Do not wait too long to put the plants in—the soil might dry and weeds may start to grow.

After digging planting holes you may choose to add some mycorrhizal inoculum. Usually, a well-grown native plant *is* the inoculum for the site. However, for compacted and overworked soils, the new mixes with *native* endo- and ectomycorrhizae and tricoderma may really help. Just follow product instructions.

Run your finger along the outside of the root ball to help break any root encirclement as you place the plant into the hole You want the roots to grow out from the ball, not continue circling. Place backfill around

Smaller container plants usually do better than larger sizes; 4-inch pots to 5-gallon containers are ideal. Most should be 1-gallon.

Leave plenty of space around the plants so they can grow to their mature size.

A 5-gallon redbud tree is planted with the root ball level with the soil surface, while a 1-gallon companion ceanothus awaits planting. Plenty of room is left for both to reach mature size.

The same tree and ceanothus less than two years later.

the root ball and tamp in solidly. Circling the plant with your feet is very effective. Bert Wilson refers to this as the "plant dance." Consider placing some 6- to 12-inch boulders right on the root ball, pressing them in. Not in a campfire ring, but actually on the root ball. Leave enough space for the trunk to grow. Placing rocks in this manner protects the plant, keeps the roots cool, prevents smothering by the mulch, and mycorrhizae may metabolize nutrients from the base of the rocks.

The most important step follows: water, water, water. A summer planting in well-draining soil may require 10 to 30 gallons of water per 1-gallon plant. Most people are shocked—these are drought-tolerant plants after all! The water is not for hydrating the soil; this is the best method for removing air pockets from around the root ball. Clay soils may only require 5 to 10 gallons per plant; wet winter soil may only require a gallon or two. It is crucial that the soil settle around the roots with no major voids. This first watering is the most important one these plants will ever receive.

Mulching

Once plants have been set and watered individually, it is time to mulch. Prior to putting down the mulch, consider applying a pre-emergent. This herbicide, usually in granular or liquid form, targets seed in the soil. It keeps the seed from germinating. Suburban environments typically harbor 10,000 to 100,000 dormant weed seeds per cubic foot of dirt. Many seeds can remain dormant up to 50 years. Pre-emergents control the upper inch or so of weed seed without harming living plants. Since they only target seed, they can be applied right over the new planting without deleterious effect. Follow the manufacturer's directions.

We do not use or recommend landscape fabric for weed control for native landscapes. It is critical to maintain a clean interface between the mulch and soil. Volatile organic compounds contained within polymer-based fabrics may disrupt the signal pathways telling mycorrhizal hyphae that it is okay to colonize plant roots. From a practical standpoint, weeds often send a thread of taproot through the pores in the mat, only to lodge in place as the weed grows. Extracting this firmly wedged weed pulls up the fabric and displaces the mulch around it, making a mess.

Mulches, also known as top dressing, are any organic or inorganic substance placed on top of (not mixed into) the soil. In most native plant communities, a natural organic duff layer forms from falling leaves, bark, flowers, seed husks, etc. As it builds up over time, it creates a consolidated covering on the soil helping to prevent weeds and sustain mycorrhizae. The exceptions include coastal strand, grassland, and desert plant communities where the mulch layer is usually inorganic.

While an undisturbed plant community had thousands of years to develop its ecology, creating a new native landscape means we must break into the cycle and reconstruct the essential components necessary to jump-start that ecosystem. Therefore, it is crucial that the mulch resemble the real duff layer as closely as possible. For most plant communities, shredded redwood bark, also known as "gorilla hair," is the closest at emulating natural mulch. The redwood forest community is integrated with chaparral, coastal sage scrub, and oak woodland communities. Redwood breaks down very slowly. This extended decomposition is ideal for proper mycorrhizal development. For those concerned that the gorilla hair "robs nitrogen" in its slow decomposition, this is not a worry with native plant communities. They have evolved in highly inorganic soils nearly devoid of organic matter and are not dependent on intrinsic soil fertility to thrive. They do better without it.

After applying pre-emergent, lay down a 3- to 4-inch layer of redwood bark. Because of the "fluff" factor, gorilla hair can spread much farther than most other mulches, covering up to 200 square feet per cubic yard— a good rule of thumb when calculating the quantity needed for the landscape. Use tubs or trash cans to carry it. Spread the mulch evenly, but do not smother the plants. Pull it back 4 to 6 inches from the base of each plant. If there are boulders, mulch up to the rocks. Once the mulch is down, turn on the irrigation for as long as the landscape will tolerate without leading to erosion. This both dissolves the pre-emergent granules, which generally require the equivalent of a half-inch of rainfall to properly incorporate, and mats down the mulch. Consolidating the mulch is

Gorilla hair mulch represses weeds and stabilizes slopes.

Apply pre-emergent directly to the soil and water in before laying down mulch.

critical to fire safety, creating a poorly oxygenated fuel. Shredded redwood bark has tremendous moisture capacity and is a wonderful erosion-resisting material.

Other materials are available for mulches; however, we follow the axiom, "The plant community begets the mulch, and the mulch begets the plant community." It is a chicken-and-egg cycle that we are breaking into to develop an ecologically based native landscape. For example, shredded cedar looks similar to shredded redwood. Nevertheless, the biochemistry of cedar would drive the ecology toward a white fir, black oak, or incense cedar forest. That is fine if you live in those woods; however, it is quite different from a typical chaparral or coastal sage scrub ecology appropriate to most coastal populated areas. Chipped fir and tree trimmings are inferior to redwood, but not totally out of the question. Chipped oak and/or pine are quite good. The worst organic mulch for natives is dump mulch, which breaks down quickly and contains all manner of weeds, grass, plastic, and chemicals. Use shredded rubber products only on playgrounds.

Desert plants with inorganic mulch.

Inorganic mulches are targeted to desert, coastal strand, and grassland communities. They include boulders, rocks, pebbles, gravel, decomposed granite, and sand. Mixing these components can create a very convincing "desert-pavement" look for a southwestern-style landscape. Using just a gravel or cobble top dressing is appropriate for a stylized look. Anticipate the dense nature of these mulches when planting, otherwise you risk creating hollows that collect water and can drown the plants. Therefore, plant the plants about 2 inches high, then add the inorganic mulch up to the sides of the exposed root ball at roughly the same level or slightly below the root crown.

CARE AND MAINTENANCE
A less intensive schedule

The long-term care and maintenance of a native landscape requires a different approach from a conventional landscape. You may have to find someone to buy your old lawnmower! The edger will probably go, too. In fact, most of your garden equipment will fit into a much smaller space. You will be spending less time maintaining and more time enjoying your new landscape.

Occasional maintenance promotes vitality and crispness in the native landscape.

ALTHOUGH THERE is no such thing as a completely maintenance-free landscape (at least if you intend to impress the neighbors), native gardens come pretty close. The little upkeep required is purposeful and directed. The emphasis is on weeding (which diminishes with time) as well as pruning for shape and removing dead flower heads (deadheading). The whole process is more peaceful than pushing a noisy, polluting, and dangerous lawnmower around weekly. It's not uncommon to be accompanied by native birds, butterflies, lizards, and insects as you are at work in the landscape.

This section is a general overview of basic maintenance concepts for native landscapes. It is okay to make mistakes—that's how we learn—but by following these principles and practices, soon you will begin to get to know your plants in your yard and will reap the rewards of a beautiful, easy-care landscape. Remember, California native plants rely on a symbiotic relationship with microorganisms in the soil to a much greater extent than plants from other areas. This relationship of plant roots with mycorrhizae enables the native plants to thrive in an environment that is difficult for other plants.

Fertilizer: Yes or no?

Fertilizer is not typically needed for California native plants. Remember, California native plant communities have had 40 million years to adapt to lean, inorganic soils. Trying to "juice them up" on fertilizer is a fool's errand that often ends in disaster. The focus is on recreating the native ecosystem as best we can. The only place high fertility comes into play is in wetland plantings. Wetlands are nourished through constant soil disturbance and erosion upstream that naturally feeds into the system. Fertilizing a native plant landscape typically leads to mycorrhizal disruption and results in conversion to a bacterial-based ecology. The now-vacant root nodes of the native plants are opened to infection by bacterial and fungal diseases, typically leading to an overnight ecological collapse.

What about mycorrhizal soil inoculation?

This issue of mycorrhizal soil inoculation is a tricky one that is still requiring a lot of research. Mycorrhizal spore is everywhere—airborne, on our shoes, on garden tools, in gopher fur—readily available for colonization, given the right overall conditions. A healthy, properly grown native plant in a pot should already be mycorrhizal and serve as the inoculum for the site. Under good conditions, native mycorrhizae colonize about 3 to 6 feet per year. However, when conditions are not ideal, such as in highly disturbed or rancid soil, supplemental inoculation may prove useful. Ten to fifteen years ago, when inoculums were first being marketed, much of the spore was generic and not native to California. As the industry has developed, however, more appropriate native spore is being used. Currently most inoculants have a mixture of endo- and ectomycorrhizae, along with other beneficial microorganisms like tricoderma. Rudimentary testing indicates that new inoculums may be beneficial, especially for really poor, disturbed sites and for native plants struggling to establish themselves. Tested against fertilizers, the inoculated plants gain permanent vigor after a few weeks to months. Fertilized plants may show a short-term positive response only to subsequently collapse and die.

Watering

It is commonly assumed that because a plant is native, it somehow doesn't need supplemental moisture. A heck of a lot of plants have bitten the dust on this assumption. Keep in mind, it takes time for mycorrhizae to kick in and young plants are vulnerable as they begin to grow into the landscape. The better you address their needs, particularly during the first one to two years, the stronger they will grow and the less you will have to do in the future. A newly planted native landscape generally requires watering just like any other new planting.

Establishment

On planting day each plant requires a significant amount of water immediately upon being placed in the soil. It is critical to remove air pockets from around the root ball because air pockets dry out the newly growing root tips, setting back new growth significantly. Use this first watering to saturate and settle in the soil and flush out any remaining air. This can require gallons of moisture per plant, especially in well-draining soil during summer months. To assure full saturation, create a temporary basin surrounding each plant and fill it fully. Keep the basin in place for a couple of months until the plant is established, then take a finger or trowel and break the basin wall to let the plant drain naturally.

Use the "Interval" setting on your irrigation timer, rather than watering on specific days of the week. This way the interval between watering can be easily increased over time. The amount and frequency of water required through the first summer of establishment depends on the type of plant, location, soil type, and time of year. If the plants are native to a moister area, they will always require supplemental watering. Inland plantings experience greater extremes in temperature than coastal. Porous soils usually require watering longer and more frequently than clay soils.

Create a temporary basin around each plant and fill it fully. Keep the basin in place for a couple of months.

Planting during a consistently wet fall or winter may mean that the irrigation system stays off until the weather warms. Caution: be prepared to run the irrigation during the first day of each strong Santa Ana wind. This California weather extreme quickly pulls the moisture from the leaves of even the most drought-tolerant plants.

The key is to get the plants to survive through the first summer. There is a common notion that California natives cannot be planted during the summer. While it may be easier to plant in late fall or winter (especially on those doing the planting), native plants can be installed year-round. In summer months they require more water only at first, like any other landscape planted during the hottest part of the year.

The most challenging scenario is a sandy inland or desert installation in July through September, but it is possible. It may require an initial irrigation schedule of two to three times per week, with the equivalent of up to a half-inch of precipitation per watering.

Set the initial water cycle to once every three to five days during a summer planting, and about once per week during winter, depending on the weather. Watering application is typically a fifth to two-fifths of an inch of equivalent precipitation. Utilizing an MP Rotator–type irrigation system, this equals 30 to 60 minutes per cycle.

Establishing a native planting means weaning the plants from their water dependence. The best way is to respond to the plants as they grow, supplying just enough water to support survival—not pushing them to grow too quickly. Try increasing the interval by a day every couple of weeks. A good target is to reduce watering to once every seven days through the first summer, turn off the irrigation after the weather cools and the rains start, then turn the system on again when the weather warms in May–June. Begin watering once a week, then try to push the plants to once every 10 to 14 days during the second summer, with about $\frac{1}{5}$ inch of equivalent precipitation per watering.

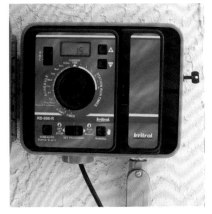

Set the initial water cycle to three to five days during a summer planting.

Post-establishment watering

It is technically possible to create a landscape that requires no supplemental irrigation once established by selecting plants native to the garden location. Near the coast, where summer fog, higher humidity, and lower temperatures are the norm, it is possible and appropriate to allow your native landscape to naturalize. However, light irrigation is advisable through the warm months of the year for inland locations. Do not to saturate warm soil; instead, think of emulating a summer thunderstorm or a fog drip, which wets only the leaves and mulch. Irrigating about a fifth of an inch per cycle is usually sufficient. The goal is to water once every 10 to 14 days in the summer. Light, overhead irrigation keeps plants dusted off while supplying foliar moisture. This type of hydration keeps plants looking their best without compromising their ecology. It also promotes fire resistance in drought-tolerant natives. In fact, lightly hydrated native landscapes, far from being firebombs, may provide the greatest fire resistance. Under extreme stress from radiant heat, these plants retain their moisture instead of transpiring it away, despite leaf scorching or searing.

Watering an established native landscape in summer means "spritzing" it off every two to three weeks. Because the soil is not soaked, the irrigation has minimal effect on precipitation at the plants' roots. Remember, the rains of November through April (except for desert plants) provide most of the deeper root-level moisture. Determine how much water the plants receive in their native locale and use that amount and timing as a guide for watering. If you are using plants from an area of greater rainfall, supplement irrigation during the wet months (March through May), especially when the preceding winter has been drier than normal. For most non-desert plant communities, the key is to apply deeper irrigation before the soil has warmed up in summer.

A good resource on annual rainfall requirements is the Las Pilitas Nursery website, www.laspilitas.com. If you use plants from similar plant communities but different areas of the state, find a happy medium between the lower and higher water requirements. Some plants may be receiving minimum rainfall requirements while others may be at their upper limits. With good drainage, the upper limits are often testable.

Desert plants have a different precipitation schedule. Overall, desert plants receive less annual rainfall; however, it is more evenly distributed than in coastal and mountain communities. Where chaparral plants receive little to no rain in the summer, our deserts receive monsoonal moisture through thunderstorms. Accordingly, separate the irrigation system for desert plants from the system for chaparral plants. Desert species can handle light summer watering as long as there is good drainage and no organic mulch is applied around the plants. As in the case of any native plant, targeting the upper range of the plant's natural rainfall total is usually acceptable if you are trying to reach a happy medium for all plants in the group.

Keep the distinction between desert and non-desert plants firmly in mind. Desert natives typically can be watered during afternoon hours. As long as the soil drains well, they tolerate heat and moisture. Desert summer thunderstorms often occur in the late afternoon. Water non-desert native plants when the soil is coolest; early morning is best.

Trimming and pruning

A native landscape requires very little maintenance compared to weekly summer lawn mowing. However, unless your front yard is just gravel and rocks it will need some targeted maintenance to look its best. A typical well-designed native landscape smaller than a quarter acre usually requires quarterly maintenance. This means: a landscape of natives of appropriately sized and placed plants, with good quality mulch deep enough to suppress weed growth and retain moisture, overhead irrigation, and approximately 70 percent evergreen backbone plants, with colorful perennials placed along paths and edges for easy access. The following sections describe guidelines for the typical trimming and pruning required for grasses, perennials, shrubs, and trees.

Grasses

In the last decade, landscape design has significantly increased the use of grasses. Grasses are dramatic in their individual spiky verticality, yet create flowing softness when massed. The price of this beauty and versatility is intensive maintenance. They need a haircut every year or two. Regular lawnmowers are incapable of trimming taller bunch grasses. While trimming back an individual clump or three is manageable, mass plantings are challenging. If left untended over time, dead thatch builds up, leading to a weedy bird nest look. Untrimmed, large plantings can create a major fire hazard from accumulated biomass.

One multi-acre commercial installation in southern California utilized thousands of plugs of deer grass (*Muhlenbergia rigens*). The maintenance budget was insufficient to properly prune all the grass, resulting in an untended gray mass of dead straw—the perfect poster material to dissuade the public from using native plants in their landscapes.

Native Americans all over the West managed their stands of deer grass (an important source material for basketry) by periodic burning. This renewed the plants and promoted straight, supple culms used to create their baskets. Since burning is generally discouraged, periodic pruning is the best way to maintain appearance. Avoid creating straw "balls" of any height. Instead, prune aggressively to the same height, even as low as within an inch or two of the ground. Low pruning assures complete plant renewal. On average, trim aggressively once every two years. Late summer

Cut deer grass closely to the ground every other year.

is a good time, when the grasses begin to look disheveled. More frequent cutting may weaken the plants.

Some commercial operations with large plots are experimenting with an old European and early American method of bringing in sheep to trim lawn grasses. Sheep crop the grasses evenly low to the ground, leaving an expanse of short green groundcover. This is *not* recommended for native landscapes. Grazing livestock in the backcountry have vastly diminished native grasses and vegetation over the past 50 years. Sheep eat everything, grazing too close to the ground for natives to recover. Goats eat anything—lawns, shrubs, flowers, paper. Llamas eat everything good (natives before weeds). Horses love native grasses. Cows target the non-native fodder originally brought in for forage.

Perennials and sub-shrubs

Plant the more labor-intensive, colorful perennials along the edges of the landscape. The color is concentrated in front for viewing, and they are easily accessible for deadheading the spent flowers. Deadheading is not essential for the health of the plants, but it greatly enhances the garden appearance and can promote reblooming in some plants.

Perennial plants live longer than two years and bloom annually. Their stems are soft and they may (or may not) experience a period of hard dormancy. "Herbaceous" perennials lose their leaves during part of the year (usually during the late summer months). An example is blue-eyed grass (*Sisyrinchium bellum*). This monocot, in the iris family, can resemble a ball of purple when in bloom, but disappears without a bump by the end of summer. Other perennials are more or less evergreen, such as Pacific Coast iris (*Iris douglasiana*). Larger perennials with a woody base are known as sub-shrubs, such as coast sunflower (*Encelia californica*).

Truly herbaceous perennials, like blue-eyed grass or the wetland species yerba manza (*Anemopsis californica*) usually die to the ground in late summer. Just remove the dead matter after their cycle. Do not use these perennials for foundational massing; instead use them along edges as color spots or mix in with evergreen plants (like sedges or yarrow), which will provide cover during their dormancy. Hummingbird fuchsia

(*Epilobium* sp.) is a popular color perennial that goes dormant during late fall and winter. Cut its dried stems to the ground to reveal newly emerging shoots at the base. You will have a clean mound of fresh growth by spring, covered in scarlet blossoms in summer and fall.

Other perennials maintain nearly evergreen leaves despite dry flower stalks when they set seed. The seaside daisy (*Erigeron glaucus* and selections) exhibits a low-growing mass of evergreen foliage covered with lavender flowers starting in early spring. As the multiple flowers fade, the whole stem will start to yellow. Remove the entire stem down to the base. Simply cutting off each flower leaves the plant studded in dead stems resembling an unattractive seaside porcupine. Interestingly, this method of deadheading usually forces seaside daisy into additional flowering cycles. Similarly, cut yarrow (*Achillea millefolium* var. *lanulosa*) flower stalks back to the base; otherwise hard, sharp, woody flower stems will remain. 'Margarita BOP' foothill penstemon (*Penstemon heterophyllus* 'Margarita BOP') flowers are held in clusters above the foliage. As the flowers fade, cut the entire stem down to the most vigorously budding leaf axils on the stem. This ensures strong basal growth rather than suspended aerial branching. Repeated cycles are rare for this plant, but deadheading may help prolong

Strip old leaves off mimulus by running your hands up the stem.

the initial bloom period. Mimulus are the exception, just pull your hands along the stem to strip dead leaves.

Maintain sub-shrubs similarly to perennials. Sages are a classic example. Salvia flowering stalks often occur as three branchlets (*Salvia clevelandii*, for example). When they finish blooming cut stalks back below the trident to the new leaf buds. A handy rule of thumb is to leave two leafed-out nodes. Up to half of the plant can be removed this way; however, avoid cutting into old wood, which usually doesn't resprout. Prune in late winter to early spring. Pinch off central vertical stalks of groundcover sages that could lead to mounding and ultimately a woody center. Avoid cutting off actively growing horizontal branch tips, unless necessary for clearance. Groundcovers trimmed around the edge push their growth habit vertically. If you need to edge groundcover type plants, avoid shearing back the encroaching stems all at the same point. Instead, prune branches individually giving the edge a softer, more natural appearance and discouraging new stems from forming along the same line. Shearing from one point can also reveal an unsightly pile of dead undergrowth along the edge.

Popular examples of other native sub-shrubs include apricot mallow (*Sphaeralcea ambigua*), woolly blue curls (*Trichostema lanatum*), and bush

In deadheading salvia, cut back the bloom stalk below the trident to new leaf buds.

mallow (*Malacothamnus*). Like perennials, the general rule is to cut down old flower stalks to an actively growing leaf bud. Deadheading immediately after flowering is best.

Sometimes perennials and sub-shrubs become leggy or woody in the middle. Tipping pinches back the ends of branches to force growth in the middle. It is similar to deadheading, except it targets actively growing stems rather than spent flowers. Remove only the growing tip and at most a couple of leaves. This encourages buds along the lower part of the stem to grow.

Shrubs

Prune shrubs to improve structure, for shaping, or to correct unsuitable growth. Appropriately placed shrubs in the landscape will not require constant pruning for size. Remove overcrowded shrubs to thin out the planting. Individual shrubs may have imbalanced growth or may require shaping. Some shrubs need thinning to reveal the underlying structure or to open them up for more air and light.

Pruning and shaping tools include: hand (bypass or anvil) pruners, pruning saws, pole saws, loppers, hedge shears (especially long-handled

Trimming back ceanothus at the edge of the walkway.

versions), and chain saws for large limbs. Keep all tools sharpened; dull blades bruise, crush, and macerate foliage, severely wounding plants. Keep a spray bottle of 10 percent bleach solution or rubbing alcohol nearby to sterilize all pruning surfaces between cuts. Always clean tools before

Deadheading eriogonum by trimming stems to the desired length.

Cutting back eriogonum significantly at the end of the season.

moving from one plant to the next. This prevents transmitting disease and is a good general practice even among healthy plants.

The two principal shaping techniques for shrubs are heading back and shearing. Heading back means trimming individual stems back to a desired length. Heading back just the tips of the plant emulates the browsing that a deer would do. Most native shrubs tolerate this treatment. However, do not remove more than about a third of the mass at any one time. Extreme pruning can stress or even kill plants.

Some native plants tolerate severe cut backs, even to the point of coppicing—removing all growth down to the base. Plants that tolerate coppicing are generally fire followers or are riparian, adapted to either fire or flooding by stump sprouting. Be careful. For instance, only certain manzanitas resprout from a basal burl, including eastwood manzanita (*Arctostaphylos glandulosa*). Many more, like bigberry manzanita (*A. glauca*) die when burned to the ground and do not tolerate drastic pruning. This is why many manzanitas are the first to disappear after frequent fires. When pruning, it is best to "make like a deer" rather than a chainsaw massacrer.

Shearing is used to form hedges or topiary shapes. Rumor has it that the English have been growing lemonadeberry (*Rhus integrifolia*) hedges for

Deadheading ceanothus after blossoms are spent.

years. Unlike pruning, shearing slices through planes of vegetation, leaves and all. Many plants cannot tolerate this, dropping leaves and branches as a result. Yet, numerous evergreen shrubs can withstand shearing, including species of rhus, prunus, arctostaphylos, quercus, myrica, rhamnus, umbellularia, and ceanothus. Even some salvias tolerate shearing. However, exercise care with ceanothus because cutting larger stems (half-inch or greater) often leads to infection by airborne pathogens spread by rain or overhead watering. Some suggest using a sealant on newly cut surfaces to protect against exposure.

Use selective pruning to thin out dense internal branching, to redirect branches, to remove stems like water sprouts (rapidly growing suckers that sprout near major cuts) that compromise the integrity of the shrub, or to reveal the underlying structural lattice of the plant. Pruning cuts must be made correctly. Always sterilize pruning tools between cuts using your spray bottle filled with 10 percent bleach solution. Cut as near to the branch or trunk as possible, usually with the cutting blade facing downward. Keep cutting tools sharp to avoid tearing or crushing the plant tissue.

Most native shrubs tolerate selective pruning well. Manzanitas, as a group, are known for dramatic branching structure and appearance.

Although not generally recommended, sealing cuts to ceanothus branches over a half inch helps prevent infection by pathogens.

Pruning out lower stems, crossing branches, and dead wood helps expose the smooth, mahogany red bark and sculptural quality of the superstructure. Manzanita branches terminate at each flower cluster. New growth occurs along a side bud immediately underneath the inflorescence creating the dramatic crooked character of manzanita branches. Other related plants like mission manzanita (*Xylococcus bicolor*), summer holly (*Comarostaphylis diversifolia*), and Baja bird bush (*Ornithostaphylos oppositifolia*) also benefit from selective pruning to reveal the impressive structure and beautiful bark. Setting branching forms against attractive rock, masonry, plaster, or wooden walls enhances their sculptural effect.

Other strong branching plants include: lemonadeberry (*Rhus integrifolia*), New Mexico olive (*Forestiera neomexicana*), and mountain mahogany (*Cercocarpos* spp.). Some larger wild lilacs (*Ceanothus* spp.) can be pruned to reveal branching character or even sculpted into standard, single-trunk trees. However, use a sealant on cuts of a half-inch or greater diameter to discourage rain-spread airborne fungi. Deadheading ceanothus blossoms immediately after flowering can discourage rangy growth.

Trees

Trees are designated as either evergreen or deciduous. "Evergreen" plants retain foliage throughout the year, whereas "deciduous" trees go dormant, losing all their leaves for a period of time. Evergreen trees include conifers like cedar, pine, and redwood, as well as trees with more traditional leaves, such as a number of our California oaks.

Use evergreen trees for year-round shade or foliar effect. In many cases, "evergreen" is actually "ever-dropping" since the oldest leaves are shed gradually throughout the year. Coast live oak (*Quercus agrifolia*) is notable for the depth of mulch created by this constant leaf drop. Many people remove dead leaves from the landscape for appearance, however they should be left in place to create an ecologically beneficial mulch. In fact, adding additional mulch creates a visually definite and intended groundcover.

Although relatively unknown and rarely used, another great, evergreen oak is island oak (*Quercus tomentella*). This beautiful, fast-growing oak is a wonderful choice for landscapes. It has giant, luscious leaves—flat, serrated, and several times larger than those of its cousin, the coast live oak. Island oak also has huge acorns. Principal maintenance at maturity is occasionally cleaning out old dead and crossing branches. Again, the leaf-drop mulch is beneficial and should be left in place.

The popular Engelmann oak (*Quercus engelmannii*) is semi-deciduous, dropping its leaves just as the new ones emerge in spring. It can also be stress deciduous, dropping its leaves in response to drought.

Other native evergreen trees include: tanbark oak (*Lithocarpus densiflorus*), California bay laurel (*Umbellularia californica*), and Santa Cruz Island ironwood (*Lyonothamnus floribundus* ssp. *asplenifolius*). Island tree lilac (*Ceanothus arboreus*) forms a nice small single- or multi-trunked tree in about five years. Prune these trees after blooming in the summer by shaping, thinning, and removing dead wood. Leaf drop for these species is generally tolerable, forming important mulches for the trees' ecological health. Umbellularia and lyonothamnus can be coppiced if necessary, but only if the tree is greatly damaged or so misshapen it requires starting over.

Deciduous trees are nature's air conditioners—perfect for creating shade during summer while allowing sun to penetrate during the winter. They drop their leaves once a year, usually in late autumn. California has many native deciduous trees.

California sycamore (*Platanus racemosa*) is a majestic, large, signature tree of the California landscape. It is colorful with mottled bark revealing patches of tan, gray, sage green, and white and large, luscious leaves that often turn bright yellow in fall. As beautiful as sycamores are, however, carefully consider all the characteristics before adding one to the garden. Inappropriate for a small garden, a sycamore can grow over 100 feet tall and wide in 10 to 15 years. Fall leaf drop is considerable, and the thick leaves do not break down quickly. When raking sycamore leaves, always use a dust mask to keep the stellate hairs from entering your respiratory system, where they cause irritation and coughing. Do not cut large branches over 6 inches in diameter. Large cuts open the branch and trunk to rot and potential catastrophic loss of major branches. Finally, sycamores are susceptible to anthracnose, which causes the first flush of leaves to drop especially in wet springs. If you wish, treat anthracnose by applying a copper mixture spray to the buds prior to leafing, though the problem usually resolves by summer, and proper watering techniques, along with restriction of fertility, can help minimize the leaf drop.

White alder (*Alnus rhombifolia*) is another large, fast-growing, majestic deciduous tree. There is nothing drought tolerant about this plant. It grows with its roots next to or even in a creek. However, white alder can be useful in damp areas or in the middle of a lawn. Its leafless period is usually short, often sprouting new leaves as the previous year's leaves are dropped. The alder has beautiful silver bark, the trunk marked by "eyes" where older branches have been shed. A grove of alders is a very dramatic landscape feature. Do not plant this tree anywhere near a septic system or sewer line. It has large and aggressive roots. It grows fast, as much as 10 to 12 feet per year. The alder may be pruned to keep the main leader straight and single. Otherwise, it requires very little pruning, just for the removal of old dead branches. The best time to prune, as with most deciduous trees, is during the winter, dormant season. Pruning cuts or scratching the bark reveals a bright orange sap once used by the Indians for dye.

Cottonwood (*Populus fremontii*) is another aggressive-rooting deciduous tree. Like the alder, it is extremely fast growing. Unlike the alder, however, it can become drought tolerant as its roots locate deeper moisture. It soon outgrows the height at which branches are easily pruned. It is heat tolerant and is well adapted to the desert. Consider carefully before planting a cottonwood. Like the sycamore, it can grow to over 100 feet in height and is inappropriate for a small garden. Never locate a cottonwood near sewer or septic lines. Cut back shoots and water sprouts to help maintain its form.

Valley oak (*Quercus lobata*) is another large deciduous tree to consider. Valley oak is the largest and fastest-growing native oak. Cut back vigorous side shoots to maintain a single trunk. Prune in winter. As in the case of all oaks, the leaf litter mulch is important to the ecology of the plant and should be left in place.

Numerous smaller deciduous trees are better scaled to a typical residential lot. Two wonderful, colorful, fast-growing but easily maintainable trees are the desert willow (*Chilopsis linearis*) and its intergeneric hybrid cousin the chitalpa (×*Chitalpa tashkentensis*). In the trumpet vine family, both have showy, tubular flowers for months, starting when the weather warms in late spring. Both have nice form as small trees and need little maintenance. When deciduous, many varieties of desert willow retain long dry seedpods. Most people remove these to maintain nice appearance. Seedless varieties are becoming more available. Chitalpa is seedless. Both of these trees prefer well-draining soils and inland heat. Those planted on or near the coast can develop mildew or verticillium wilt in heavy soils.

Western redbud (*Cercis occidentalis*) is another small, handsome, multi-trunked deciduous tree. It grows best in inland locations, especially at higher elevations where the winter chill promotes heavier flowering. In spring, prior to leafing out, it is covered in magenta, edible flowers. This plant requires little maintenance. You may prune out the oldest branches in late fall if the tree starts to lose vigor. If it appears to require complete renewal, it can also be coppiced.

Mexican elderberry (*Sambucus mexicana*) is a large shrub requiring assistance to be maintained as a small tree. Remove basal sprouts as soon as they form, especially in young trees. This plant grows quickly, so early attention ensures a nice canopy later on. Because it is twiggy, crossing branches can be a problem. General thinning is a good practice. Wildlife feed and nest in elderberry. It can form a nice small shade tree in just a few years, so long as it is properly pruned.

California walnut (*Juglans californica*) is a medium-size deciduous tree with nice form, attractive bark, and compound leaves. It looks good in a place where it stands alone. It is a true walnut with small, hard-shelled, edible nuts. To avoid permanent black staining from dropping tannin-laden fruit and leaves, plant well away from sidewalks and hardscape features. Do not plant a flowerbed under a walnut; the roots secrete chemicals inhibiting the growth of all but the appropriate understory native plants.

Conifers have evergreen, needle-like foliage. Major classes include pine, cedar, juniper, cypress, and sequoia. They rarely require pruning unless a specific shape is desired, as in Japanese gardens, or to create a windswept or open architecture. They can be pruned year-long, though it is best to prune foliage after the new growth has hardened off. Do not cut back to old wood, as they usually will not resprout. It is important to give these trees plenty of room. Branches deeply shaded or touching other trees will usually die and never come back.

Weed control

One of the greatest enemies of native ecology is weeds. The uncontrolled spread of exotic species in California is causing mass destruction of native plant communities, habitat, and ever-increasing wildfire frequency. Conversely, eradication of invasive exotics (alien weeds) can help lead to rapid recovery of these ecosystems. Numerous strategies are available in the war on weeds.

Preventive measures

Be certain the plants you bring home are weed free. Or, at least, pull out the weeds by the roots before planting. Take the plant out of the pot and gently tease the weeds out while the root ball is exposed. Minimize root ball disturbance.

Weeds like spurge (*Euphorbia* spp.) and wood sorrel (*Oxalis* spp.) are extremely invasive if not removed at planting. Because they grow so close to the plant, later removal is more difficult. Some weeds eventually can kill the plant outright or cause the plant to be killed during attempted weed eradication.

Check sources when importing soil, as you may end up importing a lot more than just dirt. "Fill dirt" may require herbicidal control as either pre-emergents or later weed control. Most amended topsoil is fairly clean, but it is always smart to check with the supplier first.

Another potential source of weed contamination is unclean tools. Make sure that all your tools are thoroughly washed prior to using them in your new planting bed. Remember your shoes and boots, as well. Seed can be incredibly small and hard to detect, so if you have been working in a really weedy area, take time to wash everything off. You will thank yourself later.

Sometimes we are our own worst enemy; we may already have invasive plants in our garden palette. Some beloved but highly invasive plants that can become ferocious weeds include: mint (*Mentha* spp.), Mexican evening primrose (*Oenothera berlandieri*), periwinkle (*Vinca minor/major*), and Jupiter's beard (*Centranthus ruber*). Removal by chemicals may become the only practical means of eradication. Better to plant the invasives you love in pots or beds that are separated from other planting areas.

Applying good-quality mulch (shredded redwood, cedar, or clean tree trimmings) is important for the health of most native landscape ecosystems. It is also an important weed preventative measure. Combined with the plant community ecology, these good quality top dressings help natural weed inhibition. Ironically, using poorly composted dump mulches can promote weed activity due to undigested weed seed and high fertility associated with grass and perennial trimmings.

Manual and mechanical control

Having some weeds in the landscape is a given. The density of the weeds and the size of your property may determine what methods you will use to control them. There are many alternatives, from hand pulling to chemical

Removing oxalis from the container can prevent introducing this noxious weed to your landscape.

application. Whatever method you decide to use, our recommendation is that you remove the weeds as soon as possible. Once they have matured and set seed, your problem will only be compounded in subsequent years.

HAND WEEDING Pulling weeds is a part of gardening. Once you begin to recognize the bad plants, you may become a compulsive weed puller—even beyond your own yard! There is a positive ethic associated with this practice. Manual weeding doesn't involve chemicals. It is most effective in small areas. It is best to attack weeds when they are seedlings, before the root systems have developed.

Remove the entire weed, roots and all. Most weeds can grow back if rhizomes or tubers are left behind. Unfortunately, pulling the newly emerging shoots of rhizomatous/tuberous plants like Bermuda grass, wood sorrel, or Mexican evening primrose does nothing to control them.

Some situations preclude manual weeding. It may be impossible to pull out the roots with the plant in dry soils. It may be impractical to weed large areas (greater than 1000 square feet) manually. Sometimes soil disturbance and compaction from manual weeding may be more detrimental than beneficial. Pulling out a weed can bring up and activate more weed seeds. In pristine areas, walking around, compacting the soil can adversely affect delicate native ecology to the advantage of alien invasives.

HAND TOOLS A simple dandelion fork is an invaluable asset for manual weeding. This tool is actually a "repurposed" asparagus harvesting knife, useful for cutting and prying taproots or root masses below the root crown. When working in native landscapes it minimizes soil disturbance, reducing the potential for bringing up more weeds later on. Another important tool is the Dutch or hula hoe, a loop of sharpened metal strap pushed or pulled underneath the soil surface, cutting off roots below the root crown. Use hula hoes when weeds cover the soil. You can clear a large area much more efficiently than by hand weeding. Although it does disturb the soil minimally, the soil surface strips are relatively intact compared to the chopping action of a conventional hoe. Weeds are easy to pick up from the strips.

Flaming and foaming tools are interesting weapons in the weed wars. Both kill weeds with heat without disturbing the soil. Flamers are usually butane or propane torches that quickly heat the plant to boiling, destroying the tissue. Weeds collapse in minutes. Although effective with leafy weeds (not so much on grasses), do not use along the wildland interface nor in high winds.

Similarly, foam tools use a froth consisting of sugars and superheated steam to boil vegetation. However, there is no risk of fire, nor is there a requirement for applicator licensing. It is like spraying with an herbicide. However, sugar surfactants may harm aquatic organisms, and the high cost and specialized equipment are not practical for non-commercial applications.

POWER TOOLS The most used, least effective power tool is the weed eater. This power device at the end of a handle spins a nylon whip at a high RPM to cut back weeds, while the head is swung horizontally just above the ground. It can be used vertically for edging. This is a last resort tool when weeds have grown excessively tall and need to be cut back prior to fire season. Unfortunately, it is often applied after the weeds have already gone to seed. Weed whipping then simply disburses the seed in all directions, assuring a good crop to be weed whipped again the following year.

Rototilling or discing is not recommended for any type of native planting. Nor is it recommended for soil preparation, since the massive disturbance and mixing of vegetative matter into the soil creates the perfect conditions for weeds to germinate and thrive. Discing on a large scale has been used annually for weed abatement in communities for years. This process completely destroys native ecology, contaminating the soil with organic matter, making any potential restoration excessively difficult, and assures bountiful crops of flashy fuel annual weeds year after year, in perpetuity. Better to leave the soil as undisturbed as possible and use the least destructive methods to destroy the invasive exotics. A much better approach is to mow these areas before seed production, minimizing soil disturbance and reducing favorable weed ecology. When mowing in hot, dry months, have water available; if a blade strikes on rocks it can spark and start a fire.

TOP DRESSING AND SOLARIZATION   Temporarily covering the soil surface with black plastic, old newspapers, rugs, or any other contiguous solid, opaque covering is an effective way of smothering weeds prior to planting. It is chemical-free and denies light and aeration to the weeds, which can die in a matter of weeks to months. Unfortunately, this method is ineffective for deeply rooted rhizomatous plants like oxalis and Bermuda grass. In fact, they may return in even greater numbers when the competition has been eliminated. Nevertheless, it is a valuable tool for killing most annual and shallow-rooted pest plants.

Soil solarization is another pre-planting weed-control method that amplifies the heat energy of the sun to create a small-scale greenhouse effect. It uses clear (not black) plastic to allow ultraviolet energy to penetrate the soil while trapping infrared heat. The plastic is sealed with soil completely around the perimeter, and then left throughout the summer months. The temperature goal is approximately 130 degrees to a depth of 6 inches. This helps destroy living plants, dormant weed seed, and also pathogens in the soil. Solarization has proven effective against many weeds; however, again, it is not effective against deep rhizomatous plants or deep-set bulbs and tubers. The additional heat may stimulate these plants. In the absence of these actors, however, it can be effective for weed control for up to two years.

Biocontrols

In recent years, insect biocontrols targeting invasive exotics have been introduced in the war on weeds. There is new hope for effective control of many aggressive exotic weed species, including: starthistle (*Centaurea sulphurea*), Canada thistle (*Cirsium arvense*), spurge (*Euphorbia* sp.), and loosestrife (*Lythrum salicarica*). Over the centuries, in plants' native locale, they achieve an ecological balance with local pathogens and biocontrols. Exotics transported into completely new environments often run rampant, in part due to the lack of these natural controls. Rather than relying exclusively on chemical controls, scientists now consider the introduction of biocontrols from the invasive plant's origin. These new introductions have potential to help even the score.

While we most often think of biocontrols as insects, one effective bio-control has existed in California since early European settlement. Grazing cattle, placed on newly burned and cleared California plant communities, spread the seed of the pasture plants imported to feed them. Seeds of hay, filaree, clover, oats, and other plants introduced from European pastures were transported in the fur and manure of the cows. Within 75 years of initial settlement, much of the type conversion from natives to alien pasture was complete. Within this cataclysm, however, is the mechanism of revitalization. It turns out that bovines have selective palates. They prefer eating the same weeds that were intentionally introduced for their survival. They usually consume many of the pasture weeds before they touch the native plants. The casual observer may note that some of the best wildflower displays remaining in California are actually within the cattle pens.

Never consider grazing cattle in a pristine area. However, in areas overrun by weeds, the introduction of small numbers of cattle may provide a low-cost method to help keep a favorable balance for natives. If low-density grazing is employed, with cross fencing to sectionalize the areas, cows can be progressively moved to the next paddock as they have finished eating the non-natives and begin eating the natives. Vigilant observation is required. Horses are also somewhat effective at targeting the non-natives, although they have a strong appetite for our rich native grasses. Nevertheless, they may be better used where native grasses are not a major component of the ecosystem. Responsibly grazed plant communities often provide some of our cleanest habitat, but for the occasional cow patty.

Herbicidal controls

Many situations are too large or aggressive to practically apply physical controls. Nor do most people have a cow in their front yard. Therefore, it may be necessary to consider chemical controls. There are many effective herbicidal controls that, used according to their directions, are relatively safe and effective. This is not a blanket endorsement of all herbicides; some are safer than others. The key is to exercise basic precautions, and, above all, *follow the instructions*—the labels are there for a reason. Keep chemicals in their original containers, locked away and out of the reach of children. Follow all labeling instructions for handling and application. Avoid accidental drift onto desirable plants or beyond the immediate area of work. It is illegal to spray in areas designated as habitat for endangered species.

POST-EMERGENT HERBICIDES As the name suggests, post-emergent herbicide is applied to growing plants that have already germinated. If the herbicide kills all plant species, it is designated as non-selective. A good example is glyphosate, which kills most types of plants. Several brands are available—look on the label for this ingredient. It is an effective tool, as long as spraying is confined to only the target plants. Glyphosate is biodegradable when exposed to ultraviolet energy (sunlight) for a length of time or if it contacts soil. It must be applied to living green leaves in order to be absorbed and translocated into the roots, where it kills the plant. This characteristic is extremely valuable for species that spread by deep rhizomes, like Bermuda grass, which are nearly impossible to control by other means. Glyphosate may be toxic to aquatic organisms. Research has shown that the problem is not the active ingredient, glyphosate, but the soap-based surfactant that is added to make the solution adhere to the leaves for absorption. There are alternative formulations available without any surfactant, which should be used around bodies of water. Do not use surfactant-based mixtures where runoff could potentially carry them downstream. Always follow the label instructions and comply with any cautions or warnings on the label.

One selective post-emergent herbicide, Fluazifop-P-butyl, is a grass-specific herbicide that kills grasses but not broadleaf plants. Many native plant communities are being overrun by non-native grasses, making this an extremely effective tool for restoration work. It is sprayed directly over leafy species to kill the grasses that are infiltrating them. It can be used in the native landscape the same way. It is even labeled to kill Bermuda grass in fescue lawns.

Beware of herbicides containing 2,4-D. This selective post-emergent herbicide kills broadleaf plants while sparing grasses. While it may be useful in specific horticultural applications, it has the potential to do great harm in most native landscapes. This chemical remains residual in the soil and can be taken up by desirable plants. It also may be capable of moving through mycorrhizal fungi.

PRE-EMERGENT HERBICIDES These herbicides control weeds by inhibiting them from germinating from seed. Many suburban and rural soils contain from 10,000 to 100,000 dormant weed seeds per cubic foot. Used according to the label, pre-emergents can significantly reduce this potentially endless and toxic weed bank. With few exceptions, pre-emergents do not adversely affect actively growing plants. They can be applied over new plantings—just wash off the leaves after application. If the area is weedy, remove the weeds before applying the herbicide. Pre-emergents work best when applied over bare dirt.

Pre-emergents typically require about a half-inch of equivalent rainfall to dissolve into the soil. Water immediately after distributing the pre-emergent to wash it off leaves and soak into the ground for maximum effectiveness. An ideal procedure is to plant, watering each plant individually, broadcast the pre-emergent, and then cover the ground in mulch. Finally, water the area equivalent to at least a half-inch of precipitation. Calculate by measuring the application rate of the sprinklers over the surface.

One caution: Pre-emergents should not be used within four months prior to bulb emergence, otherwise bulbs may be killed as they begin to sprout. Treat bulb areas separately, right after they have died back, or avoid them altogether.

Ironically, pre-emergents can promote the spread of rhizomatous invasives, such as Bermuda grass (*Cynodon dactylon*) and oxalis (*Oxalis californica*), which are not affected by these herbicides. Without the competition of annual weeds, these plants thrive. Be prepared to use a post-emergent herbicide if these types of weeds are present.

PESTS AND DISEASES
Unwelcome encounters

9

When was the last time you saw whitefly in the chaparral? Or snails in the sagebrush? Pests and diseases that afflict native plants in a landscape are primarily a horticultural phenomenon—a result of overwatering and fertilization. As one gets away from populated areas into the surrounding natural plant communities, many pest and disease issues disappear. In an urban-created landscape of native plants these issues, in and of themselves, are symptoms of underlying ecological problems, rather than causal. Address the problems, and the symptoms resolve themselves.

A disease-free *Ceanothus* 'Joyce Coulter'; this plant can become susceptible to disease and pests when native ecology is lost in the landscape.

Pests

In a pristine, natural environment, California native plants are typically pest free. Verify this the next time you are out hiking in healthy chaparral. There is usually not enough moisture in the system to support most of the invertebrates like snails, slugs, and sucking insects. Additionally, leaves of healthy native plants secrete phytotoxins distasteful to potential pests. Dry, undisturbed soils discourage burrowing animals like gophers. Deer typically nibble and browse but do not destroy plants (especially plants lacking in moisture). Native plants only become vulnerable when they are brought into a landscape situation. Even if your landscape closely emulates a natural ecosystem, pests arrive in droves from the neighbors.

Pests are generally categorized into two categories: Vertebrates, which include deer, rabbits, and rodents; and invertebrates, some of the most harmful of which include ants, mealybugs, scale, aphids, whitefly, borers, snails, and slugs.

Vertebrates

These are big pests with backbones, herbivores running rampant. With the abundance of weedy, disturbed sites and diminished numbers of predators, their populations are exploding. Take deer, as an example. Once it was a rare treat to glimpse a deer, now they seem to be everywhere. Even if you don't see deer, they leave plenty of evidence behind. Plants are pulled from the ground, eaten to a nub; or trees, nearly leafless to a certain height, exemplify deer damage. Individual plants may be protected by tall cages covered with chicken wire or hardware cloth, resulting in a cylindrical plant that conforms exactly to the cage. Effective deer control often requires 8-foot-tall chain-link fencing or 5-foot-tall electrified fence. One deterrent is a double fence separated by about 3 to 5 feet; the outer fence about 5 feet tall and the inner one about 8 feet tall. Another alternative is an 8-foot fence that tilts outward at a 45-degree angle. In all cases, the footings need to be at least 2 feet deep. Planting really fragrant plants like sage (*Salvia* sp.) or pearly everlasting (*Gnaphalium* sp.) around the perimeter creates a barrier of distasteful plants to help deter Bambi. Unfortunately, repellants don't work if the deer are hungry enough. You might have better luck with a barking dog.

Rabbits are a big problem in many areas. What seems to be a failing landscape may be the result of rabbits constant nibbling. They can destroy woody shrubs and trees by eating away the bark around the trunk, girdling the plant. Eventually plants die from such constant abuse. Caging the plants individually usually saves the plant; however, any shoots outside the cage will be eaten. Three-inch-wide hardware cloth with half-inch holes, buried a foot deep and attached to the base of fencing, can keep the rabbits out of the property. This type of fencing can also be mounted to 3-foot stakes driven around the perimeter of a planter. Use nylon ties to secure the wire against the stakes. It is essential that *all* holes are covered. Rabbits can and will squeeze through any opening over 2 inches in diameter. There are also live traps for catching and relocating rabbits. If you are being overrun, however, barrier methods are probably more effective.

Squirrels and wood rats can play havoc with a landscape. These creatures are extraordinary climbers, so their damage begins at ground level and moves up. They sever and gnaw branches, eat flowers and fruits, girdle plants, and chew up irrigation hose. Sharply pointed cuts on branches indicate wood rats. They can completely "lace out" a shrub in an evening, carrying branches back to make hut-like dens (sort of like land beavers). They are extremely destructive because they remove large portions of the plant.

Ground squirrels are terrestrial dwellers that hollow out extensive holes under anything large that covers the ground, especially boulders. They create the same damage as their arboreal cousins, and also destroy many plants in their burrowing activities. In most cases, safe control involves trapping (live or dead) to relocate or kill these pests. If using dead traps, the body can be placed outside where it will almost always be found by scavengers (returned to the food chain). Avoid poison, which could kill the same scavengers.

Gophers live in both rural and suburban settings. They frequent weedy areas and disturbed soil, and can completely undermine a fill slope. Plant damage, especially to young plants, can be catastrophic. Many gardeners have seen a favorite perennial quiver and disappear before their eyes as the plant is eaten from the roots and pulled into the tunnel.

One gopher deterrent is to set a 3-foot-diameter hardware cloth cage around and below the root system of the plant or planting area, leaving about a foot above ground. Use 1-inch-diameter hardware cloth or smaller, as gophers can easily squeeze through anything larger than 1 inch. This type of cage may eventually girdle the root system. Another possibility is a 4-foot-wide hardware cloth barrier completely around the perimeter of the property at the base of the fence, in a manner similar to rabbit fencing. Bury the wire at least 2 feet deep. This is laborious, expensive, and fraught with potential entry points at 1-inch or larger breaches.

In most cases, the best alternative for removing gophers is trapping. Eradicate the rodents back to the perimeter of the property, and then keep them from reinvading. A very effective dead trap is the "hole" type—cylindrical or boxy and black—that is placed in the tunnel. When tripped, a spring-loaded loop instantly kills the rodent. To set these traps successfully, you must find and dig down to the main run—not lateral tunnels with mounds, but the main run connecting them. Set two traps in opposite directions, since there is no way to know which direction the gopher may be traveling. Bury everything but the end hole of each trap. When the gopher scurries to plug the breach, it is killed instantly (usually by the following afternoon). The dispatched gopher can simply be laid out to quickly become part of the food chain. Reset the traps, as many gophers often utilize the same tunnels.

Invertebrates

These are annoying small pests without spines. Think creepy, crawly insects, slugs, and snails raising havoc among the plants, especially in suburban areas. Many invertebrates have been introduced to the landscape with exotic plants, but have begun attacking native gardens surrounded by conventional horticulture. Proper native culture will go a long way toward minimizing the damage. However, sometimes population pressures require active intervention to prevent serious injury or death among the natives. In keeping with Integrated Pest Management practices, pesticides should be used only as a last resort. They can do more harm than good, as beneficial predator insects are taken out in the crossfire. Traps and barriers, non-toxic surfactant washes, and targeted baiting are usually the best approach. As with many exotics, often the first line of defense is a strong stream of water to knock the insects off the plants.

One of our worst ecological problems comes in a tiny package: the Argentine ant. This small, South American species has formed a super colony over much of the southern United States. They have wrecked havoc wherever they appear, displacing native ants, becoming nuisances in households, and supporting nearly every type of sucking insect such that these additional pests are gaining footholds in areas once unaffected. These ants have an intense symbiotic relationship with nearly every sucking insect. Whether mealybugs, aphids, whitefly, or scale, Argentine ants feast off the honeydew secreted by these pests as a waste product from their sucking. The sugar produced by the insects is evidenced by black sooty mold that grows over their secretions. Sooty mold may be the first visible sign that your plants are under attack by sucking insects. If you see sooty mold on your stucco, look up. Probably a tree or shrub infested with sucking insects is right above you. These insects feed on natives and introduced plants alike.

Scale is harvested by ants.

The ants protect and cultivate such creatures for their honeydew food source. Yes, they farm sucking insects! Ants place the insects on new growth and protect them from predators. If ants are heading for a native plant, it is most certainly infested with some form of sucking insect. When ants are controlled, the sucking insects are left vulnerable to attack by natural predators.

Spraying "instant-kill" insecticides can fragment the colony and make the problem worse. It is more effective to introduce bait for worker ants to carry back to the queens. Bait stations purchased over the counter may contain a mixture of molasses and arsenic, which workers collect and take back to feed the colony. Other ant baits use a combination of sugar and boric acid. You can make your own with the following recipe: ¼ teaspoon boric acid powder, 3 tablespoons hot water, and 1 tablespoon sugar. Boric acid powder will only dissolve in hot water. You can mix it with hot water or put it in a microwave to heat it up. Place the mixture in a shallow dish near the ant nest.

Reduce ant populations by making the area less attractive. Ants nest in moist, covered areas, so remove any moist debris from the trunk base of trees and shrubs. Inside the house, put food in sealed containers. Ants' preferences vary at different times of year: sugars, proteins, fats, or moisture. See what they are attracted to and reduce the source of their desire.

Another way of controlling ants on trees and shrubs is to restrict their access to the plant. To accomplish this, wrap the trunk tightly with a strip of fabric, nursery tape, or plastic at least 3 or 4 inches wide. Then apply a thick coating of a sticky petroleum-based product to the wrapping completely around the trunk. Do not apply the goo directly to the bark as it may damage the plant. The ants cannot cross the barrier so are cut off and unable to tend their symbiotic partners. Check the barrier often to make sure it has not become saturated with dead ants, creating a bridge for their ant buddies. Replace periodically at a different point on the trunk. Be aware that if any branch is touching another plant, building or fence, the ants will find an alternative route to their food source.

Aphids are common and may occur in large numbers; though for all their sucking, they rarely cause permanent damage to established plants.

Control the ants that support them; the aphids can be blasted with pressurized water or sprayed with insecticidal soap.

Mealybugs are similar to aphids but hairier, and can be treated the same way. Horticultural oils can also be used to control aphids and mealybugs. Read the label for use and application. Make it a practice to read the label for every substance you use in the garden and carefully follow the instructions.

Manzanita leaf gall aphids cause the leaves of certain arctostaphylos species to curl, swell, and redden brightly. Check the cultural conditions first. This reaction also can be a sign of stress, such as too much water or fertilization, or using a plant that's inappropriate for the site. As soon as you see infected leaves, especially on new growth, pull them off and dispose of them. Look around—there could be other infected plants nearby. In the worst case, it may be necessary to treat the infected plants with a systemic pesticide containing Merit (not recommended for any other aphid infections). Merit should only be used as a last option. And, as is always the case with aphids, control the ants.

Scale and whitefly are more destructive and can be difficult to control. Whiteflies invade in swarms attacking more leaves than aphids and can kill an entire plant; scale live under protective shells that closely adhere to bark and can suck the sap from branches killing whole limbs. Ceanothus branch dieback is often due to scale. Locate the scale, take a rag, and rub as much of it as possible off the branch. One or two good swipes with old toweling should greatly reduce the infestation. Look closely to find it all. Knock off the scales and aphids with a blast of pressurized water. Whiteflies have several instars; once knocked off, their reproduction is interrupted, reducing future populations. They do not climb back up the plant. Remove the filament secreted by whiteflies. Filament protects whiteflies from direct contact with insecticidal soaps and oils. A good protocol for control is to wash off the scale and whitefly first, then apply the insecticidal soap and oil, finally respray with water to clean off any remnants. Check and respray with water every couple of weeks, as necessary. Always treat for ants, which will bring more sucking insects back to the affected areas. The last resort to save a badly infected plant, when all other methods have been exhausted, is a Merit-based systemic pesticide. If it doesn't work it can actually create resistance in these bugs and make the problem worse, so it is not usually recommended.

Flathead borers attack woody trees and shrubs. Normally, healthy trees typically outgrow areas that have been injured and are rarely attacked by borers. Infected plants are often already stressed, so borer infestation is usually symptomatic of underlying ecological problems. Beetle larvae form tunnels (called galleries) throughout the living cambium layer just under the bark, eventually girdling the tree. Treatment includes removing any infested or dead branches, and addressing the underlying ecological problems causing susceptibly to infestation.

Southern California oaks (*Quercus* spp.) have recently come under attack by a new pest, the gold spotted oak borer (GSOB). This pest, native to southeastern Arizona, apparently arrived in firewood. Infestation is evidenced by loss of the upper leaves of the oak (crown thinning) and D-shaped exit holes where the adult GSOB beetles leave the host. GSOB is responsible for most of the mortality in southern California's oaks. Treatments are still being developed, but focus on pesticides and/or importing natural biocontrols from Arizona, where GSOB live in equilibrium with their natural enemies. Scientists are investigating whether degraded habitat in combination with fire and drought may be desiccating oak woodland ecology, leaving these oaks more vulnerable to attack.

Pine bark beetles impact pines (*Pinus* spp.) like GSOB does oaks (*Quercus* spp.). The larvae attack living cambium layers just under the bark, their galleries completely girdling and killing infected trees. Since the recent drought, huge stands of native pines have collapsed from pine bark beetle infestation. Drought-stressed pine trees no longer produce enough sap to repel the tunneling larvae. As in the case of GSOB, researchers are investigating whether the heavily degraded, weed-infested condition of many post-fire pine plant communities is contributing to this process of desiccation. In a landscape situation, maintaining healthy native cultural conditions can mitigate or discourage attack.

Gastropods (snails and slugs) typically attack soft perennials and annuals. They like moist conditions and usually are not disruptive in appropriately watered native gardens. However, planting perennials and wild-flowers closely together enables the gastropods and their eggs to survive. Evidence of attack includes damaged and missing leaves and stems, usually covered with slime trails. They can completely destroy young plants and seedlings.

Control gastropods by hand picking or collecting them under old fruit rinds or moistened paper. Or, put a board in the garden and water under it, they will seek the moisture. Collect them in late afternoon or early evening before they disburse. Begin by checking daily; frequent checking and disposal are crucial. They are purportedly attracted to shallow dishes of beer, death by drowning. Commercial emulsions and baits can be distributed around vulnerable plants. Most of them contain metaldehyde, which is toxic and must be keep away from children and pets. Surrounding bases of plants with copper bands is also deadly to slugs and snails, with far less impact on the environment—there is nothing to flow downstream. A safe snail bait, with the active ingredient of iron phosphate, kills by ingestion; that which is not eaten will biodegrade into harmless components in the garden.

Diseases

Healthy ecosystems rarely succumb to diseases. Susceptibility to disease is often a sign of underlying ecological problems. A major exception is sudden oak death (SOD), which is killing thousands of acres of old growth oaks and forest companions in Northern California. Many apparent diseases like galls and drippy oak are actually secondary damage from native insects and are generally part of the ecology. Environmental conditions also cause plant damage including: salt burn, overwatering resulting in mineral deficiencies or rot, and even sun scald. Following is a list of some of the most common afflictions and what, if anything, can be done to treat them. Foliar, non-systemic fungicides, used according to their instructions, can be applied at any time for fungal problems without fear of affecting beneficial mycorrhizae. Systemic, soil drench fungicides, however, can damage mycorrhizae and should not be used unless packaging indicates specifically that the product will not harm mycorrhizae.

Anthracnose

This suite of many similar fungal diseases causes leaf spotting, followed by early drop of the first flush of leaves on deciduous trees like sycamore (*Platanus racemosa*) and many others. Sycamore anthracnose led to the unfortunate moniker "sick ever more" being attached to these beautiful trees. Late-winter to early-spring rains with temperatures below 55 degrees cause the worst infections. The disease is rarely fatal. Clean up dropped leaves and twigs as soon as possible. Poor horticulture—overwatering and feeding—promotes bad infections. Cankers may form, causing the tree to lose limbs or even die. In severe cases, where the health of the tree is in jeopardy, call in licensed professionals to spray copper-based fungicide on the dormant buds. Always use licensed professionals to care for large trees and severe infections.

Blights

Fire blight is a common bacterial infection of plants in the rose family (Roseaceae). Toyon (*Heteromeles arbutifolia*) is its best-known native victim, although other plants in this family are susceptible. This is a rare disease in nature but is common on plants grown in a horticultural setting. Toyons that are overwatered (especially on drip) and fertilized are more

Anthracnose-infected *Cercis* leaves.

susceptible. New growth, buds, and flowers suddenly shrivel and blacken, appearing burnt. Prune out the infected growth well back into the healthy part of each branch. Dispose of infected material immediately. Do not put it in with your green waste, but in the regular trash. Sterilize pruners with a 5 percent bleach solution between cuts. Treat severe infections with a copper-based fungicide or Bordeaux mixture of copper sulfate and lime.

Oak twig blight is an occasional disease of coast live oaks (*Quercus agrifolia*) that causes twigs scattered throughout the canopy to suddenly die. It is worse in high rainfall years. Treatment is the same as for fire blight.

Canker

Cankers are areas of sunken tissue that exude dark or resinous sap and are often ringed by callus tissue. Pitch and cypress canker are two of the most deadly, easily infecting pines or cypress. Control these cankers by cutting out infected parts well into healthy tissue. Remove and dispose of dead trees. Always sterilize all equipment after cutting infected plants.

Other cankers will infect stressed plants. That's why it is so important to maintain healthy native cultural conditions. Do not overwater or fertilize. Use the appropriate plants for your area. Botryophaeria is a canker that infects trees like madrone (*Arbutus menziesii*), sequoia (*Sequoiadendron giganteum*), and incense cedar (*Calocedrus decurrens*) when they have been planted in a climate that is much hotter than their native range. Treat by destroying and disposing of the infected parts of the plant.

Chlorosis

New leaves emerging as yellow with green veins are chlorotic, deficient in iron or other nutrients necessary to produce chlorophyll. Lack of iron uptake is a reliable sign of overwatering, because plants are unable to extract iron from saturated soil. Chlorosis can also indicate high soil alkalinity. Normally plenty of iron is available in California's soils, so the problem is typically cultural. Moist, heavy clay soils can tie up iron, causing chlorosis in plants. Always check for overwatering first. Applying chelated iron will address the immediate symptoms, but you must examine long-term cultural issues.

Yellowing leaves can also indicate mineral deficiency. Straight yellowing may be a sign of low nitrogen, while lack of leaves may indicate low potassium. Phosphorous deficiency causes stunted stems and lack of flowers. Some native soils are legitimately low in potassium. Invest in a soil analysis before adding potassium sulfate. Other mineral deficiencies are almost always a sign of overwatering and should be addressed as such.

Leaf burn

Salt toxicity and sun scald are two primary causes of leaf burn. Salty soils can occur naturally, especially near the coast or in the desert, or they can result from over-fertilization or application of poor fill soils. Reliance on reclaimed water has created problems with salt toxicity in native plants; typically reclaimed water is high in sodium and nitrates. Salt-toxic leaves typically burn along the margins. Mature, established leaves turn yellow down to the green veins prior to burning or dropping. Address salty conditions by using plants that have higher salt tolerance, leaching with fresh water, mulching soils to drive the salts down, and using potable water to irrigate native plantings.

Sun scald

Sun scald results from change of environment. It occurs when shade-tolerant shrubs are suddenly exposed to too much light, often by moving from a shade tree or structure, or by over-pruning a plant, suddenly exposing internal shaded leaves and branches to sunlight. Both leaves and bark may scald. Set up a temporary shade structure of nursery shade cloth to help ease the transition for a beloved plant, and be wary of over-pruning. Scalding bark may be severe enough to cause secondary infections of canker fungi. Be careful when pruning.

Leaf spots and holes

Some fungi besides anthracnose can cause spotting or holes in leaves of plants like toyon (*Heteromeles arbutifolia*), cherries (*Prunus* spp.), and cottonwood (*Populus* spp.). These are typically not fatal. Copper-based treatments can help in the worst cases. Remove fallen, infected leaves and twigs as soon as possible.

Mildew

Powdery and downy mildew are groups of fungi that form white or gray patches on leaves. These cause distortion and discoloration on leaves and shoots, which ultimately die. In native plants, mildew is a symptom of poor cultural practices or lack of air or light circulation. It forms when cool moist nights are followed by warm sunny days. In warm weather, wash the mildew off the leaves. Prune severely infected stems with sterilized equipment. In extreme cases of mildew, you can apply neem oil for treatment and prevention. Neem oil is a traditional botanically based oil from the Indian neem tree (*Azadirachta indica*).

Root rots

These fungal-based maladies cause native plant enthusiasts much grief. Many a wild lilac (*Ceanothus* spp.) has collapsed seemingly overnight to the ravages of rot, as have flannel bushes (*Fremontodendron* spp.) and coffeeberry (*Rhamnus californica*). There are no practical methods for treating root rots other than prevention through proper cultural practices and the use of resistant plant varieties. Root rot is not typically seen in the wild, with the exception of sudden oak death.

Leaf spot on toyon.

Armillaria root rot

This root rot (*Armillaria ostoyae*, formerly *mellea)* is a decay fungus associated with oak trees (otherwise known as oak root fungus). It exists naturally as a component of the oak woodland. Interestingly, it is theorized that these types of fungi are an important part of the ecosystem helping to prevent exotic or inappropriate species from getting established while negatively impacting the very tight-knit oak woodland plant community. Large golden brown mushrooms form at the root crown of the tree. Root-like structures called rhizomorphs form around the base, distinctive from real roots because they are soft and pithy. Mats of white fungus occur underneath the bark on the trunk. The tree usually drops its leaves—lower branches and trunk rot away.

Root and crown rot

Phytophthora spp. loves warm, wet soil. It kills many beloved native species, such as fremontia (*Fremontodendron* spp.), coffeeberry and redberry (*Rhamnus* spp.), and redbud (*Cercis occidentalis*). It may also kill wild lilac (*Ceanothus* spp.). Plants wilt and branches die back as the roots are killed. In southern California, avocados are a main host for *Phytophthora cinnamomi*, and since avocados have been a major crop in the back hills, this disease is fairly common. The fungus spreads easily on the bottom of shoes. Fortunately, good native cultural practices—particularly reducing irrigation—can help plants resist this disease. There is some evidence that it does not persist in the soil as long as appropriate watering is maintained.

Sudden oak death

Phytophthora ramorum exudes a reddish ooze from the tree bark, almost as if the tree was bleeding. It typically targets oaks (*Quercus* spp.) and tanbark oak (*Lithocarpus densiflorus*), although many other species are susceptible. Most infected plants die. Efforts are focused on controlling the spread of disease by removing and disposing infected trees and leaf litter. Phosphonate fungicide shows promise as a preventive measure to stimulate immune responses in susceptible trees. In California, sudden oak death only appears active in areas of higher rainfall, from Big Sur north.

Southern California occurrences have not been verified; these deaths are possibly due to root and crown rot infections (*Phytophthora cinnamomi*) and not SOD.

Dematophora root rot

Dematophora necatrix principally affects and kills wild lilac (*Ceanothus* spp.). This disease causes ceanothus to die quickly while still retaining its dead leaves, as if the plant "flamed out." Sometimes only a segment of the infected plant dies. Immediately stop all watering and allow the soil to dry out. This may save the plant. This problem often occurs with ceanothus on drip systems during the summer. While they will abide some light, overhead watering, established plants do not tolerate wet, warm soil at all. If the trunk darkens just above the root crown, anticipate plant death. There is no cure. Early detection and allowing the plant to dry out can occasionally save a plant. Remove and destroy dead plants.

Rust

Aptly named, rust fungus infects deer grass (*Muhlenbergia rigens*), currants and gooseberries (*Ribes* spp.), cottonwoods (*Populus* spp.), and other plants. It forms a powdery orange coating on the underside of leaves. If it spreads to the entire plant it can kill the plant. In the worst cases, the plant may develop cankers. Rust is usually caused by too much humidity and moisture in early spring. Remove and dispose of badly infected leaves and branches. Allow the plant to dry out. Spray with neem oil to kill the fungus.

Wilts

Two major bacterial wilts affect native plants: verticillium (*Verticillium dahliae*), which infects woody plants in their vascular tissues; and fusarium (*Fusarium oxysporum*), which typically infects perennial herbaceous plants and Canary Island date palms (*Phoenix canariensis*, not native). While superficially resembling each other, their hosts differ. Verticillium wilt infects the stems of woody plants by plugging the water-conducting tissues know as xylem. If you cut through a stem, it shows dark discoloration

Salvia 'Bee's Bliss' with dead portions from wilt.

in the internal vascular tissues. Since this wilt moves vertically through a plant, it can infect one portion while leaving another side unaffected. Eventually it will spread to the whole plant. Sonoma sage (*Salvia sonomensis* and hybrids) is notoriously susceptible to this pathogen. There is no known cure. Cut out the infected portions using sterilized tools and maintain good cultural practices to keep the disease in a chronic, "treatable" state. Verticillium is known to survive in soils for years. Replace susceptible plants with resistant varieties or non-affected species, such as *Arctostaphylos* spp.

Fusarium wilt infects perennials and annuals. Similar to verticillium, it plugs the vascular xylem, which cuts off fluid flow, often on just one side of the plant. Ultimately, the plant wilts and dies. This bacterium also survives for long periods of time in the soil, so the best approach is to use resistant varieties of plants. Interestingly, fusarium is killing most of the Canary Island date palms in southern California. Removing infected palms is an expensive process, requiring isolation and careful disposal of the debris. Unattended, the infection can spread. This is yet another good reason to avoid using palms in the landscape.

For more extensive information and photos on the latest pests, diseases, and weeds, the University of California has an excellent website with up-to-date research and information at www.ipm.ucdavis.edu.

THE BOTTOM LINE, California native plants are susceptible to numerous pests and diseases, many of which can be completely avoided with proper landscape care and maintenance. With native plants, not only do you save money on water, you also have more free time to enjoy your yard, rather than being a slave to it. Weeds may seem daunting for the few years after you have converted to a native landscape, but they will diminish as your healthy natives reestablish a healthy ecosystem. Regular quarterly maintenance keeps you in touch with what is happening in your garden so you can be aware of any problems before they become serious. Keep your cuts straight, your tools clean and sharp, and dispose of diseased or infected plant material responsibly.

WEEDS AND THE NATIVE LANDSCAPE 10
Adventitious aliens

In California we are losing native habitat at an alarming rate. Weeds are most of the problem. Weeds are competitive, while most native plants are mutualistic—living together in general harmony. While over-generalized, this simple statement captures the essence of the difference between California's indigenous plants and the exotic, aggressive invaders that are destroying our fragile ecology on a daily basis. It used to be said that a weed is "a plant growing where it is not wanted." We propose that this definition should be embellished to include: "a plant that is typically not native, that displaces and/or destroys the indigenous ecology while putting all of its life energy into reproducing itself, vegetatively or sexually, often producing enormous quantities of seed that may remain dormant up to 50 years."

This beautiful, pastoral scene is marred only by the presence of non-native grasses, which may one day destroy these magnificent valley oaks.

INTERESTINGLY, some of our worst weeds are fairly minor components of their own native ecologies. Kudzu vine, the plant that ate the South, is hard to find in its home range in Asia where insects and pathogens check its rampant growth. Eucalyptus and oleander have been fail-safe "no-problem" landscape plants in California for 100 years, bothered by neither pest nor disease. In the last decade, pests indigenous to their native habitats were introduced and have proliferated, sending scientists and horticulturists scurrying to find additional biocontrols for the newly introduced pests.

Ironically, some of our California natives are aggressive weeds in other locales. The California poppy (*Eschscholzia californica*) is a fiercely invasive weed in India. Some native species we find difficult to grow are problem-free in other areas of the world. Flannel bushes (*Fremontodendron* spp.) grow to 20 feet in Ireland. California lilac (*Ceanothus* spp.) is a garden staple in England.

Weeds destroy our fragile ecology because their own native ecology is so different. Most California native plants are mycorrhizal. Namely, soil microorganisms live in symbiosis with the roots of native plants increasing their efficiency to extract minerals and water from sparse soils. In contrast, most exotic invasive species are non-mycorrhizal or facultatively so (becoming mycorrhizal when it benefits them). The exotics do not depend upon a delicate relationship with a fungal partner in order to survive. Some plants temporarily hook into the fungal network, rape it of all nutrition and moisture, collapse the native plant community, and take over. In either case, weeds survive on the innate soil nutrition and seasonal moisture, then die or go dormant as the rainy season ends. By August, the dead carcasses are ready to burn as flash fuels. This facilitates increased fire frequency, which hastens the decline of the native plant communities already under siege.

Many weeds flourish in disturbed, wet, rich soils that are the anathema of native ecosystems. Relatively rare in California in nature, these soil types of have become more prevalent due to agriculture and development. They represent the ideal in traditional horticultural technology, which applies water and fertilizer for optimal ornamental plant growth. Moist, nutrient-rich soils are often coated in green algae and have an unpleasant odor due to anaerobic bacteria actively decomposing plant debris. The closest natural analogy is a swamp. It is lethal to our natives (except swamp plants), while weeds, free of limiting pathogens and biocontrols, are able to thrive in it.

Habitat disruption and destruction

Native ecosystems, when mature and undisturbed, inhibit the establishment of foreign plant species. The strong native symbiotic ecology excludes weeds. Absence of weeds is a prime criterion for evaluating native habitat health. Taking a hike in healthy chaparral provides observable demonstration of the difference. The understory is extraordinarily clean. Indigenous people purportedly could walk 200 miles barefoot through much of California prior to European contact. Nowadays, anyone would be ill advised to walk barefoot even 200 feet through a typical open field.

Soil disturbance promotes weed infection in a healthy plant community. It often initiates when a trail or road is cut through the plant community—analogous to a cut on your arm becoming infected. The weeds act like the bacteria—seeds are already present but harmless until there is an opportunity to enter the organism; a break in the skin or crust allows them entry or germination. Old-growth stands may be completely clean, while the trails or roads cut through them are usually lined with weeds.

Further disturbance is required for weeds to spread. Unfortunately, there is no shortage of weed-spreading mechanisms. Clearing vegetation mechanically, especially with heavy equipment, is akin to running a plow through the forest, usually leading to massive infection. Old-growth plant communities can be converted to weedy "cow pasture" in just a season or two. Once the ecology is lost, it can be very difficult and costly to restore.

Frequent fires are one of the most common and insidious ways in which native plant communities are replaced by invasive exotics. Imagine a person with third degree burns all over their body. A victim exposed to unsanitary conditions suffers massive infection. After fire, the weeds, once confined to the vicinity of the trail, are now free to seed themselves over open soil enriched by carbon ashes. Worse still, seed may be *deliberately* introduced in a misguided attempt to control erosion. One example is aerial seeding of non-native species after a fire, just when the natural plant community is most vulnerable. This is akin to a doctor coming in and spreading germ cultures all over the flesh of the burn victim.

Native plantsman Bert Wilson has observed the ecology of the landscape over many decades. He took note of a burn area that had been aerially seeded with non-native grass mix containing star thistle seed. In subsequent seasons he watched the burn area "degrade terribly, the weeds spread, the fires increased, and the water-holding capacity of the land decreased." Wilson describes the strong symbiosis between mycorrhizal fungi, associated microorganisms, and the native plants. The microorganisms supply micronutrients metabolized directly from inorganic soil and rock, store water, and move the water and nutrition around to where it is needed in the plant community. In addition, the soil biomass helps create structure that increases the moisture and air capacity of the dirt. The plants, in turn, provide essential sugars to the soil biota (plant and animal life) that they cannot produce themselves.

Wild mustard destroys the mycorrhizal grid, ultimately replacing native species.

After a fire, the aboveground, sugar-producing vegetation needed for survival of the mycorrhizal fungi and associated microorganisms in the soil is gone. As Wilson notes, these microorganisms are in desperate need of carbohydrates and will only last a few months in their absence. In nature, salvation comes with the winter rains, as fire-following native annuals (wildflowers) connect to the underground organisms and supply them with carbohydrates. The mycorrhizae and microorganisms start feeding the damaged perennial plants so that they can regrow. While complete recovery takes years, this amazing response to fire has evolved over millions of years to recover the plant community, but at a natural fire frequency of every 60 to 120 years, not the 5 to 10 years occurring now.

Weeds displace fire-following native annuals when there are no biocontrols or pathogens to control weed growth. They germinate more rapidly than wildflowers. They thrive in the carbon-rich, post-fire soil, utilizing the nutrients, but not connecting to the soil microorganisms or returning any benefit to them. Even worse, some weeds connect and rape the mycorrhizal grid of its reserves, while mustard toxins actually destroy it.

Starved of vital carbohydrates, the soil microorganisms begin to die off. Without the means to survive, they are unable to provide micronutrients to the recovering native plants. The whole native plant community collapses, to be replaced by non-native weeds and grasses. Unlike native wildflowers, which are readily absorbed back into the ecology, the nutrition utilized by the alien weeds is held above ground in their dead, dry carcasses. These woody weeds are full of lignin, which decomposes very slowly. The resulting thatch is dead and ready to burn again by August,

Alien grasses and flowering marguerite line disturbed edges of this trail in the native area of Balboa Park.

promoting more frequent fires and further destroying the remainder of the native ecology. As the type-conversion continues, the soil loses fungal biomass, structure, and moisture-holding capacity. Progressively, erosion increases and the lack of retained moisture in the ecosystem leads to desertification. This process, unfortunately, is happening all over California and has been promoted, unwittingly, by our own ill-advised management practices.

Why are our oaks dying?

Some of the most conspicuous casualties of this invasive exotic invasion are majestic native oak trees. What may first appear to be an "oak savannah" is usually a cow pasture with a few oak trees in it. Their associated ecological partner communities, like chaparral and coastal sage scrub, are long gone. As a result, oaks are dying throughout the state. As the trees degrade they begin to look unhealthy. Leaves on normally evergreen trees start to yellow and drop. Whole branches become bare, as their bark cracks and exfoliates. Finally, the entire tree collapses, leaving only a central, dead trunk, surrounded by a carpet of weeds.

Even worse, few seedlings are available to replace these lost treasures. Oak trees have stopped reproducing. Again, the culprit appears to be weeds. Weakened trees are far less likely to flower and set acorns. Additionally, weeds prevent the few acorns that form from contacting the all-important litter layer of dead oak leaves. And finally, the miniscule numbers of acorns that root are completely overwhelmed by aggressive thatch and soon die. Fires, promoted by the dead dry thatch in summer, also destroy what few volunteers made it that far.

Evergreen, or live oak trees, are probably the most weed resistant, as they have the ability to shade out alien species while setting down an ever-dropping layer of dead leaf mulch. You can often see an exact shadow of the canopy, devoid of weeds, out to the drip line of the tree. The few weeds that survive under this type of oak are usually poorly rooted (often just in the mulch) and easily pulled out. Actually, most vegetation growing under the evergreen oaks is native and plugged into the highly symbiotic ecology. Some describe a healthy oak forest as a "fairy woodland."

Unfortunately, not all evergreen oaks are healthy. If a thick thatch of weeds has been able to establish under a live oak, that tree is in serious trouble. It means that the alien invasives have overwhelmed all defenses, and the tree is in the final stages of collapse. Saving oaks in this condition requires rapid intervention.

Deciduous oak trees are less weed resistant. Because they are bare-branched for part of the year, much more sunlight passes through, helping weeds get established. Their mulch is not as thick, which also promotes weed growth. Weedy thatch further discourages the formation of the litter layer. Progressively less nutrition is available for native soil microorganisms that metabolize the litter layer and pass nutrients along to the oak tree. As the weeds continue to use up the available moisture and nutrients without benefitting the oak, the whole system collapses. When the mycorrhizal partners are lost, the tree becomes vulnerable to all manner

Dramatic comparison illustrating the impact of alien weeds killing a native oak while weed removal has allowed the oak in the foreground to thrive, producing copious yellow blossoms.

of pathogens, some of which plug the ability of nutritious sap to travel back to the roots. The back pressure can rupture the bark, forming exudates often misdiagnosed as sudden oak death. Untreated, the oak tree eventually dies.

With active intervention, this deadly process is often reversible. Removing all weeds from approximately 1½ times the diameter of the drip line can result in visible recovery in a matter of months. The whole appearance of the trees changes as they stop dropping leaves and branches, the dull green and yellow leaves are replaced by dark green, healthy, shiny leaves, and the tree may even go into bright bloom in spring. Planting appropriate oak woodland understory plants enhances this recovery. Secondary natives produce carbohydrates for the soil biology, which helps supply nutrients needed by the overall plant community. When the oaks go into vigorous bloom, acorn production abounds. Lots of acorns lead to lots of seedlings, which are free to develop in the absence of weeds. Native squirrels further distribute the acorns. Clients have reported seeing carpets of oak seedlings in the weed-free zone, whereas the weedy areas immediately adjacent are devoid of volunteers.

A lineup of the worst offenders

It is amazing just how many malicious weeds have invaded and are destroying California's beautiful, delicate ecology. Some have been here for so long that people are surprised to find out they are not native. Here is a sample of some of the most common and aggressive offenders.

Grasses

When you look out over the emerald green grass-covered California hills in spring, you probably think you are looking at native grasses. In fact, virtually none are indigenous. Most are exotic species introduced from Europe, Asia, or Africa as a result of grazing, agriculture, or ornamental horticulture. To think that the landscape resembles the hills of Ireland is not far from the truth. Almost all non-native grasses proliferate in the presence of burning, thus leading to ever-increasing fire cycles.

Wild oats (*Avena sativa*) and brome grass are some of the most common annual weeds, having spread on a large scale through grazing and fire. As the name suggests, ripgut brome (*Bromus* spp.) is especially dangerous to cattle as it can perforate their digestive systems. Foxtail (*Wodyetia bifurcata*) or red brome often ends up on socks and in pet ears. Veldt grasses (*Ehrharta* spp.) were introduced by cattleman for range improvement in the 1940s. However, they are extremely invasive and can reseed in a matter of weeks. Just a few individuals can lead to total colonization in less than a year. The same is true for the aggressive rabbitsfoot grass (*Polypogon monspeliensis*). These require *immediate* removal when encountered.

Pampas grass (*Cortaderia selloana*) is a highly invasive, gigantic perennial that is aptly called sawgrass. It is so huge that removal often requires a backhoe. Its leaves are razor sharp. All parts have to be killed, or it will regenerate from the smallest segments. Its tall, beautiful plumes contain millions of seed easily spread by wind, leading to logarithmic population explosions. It displaces huge areas of chaparral and coastal sage scrub, while increasing fire frequency, in turn leading to greater spread.

Fountain grass (*Pennisetum setaceum*) and buffelgrass (*Cenchrus ciliaris*) from Africa are also aggressive perennial grasses that thrive in arid

Pampas grass.

Fountain grass.

climates. Many people find pennisetum seedheads attractive and bring them home to grow, not realizing they are spreading a destructive weed that could help burn down their home! These grasses love fire and proliferate after a burn. Unfortunately, years ago, fountain grass was seeded along road cuts by Caltrans and other agencies for erosion control. Buffelgrass was another grass brought in by the cattle industry. Both have since spread far and wide, destroying enormous areas of habitat, especially in the desert.

Another voracious perennial grass is Bermuda grass (*Cynodon dactylon*), which reproduces aggressively in multiple ways. Its seed remains viable for years. Aboveground stolons root at the nodes, while it can multiply by belowground rhizomes, some of which reach a depth of 10 feet or more, and are nearly impossible to remove mechanically. Herbicides are often the only means of eradication.

Filaree

Filaree (*Erodium* spp.) is in the geranium family and includes many non-native Eurasian species. Feathery shaped leaves form a low rosette. Showy flowers range in pink and magenta tones. They were intentionally brought

Filaree.

here as cattle forage and are still valued for their high nutrition. Unfortunately, they are perfectly adapted to California ecology and in some areas they have aggressively and completely displaced all native plants. Their coiled seeds contract in dry weather and expand with humidity, actually drilling into the soil. Seeds easily freeload on fur and socks, thriving in warm weather. By summer's end the plants form spiny masses, painful to remove. Filaree can be difficult to eradicate once established. If it is in your garden, hand pulling works well. Do so before the plants set seed. Herbicides are usually required for larger infestations.

Mustard

Non-native brassicas or mustards fill the landscape with yellow in the spring. There are actually two: black mustard (*Brassica nigra*) and short-pod mustard (*Hirschfeldia incana*). The first is tall and annual; the second is a short, pervasive, tough-rooted perennial. They are some of our earliest invaders, brought here for seasoning by the Spanish. Mustards have been here so long, they seem like just another part of the ecology. Many are antagonistic to our delicate ecology, producing chemicals that actively suppress and destroy mycorrhizal fungi, leading to the destruction of the native plant community. This is why you often see a monoculture of mustard and nothing else.

A common beloved annual flower with a sweet scent is actually an aggressive form of mustard. Sweet alyssum (*Lobularia maritima*) is found in many seed mixes and is sold in pony packs as a color spot. Just a couple of years in your garden, and the once-varied seed mix of flowers becomes a monoculture of alyssum. It is peculiar to see seed packets of native wildflowers (the least aggressive wildflowers of all) mixed with alyssum for quick fill. The native wildflowers are usually gone by the second or third year.

A golden field of mustard.

Newly introduced, one of the worst mustards is Sahara mustard (*Brassica tournefortii*), now rapidly destroying huge swaths of desert, until very recently covered in wildflowers. Like most mustards it knocks out the delicate soil ecology and takes over. When dead, seedpods delay opening until the dry plant has scattered across the desert like tumbleweed. Sahara mustard creates a tremendous amount of dry, readily flammable biomass, especially when accompanied by noxious cheat grass (*Bromus tectorum*). Native desert vegetation is not adapted to fire, so any fire can lead to complete loss of habitat. This is a dangerous, vile weed in desperate need of control.

On a small scale, mustards can be controlled by hand pulling or mechanical means. One effective method is to use a pointed shovel to quickly cut through the taproot a couple inches below ground. Once cut, remove all vegetation. Mustard infestations can be incredibly widespread and often require herbicides for control. Some invasions, such as Sahara mustard, are so prolific that control strategies have yet to be developed.

Spurge

Euphorbia is a large and diverse genus of plants. It includes beloved plants like poinsettia and candelabra tree, but also damaging noxious weeds like

Petty spurge.

spotted, prostrate, and petty spurge (*Euphorbia nutans*, *E. supina*, and *E. peplus*). All are identifiable by their distinctive flowers and milky, poisonous sap. The low-growing spotted and prostrate varieties produce copious amounts of seed within weeks of germination, which is then collected and spread by Argentine ants. When you pull out this weed, there is almost always a swarm of ants underneath. Spotted and prostrate spurges look similar. However, the spotted type emanates from a central taproot and can be easily pulled from moist soil, whereas the prostrate variety roots at the nodes as it grows and requires persistent removal.

Petty spurge is a more upright annual that looks like a miniature tree in bloom. It sets copious seed and completely takes over any open area, discouraging the growth of native plants and wildflowers.

Hand pulling is usually effective for yard-scale infestations of spurge. They need to be pulled *as soon as they are detected*, because they set seed very early in their development. Spotted and prostrate spurge set seed at every stem node. Larger infestations often require chemical intervention, including pre-emergents that target their enormous seed bank in the soil, rather than the growing plants. The ants will be waiting!

Thistle

Thistles, in the family Asteraceae, are another large group of annuals and perennials with non-native weedy representatives. They form rosettes with toothed or spiny elongated leaves. The often-showy flowers form at the end of single to branched central stalks. It is important to remove the plants before they set their enormous quantities of seed. Several aggressive varieties have become widespread pests that are difficult to control.

Sow thistle (*Sonchus oleraceus*) and dandelion (*Taraxacum officinale*) are two invasive common garden weeds. They spread locally; however, they can be controlled by hand weeding. Post- and pre-emergent herbicides also work well for eradication.

Perennial Canada thistle (*Cirsium arvense*) can survive under oak trees, and is often the first pioneer of weed infestations that lead to oak downfall. It is an aggressive seeder with painfully spiny leaves. Prior to flowering, it can be easily plucked from the leaf litter by hand, with strong gloves.

Artichoke thistle (*Cynara scolymus*) is the wild form of the culinary plant, reverted to its spiny origins. Prickly leaved, heavy seeding artichoke thistle is completely displacing large tracts of disturbed coastal sage scrub and chaparral along the coast. Easily recognizable, it has large, spiny, silver leaves and striking purple flowers. Prior to flowering, localized infestations can be hand pulled, with gloves. However, huge-scale invasions preclude even mechanical control. Herbicides are frequently necessary.

Yellow star thistle (*Centaurea solstitialis*) is an extraordinarily aggressive annual that has invaded millions of acres in California. This plant can fill in areas with monotypic stands forcing out all else. It promotes and is promoted by fire. A contaminant in hay, yellow star thistle is often an indicator of prior horse activity. This plant must be addressed prior to flowering. When it is still a low rosette of lobed leaves it can be mechanically removed. This weed is so widespread that herbicide intervention is often required. The science community is exploring biocontrols, like European weevils, as possible agents in stemming the tide of this menace.

Oxalis

Many species of oxalis inhabit California, some native and some weeds. Native varieties tend to be mild mannered, like redwood sorrel (*Oxalis oregana*). Non-natives, on the other hand, can be incredibly voracious and a challenge to control. One variety that has colonized most of coastal California is Bermuda buttercup (*Oxalis pes-caprae*) with handsome yellow flowers on erect stems. Many people find it attractive (at first) so control is often delayed until it is too late. Another name, sour grass, describes the sour-tasting flower stalks, full of oxalic acid and attractive to children to suck on—harmless in small quantities, but not recommended in large amounts. This oxalis has deeply rooted bulbs and bulblets making hand pulling futile.

Oxalis.

Burclover.

Another weedy oxalis is wood sorrel (*Oxalis corniculata*), which seeds aggressively and sends rooting stolons along the soil surface. This, too, is a persistent perennial. Hand pulling is more effective for this plant, but the roots run deep. Herbicides can be effectual with repeated applications. There are products specifically targeted for oxalis control.

Clover

Yes, the clover family has weedy representatives. The worst offender is California burclover or *Medicago polymorpha*. Despite its common name, it is not native and has spread throughout the state. In the pea family, the leaves look like common clover. This annual grows rapidly from a central taproot. A single plant can spread for 5 feet or more in all directions. The seedpods will hitch a ride on anything that moves—your pet's fur, your clothes, especially socks; the burs can even devalue the price of wool. Each nasty pod contains several bean-shaped seeds. Pull by hand or treat with herbicides *before* the seed ripens. Control burclover as soon as you see it, because it matures quickly. Trace the leaders back to the central taproot. A tug at the center usually pulls burclover up easily.

Another fairly common weed is sweet clover (*Melilotus albus*), which has now invaded all 50 states. This plant gives off a distinctive, sweet fragrance, hence its name. Another plant brought here as cattle forage, it is a biennial, putting all its energy into root production the first year, then flowers and seeds the second. Less aggressive than burclover, it can be controlled effectively by hand weeding or herbicides. People with traditional lawns often plant sweet clover to add nitrogen to the soil to achieve the look of a traditional East Coast lawn. Native plants have little to no need for extra nitrogen in the soil.

Other nasty weeds you should not be planting

Many attractive plants used in landscapes, just like sweet alyssum and pampas grass, have escaped to wreak havoc in the wilderness. Unfortunately, unaware of their potential to destroy native habitats, nurseries still sell these weeds for their ornamental appeal.

Periwinkle (*Vinca major*) is an evergreen spreading perennial with lovely purple flowers. It is gaining a foothold in many oak woodland and riparian sites. Periwinkle, deep rooted and difficult to control, is still sold as the ultimate shade-tolerant groundcover by most nurseries. Even direct, repeated application of the herbicide glyphosate may be ineffective. Sometimes the best and only treatment is to dig it out, a laborious task that can do real damage to the roots of established trees where it grows. Better yet, don't plant it!

For decades, succulent Hottentot fig, or ice plant (*Carpobrotus* sp.), has been used as a slope groundcover, only it is a lousy slope stabilizer. Ice plant–covered slopes frequently slough off under heavy irrigation or rain. Its weightiness, particularly after seasonal rains, shallow roots, and lack of soil-stabilizing fungi, all contribute to its propensity for downhill travel. Ice plant was an early immigrant and voracious escapee, a contaminant in ship ballast, long cultivated as a favorite slope cover by road engineers. It became so prominent in the wild that it was once believed to be native—a fact disproven by pollen studies about 15 years ago. Fortunately, it can be peeled off the surface of the soil fairly easily, or sprayed in place with herbicides. When removing ice plant manually, pile it up for a week or two to allow it to dry out. This will save your back and reduce the weight

Spanish broom.

and cost of disposal. If you spray with herbicide, ice plant can generally be left in place. Once it is dead, it is not likely to return. Just clear 3-foot-wide holes in the debris to plant native groundcovers. Mulch over the top of the dead ice plant and it will compost into the ground.

Broom species (*Cytisus*, *Genista*, *Spartium* spp.) are becoming serious weeds. These striking plants have longitudinal leaves and brilliant yellow flowers. Seen growing in the wild, people can't wait to dig them up to plant in their own yard. The problem is, they rarely stay in one yard. This highly invasive group of plants is making major impacts in the chaparral and coastal sage scrub plant communities. The rapacious root system is challenging to remove. Herbicides are the best control.

Peruvian and Brazilian pepper trees (*Schinus molle* and *S. terebinthifolius*) are serious pests in many areas. Peruvian (aka California) pepper trees were introduced so early, and are so integral to Old California folklore, that many people assume they are native. *Schinus molle* spreads aggressively in drier areas, whereas *S. terebinthifolius* likes wetter, riparian areas. Peruvian pepper spreads by seed; Brazilian pepper spreads by root suckers. Of the two, Brazilian pepper can be more difficult to remove because cutting the trunk activates the suckers and the surrounding area becomes a carpet of shoots. Removing a Brazilian pepper requires extensive root excavation and/or the use of fairly harsh herbicides. Peruvian pepper can usually be dug out at the root crown.

Finally, there is the perennial garden favorite, fennel (*Foeniculum vulgare*)—much like the artichoke, this plant has escaped garden cultivation and reverted to its wild ancestry. Fennel is now a widespread weed, invading hundreds of thousands of acres, forming nearly monotypic stands. Camp Pendleton, in southern California, is covered in fennel. It promotes very hot fires and contributes to fire frequency. Few animals will eat it. Fennel is best controlled by digging or with herbicides.

Not mere annoyances, weeds are extremely destructive to the California native habitat and to our lifestyle. This is a problem of our own making that has been growing worse through decades of abuse, neglect, and improper management. Aggressive weed control, not only in the native landscape, but also in our undeveloped spaces, can reclaim our once-healthy environment, enable it to retain precious water resources, reduce fire frequency and intensity, and fight back desertification. The regained habitat for California native plants will also encourage native wildlife species for the joy of our children and their children after them.

FIRE
Lessons learned from Southern California

11

Disaster movies cannot hold a candle to awakening to an orange sky, ash snowing down, and the inescapable stench of acrid smoke. Senses tingle from the ominous dry electricity of Santa Ana winds, roaring hell bent through crackling, groaning trees. Before words can form, your being knows at the most primitive and encompassing level that life may never be the same. This is the primeval response to overwhelming, life-threatening fire.

Well-maintained, irrigated native plantings and ample hardscape create defensible space around this home.

For most urban and suburban dwellers, fire was something contained for warmth and visual delight until the major firestorms in southern California in the first decade of the new century wiped out vast swaths of developed land. San Diegans woke up to this scenario on 26 October 2003, and, sadly, again on 21 October 2007. Los Angeles–area residents experienced those same disastrous seasons. In August 2009 over 100,000 acres of forest around Mount Wilson went up in flame while four additional fires raged along Crest Highway, above Azusa, in Rancho Palos Verdes, and at Cottonwood, east of Hemet. Santa Barbara was affected in mid November 2008, with the Tea Fire licking the city and destroying a good portion of the Santa Barbara Botanic Gardens. After three years of drought, a severe dry-lightning thunderstorm on 20–21 June 2008 ignited over 2000 fires in northern and central California. The Basin Complex conflagration alone scorched 254 square miles.

Those living directly in the path of the wildfires were confronted by impenetrable, suffocating smoke and embers flying like the firefalls of Yosemite in a wind tunnel. Small wild animals, aflame, scurried for protection, only to spread additional fires. Many residents had only minutes to make heart-wrenching choices of what to throw into their fleeing vehicles and what parts of their lives would be left to burn. Some didn't have even that much time. Some didn't make it out at all.

The physics of fire

The traditional descriptive for the physics of fire is the "fire triangle." It is a simple model that depicts oxygen, fuel, and heat as the three legs of an equilateral triangle. All three components are necessary to have fire. Remove one and the fire goes out. Deprive the triangle of oxygen and the fire is extinguished. Adding water diverts the heat, which changes the water to steam, reducing the heat available for the fire, so the fire goes out. Remove the fuel, and the fire stops. The chemistry is interesting; hydrocarbon molecules (CH) combine with oxygen (O) in the atmosphere to produce water vapor (H_2O) and carbon monoxide/carbon dioxide (CO/CO_2). The reaction looks like this:

$$H_2C - CH_2 - CH_3 + 5O_2 \rightarrow 3CO_2 + 4H_2O$$

This reaction is exothermic, meaning it gives off more energy than it uses from the fuel, releasing the additional energy as heat and light. Wildland fire suppression theorizes that removing the hydrocarbon fuel—i.e., chaparral—from this equation will stop the fire. Apparently one of the triangle's legs has been taken away. However, the reality is much more complex.

Wholesale chaparral removal usually results in replacement growth by highly combustible annual weeds. Dry weeds ignite more quickly to produce a less intense fire but one that moves extremely rapidly. Dry weeds are referred to as "flashy" fuels. When they come into contact with other fuel sources, such as remnant chaparral, a wood fence, or your house, the fire can climb (called laddering) into and ignite taller structures with greater fuel volume. Currently much of California is degraded chaparral surrounded by dry annual weeds. This is the worst of all situations, in which dry winds can spread fires a thousand acres in less than an hour.

Even if weeds are controlled following chaparral removal, a house surrounded by bare mineral soil and nothing else is still vulnerable to fire. Catastrophic burn events are accompanied by fierce winds (40 to 70 miles per hour) and low humidity (less than 15 percent). As fire nears the cleared zone, quantities of high-flying embers are carried toward structures. Traveling over smooth ground, there is nothing to block their flow—except maybe your house. As fire ecologist Rick Halsey explains, "you have created the perfect bowling alley for embers." This is how fires cross freeways 150 feet wide or more. On the other hand, hydrated vegetation appropriately spaced around the house can block, disrupt, and cool an otherwise uninterrupted flow of embers and debris.

Heat rises and fires move in interesting ways. Structures' locations can be key to their vulnerability. Californians often build houses on the edges and ends of box canyons. When fire moves up these canyons, it rolls horizontally as it sweeps up the slope. This destructive scouring action is difficult to control. Buildings situated at the top of ridges above the canyons are sitting ducks for fire. Even worse are homes built on top of peninsulas with the land dropping down on three sides of a narrow residential cul-de-sac. Fire rolls up the slopes on both sides and the end of the street, igniting nearly everything in its path. Fire crews have difficulty accessing these areas. They are blocked by fleeing residents, then multiple structures flame up as the fire reaches the crest. In response to this scenario, some countries, like Australia, have mandated open space and parks at the ends of their canyon-formed land peninsulas.

Increased fire cycles

The average natural cycle of major chaparral fires in California, prior to human habitation, was approximately once every 75 to 150 years. There are few natural ignition sources for wildfire: the millennial volcanic eruption, lightning, a spark from a falling rock, and the occasional rubbing of tree branches. In California, lightning storms seldom occur between the mountains and the sea. It is not like the Midwest, where you can set your watch by the daily thunderstorms on hot humid days in late summer. Furthermore, how often do lightning strikes occur during Santa Ana winds? Catastrophic fire events rarely occurred before humans came to California. Perhaps lightning would strike and ignite vegetation in late summer, which would then smolder (somehow) for weeks until a fall Santa Ana wind whipped up the fire. Once started, there would be no stopping the conflagration, until it finally reached the sea. Fires could burn over a million acres at a time, but were so infrequent that the chaparral ecosystem recovered fully between burns.

Indians represent the first human habitation affecting fire cycles—fire that was not a part of the evolved ecology. Some argue that Native Americans used fire to manipulate ecosystems for their own benefit as proof of more frequent fire cycles, but there is no evidence that these fires were intended to be large events. Why would they deliberately destroy their food sources, their neighbors, or their own villages? Native people used

Clearing everything to bare ground around this house only created a perfect bowling alley for embers.

Numerous houses were lost as this peninsula left no access or escape during 2007 fires.

fire to entrap game, clear areas for settlement, promote bulbs and grasses for consumption, etc. In fact, using fire to make clearings was a form of early agriculture. Of course, accidents—sometimes catastrophic ones—must have occurred. But there is no reason to believe that the early people were any less respectful or careful about the power of fire than we are today, and probably were more so. The indigenous people have lived in California perhaps 12,000 years; chaparral is over 40 million years old.

Chaparral plants developed adaptations that allow the community to regenerate after a catastrophic fire event. It is their insurance. Saying chaparral "needs" to burn is like saying your house "needs" to burn because you own fire insurance.

A different fire regime exists high in the mountains where summer thunderstorms are more frequent. These are true forest fires, which are less intense and typically burn understory plants without destroying the crowns of mature trees. Generated by lightning, they burn themselves out in the absence of Santa Ana winds. Many trees, such as Ponderosa pine

Once-healthy chaparral is being replaced by weeds.

(*Pinus ponderosa*) have adapted to these more frequent, lower-intensity fires, surviving with little or no damage.

Some plants, such as lodgepole pine (*Pinus contorta*) or manzanita (*Arctostaphylos* spp.), have cones or seeds that require fire or smoke in order to germinate. This begs the simple question: How often do you need to regenerate a manzanita or pine tree? How do they achieve such great size if they are getting burned up every few decades? The seeds of bigberry manzanita (*Arctostaphylos glauca*) require an accumulated duff layer over the seed to keep the seeds from burning up at the same time as the mother plants. This particular manzanita is not a stump sprouter, so it is killed by fire. About 40 or more years are required to allow for sufficient duff buildup, by which time the plants attain large mature sizes.

Humans have had a huge impact on fire frequency, leading to a tenfold increase in the number of fire events. A map depicting fires in northern San Diego County over the last century revealed that not even a single event was naturally caused. Frequent fires have converted many native ecosystems into weedy cow pastures. It is the non-native systems that are made to burn. Introduced grasses and weeds come from areas with frequent summer thunderstorm activity, and are therefore adapted to recurrent fire. Conversion to flashy fuels has become a self-fulfilling fire prophecy.

Effect of invasives

Frequent fires and weed invasions combine to destroy and convert native ecosystems. Historically, when chaparral burned, wildflowers would proliferate in the carbon-enriched soil, providing the necessary carbohydrates to sustain the mycorrhizal grid. This was essential when none of the chlorophyll-producing shrubs were available to supply the necessary sugars. The mycorrhizae, in return, provided minerals and nutrition to the recovering shrubs—those that can stump sprout after fires. Non-stump sprouters began to reproduce from the seed, which was protected under a heavy layer of duff. The whole ecology experienced a phased recovery, going from pioneer plants (wildflowers, perennials, and seed-sprouting shrubs) through sub-climax species (fire-adapted shrubs) through climax species (long-lived, stress-tolerant shrubs and trees). This is known as ecological succession.

Nothing disrupts this process like weeds. These invasive plants knock out the recovery process right from the start. They germinate more quickly and grow faster than non-competitive native wildflowers. The carbon in the soil provides all the nutrition they need. Weeds outcompete and completely suppress the germination and growth of the wildflowers. Weeds utilize the moisture and free nutrition in the soil, providing nothing to the struggling mycorrhizal grid. Or worse, some weeds opportunistically connect to the grid and devour all of its moisture and nutrition. In either case, the fungal network collapses, taking the native plant community with it. In this way, a whole ecosystem can be destroyed in just a couple of fire cycles.

The effect of weeds does not stop there. Cool-season annuals go to seed and die by mid summer. All moisture they utilize is lost to the system, leading to desertification, or complete desiccation of the ecology. Since the annual weeds are full of cellulose, the rich accumulation of dry organic matter above ground is tinder dry and ready to burn. These fuels are flashy, so large areas can ignite simultaneously. Although less intense than a chaparral fire, wind-driven infernos move quickly, sometimes 65 miles per hour or faster. Firefighters are often hard-pressed to get their equipment out of the way of grass fires. Conversely, the higher- and hotter-burning fires in chaparral tend to be spottier. The resulting mix of the flashy ladder fuel of weeds and debris of degraded chaparral due to annual weed invasion is explosive.

Recognizing the flammability associated with dry, dead weeds, most California communities have instituted weed abatement programs to minimize fire danger. Unfortunately, the method most commonly used is discing—plowing the field and turning the soil over. This completely disturbs the soil and incorporates all the weedy organic matter and alien seed into the ground. Thus, discing for weed eradication ensures continued weed proliferation.

A far preferable method of weed abatement is well-timed mowing.

Mowing before the weeds have set seed is the best. The soil is not over-turned or fertilized with copious organic matter, and seed in the soil is minimized, reducing the next year's crop. Mowing traditionally occurs after seed has set. This one change—to mow and use herbicidal controls prior to seed-set—ultimately helps eradicate weedy species, especially if any remnant natural ecology is left undisturbed.

The role of natives in wildfire situations

Media would almost have you believe that if you plant a native landscape around your house the natives will spontaneously combust and burn down your house, whereas in reality just the opposite is proving to be true. Native vegetation, when appropriately hydrated, can be as fire-resistant as any other form of vegetation. No one can guarantee that your home will remain unscathed in a firestorm, but well-planned native landscaping can improve the chance of its survival as well or better than any other form of landscape.

Thunderstorms, though infrequent, sometimes occur in the chaparral. Even though these are summer events, the native ecosystem is able to tolerate and even benefit from occasional downpours. Dust washes from the leaves. Higher humidity curtails loss of moisture. Water is absorbed through diffusion processes and through leaf pores in some plants. These exact processes need to be further examined through rigorous testing. However, the bottom line is that plants hydrated after a thunderstorm are less likely to burn. Native plants tolerate occasional summer hydration because there is not enough rainfall to saturate the hot soil and promote plant pathogens. A similar scenario plays out in fall, when early rains reduce or eliminate fire threat, even during succeeding Santa Ana winds when relative humidity drops dramatically.

One way to emulate the occasional hydrating summer thunderstorm, or even fog drip, is to apply light, occasional overhead irrigation throughout the warm months, from roughly early June to mid October. The amount of moisture delivered can be slight—approximately a quarter inch of precipitation per watering. That equates to about 40 minutes on a micro-rotator-type irrigation system. Set the watering interval on an established landscape to once every 10 to 14 days, depending on location and exposure. Steep inland slopes may be watered as frequently as every 7 to 10 days, depending on exposure. Each watering is well within the tolerance range of most natives (as are summer thunderstorms or fog drip). The goal is to "dust off" the leaves and wet the mulch, but not saturate hot soil, thus avoiding pathogen problems.

Drought-tolerant native plants hang onto their moisture even in the face of flames. Other plants also exhibit this property; however, it typically requires much less water to hydrate a native plant than an exotic. An interesting incident in the 2007 Witch Creek fire clearly illustrates the difference. Groundcover rosemary (*Rosmarinus officinalis*) was growing on a client's slope. A wild flattop buckwheat (*Eriogonum fasciculatum*) had sprung up as a volunteer amid the rosemary. The area where they grew received light watering once every two weeks. During the course of the fire, the rosemary was incinerated into a charred black smudge. In contrast, the buckwheat, which most consider a "fire bomb," came through the fire covered in green leaves. Clearly the rosemary was not receiving enough moisture to remain hydrated, whereas, the buckwheat was. Ironically, often the plants we consider highly combustible benefit the most

New growth on buckwheat emerges after a fire, while rosemary remains a black smudge. It takes less moisture to hydrate a native plant than a "drought-tolerant" exotic.

from supplemental watering. Climatological data confirm that southern California is the driest of the world's five Mediterranean climate zones. From empirical observation, plants from other Mediterranean regions of the world require about twice as much moisture as California native plants to maintain similar levels of hydration. Note that these suppositions should be examined and tested.

Fire resistance in natives has less to do with plant selection than with hydration. A study conducted by Bert Wilson of Las Pilitas Nursery examined the relative ignition times of selected native and non-native plants when exposed to a propane torch. The data included whether or not they were hydrated. Although not scientifically controlled, the results are useful as a relative measure. Some plants that would ignite in 15 seconds unhydrated took over a minute to do so once hydrated. Many of the ignition times for natives far exceeded those for non-natives under the same conditions. Mr. Wilson's interest in doing this experiment resulted from his experience and observations as a volunteer firefighter for San Luis Obispo County for 14 years.

Defending your home against fire

Vegetation often has nothing to do with whether or not a structure burns. Some of the most important steps you can take to defend your home against fire involve the architecture of the house itself. Important fire-defense areas include roofing, vents, eaves, windows, and secondary elements that immediately contact your house, like shade structures, decks, and fences. Your local fire department has information on fireproofing the structure of your home. Vulnerable practices such as wood shake roof shingles are now banned in most communities.

Defensible space around the home

In the panic following the great San Diego firestorm of October 2003, many agencies and insurance carriers required that surrounding property be cleared of vegetation for 100, 200, even 300 feet or more. This environmental devastation of huge swaths of land caused horrible erosion problems, and the establishment of flashy-fueled non-native grasses and weeds by the following August. Even worse, many homes whose surrounding landscape had been cleared to bare mineral soil for hundreds of feet *still* burned to the ground, sometimes amid green lawn and palm trees. This certainly runs counter to the conventional wisdom that wholesale removal of vegetation prevents destruction by fire from happening.

We repeat: Maintaining low-growing, hydrated groundcovers and shrubs disrupts and cools the otherwise uninterrupted flow of fire. Expanses of clear, mineral soil may not be defensible. Allowing thinned and maintained natural vegetation to remain, in addition to irrigated landscape plantings may, in fact, help prevent structures from igniting.

Fire Defense Zone 1

It is critical that firefighters have a perimeter or zone around a house where they can safely fight a fire. This area is known as "defensible space."

This homeowner completely cleared all vegetation for hundreds of feet, leaving the home exposed to fast-moving embers in a firestorm and erosion.

The first 30 feet is probably the most critical. A passing fire crew quickly assesses whether it is safe to stop and set up a perimeter or to move on. You want to have a considerable amount of hardscape—flagstone, boulders, pavers, cement, gravel, etc.—in the first zone. Avoid planting directly underneath the eaves of the house. It is prudent to create an apron about 4 feet out from the house simply covered in gravel or concrete. Just these aprons alone have been proven to save homes during wildfires.

Plants near the house should be either lower growing or have an open "see-through" structure to limit potential fuel for a fire. They should be hydrated with once-per-week watering. Most conventional landscape plants are appropriate. However, many native perennials and low-growing shrubs would work well in this area.

Fire Defense Zone 2

Zone 2 is the area 30 to 100 feet from your house. Zone 2 may extend up to 300 feet if your house is located on a ridge or at the end of a north- or east-facing box canyon. If there is existing chaparral growing in Zone 2, thin it by about 50 percent. This one step removes about 70 percent of the fuel volume. Clear cutting or bulldozing only creates more problems. Thinning may involve cutting the shrubs back as much as to the ground, but *not* removing the roots. Thinning prevents further erosion and soil disturbance that encourages even more weeds in the future. Chamise (*Adenostoma fasciculatum*), laurel sumac (*Malosma laurina*) growing near the house, and maybe some buckwheat (*Eriogonum fasciculatum*) and sage (*Salvia* spp.) are targeted first for thinning. Plants like manzanita (*Arctostaphylos* spp.), California lilac (*Ceanothus* spp.), hollyleaf cherry (*Prunus ilicifolia*), lemonadeberry (*Rhus integrifolia*), and bush rue (*Cneoridium dumosum*) are usually preserved, although dead wood should be removed.

Open up plants' structure whenever possible by pruning lower branches. Mulch all trimmings and then, to help suppress weeds, return the mulch to the areas where the plants were thinned out. This is also an opportunity to lace the area with 4- to 5-foot-wide paths that double as firebreaks and further open up the vegetation. Bring in benches, birdbaths, non-woody perennials, signage, and other features to transform once-impenetrable

Thin natural vegetation within 100 feet of a home. Paths and features carve out a mature native landscape.

Low-density, fire-resistant landscaping within 30 feet of a home.

chaparral into an inviting, mature native landscape. It is not necessary to destroy the environment in the name of fire safety. There are many creative, aesthetic landscaping "solutions" that lower the risk of fire danger.

Maintenance Considerations

Good site maintenance is critical for fire safety. Non-native weeds are typically annuals and perennials that are dead or dormant by August. They are rich in lignin. Their dry, dead carcasses sit on top of the soil. Compare this to wildflowers, which are reabsorbed into the soil after they die; by summer there is little evidence of the previous spring's show. Unlike native chaparral that tolerates intense but infrequent fires, non-native weeds welcome and promote frequent burning. Responsible maintenance dictates that they be controlled and removed.

Most healthy and undisturbed native plant communities, by virtue of their specialized and finely adapted ecology, do not support the growth

Rhus regrowth from stump after fire.

of non-native annual weeds. The litter layer or mulch formed by these natives kills most weeds. Additionally, most of the native plant community's nutrition is contained in the mycorrhizal fungi and is not available to the weeds (which are usually non-mycorrhizal). Disturbing the plant community opens up the canopy and makes nutrition available to invasives. Even thinning and removing 50 percent of the existing chaparral canopy, while not as disruptive as wholesale clear-cutting or removal, is like creating an open sore, allowing for weed infection—thus, the need for continuous weed control.

One home in the 2003 Cedar fire was partly saved by chaparral thinning and accompanying weed control. These measures reduced the heat and intensity of the flames. A dramatic demonstration was a mission manzanita (*Xylococcus bicolor*) that had a dead knot burned out at the base of the plant, yet the rest of the shrub was completely intact. The weeds had been controlled, so the smoldering natural duff layer could generate only enough heat to ignite the dead wood and had no effect on the living tissue.

Because this homeowner removed the weeds, only the dead knot wood of the manzanita burned, leaving the rest of the plant unscathed.

Left to their own devices, weeds will severely compromise the ecology of native plant communities by robbing moisture and nutrition from the system. Worse, they act as fire ladders into the remaining native shrubs and trees now weakened and even more fire prone. This is the worst of all possible situations—an unhealthy plant community depleted of its moisture and full of highly combustible dry tinder. Death of annual weeds by summer's end leads to desertification. Humidity levels drop in the weedy areas, because no moisture is being held onto in living tissue. Unfortunately, this describes what is happening in much of California.

Controlling annual weeds can be challenging. Using tree trimmings for mulch helps. Hand pulling may be sufficient in small areas. However, with a typical seed bank of 10,000 to 100,000 seeds per cubic foot, post- and/or pre-emergent chemical treatment may be required. Whatever method is chosen, it is essential that the site be maintained as weed free as possible once it has been opened up.

Keeping the canopy coverage pruned to around 50 percent is important for fire safety. Whenever possible, prune trees 6 feet up from their base. Keep shorter perennials and shrubs pruned to a height of about 18 inches when practical. A good rule of thumb is to provide clearance *between* tree limbs and groundcover (shrubs, perennials) of at least three times the height of the lower plants. Remove all dead wood. Most plants that have been cut to the ground annually, like chamise (*Adenostoma fasciculatum*), will regenerate from basal burls. Allow the plants to grow for up to one year, then cut them to the ground again once their newer green growth starts to become woody.

If Zone 2 (30 to 100 feet from the house) is cleared and planted in irrigated natives, the maintenance routine is straightforward. These plants should be lower-growing (under 18 inches) and spaced for final size. This prevents overcrowded plants from forming a flammable woody thatch. Mulch with shredded redwood bark (gorilla hair) matted down with water so that it is poorly aerated. Thickly applied mulch is effective at controlling annual weeds, especially when combined with hand weeding, or with pre-emergents in large, hard-to-maintain areas where hand pulling is not practical.

Fire-wise planning and planting

Zone 1 must be irrigated, ideally with overhead irrigation at least once a week. This ensures that the plants are always hydrated and less likely to burn. Install lots of hardscape (flagstone, interlocking pavers, decomposed granite, gravel, etc.), including an apron of these same materials extending beyond the eave line. Numerous native plants will both tolerate this frequent watering and provide low fuel volume. Some attractive evergreen shrubs meeting these requirements include: lower-growing manzanitas like *Arctostaphylos edmundsii* 'Carmel Sur', *A. uva-ursi* 'Radiant', *A.* 'Emerald Carpet', and *A.* 'Pacific Mist'; as well as medium-height manzanitas like 'Sunset' and 'Howard McMinn'; lower-growing, garden-tolerant wild lilacs *Ceanothus thyrsiflorus* var. *repens*, *Ceanothus gloriosus* 'Heart's Desire' and 'Anchor Bay'. Native perennials for these conditions include seaside daisy (*Erigeron glaucus*), Matole River fuchsia (*Epilobium septentrionalis*), and goldenrod (*Solidago* spp.). Monkey flower (*Mimulus aurantiacus*) may be shorter-lived, but will put on a show for the two to five years it survives. Just get a new one when it dies. A good decorative mulch is 6- to 12-inch boulders placed on the plants' rootballs surrounded by gorilla hair, but the bark must be watered down to compact it immediately after planting.

Zone 2 ideally consists of either thinned chaparral or lightly hydrated native plantings. Coyote brush (*Baccharis pilularis* 'Pigeon Point'), California lilac (*Ceanothus* 'Yankee Point'), manzanita (*Arctostaphylos* 'John Dourley'), and San Diego marsh elder (*Iva hayesiana*) are all excellent choices for this area. A smattering of larger shrubs, such as *Ceanothus* 'Blue Jeans' and 'Concha', coffeeberry (*Rhamnus californica* 'Eve Case' and 'Mound San Bruno'), and toyon (*Heteromeles arbutifolia*) are all fine. Plant them in groups of three or less to prevent creating a large fuel mass. Leave about 10 feet between these small groups of larger shrubs.

Create small firebreaks by incorporating lots of trails or paths at least 4 feet wide in this area. Fully established Zone 2 plantings must be irrigated with overhead irrigation about once every 8 to 14 days during the warm months to promote adequate hydration. It may be possible to lightly

After a 2007 fire, this native slope was scorched but not burned, saving the wooden deck at the back of the house.

Three years after the fire, the native slope has completely recovered.

irrigate existing chaparral in Zone 2 as long as the natural soil is not saturated. Test results are pending.

The importance of reversing current fire patterns

Fire in southern California is an unfortunate inevitability. Ironically, prescribed burning is used to "reduce fuel" and create a "mosaic" of age classes in vegetation. Simply looking at the reburn of many 2003 fire areas by the 2007 fires shows the fallacy of this method. Frequent intentional burns only speed up the conversion to weeds. The same is true for mastication, where large swaths of old-growth chaparral are being crushed and disturbed, often miles away from population centers.

Fuel reduction in areas immediately surrounding our communities is just as important as it is for individual properties. Mowing or thinning

Barely recovering vegetation from a 2003 fire, reburned in 2007, indicating prescribed burns may not be a useful fire control strategy.

chaparral around the borders of a neighborhood creates defensible space, as does planting fire-resistant natives in a 100 to 300-foot swath around communities. Native plants provide appropriate habitat, while permanent systems for light irrigation keep it hydrated. Such landscaping provides beautiful transitional buffers from the natural chaparral areas.

Many people, even professionals, advocate doing nothing, averring that chaparral "needs" to burn and these burn cycles are a natural part of the native ecology. Prior to human habitation, the ecology developed adaptations that allowed it to recover from intense but infrequent fires. Human-caused high-frequency fire is destroying our native ecosystems and replacing them with dry weeds. Not only has this resulted in extensive habitat loss, but the resulting desertification and dry flashy tinder is feeding even more fires in a vicious cycle. Erosion and landslides are increasing as the natural vegetation disappears. Soon the only year-round green areas will be those that are artificially irrigated. We, humans, are transforming the once-beautiful, -green, and -diverse California landscape into a dried-out hulk of its former self. We know what have to do—we can, and we must!

CONCLUSION
A vision for beautiful, healthful landscapes

We envision a new approach to landscaping in California; one that is much more purposeful, healthier, and sustainable. The new landscape is full of color, fragrance, and wildlife, yet easy to maintain and free of pollution. No fertilizers fill our waterways with algae. Yards become extensions of open space. Streets are tented by arching oak canopies providing cooling summer shade. Native birds and butterflies cavort around our homes. Water usage plummets. Beautiful scenery dominates every window.

The expanding use of natives to create ecologically responsible landscapes throughout our communities portends a bright future for us all.

U TOPIAN? Perhaps, but every life change starts with a dream, and this one is achievable with will and education. It is not a purist manifesto. Instead, it is a defined concept based on a realistic model. People can have their rose garden or poolside oasis; children will have places to play. It is simply a shift to a wiser, more natural protocol where native plants are predominant, rather than the exception. New ways of understanding and designing with California's plants mean yards can be as trim and clean, or as carefree and wild as we desire. Ironically, this "new approach" is about returning to the essence and wisdom of nature. Although we can replicate any garden style with California native plants, our natural identity and ecology will always be the basis.

The new neighborhood

Expecting all of California to suddenly convert to native landscaping is far fetched. So for now, let us consider one grassroots effort. Imagine a neighborhood that looks like it was built in the middle of a natural forest. Current housing developments have many trees, but they are principally exotics, like eucalyptus, tristania, or, worse, palms. This enlightened developer decided to do something that would benefit not only the bottom line, but also the experience of all those who would live in and pass through the idyllic housing tract. The original cost for the landscape installation was kept reasonable by using primarily 1-gallon plants placed to their mature size—the street trees were larger. The developer also utilized credits for on-site mitigation (for the environmental impacts caused by the housing tract) obtained for using an all-native, regionally appropriate plant palette. More money was saved by not having to purchase soil amendments.

New residents of the project now enjoy much lower homeowner's association (HOA) dues and do not suffer weekly noise pollution from mow-and-blow maintenance. Despite the surrounding abundance of natural beauty and park-like settings, the common areas and green space use only 20 percent of the water and 30 percent of the maintenance required by the same features in other developments.

This smart developer created quite a buzz around the project, with all its positive environmental and cost-saving features. A beautiful, rustic entry monument beckons people in, as if they are about to enter a national park. The units sold quickly, and continue to increase in value as the residents delight in the following benefits.

Lower inputs

None of the front yards have lawns; rather, they have colorful groundcovers, shrubs, and trees. Because the majority of plants are evergreen, almost no maintenance is required. The HOA holds classes on basic native plant maintenance so most of the residents are able to do their own work, which amounts to just a few hours per month. People have the option of doing what they want in their backyards, so they may have roses, veggie gardens, exotics, and even lawns if they choose. However, most people continue the native theme in their backyards since that was what attracted them to this development in the first place. Plus, they like the idea of saving work and money!

A woodland neighborhood.

A functioning bioswale full of rainwater.

Except for those who create thirsty landscapes in the backyard, the monthly water bills are negligible. Water usage is only 10–20 percent of that in neighboring developments. Since many water agencies now have escalating tiered water rates, most of the water bills remain in the least-costly first tier. In addition, such light watering allows the native plants to maintain a high degree of pest resistance (with no white fly or scale in wild plant communities). Avian and insect predators usually consume the few pests that try to attack. Fertilizer expense is spared since native landscapes do not require fertilizer. With so little effort required by the homeowners, residents spend their limited leisure time enjoying, rather than working in, their landscapes.

Less pollution

Mycorrhizal soils have tremendous moisture capacity. With so little supplemental irrigation required, there is no runoff from the landscape into storm drains. Any minimal drainage is clean and unpolluted by pesticides and fertilizer. However, those with conventional landscapes in back have additional measures in place. Bioswales in all common areas collect runoff from housing areas. These attractive swales use large boulders set in meandering courses to emulate natural dry streams. The swales catch all the runoff and allow it to stay on-site, within the development, so that it can percolate into the soil. The drainage areas are planted with riparian vegetation like sedges and willows that absorb the excess nutrients and moisture. Small field sedges adjacent to the wetter areas create open, meadow-like regions, much like turf, and can be used the same way. Not only do these areas help contain any possible contaminants, but they also create beautiful focal points full of bird life.

Increased wildlife attraction

Nothing attracts native birds and butterflies like native plants. These gardens provide all the forage, cover, and protected nesting areas that our flying friends require. Homeowners no longer need to maintain messy bird feeders that contaminate the soil with weeds while drawing rodents and non-native bird species. Particularly superfluous are hummingbird feeders, since vast numbers of California native plants are hummingbird pollinated. Homeowners delight in the amazing number of these tiny, colorful birds visiting their landscapes each day. Now the hummers receive balanced meals of gnats and nectar as opposed to getting "drunk" on sugar water. No more ants swarming beneath messy, sticky feeders that need to be cleaned and refilled regularly. No more birds suffering with nasty bill infections from communal use and feeder contamination.

Masses of butterflies visit the neighborhood to feed and reproduce. Swallowtails on sycamores, monarchs on milkweed—the housing tract is not only beautiful, it is also providing large-scale, quality habitat. People are stunned to see checkerspots, gulf fritillaries, spotted sulphurs, and the rarest and most beautiful of all, the dogface butterfly. Few residents have ever seen this gorgeous yellow, black, and pink insect before, even though it is our state butterfly. Fortunately, the visionary developer included false indigo bush (*Amorpha* sp.) in the plant palette around the sycamores and

Rarely seen dogface butterfly, California's state butterfly, may become more common around our homes as native garden habitat increases.

oak trees, attracting this beautiful insect with the lightly colored canine silhouette on each of the male's wings. Everyone is benefitting by this foresight.

Quality of life

People start to comment that coming home from work is like going on vacation. They are literally surrounded by natural California. Their homes feel more like the Ahwahnee Hotel in Yosemite than a house in a typical subdivision. As time goes by the street trees grow surprisingly fast. Oaks and sycamores begin to span the streets to form living bowers. The sounds of birds are everywhere. It is a quality of life to which so many would aspire.

Is this a dream? Not necessarily. We have the means to begin making it a reality, right now. We have the technology that can be implemented with little or no additional cost. In fact, a subdivision-scale nativescape would save huge amounts of money and resources over time. All that is needed now is the vision and determination to make it happen.

RESOURCES

Books and articles

Anderson, M. Kat. 2005. *Trading the Wild*. Berkeley: University of California Press.

Bakker, Elna. 1971. *An Island Called California*. Berkeley: University of California Press.

Balls, Edward K. *Early Uses of California Plants*. California Natural History Guide. Berkeley: University of California Press.

Barbour, Michael, Bruce Pavlik, Frank Drysdale, and Susan Lindstrom. 1991. *California's Changing Landscapes: Diversity and Conservation of California Vegetation*. Sacramento: California Native Plant Society.

Belzer, Thomas J. 1984. *Roadside Plants of Southern California*. Missoula, Montana: Mountain Press Publishing.

Bornstein, Carol, David Fross, and Bart O'Brien. 2005. *California Native Plants for the Garden*. Los Olivos, California: Cachuma Press.

Bossard, Carla C., John M. Randall, and Marc C. Hoshovsky. 2000. *Invasive Plants of California's Wildlands*. Berkeley: University of California Press.

Brenzel, Kathleen Norris, ed. 2012. *The New Sunset Western Garden Book: The Ultimate Gardening Guide*. New York: Time Home Entertainment, Inc.

Brookes, John. 1991. *The Book of Garden Design*. New York: MacMillan Publishing Company.

Civilian Conservation Corps. 1939. *Collecting and Handling Seeds of Wild Plants, Forestry Publication No. 5*. Washington, D.C.: United States Government Printing Office.

Cohen, Ronnie, Barry Nelson, and Gary Wolff. 2004. *Energy Down the Drain: The Hidden Costs of California's Water Supply*. Oakland, California: Natural Resources Defense Council.

Connelly, Kevin. 1991. *Gardener's Guide to California Wildflowers*. Sun Valley, California: The Theodore Payne Foundation.

Crampton, Beecher. 1974. *Grasses in California*. Berkeley: University of California Press.

Dale, Nancy. 1986. *Flowering Plants, The Santa Monica Mountains Coastal and Chaparral Regions of Southern California*. Santa Barbara, California: Capra Press.

De Hart, Jeanine. 1994. *Propagation Secrets for California Native Plants*. Encinitas, California: Jeanine De Hart.

Duffield, Mary Rose, and Warren D. Jones. 1981. *Plants for Dry Climates*. Los Angeles, California: HP Books.

Emery, Dara E. 1988. *Seed Propagation of Native California Plants*. Santa Barbara, California: Santa Barbara Botanic Garden.

Farnsworth, Kahanah. 2005. *Taste of Nature: Edible Plants of the Southwest and*

How to Prepare Them. Benton Harbor, Michigan: Patterson Printing.

Francis, Mark, and Andreas Reimann. 1999. *The California Landscape Garden.* Berkeley: University of California Press.

Fross, David, and Dieter Wilken. 2006. *Ceanothus.* Portland, Oregon: Timber Press.

Gilmer, Maureen. 1994. *California Wildfire Landscaping.* Dallas, Texas: Taylor Publishing Company.

Hall, Clarence A., Jr. 2007. *Introduction to the Geology of California and its Native Plants.* Berkeley: University of California Press.

Halsey, Richard W. 2005. *Fire, Chaparral, and Survival in Southern California.* San Diego, California: Sunbelt Publications.

Heinz, The H. John Center for Science, Economics and the Environment. 2008. *Landscape Pattern Indicators for the Nation.* Washington, D.C.: Island Press.

Hickman, James C., ed. 1993. *The Jepson Manual: Higher Plants of California.* Berkeley: University of California Press.

Howard, Arthur D. 1979. *Geologic History of Middle California.* Berkeley: University of California Press.

Jepson, Willis Linn. 1925. *A Manual of the Flowering Plants of California.* Berkeley, California: Associated Students Store.

Keator, Glenn. 1990. *Complete Garden Guide to Native Perennials of California.* San Francisco, California: Chronicle Books.

Keator, Glenn. 1994. *Complete Garden Guide to Native Shrubs of California.* San Francisco, California: Chronicle Books.

Keator, Glenn, and Alrie Middlebrook. 2007. *Designing California Native Gardens: The Plant Community Approach to Artful, Ecological Gardens.* Berkeley: University of California Press.

Kozloff, Eugene N., and Linda H. Beidleman. 1994. *Plants of the San Francisco Bay Region.* Pacific Grove, California: Sagen Press.

Kruckeberg, Arthur R. 1984. *California Serpentines: Flora, Vegetation, Geology, Soils, and Management Problems.* Berkeley: University of California Press.

Krupnick, Gary A., and W. John Kress, eds. 2005. *Plant Conservation: A Natural History Approach.* Chicago, Illinois: University of Chicago Press.

Landis, Betsey. 1999. *Southern California Native Plants for School Gardens*, Sacramento: California Native Plant Society.

Lenz, Lee W. 1956. *Native Plants for California Gardens.* Claremont, California: Rancho Santa Ana Botanic Garden.

Lenz, Lee W., and John Dourley. 1981. *California Native Trees and Shrubs.* Claremont, California: Rancho Santa Ana Botanic Garden.

Lightner, James. 2006. *San Diego County Native Plants.* 2nd ed. San Diego, California: San Diego Flora.

Lowry, Judith Larner. 1999. *Gardening with a Wild Heart: Restoring California's Native Landscapes at Home.* Berkeley: University of California Press.

McPhee, John. 1992. *Assembling California.* New York: The Noonday Press.

Miller, George Oxford, and Julian Duval. 2008. *Landscaping with Native Plants in Southern California.* St. Paul, Minneapolis: Voyageur Press.

Minnich, Richard A. 2008. *California's Fading Wildflowers: Lost Legacy and Biological Invasions.* Berkeley: University of California Press.

Munz, Phillip A., and David D. Keck. 1973. *A California Flora and Supplement.* Berkeley: University of California Press.

Myers, N., R. A. Mittermeier, C. G. Mittermeier, G. A. B. da Fonseca, and J. Kent.

2000. Biodiversity Hotspots for Conservation Priorities. *Nature* 403: 853–858.

Native Revival Nursery. 2000. *A Gardeners Guide to California Native Plants*. Aptos, California: Native Revival Nursery.

Niehaus, Theodore F., Roger Tory Peterson, and Charles L. Ripper. 1976. *A Field Guide to Pacific States Wildflowers: Washington, Oregon, California and Adjacent Areas*. Petersen Field Guide. New York: Houghton Mifflin Company.

O'Brien, Bart, Betsey Landis, and Ellen Mackey. 2006. *Care and Maintenance of Southern California Native Plant Gardens*. Claremont, California: Rancho Santa Ana Botanic Garden.

Ornduff, Robert. 2003. *Introduction to California Plant Life*. California Natural History Guides. Berkeley: University of California Press.

Pavlick, Bruce M., Pamela Muick, Sharon Johnson, and Marjorie Popper. 1991. *Oaks of California*. Los Olivos, California: Cachuma Press.

Perry, Bob. 1987. *Trees and Shrubs for Dry California Landscapes*. Claremont, California: Land Design Publishing.

Perry, Bob. 1992. *Landscape Plants for Western Regions*. Claremont, California: Land Design Publishing.

Perry, Bob. 2010. *Landscape Plants for California Gardens*. Claremont, California: Land Design Publishing.

Phillips, Judith. 1987. *Southwestern Landscaping with Native Plants*. Santa Fe: Museum of New Mexico Press.

Rawls, James J., and Walton Bean. 2003. *California: An Interpretive History*. 8th ed. Columbus, Ohio: McGraw-Hill.

Rowntree, Lester. 2006. *Hardy Californians: A Woman's Life with Native Plants*. Berkeley: University of California Press.

Sauer, Jonathan D. 1988. *Plant Migration: The Dynamics of Geographic Patterning in Seed Plant Species*. Berkeley: University of California Press.

Schmidt, Marjorie G., and Katherine L. Greenberg. 2012. *Growing California Native Plants*. 2nd ed. Berkeley: University of California Press.

Showers, Mary Ann. 1999. *Nursery Sources for California Native Plants*. Sacramento, California: Office of Mine Reclamation.

Soil Survey Staff, Natural Resources Conservation Service, United States Department of Agriculture. Web Soil Survey. http://websoilsurvey.nrcs.usda.gov.

Smith, M. Nevin. 2006. *Native Treasures: Gardening with the Plants of California*. Berkeley: University of California Press.

Thomas, John Hunter. 1961. *Flora of the Santa Cruz Mountains of California: A Manual of the Vascular Plants*. Stanford, California: Stanford University Press.

Thurston, Carl. 1936. *Wildflowers of Southern California*. Pasadena, California: Esto Publishing Company.

Van Atta, Susan, and Peter Gaede. 2009. *The Southern California Native Flower Garden: A Guide to Size, Bloom, Foliage, Color and Texture*. Layton, Utah: Gibbs Smith.

Wasowski, Sally, with Andy Wasowski. 2000. *Native Landscaping from El Paso to L.A.* Chicago, Illinois: Contemporary Books.

Whitson, Tom, et al. 1996. *Weeds of the West*. 5th ed. Newark, California, and Jackson, Wyoming: The Western Society of Weed Science in cooperation with the Western United States Land Grant Universities Cooperative Extension Services and the University of Wyoming.

Wilson, Bert. 1996. *Manual of California Native Plants*. Santa Margarita, California: Las Pilitas Nursery.

Online resources

The following resources do not sell native plants but include organizations with information regarding native plant horticulture.

California's Own Native Landscape Design, Escondido
www.calown.com

California Native Grasslands Association, Davis
www.cnga.org

California Native Plant Society, Sacramento
www.cnps.org

California Gardens
www.californiagardens.com

California Society for Ecological Restoration, Bakersfield
www.sercal.org

Growing Native
www.growingnative.com

Jepson Interchange, Berkeley
ucjeps.berkeley.edu/interchange.html

University of California Integrated Pest Management
www.ipm.ucdavis.edu

Sources for California Native Plants and Seeds, from the Sonoma County Master Gardener Program
ucce.ucdavis.edu/files/filelibrary/5669/33468.pdf

Regional chapters of the California Native Plant Society

Networking with members of the California Native Plant Society is a wonderful way to find out about the resources and opportunities in your area. Members are the people with their fingers on the pulse who are growing or attempting to grow local native plants. They know which nurseries carry natives, which are new, and which have bitten the dust.

Alta Peak, Tulare County
altapeakcnps.wordpress.com

Bristlecone, Owens Valley
bristleconecnps.org

Channel Islands, mid coastal, Ventura
www.cnpsci.org

Dorothy King Young, northern Coastal area, Mendocino and Sonoma counties
www.dkycnps.org

East Bay, eastern Bay Area, Orinda
www.ebcnps.org

El Dorado, El Dorado County, Placerville
www.eldoradocnps.org

Kern County
www.kerncnps.org

Los Angeles–Santa Monica Mountains
lasmmcnps.org

Marin, Marin County
www.marin.edu/cnps

Milo Baker, Sonoma County
www.cnpsmb.org

Mojave Desert, northern and eastern
San Bernardino County
www.mojavecnps.org

Monterey Bay, Monterey and San Benito
counties
www.montereybaycnps.org

Mount Lassen, Butte, Glenn, Tehama,
and Plumas counties
mountlassen.cnps.org

Napa Valley, Napa, St. Helena, and Cal-
istoga areas
www.napavalleycnps.org

North Coast, Eureka, Arcata, and
McKinleyville area
northcoastcnps.org

North San Joaquin Valley, Merced, Stan-
islaus, and South San Joaquin counties
nsj.cnps.org

Orange County
www.occnps.org

Redbud, Placer and Nevada counties
www.redbud-cnps.org

Riverside–San Bernardino
www.enceliacnps.org

Sacramento Valley, Sacramento, Yolo,
Colusa, Sutter, Yuba, and Lower Placer
counties
www.sacvalleycnps.org

San Diego, San Diego and Imperial
counties
www.cnpssd.org

San Gabriel Mountains, San Gabriel and
eastern San Fernando Valley
www.cnps-sgm.org

Santa Clara Valley, central and southern
San Francisco Peninsula and South
Bay
www.cnps-scv.org

San Luis Obispo
www.cnps-slo.org

Santa Cruz County
www.cruzcnps.org

Sequoia, Madera and Fresno counties
www.cnps-sequoia.org

Shasta, Shasta, Siskiyou, Modoc, Trinity,
and Tehama counties
www.sierrafoothillscnps.org

South Coast, Palos Verdes Peninsula
area
www.sccnps.org

Tahoe, Tahoe Basin
(no website listed)

Willis Linn Jepson, Solano County
www.cnpsjepson.org

Yerba Buena, City of San Francisco and
northern San Mateo County
www.cnps-yerbabuena.org

California native plant sources

Many of the following seed companies and propagators are wholesale; others are retail nurseries that stock at least some California native plants. Some are specialty growers of one type of plant, e.g., iris. Reviewing the websites will provide a visual and informational bounty as you learn about and seek the perfect plants for your landscape.

Acterra Wholesale Native Nursery, Palo Alto
www.acterra.org

Aitkens's Salmon Creek Gardens, Vancouver, Washington
www.flowerfantasy.net

Anderson's Seed Co, Escondido
www.seedcoseeds.com

Bay Natives, San Francisco
www.baynatives.com

California Flora Nursery, Fulton
www.calfloranursery.com

Central Coast Wilds, Santa Cruz
www.centralcoastwilds.com

Clyde Robin Seed Co., Inc., Castro Valley
www.clyderobin.com

Cornflower Farms, Elk Grove
www.cornflowerfarms.com

Elkhorn Native Plant Nursery, Moss Landing and Soquel
www.elkhornnursery.com

El Nativo Growers, Inc., Azusa
www.elnativogrowers.com

Environmental Seed Producers, Inc., Lompoc
www.espseeds.com

Far West Bulb Farm, Grass Valley
www.californianativebulbs.com

Floral Native Nursery, Williams, Oregon
www.forestfarm.com

Freshwater Farms, Eureka
www.freshwaterfarms.com

Greer Gardens, Eugene, Oregon
www.greergardens.com

Growing Solutions, Santa Barbara
www.growingsolutions.org

Hedgerow Farms, Winters
www.hedgerowfarms.com

High Country Gardens, Santa Fe, New Mexico
www.highcountrygardens.com

Intermountain Nursery, Prather
www.intermountainnursery.com

J. L. Hudson, Seedsman, La Honda
www.jlhudsonseeds.net

Larner Seeds, Bolinas
www.larnerseeds.com

Las Pilitas Nursery, Escondido and Santa Margarita
www.laspilitas.com

The Living Desert Zoo and Gardens, Palm Desert
www.livingdesert.org

Manzanita Nursery, Solvang
www.manzanitanursery.com

Matilija Nursery, Moorpark
www.matilijanursery.com

Mockingbird Nursery, Riverside
www.mockingbirdnursery.com

Moosa Creek Nursery, Valley Center
www.moosacreeknursery.com

Mostly Natives Nursery, Tomales
www.mostlynatives.com

Mountain States Wholesale Nursery, Glendale, Arizona
www.mswn.com

Native Revival Nursery
www.nativerevival.com

Native Sons, Inc., Arroyo Grande
www.nativeson.com

North Coast Native Nursery, Petaluma
www.northcoastnativenursery.com

Plants of the Southwest, Albuquerque, New Mexico
www.plantsofthesouthwest.com

Rana Creek Habitat Restoration, Carmel
www.ranacreekdesign.com

Rancho Santa Ana Botanic Garden, Claremont
www.rsabg.org

RECON Native Plants, Inc., San Diego
www.reconnativeplants.com

The Reveg Edge, Redwood City
www.ecoseeds.com/nature.html

Rosendale Nursery, Watsonville
www.rosendalenursery.com

S&S Seeds, Carpinteria
www.ssseeds.com

San Marcos Growers, Santa Barbara
www.smgrowers.com

Santa Barbara Botanic Garden, Santa Barbara
www.sbbg.org

Santa Barbara Natives, Gaviota
www.sbnatives.com

Seedhunt, Freedom
www.seedhunt.com

Sierra Azul Nursery and Gardens, Watsonville
www.sierraazul.com

Siskiyou Rare Plant Nursery, Medford, Oregon
www.srpn.net

Specialty Oaks, Inc., Lower Lake
www.specialtyoaks.com

Stover Seed Company, Los Angeles
www.stoverseed.com

Suncrest Nurseries, Inc., Watsonville
www.suncrestnurseries.com

Tarweed Native Plants, Los Angeles
www.tarweednativeplants.com

Theodore Payne Foundation for Wild Flowers and Native Plants, Sun Valley
www.theodorepayne.org

Tree of Life Nursery, San Juan Capistrano
www.treeoflifenursery.com

Village Nurseries, Statewide
www.villagenurseries.com

Wildwood Gardens, Mollalla, Oregon
www.wildwoodgardens.net

Yerba Buena Nursery, Woodside
www.yerbabuenanursery.com

Index

364

feels like
HOME

RELAXED INTERIORS
FOR A MEANINGFUL LIFE

lauren liess

PHOTOGRAPHY BY HELEN NORMAN

ABRAMS, NEW YORK

To my parents, for always feeling like "home" to me.

CONTENTS

INTRODUCTION

"Our souls are not hungry for fame, comfort, wealth, or power. Our souls are hungry for meaning, for the sense that we have figured out how to live so that our lives matter."

HAROLD KUSHNER

AS A KID GROWING UP in a divorced family, the feeling of "coming home" to my parents after being separated from them for long periods of time was almost palpable. I lived in Virginia right outside of Washington, DC, with my mom and grandparents most of the time, and spent summers, long weekends, and holidays with my dad in a suburb outside of Chicago. I always felt a little torn between my two lives and homes—loving both of my parents equally but always missing one of them. Each home meant something different to me—I think partly due to the nature of "off" time versus "school time," and also partly because of who my parents are. Life at my dad's house was unbridled, carefree, and adventurous, and consisted of lots of running through fields and time on the water, whereas life at my mom's was full of routine, time with friends, special plans to look forward to, crafting, gardening, and walks in the woods. No matter how different my two lives were, the feeling of "home" I had when being reunited with the parent and house I'd been away from was the same. It felt like safety, comfort, and an intense joy or a gratitude of sorts where I saw and felt my home through rose-colored glasses hitting me all at once. I absorbed and felt so much just walking through the door—the smell, the objects, the light, but most of all, an all-encompassing sense of "home." I would just breathe in home and let it hug me, feeling utterly and completely swept up in the moment. Home and the love I had for my parents were deeply intertwined.

After hugging and kissing my parents (and then pets!) I'd run up to my bedroom—which always had a perfectly made bed and no mess yet—and greet my stuffed animals and touch all of my things. I'd look around at my room, feeling like it was this little part of me I'd been away from. I'd start unloading my books and getting everything just right. My mom often left a fresh arrangement of flowers from the garden on my nightstand in the warmer months, and my dad's fridge was always stocked with my favorite foods—including the sausage we could only get in Chicago. They didn't have to say a word to me, because these little displays of love throughout the house let me know I'd been missed. I have forgotten so much of my childhood, but I remember these moments and the feelings so clearly, as if they've been preserved in time. These are the feelings I associate with home.

Today, many of us spend so much time, effort, and money on our homes—for what? Why do we care so much about our homes? Why do we do all that we do for "home?" It's a physical thing, a place, and most of us understand that material

opposite
I hung paintings by my kids in our dining room to show them I love them and to make them feel special. An old zinc table is a makeshift seeding and potting station.

goods aren't the path to happiness, so why does home matter so much?

Because it makes us *feel.*

Our homes touch us on a subconscious level. I still dream about my childhood homes every now and then. As humans, we understand that our environments affect us profoundly, and we do all that we can to make our homes feel right. We get that they can be positive or negative and help or hinder us. Somehow, the physical place in which life takes place shapes us and helps form us. Home is literally the backdrop for our lives, setting the stage for all that we feel and do, which is why I've done so much soul-searching and questioning about how the design of a home affects our lives and can help make life more meaningful.

I've moved a *lot*, and I don't know at exactly what point a house becomes a home or how long it takes, but I do know that at some point I go from feeling like I'm living in "the new house" to simply being "home." I've learned from every house I've lived in, and there are certain houses that still have a piece of my heart, whether because of the house itself or how I was affected by life there. Most places we've lived in have helped me grow, but I've also experienced what it's like to feel stifled by a house, knowing it wasn't right for me—which, I guess, is also an experience of growth and self-knowledge. I know what it feels like to leave a house with a lump in my throat because of the home it had become to me, and I know what it feels like to finish sweeping up and shut the door without looking back. Some houses are just a little bit more soulmate-ish than others.

As I write this in the midst of the COVID-19 pandemic and quarantine, home is more important now than ever, and carries a whole new meaning for many of us. We're spending more time in our homes than ever before, so

naturally, they're influencing us to a greater degree. Home today needs to fulfill so many functions: it needs to be a place we can wake up in, work in, educate our kids in, and cook a gazillion pounds of food a day in. We're inundated each day with difficult and often painful news, many of us experiencing emotions we've never felt before. We need a place that helps us exhale and let it all go, lets us be totally honest and unfiltered, and is an extension of ourselves. Home—now more than ever—is about what works for us and makes us feel and be our best.

As we navigate a whole host of new challenges and tragedies that have truly put life in perspective, many of us are questioning all that we think, feel, and do on the deepest of levels. So many people are slowing down and seeking more meaningful lives, making changes. Many of us are turning to the comfort of our own homes, looking to find solace in that feeling of home. There is an awakening happening like I've never seen in my lifetime. I know we'll probably go back to some sort of "normal" when all of this is over, but I don't want to forget the lessons we've learned or go back to functioning on autopilot without questioning.

As a child, I came to associate "coming home" with those feelings of safety and joy at being reunited with not only my parents, but my house. To me, it was love. I'm sure my sensations of coming home were so intense because of this Pavlov's dog–type association, but—like most people—I *do* still feel that palpable sense of home, that sense of contentment, whenever returning home from being gone. Coming home is such a key moment of illumination because we're seeing our homes with fresh eyes and hearts. The feeling is subconscious and honest. It is like a scent in that it's more detectable at first before we eventually get used to it and stop noticing it (I switch up my laundry detergent

because of this ... anyone?), so coming home calls our attention to it.

These few moments of arrival hold so much insight into how we really feel about home deep down and present a true opportunity for discovering what's working and what needs to change (if anything). The next time you come home from being gone for some time, try to grasp what you're feeling and observing ... what home feels like to you. Does it feel how you want it to feel? And if it does, how can we savor it and make it last? I've always wondered if it would be possible to sort of "bottle" that coming home feeling, that feeling where you feel intense belonging simply because you walked through a door.

And if you can bottle it, are there specific philosophies or mantras we can adopt that will make it stronger?

After writing a how-to-design-a-house-from-soup-to-nuts book with *Habitat* and then finishing a how-to-get-the-vibe-I-love book with *Down to Earth*, I continued on to wonder how, with the building blocks of design and style in place, we could consciously live our most meaningful lives at home. Home has this undeniable power to deeply affect us.... Can we not put that to use? How can we design a home so that it helps us feel and be better?

The design of our home affects our future self: our moods, our productivity levels, and our daily habits. What feels like home is different for each and every one of us, but there are elements and processes that seem to be present or have taken place in all of the homiest of homes. They are:

- ✦ Homes created with care by someone who recognized potential.

- ✦ Homes filled with only what is loved and needed.

- ✦ Homes made for today yet rooted in who we are and where we came from.

- ✦ Homes where we are free to be ourselves, where we belong.

- ✦ Homes with a palpable atmosphere that draws us to the present moment. They affect all of our senses.

- ✦ Homes that are imperfect and real.

- ✦ Homes that were designed to be truly lived in and are set up for daily habits and rituals.

- ✦ Homes that make us exhale.

Essentially, it's a delicate balance of all of these elements that transform a house into a home.

So is this a "design book"? Not quite. While I'm sharing lots of my favorite design tips and the whys behind the pretty, it's more of an exploration into how we can make our home elicit the best feelings within us, to aid us in a sort of mind-over-matter positivity. Each of us has different *wants* in a home, but we all *need* a place where we belong as our truest selves. This is the story of the homes of my past—and how they made me feel—along with the stories of some of my design firm's projects that illustrate essential characteristics of a home filled with meaning. It's an invitation to think about what home means to you; to explore why a home carries so many emotions within its walls, and how we can design our homes intentionally so that they help us feel and be our very best, and to ultimately create a more meaningful life. Just as I found a feeling of love coming home to my parents all those years ago, I hope you find love walking through your very own front door. ✦

CHAPTER 1

THE DIAMOND IN THE ROUGH

*"Life keeps throwing me stones.
And I keep finding the diamonds…"*
—ANA CLAUDIA ANTUNES

SOME PEOPLE ARE HOPELESS romantics when it comes to finding something in need of love and having the urge to fix it. I am one of these people. I love the process of finding a diamond in the rough and bringing it to its full potential. A place means more to me when I've gone through a transformation with it. As serial renovators, my husband, Dave, and I never buy homes that are "move-in ready."

A few of our houses (including the one we live in now) sat on the market for years before we purchased them. Because they needed so much work, most other people didn't really "see" the houses the way we did, as places we could have a beautiful life in. Looking back, I've realized that we unintentionally followed a basic pattern of buying houses in need of extensive work, having babies, selling our recently finished homes to buy and renovate new houses, and then hitting repeat. It was a cycle that resulted in six houses and five kids in under ten years for us.

We bought our first home, a town house, right when we got married. I was twenty-three and he was twenty-four, and we were absolutely, without a doubt, in over our heads. We plunked down every bit of cash we'd ever saved for a small down payment and began painting and decorating away. We spent weekends tiling and thrifting for furniture, art, and accessories, and I began taking design clients. We pinched every penny—my greatest skill was buying a chicken at the beginning of the week and turning it into at least three or four meals, with broth, a chicken dish of some sort, and an inevitable salad or pasta coming later in the week. We planted a little vegetable garden in our back patio, and life was sweet. From there, we had our son Christian, and the real estate market began to tank. The housing crisis hit, and a year later, we ended up selling our house for a huge loss and moved into our next project— my mom and my stepdad's basement—to try to recover financially. I decorated the basement as best I could using what we had, painting and rearranging. I was embarrassed and bummed to be moving back home with a husband and a baby, but looking back, I am so grateful for the opportunity we were given to lick our wounds. It was an incredible gift. We had time to reflect on the mistakes we'd made and tried to look forward positively instead of back with regret.

opposite
My boys playing in
our old loft

It was a learning experience, one in which we learned to forgive ourselves.

I started my blog during that time on a total whim, calling it *Pure Style Home*, writing about all of my design obsessions, sharing client projects, and eventually sharing our predicament with my (very small) early audience as we saved up for another house and eventually began house hunting. We looked all over our area, Northern Virginia, hoping to find something livable that we could afford. Most of the houses we were looking at were "tear downs" being sold "as is" for land value, and our biggest challenge was trying to figure out if we could afford to make them habitable. (The answer was usually no.) We wanted a house that we could design and use as a portfolio piece to attract more clients for my budding interiors business, so not only did it need to work for our family, it had to have the potential to be something special. I would spend hours lying in bed awake after seeing a house, rearranging the floor plan in my head, trying to figure out what it would all cost, knowing that it didn't quite matter because we wouldn't have a cent to spend after we bought the house anyway.

On one of these nights as we lay in bed, looking up at the wonky ceiling tiles in our basement bedroom, crunching numbers on how many years it would take us to save up for something, Dave threw out an idea. He wondered about getting a no-interest credit card and using it to decorate and renovate a house. The idea terrified me. What if not enough people wanted to hire me? What if we couldn't pay off the credit card before the interest was due? What if this was the same type of miscalculated risk we'd made before and we ended up back in the basement?

right
I loaded the foyer walls of our first cedar contemporary with framed da Vinci sketches I'd cut out of an art book. I had painted the front door orange on a whim for Halloween and ended up keeping it.

OUR FIRST CEDAR CONTEMPORARY

I DON'T REALLY REMEMBER how we settled on doing it—I know it had something to do with Dave's unshakable faith in what I could do if given the chance—but we decided then that we'd try to find a house that we could fix up ourselves with as little money as possible using a no-interest credit card and then photograph it for the website to attract clients and hopefully grow my design business. We found our house a few towns over. It had been vacant and on the market for years, and I was totally in love with it. It was a cedar contemporary—one of the most underrated types of houses, in my opinion—on a nice lot within walking distance to the historical part of the town of Herndon, Virginia. We said we'd take it slow, but I'm not the most patient of people—especially when I'm pregnant, which I was . . . again—and the first day after moving in, when Dave ran to the grocery store, I took sandpaper and a can of gray-green paint to the kitchen cabinets. He came home to a mess, but by Monday morning we had a "new" kitchen, complete with beadboard walls and shelving Dave had installed from Home Depot (pictured on the next page).

Now taking on more clients, I was also sharing our renovation and design process on the blog along with some of my clients' finished projects. This was instrumental because I couldn't get published in design magazines at the time, as I was just starting out, so it was a way to attract potential clients and "publish" my work. The more I shared, the more our business grew. We were able to pay off the no-interest credit card before the interest kicked in, and we could finally exhale. (My blog opened so many doors for our businesses, and to this day my advice to any entrepreneur is to give yourself a voice and use any platform you can to show what you're capable of and what you're about.)

I was over the moon when *Better Homes and Gardens* magazine asked to do a holiday story on our house, and when the issue finally came out—almost a year after it had been photographed—our business continued to grow. By this time I had hired a design assistant, and when I was pregnant with our third son, we decided we needed a project manager. Dave, a high school English teacher at the time, was already doing the books at night and on weekends, and we would have had to pay a project manager more than he was making, so we decided he would quit teaching and come to work with us full-time.

We transformed our kitchen for very little money by repainting the cabinets. Dave hung beadboard and made shelves hung with brackets we found at Home Depot. I painted the old refrigerator with black chalkboard paint, and it was one of Christian's favorite spots to play. I found the vintage light fixture at a flea market.

Groceries:
- milk
- eggs
- lettuce
- carrots

Love you!!!

I scoured Craigslist for an English arm sofa and found exactly what I was looking for from a sweet woman in DC. I reupholstered the blue striped sofa in a bright green velvet and had pillows made. It's not inexpensive to reupholster a sofa, but it was slightly less expensive than a new sofa would have been.

The dining room was small and simple. I blew up an antique Albrecht Dürer illustration and had it printed on a wall canvas to make a big impact.

I loved all the windows in this house so much. The entire back wall of the house was windows with a view of the forest behind our house. We attached an antique mantel to the wall to try to create a focal point in the space, but it was something that never quite sat perfectly with me when it was done.

I couldn't believe our luck when Dave came home one day with a vintage brass bed he had found on the side of the road. It was a double and we had a queen, but the mattress extended only slightly on each side and it worked.

The Malm dresser from Ikea is a favorite of mine (they have to be screwed to the wall because they tip), and I mixed it with a pierced porcelain ginger jar lamp that I found for twenty-five dollars at

a thrift store and bought instantly because it looked just like the ones my grandmother had in the house growing up. I thrifted the chair too for around five dollars and painted and glazed it. I tore out the pages of

a botanical book I found at a garage sale and framed them with vintage frames I thrifted for a dollar a piece. These are still favorite pieces of mine.

We worked in our basement which was part office, part family room. I painted it a pale coastal blue when we first moved in, but my neutral tendencies won out, and a year or so later I painted it white.

The family room area of the basement after I painted it white. I pulled in more green—my favorite color—and used a pair of oversize botanical prints over the sofa.

OUR SECOND CEDAR CONTEMPORARY

WHEN OUR THIRD SON, Louie, was born, we moved again, having found another vacant cedar contemporary—in Oakton, Virginia—while randomly perusing real estate listings. This time, we felt we needed a house we could more than decorate, and we planned to renovate from top to bottom so that I could design with a lighter hand and rely more on the architecture and less on the soft goods. I had been working on ground-up projects for clients around the city, but I knew that only with my own home would I be allowed to truly share my personal style, which was a bit more relaxed and nature-inspired than the work I was typically hired to do. I really fell for this house because I found myself—in the design sense—there. It was there that we figured out how we really wanted to live, with a vegetable garden and a yard and in a house that felt connected to the land it sat upon. Every last little detail—from the purposefully rusted stair railing, shown at far right, to the stucco fireplace to the vintage wooden doorknobs—was thought out with care.

Our house was long and shallow—my favorite kind of house, because it allows for lots of natural light—with high ceilings. We stained it black and added a large patio in back. Photos of the interiors of this house are sprinkled throughout my first book, *Habitat*, but I'm including them all together here for context.

To create a private shower garden outside of our bedroom, we added a rusted metal wall, right, to enclose a courtyard that was previously in the front of the house. Interior views of it can be seen on pages 38-39.

This house was an exercise in finding my personal style. Up until this point, I had been mostly designing for clients in the DC area who generally liked a more formal look than I did. When I designed our previous house, I was for the most part designing in hopes of attracting clients, so I did things a bit more formally and colorfully than I might have if it was just for myself. This time, my goal was to do my thing, in hopes that people who were drawn to more relaxed, natural, and down-to-earth houses would come calling. I also knew how much I loved working on homes from the ground up and wanted to showcase what I could do to a space architecturally. The stairs on page 25, with their square treads and rusted iron railings connected into the drywall, were my pride and joy. They were made by craftsman Tom Owen.

The tiny foyer, left, had to really function for all of us. A hall tree hid shoes, and we had hooks (not seen) for guests' coats, because we had stolen the coat closet space to create a tiny powder room.

This time around, when we needed to create architectural interest in the living room, we added a working stucco fireplace. I flanked it with a pair of large glass windows, which had a view of our side yard, and all the butterflies that were attracted by the massive butterfly bush out there.

The furniture we bought in this house has moved with us a few times, and, though it's a bit worse for wear, I still love it today.

We opened up the wall to the kitchen from the living room and expanded the footprint of the kitchen by stealing space from the dining room. When I need space to enlarge a kitchen in an older house, I often take it from the dining room, which most people use much less than the kitchen.

I designed the iron worker baker's
racks on the countertop with Tom
Owen to match the stair railings. This
was such an easy and open kitchen
to live and work in, and it was here

that I really began to take joy in meal
prep time with the family. I hung
favorite pieces of art I'd collected over
the years above the sink for interest
because we didn't have a window.

It was in this kitchen that I learned I'm OK with a refrigerator that's not in the main work zone, and I often place the microwave near it so they have their own little "station," usually near the wineglasses.

Swedish chairs given to us by my grandparents as a wedding gift sit around a big oak Parsons table. The curtains in "Moth Wing" from my textile collection softened the spare windows and added a vintage vibe.

The dining room had been made much smaller when I stole space from it for the kitchen, so I embraced its small size and went for dark and cozy in there, paneling the ceiling with cedar planks, which smell so beautiful.

Our office, far right, with much of the same furniture from our last house, was dubbed the "Room of Requirement" (from Harry Potter), and it became whatever type of space was most needed in our lives at any given time. We eventually got a design studio outside of the house, and it turned into a craft/play space for the kids. By the end, just before we moved, it had become a nursery for our fourth child, Gisele.

I have so many sweet memories of looking out into the backyard at the deer or watching it snow from the window seat in our upstairs loft with the boys when they were little. I loved cozying up and reading there, too. I used to read and collect cheesy horror novels when I was a kid—and still love reading them occasionally. They are all sorts of fluorescent colors, so I stacked them in the very shallow niches above the window seat with their spines turned inward. I used to love playing "roulette" with the collection and picking out a random book to read.

It was rarely—if ever!—picture-perfect on a daily basis at our place, and the pillows were often smashed down from use.

We stored the kids' toys in the area under the window seat, which was accessed by lift-up lids under the cushion. Their two bedrooms were off of this main room.

Our found brass bed came with us to the new house, along with our pup, Ashby. We hung my ever-growing collection of bookplates and botanicals—which had started with the first pair in our last house—all over the wall. The patterned fabrics are from my textile collection, and the pillow is made from Kuba cloth.

I remember being so intense about this photo shoot, wanting everything to be absolutely perfect so I could pitch it to a magazine for publication. As we were photographing the bedroom, Dave surprised me with a four foot high bouquet of Queen Anne's lace—my favorite wildflower—that he'd driven around and stopped on the sides of roads to gather. We plunked it in an old pewter pitcher and set it on the dresser.

Our bedroom was originally dark and closed off and overlooked the front driveway and a little rock courtyard made by the side of the garage. The bedroom was originally accessed by the front foyer, which lacked privacy. During the open house when we first saw the house, I sat on the floor here for at least an hour trying to figure out the new floor plan in my head to determine if we could make an offer on the house. I remember hopping up from the floor the moment I got the idea for a private outdoor shower courtyard and fern garden to go find Dave to tell him we could buy the house.

We added an outdoor shower, right, and used it on most days from April through October, and then occasionally in between. I loved waking up and heading outside to shower and relax in the mornings. It was so easy with the little kids, too ... we'd just throw them out there on summer evenings and hang out in the chairs while they played around in the water.

It was at this house that I discovered my love for having a vegetable garden. I had grown up gardening, but my mom was into flower gardens, and so was I. My childhood friend Danylo Kosovych had recently started a vegetable garden company, Organic Edible Gardens, and he came over and dug all the beds for us and prepared the soil with his team. This garden taught me how I wanted to live. I used to take runs on warm weekend mornings and come home to work in the garden. We'd spend evenings with the kids playing in the yard nearby while I picked vegetables. It changed our way of life. I used willow edging around the beds to separate them from the grass paths. I lined all the beds with an alternating pattern of microbasil and small boxwoods for evergreen beauty. I set potted peach trees in the centers of the gardens. Tomatoes trailed up simple bamboo poles, and Danylo taught me to prune all but the strongest vines for the greatest number of massive, juicy tomatoes.

OUR CAPE COD

THROUGHOUT THE TIME we lived in Oakton, we often thought about one day moving back to my mom's town, McLean, to be closer to her, my sister, my stepdad, and my grandparents. Three years later, when I had our daughter Gisele, we realized we were outgrowing our three bedroom home and decided to look in McLean, which was also closer the city, where the majority of our projects were at the time. We sold our house quickly, not knowing where we would go, and ended up buying a big Cape Cod on a tiny lot about five minutes away from my family, thinking we'd live there for a few years and enjoy the convenience of living close to family until we could find something that was more "us."

I liked getting to flex creatively on a Colonial home in my own way—with painted white floors, beams, and a front yard vegetable garden—but we missed the greater indoor-outdoor connection of our last house, and our bigger yard and the play space and privacy that had come with it. Within only a few months of living there, we were dreaming about moving farther out.

For so many years I had been trying to get back to my hometown, but now that we had, I realized it wasn't something I really wanted anymore. It's an incredibly expensive area, and we would never be able to afford a large property there, and though we loved being near family and loved our new neighbors, we missed our old bigger yard farther out from the city. It was then that we found our current home—our biggest challenge yet—about twenty minutes away in the Village of Great Falls, right near our design studio.

Our fifth child, Aurora, was born about a year after we moved in, and the story of that house is told in the final chapter of this book.

Vegetable gardens need to go where the sun is, and because our backyard was shaded by a forest, into the front yard our potager went! We created a pathway and a small sitting patio out of reclaimed brick laid in a basketweave pattern, something I'd noticed and loved in historical Williamsburg, Virginia. In front of a backdrop of boxwood, I planted rows of vegetables and lined the walkways with herbs. I used to set Gisele on a blanket on the patio with toys as she was learning to walk. She loved it when the sprinklers went on, and I overwatered the garden on more than one occasion so she could play in them.

We painted the woodwork and flooring throughout the house in deep ivory and did the walls in a fresh white for contrast and to accentuate the simple woodwork. We brought along all our furniture, and I took home some of my favorite pieces from my shop, including a set of mid-century botanical studies from Lancaster College. I designed the mahogany stair railing after one I'd seen in a photograph of a historical Colonial house.

In the living room I had the main wall furred out and added floating shelving made from old railroad ties to create architectural interest. I loved having a central spot to display my favorite finds. The center wall sat empty until we came across the Jesus tapestry at our friend's antiques booth at Highpoint Market.

We closed a wall between our living room and a sitting room to create a private library. We used the new wall to hold all of our books by adding built-ins. The kids used this room for painting, and Dave always had a chess game going with one of them in here. Whenever this room was being used— which was almost always for reading, music, art, or family games—I felt like life was truly sweet.

The kitchen was in the back of the house and was originally a fairly dark space, so almost everything went white to lighten it up. I centered the cooktop and oven on the main wall and flanked it with the fridge on the left and a pantry that mirrored it on the right. A massive island created a ton of workspace and often served as the dinner table. We topped it with honed Carrara marble, which we also used as the backsplash ledge behind the cooktop. At only three inches deep, the ledge added so much functionality to the space, providing a surface for my herbs and spices.

Four cozy chairs created a seating area in the hearth area of our kitchen. We did a lot of reading with the kids and had family dance parties in there.

Space was limited in our foyer, so I designed a small wall-mount iron console table, right, and had it made. We simply moved all of our existing dining furniture to the new dining room, seen in the background. I can count on one hand the number of times we used the dining room in this house in the ten short months we lived there..

EQUESTRIAN SPIRIT

THROUGHOUT THESE YEARS of moves, we've bought multiple houses despite warnings from those around us deeming them "tear downs." I remember how worried for us my mom used to get when we would house hunt because she saw the rot, the disrepair, and the problems—and the money, time, and work that came hand in hand with the aforementioned issues! I, on the other hand, was invigorated and excited by the possibilities. When house hunting, I will walk straight out of a house in good shape with a two-year-old renovation, but one with falling-in floors that hasn't been touched since it was built? That's my jam. I've realized that you have to learn to trust yourself over others.

Being able to recognize a diamond in the rough is a skill that develops over time, and through research and experience. Seeing what something could be and creating a vision for it is the first step in designing a home. Anyone can learn to see. As a self-taught designer, I've found that reading, looking at photos, traveling, visiting historical homes and properties, and working on a variety of homes has really helped educate my eye to understand what is "good." With each home I design, I gain knowledge that I inevitably take with me to the next project. Almost any home can be fixed with an unlimited budget, but it's that budget component that often determines if a project is physically doable or not. While it can become fairly easy to see what something could be, estimating how much it will cost is always tricky and requires even more practice and experience.

After years of renovating our own homes, designing all over for clients, and realizing how much we loved the process of bringing an unloved home back to life, Dave and I decided to try our hand at real estate so we could do the work we loved without having to keep moving our family from house to house. We founded a real estate brokerage with our friends, Maura and Daan DeRaedt, called Property Collective, where we rehab and sell (or "flip") properties. We're always on the lookout for homes in need of love—homes that I can get excited about and really create a meaningful lifestyle for someone in—with a low-enough price and a profit that leave room in the budget for renovating. These properties are tough to get, but every now and then we find a good one.

This particular one was in our town, Great Falls, and had been vacant for some time. We recognized that it had great bones and was incredibly livable. It was a plain, sensible colonial house with minimal updates, lots of space, and beautiful views. We bought it with Maura and Daan, planning to sell it after a "light cosmetic makeover." I now realize that I'm not very good at doing anything halfway and should probably stop pretending I'm OK with "minimal updates," because we ended up plunging ourselves into a six month-long whole house overhaul, moving walls, adding windows, and basically touching every inch of the house. It was an exhilarating, yet slightly terrifying, experience for us all.

Untapped potential lies within the walls of almost any home, and it's up to us to see it. Looking at each and every home from the perspective that it can be good with enough creativity, work, and money allows us to really see what something could be. Just as I saw diamonds in the rough in the homes we moved our family into, I approach the design of a home for a client or a flip in much the same way . . . as an attempt to help something reach its fullest potential. There are always levels of excellence to what can be created and various restrictions, so the goal is to do as much as possible with what you have. This same process of "seeing" what something could be applies to almost any home project—existing homes and even new builds, where all you have to look at is land and/or blueprints.

I have sat on the floor of many a for-sale house, trying to figure out a floor plan in my head to determine a potential scope and budget while other open house–goers saunter through, looking at me like I'm crazy. I always try to figure out what the plan could be when looking at a place to see if what I'm looking at is really a

diamond in the rough that I can afford to fix or a money pit. We have walked away from *so* many houses that I know could have been absolutely incredible because we either couldn't afford the renovations or the cost of renovating would result in an overinvestment in the home.

If you have no idea where to start with setting a realistic budget for your project, begin with a list. Write down every single little thing that needs to go into your project—each piece of tile, cabinetry, furniture, lighting, and art, and don't forget labor, painting, shipping, and any storage or furniture transportation costs. If you don't know what these items cost, look them up online at various stores. You can even create a "low" estimate and a "high" estimate, and come up with a final budget range. Once you generally know what your project will cost, you can proceed with a realistic budget in front of you. Most people who are doing this for the very first time are shocked at the total costs—I know I was!—and so if you're feeling this way, just remember that you're not alone and it can be done over time in phases if needed. Be careful not to underestimate.

Finding a diamond in the rough has as much to do with budget as it does with having vision. This first step of observation and imagination is instrumental to any design process, no matter what type of project you're working on, be it decorating a house, purchasing a home, renovating a home, or building one. Once you see what something could be, and you believe you can afford what you need to make it special, it's "go" time. Begin by looking at the home as if you don't have any attachment to it. I find taking photos to be helpful because a photo allows us to look at a space more critically. Photos don't lie, and inspecting them allows us to critique details like symmetry (or lack of it), architectural authenticity, fabrics,

previous page
Paneling the walls of the once-plain and uncomfortably large foyer created architectural interest, texture, and character. We replaced outdated tile with antique-look brick tiles laid in a herringbone pattern to add a sense of history and a nod to the Virginia equestrian community the house is a part of. I love pulling "outdoor" plants, like boxwood, inside to create an indoor-outdoor feel. They need to be rotated to get proper sunlight, which can be a challenge, but it's worth it for certain seasons or parties.

finishes, and more without being affected by the feeling of being in a space. Photos allow for a thorough, less-biased examination of what you're working with. When working with a home that already exists, I photograph all four walls of a room. When I only have existing floor plans on a new build, I either examine the floor plans and elevations or sketch them out if there aren't, so I can tweak as needed. When I'm creating the floor plans on a ground-up project, I look at photos of the land and think about the best views and where they should be seen from in the future house.

*More on how to do this in my first book, Habitat.

When looking to make changes to your own home, go ahead and photograph the room you're working on from all four sides. Get as far back as you can to get as much of the wall in the shot as possible, turn off the lights and shoot during the day with natural light, and square up the room in the viewfinder so the photo looks as good as it possibly can. You're trying to get the most accurate depiction of the space. Straighten up the room so you're judging the design, not your housekeeping skills. Put the photos into some sort of digital or physical project file. I create a document for each project I'm working on with a table of contents up top listing each room of the house and drop in photos of each room into its coordinating section.

Now it's time to really step back and "see" the room. Examine the photos of your space. Do you like it? Does it feel good to you? Does it feel like you? If not, ask yourself what's wrong with it. What's missing? Is there something (or multiple things) in it detracting from the space? And more importantly, ask yourself what's good about a room or what could be good about it. Is there a way to create symmetry on every wall? (Something I generally strive for.) Is there enough natural light? Are the windows too small, not symmetrical, even too big?

Does the style of window or door fit with the architecture? Is there a way to improve upon the woodwork or the colors? Is the flooring consistent? Brainstorm, jotting down ideas, and don't think about what things cost at this point, just think about what would make the room its best. Then make a list of those items and estimate the costs for those changes. With the Internet and estimate tools, you don't need a background in construction to come up with a fairly decent guess. Also, always overestimate, as unforeseen costs will arise and you don't want to be caught off guard.

Do the same process with the floor plan and elevations of the walls of a room. Sketch the room out to scale,* drawing in all window and door locations. If you're undertaking a renovation and have the option of changing architectural elements, examine all window, door, and wall locations to see if they should change. Really see what's there to determine if it's good or bad. If you're decorating, assess your current furniture placement and think about how it's working for you. Again, make lists and a budget.

In this particular house, my first walk-through with the team (and my toddler in tow) was an hour or two long, and it took place after our partners had already made the offer. They brought me over thinking we could simply update the finishes, but by the end of the walkthrough, I had ideas for moving walls and reassigning spaces throughout the entire house and guesstimated the budget to be more than three times the original targeted budget estimate. The scope was going to be big, and we were all nervous about the costs of the undertaking, but we sort of held our breath and dove into the project headfirst, feeling like we had to make the house all it could be.

Planning out any structural and big-picture changes is paramount when getting started, but my favorite part of the design process is what comes next: figuring out the vibe I'm after, researching, and finding relevant inspiration. Our town is known for its equestrian communities, and this house is right near the stable where I used to ride when I was a kid. Many of the people who choose to move to our town value nature and are delighted by the horses trotting along the sides of the roads, so I decided to lean into the "old Virginia" horse country thing and created a vibe that I thought someone who wanted to live that kind of life would love. The land a home sits on is a driving force behind how I typically design. I believed that the people who purchased the house would fall for the property and land as much as the home, so I made every attempt to call attention to the property itself, adding and enlarging windows and calling attention to views wherever possible. Connecting a home's design with its surrounding area and culture imparts a strong sense of place and meaning within it that gives it a feeling of authenticity and helps it ring true. I thought about classical "Virginia" elements I could imbue the house with: brick, iron, leather, classic paneling, boxwoods, barn wood, and lanterns.

I've noticed there is often an emotional attachment and feelings associated with a home people have undergone a transformation process with. I felt my own connection to this house and witnessed it with our team. At first we connect with something that has potential. Then we set about studying it from all angles so that we can dream about it. We imagine all that it could be and try out different paths until we figure out the one we'll take. We go through so much emotion when renovating, building, and/or decorating a home; there are the times we are excited, giddy, and optimistic—the times we dream and create a vision—but then there

are the times when we might feel exhausted or financially depleted. Eventually, though, a project is completed and there's that amazing feeling of achieving our goal, of reaching the finish line and getting to see our vision come to life. It's a sort of bonding experience with the project or place. These ups and downs hold so much meaning and shape us and strengthen us as people. Each and every project I've touched—whether for myself, for a client, or for sale—brings up a whole host of memories and feelings when I think of it, becoming a part of its history, filling the house with stories and meaning. These memories and feelings are almost like the prologue for the house, because its real story begins with life being lived there.

By the time we were done with the house, the entire team had all dreamt about our own families living there, but alas, this was a business, and you don't get paid if you keep the houses! We had a big party, breaking in the new kitchen, put it on the market, and thankfully, sold it right away. In a sweet little turn of events, the house ended up going to past clients of mine whom I adore. I love knowing that the house we all poured so much into is in such good, kind hands. Every house has a story, and this one is particularly close to my heart because it went from sitting empty and unloved to becoming a project we bonded with our partners and team over, to finally becoming home for a beautiful family who cherishes it and the life they live there. It was a diamond in the rough that has finally reached its full potential. ✦

The house was missing a sense of history and permanence, so I set about redoing all of the woodwork—the floors, the doors, the trim, and the walls—so that they would feel more architecturally appropriate and authentic to the home.

We paneled the once-ho-hum living room and painted it a deep moody gray to create depth and interest. There is an open and airy family room in the back of the house, so I wanted to create a cozy and darker space out of the living room for a variety of spaces and practical uses.

I love using a deep backdrop to "set off" lighter or brighter objects in a room so that they almost seem to glow, such as the vintage brown leather chesterfield sofa and antique Belgian painting with original gold frame. A moody gray also beautifully contrasts with bright yellow-green, so I brought in some of my favorite plants that I knew would "glow" in here: asparagus fern and a lemon cypress topiary. HINT: Christmas tree–shaped lemon cypress plants are inexpensive and easy to come by, so I buy them and then trim up the bottom of the tree to create a topiary shape, as seen on the coffee table.

We created a library out of what was once the dining room. I love making tucked-away little libraries or offices in houses, where I envision books and projects can stay out and not need to be cleaned up before dinner. I learned to love these types of spaces because of our Cape Cod library, shown on page 47. Sometimes it's even built-ins or a game table in a living room, but it's really nice to be able to get creative and not have to "put away" a project every day.

A tiny antique oil painting hangs above a vintage birdcage filled with potted ferns. Quirky pieces bring personality to a space, and I find "weird" so much more interesting than "pretty," because it makes me wonder and think. A pair of turned-leg woven chairs adds that natural warmth and stands out against the deep gray walls.

We opened the wall of the kitchen to a sitting room and converted it to a dining room for a large, open, casual dining space.

Herringbone brick floors, rustic cabinetry from my collection with Unique Kitchens and Baths, and simple porcelain tile from my collection

with Architessa mix in the kitchen. I selected finishes that felt worn-feeling for a sense of patina and age. I didn't want it feeling like a "new" house.

The sink is from my collection with Atmosphyre, and we had a barely there imprint of a fern fossil I had found set into its surface, above. I love "secret" little design details like this and often do them in my textiles and patterns.

We had iron shelves made, seen at far left, to fill in the opening between the kitchen and the family room, providing storage for tableware and glasses. We replaced the back wall of the kitchen with a twelve-foot-long window to add sunlight and views of the beautiful backyard.

The kitchen, above, is now open to what was turned into the dining room. I pulled in black lanterns and caged lights throughout the kitchen for a strong rustic feel, and to contrast with the softer, aged finishes throughout.

We squeezed in a simple painted bench with hooks and shelving above to create a small mudroom space, right, by the garage door and the laundry room, which is behind the closed black door. This is a fairly simple and inexpensive way to create a mudroom out of a very small amount of space. HINT: Baby's

breath is almost always available at the grocery store, and it's one of my favorite flowers to use around a house, because it has the humble feel of wildflowers when it's on its own. It's pretty both fresh and once it dries. I styled the mudroom with our own boots and riding helmets to help tell a story to potential buyers.

The new dining room leads out to a flagstone patio we built. Because of all of the brickwork we added throughout, I had the (very red) fireplace brick painted white so the disparate bricks wouldn't compete with each other. We stacked logs in a niche beside the fireplace, one of my favorite design elements for creating a casual, rustic vibe. (Bugs don't scare me, and I've never had an issue, but it's something people always ask about, and for sure, critters can live in the logs!) At the table I mixed a pair of antique English chairs with contemporary black iron ones for a modern feel with an antique twist.

An antique Spanish leather chair is sculptural and feels like a work of art when set against clean white paneled walls in the dining room. Mixing eras and styles creates an interesting, collected space. I found the iron fox above the fireplace at Lucketts, and he stayed with the house.

The family room was originally
yellow, and almost everyone who
walked in had a problem with
the wood ceiling and the stone
on the fireplace, but as soon as
we introduced a neutral palette,
the materials felt right at home.
Sometimes all it really takes
is the right white paint! Simple
sofas and an earthy palette of white,
brown, and black create a relaxed,
natural vibe.

The fireplace anchors the room, and I brought in a pair of mid-century woven chairs and mixed them with an outdoor teak table and a pair of simple linen sofas. The stone has so much movement that I wanted most everything else in the room to be "quiet" and calm down the space.

In the guest bedroom on the main level, I hung a salon-style gallery wall filled with art that our partners collected on their travels to Belgium. A tapestry painted by Lauren Rose Jackson hangs above the chair.

We paneled the walls in the main bedroom to create architectural interest and cohesion with the foyer and hallway. I like the rooms in the house where people will be spending the most time to be interesting and layered. Wall treatments add so much depth and character to a space.

A spare wrought-iron bed is sculptural against the white paneling. The bed is layered with soft, natural textiles from my collection.

A dark horse painting by Lauren Rose Jackson hangs above an antique dresser.

A pair of vessel sinks sit atop a primitive wooden vanity in the bathroom. Rustic wall-mounted outdoor hanging lanterns flank the custom mirror.

WORDS TO LIVE BY

Quiet your mind to "see" what something can be.

Open up to the **possibilities** of what something can be first, and then figure out if you can afford to **tackle** it.

Think of the **experience** of dreaming about, building, renovating, or decorating a home as the first part of your **story** with it.

Try to **embrace** the process so you come out better on the other side.

Checklist of questions to ask yourself when you are thinking of purchasing a diamond in the rough

+ Do you like it?
+ Does it feel good to you?
+ Does it feel like "you"?
+ What's wrong with it?
+ What's missing?
+ Is there anything detracting from the space?
+ What's good about a room, or what could be good about it?
+ Is there a way to create symmetry on every wall?
+ Is there enough natural light?

+ Are the windows too small, not symmetrical, even too big?
+ Does the style of window or door fit with the architecture?
+ Does the style of woodwork fit the architecture?
+ Is there a way to improve upon the woodwork or the colors?
+ Does the flooring fit with the architectural style of the home?
+ Is the square footage of the finished house is large enough to justify the cost of the house?

A PROPERTY COLLECTIVE HOME BUILDER KELLEY HOME IMPROVEMENT

CHAPTER 2

YOUR OWN KIND OF MINIMALISM

*"It is preoccupation with possession,
more than anything else, that
prevents men from living freely and nobly."*

—BERTRAND RUSSELL

I WAS A WEIRD KID. Whenever I made a new friend and visited her house for the first or second time, I'd get to work on redecorating her bedroom. I never had intentions of doing it, but it would start something like, "Hey, want me to help clean your room?" and before she knew it she was getting a bedroom makeover by yours truly.

We'd begin by decluttering and getting rid of all the stuff she didn't love, making piles in the hallway, and pawning things off to brothers or sisters. We'd rearrange all the furniture and rehang the art. We'd make the bed and fluff pillows and then head outside to pick plants to "decorate" with, or even walk to the grocery store to buy potted plants with allowance money. I am quite positive their parents thought I was nuts, but luckily, I was always invited back.

Whenever I visited my dad's (always very messy) office from about the age of five or six on—and I was left alone to my own devices—I would organize and clean it, straightening up the jumbles of papers and stacking them into piles and spraying down the table and cleaning it with the help of his secretary. I'm pretty sure I made life more difficult for him, messing up his piles and whatnot—the most annoying thing I am now realizing I did to him (because my kids now do this to me at my office today) was make a paper clip chain out of all the paper clips I found around—but my sweet dad always seemed lifted by the sight of a pretty and organized-feeling space, and I always felt like I'd helped him, even if he did have thirty minutes of disconnecting paper clips ahead of him.

I'd been given a lot of freedom as a kid when decorating my bedrooms at both my mom's and dad's houses. They let me select the paint colors and do the painting, and I got to choose the bedspreads and curtains—which inspired a love affair with Laura Ashley! Both parents even let me help pick out furniture and fabrics throughout their houses—or at least made me feel like I was helping—and I loved it. I think I came to understand how fixing up a place made me feel like I could go out and do anything, and I wanted my friends and family to feel that, too. Let me be clear: I trashed my room like the best of them, but I understood that when our homes were organized and good to go, so were we.

above

Simple and easy-breezy, our clients' family room is a combination of newer furnishings made out of natural materials—such as seagrass, petrified wood, and linen—mixed with vintage and antique art and accessories. Fabrics are from my textile collection.

YOUR OWN KIND OF MINIMALISM   81

When just getting started with decorating a home or looking to improve upon what is already there so that you really feel your best, I recommend a more in-depth version of my childhood pastime of inserting myself into other people's personal spaces and "cleaning house." Begin by taking stock of *every* little thing. Go through every closet, bookshelf, and drawer, and give away as much as possible. Keep only what you love, what's working for you, and what means something to you. We cannot have true freedom at home when we are living with more than we need. The unimportant clutter pulls our attention and energy away from the things we do care about. I have spent countless Saturdays of my life cleaning and reorganizing various parts of my house—simply because we have too much stuff—rather than playing with my kids or doing something I'm passionate about.

At one point in my life, in our second cedar contemporary house, I realized that I was waking up on Saturday mornings—quite possibly my favorite time of the week, rivaled only by Friday nights—ridiculously excited about being off of work only to begin cleaning up the house with a vengeance because we'd trashed it during the week. Instead of lazily making eggs in my pjs and cuddling with the kids, I was barking orders left and right at everyone in the house to put this or that away. At some point—after I'm not sure of how many Saturdays—I realized what was happening and dubbed myself in this state as "Saturday Morning Mom." I would announce that Saturday Morning Mom was here and those kids hustled! No toy was safe from Saturday Morning Mom. Along with the realization of my neurosis came a freedom of sorts in which I could simply let go of the tension surrounding Saturday mornings (they say admitting you have a problem is the first step!) laugh about it,

and take steps to actually solve the root issue that was causing it.

We got rid of so many of the extra things we had—clothing, clutter, and rarely played with toys—and it got easier. (I remember blogging about this so many years ago and people commenting that I was a horrible mother for not letting my kids have a lot of toys, but with five kids I stand by the decision to keep our kids' toys at bay. It gives us all more time to be together and encourages them to get a bit more creative, making things—I have seen so many cool things constructed out of sticks, string, and cardboard boxes—and turning toward nature and outdoor play.) We also attempted to clean up the house on Fridays right after work so that Saturday Morning Mom had no reason to pay a visit. Soon enough, she stopped coming altogether, but today, all these years later, she is still the *best* catalyst for a clean house. All I have to say now—on any day of the week—is, "Saturday Morning Mom is coming! This is NOT a drill!" and things get picked up pretty quickly. She still makes us all laugh, but we also know she means business. Our friends have used her to help with their houses too, and she's even become a verb. Every now and then I'll get a text from a girlfriend saying she "Saturday Morning Mom'd" or was "Saturday Morning Moming So Hard." Keeping things simpler and having less has made life easier for us. Simplicity lies at the core of living a more relaxed and meaningful life at home. To appreciate what matters, we need clear minds and mental and physical space that leaves room for the important things in life—our passions and people. Clutter and unnecessary stuff causes stress and tension (and might possibly result in a house-cleaning alter ego!) Think of the feeling of pulling out a shirt on a hanger in the closet that's wedged tightly between the other hangers—when it falls off and the shirt behind falls off—and compare that with how it feels when pulling out a shirt on a hanger that has breathing room on both sides of it, barely touching the shirts next to it. We have the choice of creating these feelings of "difficulty" or "ease" throughout our homes. Just as we probably have lots of items in our closets we don't use or wear, many of us have so much in our homes that we don't use or need, wasting valuable physical and mental space.

We often lead busy, plugged-in lives, and our houses need to help us function smoothly on a daily basis, aiding us in our activities rather than hindering us by being disorganized, cluttered, or visually distracting. I am by no means a technical "minimalist," but I've developed my own form of minimalism, one that would probably look "maximalist" to a true minimalist but is manageable for us. That's not to say it comes easily, as I still find myself feeling like we have too much. As the years go by, I can see that I yearn to have less and less, so that my time and life are less and less monopolized by my things. My discipline waxes and wanes (along with the comfort level of my home when I'm not as disciplined), but I've noticed that I feel happier and more clear-headed when I've been tough on my stuff and cleared out as much as possible, because rather than spending my time putting stuff away and organizing, I get to spend that time with my family.

There always seems to be so much "stuff" coming into our house, be it projects and random toys from the kids' school, birthday gifts, artwork, etc., and if we don't *constantly* clear out and put things away, our house begins to get overtaken. We have "donate" bags and boxes going at all times, and having less in the house makes daily living more carefree. Even buying nothing, little things will start accumulating on the kitchen countertops, in the mudroom, and on the stair railings. (*Saturday*

Morning Mom tip here: I've taken a serious stance with my kids on their stuff and charge them a dollar for every time I find their clothes on the floor. A towel on the floor is five dollars. Toys left on the island can easily get brushed into the trash can—which is conveniently located on the island. Needless to say, my island is almost always clean. I've found, ironically, that the more ridiculous a method I can find

for disposing of their toys, and the funnier and more light-hearted it is, the more they remember it. There are lots of "remember when . . ." stories that work to my advantage.)

Along with simplifying and decluttering at home on a regular basis, we don't shop for the house unless we actually need something. When I have to buy something—for example, a toothbrush—I try to make sure it's something I actually like

the look of. It drives me crazy that toothbrushes come in bright colors that totally clash with the bathroom, and we often have those at home, but I'm always on the lookout for white or neutral ones and get them when I can. (I can't even tell you how many times I've daydreamed about calling up toothbrush manufacturers and begging for prettier toothbrushes!) There is almost always a choice for anything we have to bring into our homes, be it a tea kettle, Tupperware container, or even a broom. I know how intense it sounds that I won't even buy a sponge for my kitchen if I don't like the color (I go for the neutral brownish ones), but this discipline with shopping—or lack of shopping—has left me with so much more physical, visual, and mental free space so that I can focus on what really matters—people and life. In the best scenario, our homes should be clear and "at the ready," so that we can get up on any given day and work and function at our very best.

My own bedroom is simple and spare, because when I wake up to an emptier-feeling space that has more breathing room, my mind is freer, and I feel better equipped to think, create, and go on with my day. My bed is made sparsely without decorative pillows or throws, because at this particularly busy stage of my life, I don't want to spend even a single additional minute fluffing or fixing my bed in the mornings.

All of that being said, your own personal form of minimalism does *not* mean you have to design simply and sparely. It just means you have less than the amount that you have found hinders or overwhelms you; essentially, having only what you need and love. We each have our own threshold for how much stuff we can handle in our homes.

Along with shopping as little as possible, I try to make sure that everything in my home has a place to go, and if it doesn't, it's gone. Like, really

gone. It's disheartening to try to put things away when you can't fit them in a drawer or have to squeeze them back into a closet. I try to keep all of my storage areas—drawers, closets, etc.—only partially filled so cleaning up is easy and stress-free. The kids do a better job of cleaning up after themselves, too, when things can be easily put away and fit into the places they are stored in. If putting something away is a struggle, it often doesn't get done.

I find that I never regret taking an extra ten minutes straightening up after getting ready in the morning, before heading out the door for the day, or before going to bed, because when I return home (or wake up), I am relaxed and the space is waiting at the ready for me. Inviting order into our spaces reduces chaos, uplifts our spirits, clears our minds, and makes us more productive. When we return home to a house that's in order, life somehow feels more manageable and we are empowered to be our very best selves. Creating order in our living spaces and nesting is one of the first and most essential steps in making a home—and by effect, those in it—feel good. Whenever I'm involved in a situation where a friend or loved one needs help, I start with straightening up and cleaning his or her house. When I have seemingly insurmountable deadlines ahead of me, I do the same thing, giving special attention to my office or the room I'll be working in so I can think clearly. It makes me feel ready to accomplish the task at hand. This entire process is made easier (or unnecessary) by having less stuff and by subscribing to your own form of minimalism, one in which you need and love everything in your home and nothing else is kept. ✦

NATURAL CHARM

I'VE BEEN LUCKY ENOUGH to get to work on a few homes with people I already know and love, and the project on the following pages is one of them. We'd been good friends with our clients for years after having met through close mutual friends at a dinner party and hitting it off. She's my late-night dancing and singing partner, and he and Dave have a beautiful bromance. When they asked us to help redesign their charming historical farmhouse (I happened to have been obsessed with), including the out-of-date addition on the back of it, I was beyond excited to dig in and help it become the place I knew it could be.

They weren't asking to become minimalists, but the very first step taken when designing a home with clients is to have them look at everything they have and then keep only what they truly love and need. It's the grown-up version of what I used to do as an overzealous-yet-well-intentioned kid, and I love it because I know how freeing it is for people. Our friends kept only what they truly use and what matters to them, setting themselves up for their own form of minimalism.

Our friends had lived in their house for years with their five children, knowing that the square footage they needed was there, but that the house wasn't working for them in the way they knew it could. They didn't have a place for everything and proper functions for the rooms in the house. I think of floor plans almost as algebraic puzzles that can be solved, and I can't rest or stop working until I've gotten them figured out. I looked for ways to square off awkwardly arranged rooms, assign new functions for underutilized spaces, make strong focal points, introduce symmetry, create cohesion between the original house and the addition, and introduce more of an indoor-outdoor connection with more flow to the outside of the house. It's not a large home, and it had to be able to function for a family of seven, so organization and storage solutions were paramount. Fixing this one was truly satisfying because it fell so perfectly into place.

Once the floor plan was in order, and the flow of the house made sense, we dug into the materials, palette, and finishes. There was a major style discrepancy between the original farmhouse, with its worn heart pine flooring

opposite
A collection of old bookplates is set off by the mossy green paneling in our clients' study.

and quaint proportions, and the large, outdated 1990s addition on the back of the house, filled with odd angles and once-trendy materials—including a large wall of imposing cherry cabinetry—that made the house feel completely disjointed. We set about selecting materials and finishes that would make the addition feel like it could have been a part of the original farmhouse.

The house underwent a yearlong renovation with our other good friend, contractor Mike Carr, and his team, and when we were finished, the house felt both older and more authentic, yet fresh, comfortable, and ready for the modern life of a large, busy family. On "reveal day," we showed our friends and the kids around their "new" place, broke in the new sofa with its first (I'm sure of many) dance parties, and lip-synched into limelight hydrangea microphones from the arrangement I'd made on the coffee table. It's *exactly* how I pictured their house getting used—with lots of love, laughter, and fun—and nothing being too precious or off-limits. ✦

My beautiful friend and her little boy seen through the wallpapered foyer, right. We turned the piano room, far right—a smaller, rarely used room on the side of the house by the driveway—into the mudroom by adding French doors and personal "locker" cabinets for the family's gear. This change helps the family stay organized, as now that there is a clear and useful family entrance, the rest of the house can breathe more easily and function better.

Our friend is an incredible home chef, taking special care to find the very freshest of ingredients and always experimenting with new dishes, so this kitchen had to really *work* for him. We opened the original kitchen up to the once-dark dining room and made the entire space one large eat-in kitchen, with storage in both the working kitchen area and in the dining area. By bringing in function and order and simplifying the existing spaces, the family can live and work more easily, which leads to a sense of peace and ease. We are happier when we can work productively and efficiently.

We had the island made by Carmichael Construction to look like an old English island, and a couple of inches higher than typical counter height to make meal prep more comfortable for our friend, who is tall. The simple white cabinets emulate those in old farmhouse kitchens, with their simple rounded faces and exposed antique brass hinges.

A large Carrara marble farm sink, right, is paired with matte pale gray quartz concrete-look countertops. I try to specify timeless details whenever possible to add a sense of history and evergreen appropriateness. There is no toe-kick space under the cabinets in this kitchen, but rather a baseboard along the bottom, which feels more authentic and appropriate to the architecture of the farmhouse.

An antique farm table, far right, with the softest timeworn finish was combined with Windsor chairs from the "existing furnishings list" that we painted black for a classic update. We layered a no-stress, easy-to-wipe cowhide with a graphic zebra markings under the table to add energy and pattern into the room.

Beadboard ceilings added to the original portion of the farmhouse create architectural interest and character. The vintage pendant over the dining table, far right, feels spare and modern in its restraint. New built-ins in the dining area dramatically increase the storage space and allow for display of my friend's antique ironstone collection.

We added doors and a large deck off of the family room—which is open to the kitchen—for increased flow to the outdoors, making the entire house feel more connected with nature. A new plaster fireplace and beams simplify the once dark and outdated space. A pair of extra-long English arm sofas from my collection are slipcovered in light machine-washable fabric, so spills aren't a problem. An antique Ming dynasty coffee table feels at home in the farmhouse because of its primitive shape and natural patina. Mixing eras can come easily once you understand the vibe and language of your project. This farmhouse is pure, simple, and humble, so primitive pieces across various cultures and time periods all blend seamlessly.

Pillows in a mix of vintage and new fabrics layer over the sofas, which are covered in machine-washable slipcovers, which are amazing for families with kids—and moms who like red wine! A vintage kilim is layered over a seagrass rug, creating textures and layers. Reclaimed beams added instant character and age to the new addition.

Our friend planned to be working from home a lot and didn't want to have to be far away from the family all the time, so we created a sort of hidden "office" in the living room for him, with a printer and supplies behind cabinetry and a cozy built-in bench.

My friend has the prettiest long red hair, and she loves green and nature, so our palette of layered greens and warm browns was a no-brainer. The kids' playroom also does triple duty as an additional workspace and sometime guest room, with a pull-out sofa and pocket doors that can close for privacy. Bookshelves currently hold toys, but the space can transition into a true study when the kids are older.

Knowing what colors make you feel good is so important when working in your own home. Because the majority of the house was light and airy, with green accents, we reversed the palette in the playroom and painted the walls a darker, saturated green.

A rarely used loft over a portion of our friends' bedroom was removed to create soaring ceilings, clean lines, and symmetry. We added beams and four large green metal pendants for interest and kept the furnishings intentionally spare and simple for a stress-free, minimal feeling. A small pair of brass tables with mounted wall lamps flank the traditional spool bed, taking up minimal space. The rug is a vintage Moroccan Beni Ourain, and the green tassled throw is also Moroccan.

The bed faces a new austere-feeling stucco fireplace (echoing the one in the family room) and large views of the backyard. A pair of striped wing chairs make for cozy fireside moments and add a classic bit of pattern. Vintage art is juxtaposed with bright white walls.

We had a small dormer added to the house to make space for the main bathroom. A graceful soaking tab is flanked by his and hers vanities. A deep gray-green on the walls and all trim feels warm and rich, and contrasts with the bright white and grays in the tile and vanities.

We wrapped a fern wallpaper on the walls and ceiling of the kids' bathroom for a charming, enveloping feeling, and installed vintage-inspired subway tiles and hexagonal floor tiles with a dark grout that calls attention to the shapes. I love using patterned wallpaper in rooms with angled ceilings.

WORDS TO LIVE BY

We cannot have true freedom when we are living with **more than** we need.

Shop for only what you **need** and with intention.

Always be **decluttering**.

Make sure everything has a **place**.

Clear minds start with orderly surroundings.

Keep only what you **love** and what is **functional**.

Have a **place** for everything.

Be a fierce **editor** (declutter constantly!).

Shop less and with **more purpose**.

Create **room** for life.

Tidy up daily.

BUILDER CARRMICHAEL CONSTRUCTION

right
I use tall arrangements on a coffee table to make a house feel loved. Cut carrot blossoms in a rustic amber jug mix with collected objects and family photos to create a personal moment.

CHAPTER 3

LIVING HISTORY

*"Life is divided into three terms—
that which was, which is, and which will be.
Let us learn from the past to profit
by the present, and from the present,
to live better in the future."*

—WILLIAM WORDSWORTH

I HAVE TWO FRAMED old black-and-white photographs on the bar in my living room. One is of a strapping young blond guy in his army uniform, and another is of a handsome dark-haired man in a skinny tie. The photos are of my dad and Dave's dad when they were young. They live there on our bar, frozen in time. We're now older than they were when those photos were taken—and we were only the proverbial twinkle in their eyes—but these young men are our history, and displaying their photos connects and roots us. It makes me happy to see our dads "hanging out" at the bar together.

Next to the dad photos sits the grolla. An Italian Alpine drinking bowl, or "friendship cup," it's a wooden bowl with a lid and multiple drinking spouts—traditionally used aprés ski or after dinner—into which hot coffee and liquor are poured. Sugar is crusted around the rim of the bowl, lined with liquor, and then lit on fire. It's quite the spectacle, and my rowdy Italian family has always loved it. After we put the lid on to extinguish the fire, each person goes around in a circle and makes a toast before taking his or her drink, keeping the same spout as the grolla comes back around. It's a warm, fuzzy drink

meant to keep people toasty (or toasted!) on cold mountain nights, and you definitely feel the heat in your chest. I remember it coming out after dinner at family celebrations when I was a kid, and repeatedly making my dad and uncle relight the fire. I have the best memories of enjoying it with my cousins when I was older, so when I came across one at a thrift shop a few years ago, I snapped it up, instantly flooded with nostalgia and good vibes upon seeing it. It's just an object, a thing, but it's steeped in memories of good times with the people I love and makes me smile.

Our memories connect us with our history and our past, and remind us of why we are who we are today. Having nostalgic things in our homes brings up those memories. And there's emotion tied with our memories. We can feel sad or wistful or grateful or happy, depending upon the object and the story behind it. Think about recalling stories with an old friend, one of you reminding the other of something you'd forgotten. There's lots of "yes" and "I'd forgotten that," and laughing at the memories. It feels good to reminisce, because we are connecting with our past and bringing it right into the present. It's like our brains are

reconnecting all the dots. We feel whole. Just as we feel a deep satisfaction when recalling old stories, we can feel that same sense of nostalgia with objects—including clothing, cars, paintings, photos, fabrics, toys, furniture, grollas, you name it—that remind us of our past because they too, just like an old friend, can take us back and help us connect the dots. Are things what's most important in life? No. But can they induce a memory that makes us feel grateful for life? Absolutely.

What can an object mean to us? We often feel sentimental toward an object that was once owned by someone we love, has a story or memory behind it, or reminds us of something or someone. There are times when I present a

product to clients and they tell me it reminds them of something from their past, and I can see how excited they are to have it in their home. Objects bring out the nostalgia, that little bit of joy within us, reminding us of something, taking us back. Nostalgia often just touches on the tinge of our consciousness. We often try to grasp it and can't, but when we can harness it and bring it into our homes, there is a beautiful and meaningful melding of our past and present. Suddenly a simple object, fabric, or piece of art is elevated into something that holds meaning and history for us. Picking an object to decorate a room with can be as simple as choosing something that's pretty, in a color that works with the rug, but if we wish it to instill meaning

Our clients' office is a mix of new and old. Black walls set off pieces that have been faded over the years, along with the bits of brighter blue throughout the room. Our client loves to travel and collects art along the way. Right, an antique grandfather clock adds a sense of history to the room.

in our homes, we can select art and objects that are connected to the people who live in the house, whether it's because they so strongly embody a vibe, express a passion or sentiment of those who live in the home, or is somehow tied to their past. It's partly for this reason that I try to include lots of vintage and one-of-a-kind pieces made by artists in homes; they often come with their own stories. But not everything needs to be steeped in memory or precious to us. There is a balance, and we each have our own. On my bar next to the dad photos and the grolla is a stainless steel drink shaker I found at Target. It's all about the mix that works for you.

When I think about products I've designed, such as fabrics or tile, I realize how much things from my childhood—the plants, the land, the patterns and color palettes of fabrics, tile, wallpapers, and even linoleum—have influenced me. So many of them have stayed with me over the years, and I have this desire to reinterpret them, as if creating them anew allows me to sort of solidify my memory of them and hold on to it. Seeing one of these objects, plants, places, or fabrics reminds me of the past and the point of life I was at when it was in my life. It takes me back. The fabrics and patterns from my childhood are so ingrained in my memory that they've influenced my design aesthetic. We are sponges when we're little, picking up everything around us and taking it all in. What we buy for today affects not only our present, but is also the backdrop for our future memories. It makes me wonder how my kids will be influenced by the home I've created for them . . . how it'll affect their taste, style, and future memories. The brand-new art and objects in my house today could one day become the bits of nostalgia that will make my kids smile. (Time to go light that grolla on fire and make them some memories!) ✦

URBAN SANCTUARY

opposite
Freshly picked ferns are grouped in vintage bottles arranged around an old brass grasshopper that belonged to my friend's late grandmother, given to her by her aunt. It eventually made its way into their son's nursery, and as he got old enough, he started asking to hold it and play with it. Though he never met his great-grandma, seeing him hold and play with this object makes my friend so happy.

THIS PARTICULAR PROJECT was one in which my clients' desire for connection with their past really drove the design. When your best friend's best friend—who is also a kindred spirit and dancing partner at parties (yes, it's a thing)—calls you and says she and her husband are moving into a new condo in the city and needs your help, you jump at it. Beginning any project with people you already know and love gives you all a leg up because there's already a built-in trust and relationship. You can present things that are a bit "off" and your clients are much more likely to trust you even if they don't quite get something at first, and you're more likely to push the envelope because you know that trust is already there. And then, of course, you've already sort of "gotten" them before you even do any style-digging, and the project itself is incredibly fun and personal.

Our friends lead busy lives, with demanding corporate jobs, frequent travel, and lots of family and social engagements, so they wanted a home that would help them relax and slow life down a little . . . a place that would make them exhale and feel safe . . . somewhere they could recharge. They wanted a home that reflected who they are and where they came from. He's from New Delhi and grew up in Nigeria, spending summers and winter breaks in New Delhi, and she's from northern Virginia. They travel to Bali frequently; it was where they went on their first international trip together as they were falling in love, and a few years later, they were married there. Home for them is a place that embodies their love for travel and heritage. The materials and fabrics we used were inspired by their travels and remind them of the incredible places on this planet that mean so much to them. To our friends, "coming home" is about being with the ones you love in a place where you can completely be yourself and let your guard down, all the while being surrounded by things that remind you of where you came from and how you grew up... bits of nostalgia from the past that made you who you are today. Coming home now, they can feel all the love and heritage of their past combined with the beauty of their present life and love. This completely raw and honest way of living—to simply "be" without any pretension and an embracing of who you are and how you got here—allows us to go out into the world as our very best and truest selves. ✦

Chairs in a mix of eras and styles are unexpectedly grouped together around the dining table. Each chair has its own story and unique form and personality. Guests enjoy picking "their" chairs for dinner.

A natural live-edge table is juxtaposed with the boxiness of the apartment and its sleek white walls. Our friend bought the piece over the sideboard at a market in India with his mom years ago and had it shipped to the US before they moved into the apartment. It embodies and inspired our friends' design aesthetic, which is centered around culture and their love for travel.

The condo has breathtaking views of the Potomac River and lots of natural light, and is right in the heart of the Wharf, a burgeoning DC waterfront area. Deep, comfortable upholstery is cozy and cocoon-like in the starkly open space.

When our friends moved in, they decided to keep the walls in the family room niche empty until they could find art that meant something to them. Later that year, they took their then seven-month-old along with them to Bali and visited galleries in search of art. They eventually found their way into a small shop in Ubud loaded with paintings, where they were both drawn to pieces by a young local artist named Sugita. They loved his style, colors, and textures, and the way he incorporated the harmony between the Balinese people and nature. They ended up with six or seven paintings by Sugita that are now stored away for when they might have a larger space one day. It took them months to select which paintings to hang and frame, and looking back on it, they say the process of waiting and debating was just as fun as eventually enjoying the art.

In the main bedroom, right, pressed botanicals by Ann Blackwell hung from a track with wire hang above the bed and are flanked by a pair of rattan lanterns, calling to mind rustic handwoven baskets.

WORDS TO LIVE BY

What we put in our **homes** today **affects** not only our present, but it is also the **backdrop** for our future **memories**.

Find your **balance** of **meaningful** and **practical**.

Nostalgic objects bring **meaning** into our homes.

Live for **today** while **appreciating** the past that made you who you are.

opposite
The breathtaking Potomac views seen from the apartment. Vintage chairs were reupholstered in a Virginia Leratt Textiles fabric.

IN FABLELAND

THE RETURN OF THE NATIVE   HARDY

CHAPTER 4

DO YOU

*"To be yourself in a world that is
constantly trying to make you something else
is the greatest accomplishment."*

—RALPH WALDO EMERSON

MUCH OF WHAT GOES INTO creating a home is logic, careful planning, and attention to balance, scale, color, and harmony, but then there is another part of it that comes from the heart. And that emotional aspect can't be forced. Like any work of art, a home is more meaningful when it's real and honest and comes from a desire to create something that expresses a point of view; when it sparks a feeling, is insightful and reveals a truth of sorts, and when it tells the story of the people who live there. Our homes—when done thoughtfully and with honesty—innately express a way of looking at the world and have the power to create a mood and to set the perfect (in the realest sense) backdrop for our own lives.

Some people are gifted at observing what is around them and communicating their insights. When we laugh out loud because of something we think is funny, we often find ourselves saying or thinking, "that's so true." We might cry because a book or a movie or even a commercial is sad or touching, but ultimately because someone created a piece of "art" that got put in front of us and we reacted to seeing the truth

in it. Honest representations have meaning or truth behind them, and we deem them "beautiful" or "hilarious" or "tragic" or whatever other adjective we'd use to describe something that has the power to move us. Humans innately recognize authenticity, and we appreciate it.

The same can be said for a meaningful home that represents the people who live there in a way that exposes the truth of who they are. A home filled with meaning comes from a place of understanding those who live in it. Because each person, each family, and each house is different, homes are better enjoyed and feel "real" and in harmony with us when they reflect our uniqueness, rather than attempting to be a copy of something else or trying to be "on trend" or "perfect."

In the restroom of my old design studio, I hung a vintage painting of a woman above the toilet. She was life-size, and I hung her at eye level so she was "smizing" right at you. I named her Dr. Lalondi after one my dad's doctors who I thought she looked like. Without fail, almost all of my clients would come out of the bathroom shaking their heads or laughing

opposite
An old wooden spoon collection is like a beautiful art display on the kitchen counter.

about Dr. Lalondi, wondering who she was and cracking jokes about not having any privacy in there. She was an icebreaker, and lightened up people's moods because of the absurdity of her smizing in the bathroom. It also gave clients a bit of insight into my sense of humor and my philosophy of not taking design too seriously.

Many of the spaces that we (design lovers) fall in love with are both highly personal and beautiful. The keen observations and honest expressions made in highly personal homes are interesting to us. We might take inspiration from these rooms and refer back to images of them frequently. The inspiration can then translate into learning, reinterpretation, and personalization, rather than copying, so that we go on to create something new and unique; something that wouldn't have existed if we didn't create it; something that is our own. Creating something honest and real with a relationship to you is going to have the most powerful effects and ring the truest. Be who you are and let your home be what it is.

One of my favorite parts of meeting new clients is helping them figure out their personal style and working out the vibe for their homes, all while taking the architecture into account to come up with a project language that encompasses it all. It's basically a description and lists of words describing how we want the house to feel that helps all teams involved make decisions and selections.* Taking the time to do this, and to quiet ourselves and shut out all the noise of trends to listen and see who we really are, allows us to create something much deeper and more real than simply buying to buy or copying trends. Don't worry about doing what everyone else is doing or what's "in" or "out." Everything in the home needs only to appeal to you. Getting to know ourselves, our style, and the architectural style of our homes is key in

creating an honest representation of who we are in our homes. Forget about the trends. Good design is timeless and transcends. But just as important as not letting trends dictate your home is making sure you aren't forgoing doing something you love simply because it is a trend and has been done before, because in that way you are still allowing the trends to dictate what you do. I have found myself doing that in the past because I so badly wanted to do something original. Turn off the noise surrounding you and be true to yourself.

"Do you" is the advice I often give to aspiring designers. If you want to set yourself apart, you have to do your own thing and do what you love. You have to not care what others think. This honesty and commitment to "doing you" takes vulnerability and requires having the strength to expose ourselves for judgement and critique. Not everyone is going to like what we do when we're putting out a personal point of view . . . and that's OK. Having confidence in ourselves and asserting our independence from the opinions of others allows us to forge our own paths and to feel a freedom like we've never known before. It allows us to belong in our own world without needing to belong or subscribing to another's idea of how a life should be lived. Nowhere does it affect us more on a daily basis than in our own homes.

The best results come from making our own observations and coming to our own conclusions. There is a choice in *almost* every design decision we make. Forcing ourselves to verbalize *why* we are choosing something ensures that we have an understanding of what we're doing. Every little choice can reflect taste and personality, so choose carefully. Whenever there is a decision to make, there is an opportunity to make a home more "you." It's an exercise of self-expression. The more

thoughtful we are about it, the more satisfied we are in the end with what we have made.

The things that make me love my home the most are the "risks," the "sparks of interest," and the truly personal statements for me in the rooms—such as sanding down my trim, plastering the walls, the yellow grandma floral curtains in my dining room, loading on the brown throughout, and the pieces of religious art and sculpture we have collected and displayed throughout our home . . . the things with personality. These are also the things that might make other people not like my home. And that's OK. Not everybody has to like what you do in your home. You don't need to please anyone other than yourself. Not everything needs to be a showstopper. Basic pieces, such as a simple neutral sofa, a natural fiber rug, or a classic farm table, can provide the backdrop for those special moments, such as a crazy cool coffee table, a statement fabric, or amazing stone fireplace. On the other hand, you can do a bright green sofa and keep your walls simple. At the end of this chapter, I've listed some of my favorite basic "building block" pieces that can then be built on with your own "do you" selections.

We all know what it's like to be somewhere feeling out of place or uncomfortable. When I first started designing for clients and I visited the Washington Design Center, I felt like *such* an amateur and was sure that I stuck out as an imposter. I remember being in a design showhouse way back when, being called a "mommy blogger" by another designer behind my back. It was slightly comical (I didn't quite know whether to be insulted or honored!), but also made me feel like maybe my work was less than the others' work, and I did question myself and feel like maybe everyone else had something I didn't have. Throughout our lives, we will all experience these types of moments where we feel like we're on the outside looking in—and they are essential for our growth and development of mettle—but the beauty of home is that we never have to be outsiders within its walls; we never have to hold up a wall of strength there. Talking with my clients throughout the years, the one thing I hear the most is that home is where they are "free to be" themselves, to "let their guards down," and to simply "be." They can relax and let go and be protected from the outside world within the walls of their own homes.

When designing a home, we often come to know ourselves better by the time we have come out on the other side. We have learned about ourselves, understanding our wants and desires because we've studied how we live and figured out how a home can best help us. Epiphanies come to us as we're designing— and then as we're living in a house—that we can't unknow, and we take them on to future decisions. I've watched my own opinions for what I want evolve and solidify as I've lived in multiple houses over the years and as my family has grown, or we have moved. My sink gets bigger at every house we move to, and my gardens become more integral to living. Each time, I don't want to lose the good things that we have already created, but I want to add a new, more improved aspect to our life, such as a bigger yard or fire pit, etc. Living somewhere teaches us what we love in a house. ✦

At left, our client's family photo wall mixes moments from past and present.

*I delve into how to do this in detail in my first book, Habitat.

VINTAGE GRACE

opposite
Simple upholstered pieces in machine-washable linen slipcovers are relaxed and practical. Vintage-inspired patterned curtains have a yesteryear quality about them that fits the house.

CLIENTS OF OURS HAD a similar experience of getting to know themselves and figuring out exactly what they wanted in a home. We finished renovating and decorating a home for them, and after living there for just a couple of short years—and their children getting a bit older—they thought about having a bigger yard and space for a pool, so when a nearby beautiful old Queen Anne Foursquare built in 1916 filled with original charm and 1980s "updates" came on the market, they jumped at it.

I know what it's like when you've recently finished a house and then decide to move again . . . you are questioned, and people think you're crazy. It's a funny phenomenon, but I've heard people looking at the situation from the outside say it "exhausts" them, which always makes me laugh, because I think, "Shouldn't *I* be the one who's tired?" And trust me, it can be exhausting. You've done it before so you know what you're getting into, but you also know how worth it it will be on the other end and are willing to do it all over again. I've realized that it's the times when we go our own way and write our own story that we feel our freest and happiest, no matter what others may think.

After already having gone through an extensive renovation and design project in the recent past together and becoming close with my clients, we'd all developed a trust and a shorthand which we took with us onto the next house. They've always been confident in decision-making because they know themselves well, but we were able to move even more seamlessly this time around because we already understood the way in which they lived and desired to live and could dive right into the nitty-gritty. Cunningham Quill Architects reworked the floor plan of the house while we selected all the interior details and finishes that would keep the house feeling true to itself—the pine floors, the traditional moldings, the stair railings, the cabinetry, the tile, etc. CarrMichael Construction got to work (again), and we began to decorate the rooms, using as much as we could from the last house, bringing in new furnishings where necessary.

Our clients wanted to create a home where they felt they and their children could live life to the fullest. They are determined, busy people who understood how a house needed to work for them in order to comfort them and make life easier.

They don't care about impressing others—and that's not to say that the house doesn't feel welcoming or isn't geared toward entertaining (because it does and is!), but that it's so personal and innately honest and was made just for them. It's filled with pieces from their past and present. They know what they like and don't have any fear of doing it. They aren't trying to impress a single soul or stay "on trend." We designed for them with no regard for what others think.

+ "Busy" wallpaper? Check.

+ Grandma florals? Check.

+ Victorian furniture? Check.

Fearless floral "granny" chintzes mix with linen ikats and block prints. Mid-century pieces are paired with Victorian ones. It's about what they love, not about what's "in." They know that their home is for them, and that it's the place where they can let their guards down, relax, and just be themselves. The only way to get the emotion and truth out of a house is to take risks and "do you" without regard to what anyone thinks. +

The exterior was changed as little as possible. Jennifer Horn's land-scaping and garden designs for the house were simple and timeless. We designed the new stair railings with a combination of elements from the home's original stair railings and those at the historic Inn at Little Washington, a favorite spot of our clients.

In the living room, original doors with cremone bolts and wavy glass lead out to the porch. We paired a new pale blue English arm sofa with a velvet sofa from the old house. The walls are papered in a small-scale blue-and-white playful block print. We wanted to remain true to the original house and to keep all of the charm and "yesteryear" qualities it had, all while turning it into a practical, livable family home for today that expresses our clients' personality and style.

A pair of newly reupholstered antique bamboo chairs and a small game table with a lamp create an intimate moment in the living room. I love how the light filters through the unlined hand-block-printed curtains by Les Indiennes. This room is all about pattern on pattern, and the key is mixing the size and scale of the patterns so that they work together instead of competing.

Rhododendrons grow all over the property, and so we commissioned rhododendron botanicals by artist Emily Morgan Brown, which fill the wall in behind the sofa and contrast with the small scale of the block print wallpaper.

The traditional blue, brown, and gray-green chintz on the dining room curtains inspired the palette of the house. The side chairs were inherited with the house, and we had them reupholstered in a blue ikat to contrast with the green velvet host chairs, which were brought over from their old house, along with the table. The rug is an antique Chinese piece. A collection of antique paintings lines the walls.

I love seeing my client cook. I've watched her meal prep for the family throughout the years as I've been at the house and have had the pleasure of a few meals that she's made, and every single one is just pure, simple perfection. She always seems to use such fresh, beautiful ingredients, has

such an organized, measured way of going about cooking, and it makes me happy seeing the ingredients spread all over the kitchen as it's in use. I always go home inspired.

CarrMichael Construction built the island out of reclaimed wood. Drawers are tucked into the apron, and pots

and vegetables are casually stored on the lower shelf.

A traditional apron front sink faces the backyard. Simple subway tile with black grout to accentuate the tiles is run up to the ceiling. Rise-and-fall pendants over the island are both practical and beautiful.

A vintage brass globe light fixture hangs over the kitchen table and chairs, which were brought over from the old house. With the window at the back of the dining nook, I went for simple, spare pieces that would silhouette against the sunlight. I often place hide rugs under dining tables where little kids dine frequently because they can't be damaged by spills and are easy to wipe clean.

Eras and styles mix in the family room—which is open to the kitchen—for a relaxed, fresh, collected feel. The chaise is an antique Victorian reupholstered in a linen fern print. The new addition in the back of the house allows for a big, open family and dining/cooking space where they can all be together. The house now makes so much sense for our clients. It might not be easy for everyone to understand why someone might make a decision like this—moving and renovating again when they'd just finished another beautiful house only a few years before—but our clients understood deep down exactly how they wanted to live and so they went for it. They took their own path and created exactly what they knew would make them feel the most at home.

The back of the house—where the family spends the majority of their time—is more casual and relaxed than the more formal entertaining spaces in the front of the house. We planked the ceilings in reclaimed wood and had them whitewashed.

The main bathroom is a mix of old and new, with bold iron shower doors and bordered marble floors, a vanity fashioned after an antique dresser, and simple linen café curtains.

The laundry room is minimal and serene, with nickel board walls, vintage-inspired lighting, and unlined linen café curtains.

The pool house is part pool house, part potting shed. Zinc countertops and open shelving layered with plants, cloches, and pots create a potting shed feel in the pool house.

The design of this space began with a vintage cast-iron sink with drainboard and had CarrMichael Construction build a rustic base out of reclaimed wood to set it into. Slate floors in a French pattern are durable and maintenance-free.

WORDS TO LIVE BY

Do *you*.

Forget the trends.

Trust yourself.

Mix design styles and
eras *fearlessly*.

Take your own *path*.

BUILDING BLOCKS

+ Simple neutral linen
  or leather sofa

+ Natural fiber rug

+ Basic end tables

+ Farm table

+ Parsons bed

PERSONALITY MOMENTS

+ Art

+ Statement rug

+ Chairs

+ Coffee table

+ Fabrics

+ Lighting

ALL OF THAT BEING SAID, I love a crazy, patterned sofa with lots of personality or an incredible statement-making dining table. In the end, it's all about the balance of what's clean and simple mixing with what's quirky and personal. We each have our own desired ratio of statements-to-basics in any given room. To each her own!

ARCHITECT CUNNINGHAM QUILL ARCHITECTS

BUILDER CARRMICHAEL CONSTRUCTION

LANDSCAPE DESIGN JENNIFER HORN LANDSCAPE ARCHITECTURE

right
A prep sink
for drinks
and cleaning
vegetables is
tucked in the
corner of the
kitchen.

CHAPTER 5

COMPOSING ATMOSPHERE

*"Create an atmosphere
in which anything is possible."*

—THOMAS RAYMOND KELLY

WHEN I WAS WRITING this book and thinking about how home makes us feel, I asked my kids, ranging in ages from three to thirteen, "What is home to you?" They all thought a bit and then answered with words like "cozy," "happy," "warm," "joyful," "relaxing," and "safe and snug." My five- and three-year-old daughters said, "Home is fun," and when I asked them why, they said because their bikes and scooters are there. (Ah, of course! Priorities.) But not a single one of them said anything like "stylish," "pretty," "beautiful," or "well-built." No one commented on my curtains or furniture . . . or my pretty throw pillows. Not a word about the style of the house or its design; the words they landed on were rooted in emotion, on how home made them feel.

I'm fascinated by the fact that something like a house that is in and of itself a physical *thing* brings up so much emotion in us. A house is a building . . . walls, floors, ceilings, and things . . . wood and drywall. Places have a power over us, because each one has its own atmosphere that surrounds us and influences us. Most of us want to elicit positive feelings within ourselves and our loved ones at home, and it's for this

reason that we're so careful and thoughtful about the design of our houses. We know that they're made up of material goods, of "stuff" and design choices, but those physical things—the materials—and our choices have the power to make or break our moods.

We all have different ideas of what we want home to feel like. Some of us want warm and cozy, some of us want cool and edgy, and some of us want soulful and romantic. We can begin to determine our desired atmosphere by figuring out what we feel the freest to be ourselves in; where we feel safe just being who we are.

I personally feel my best when my home has a relaxed, down-to-earth atmosphere. (My second book, *Down to Earth*, is entirely about achieving it.) Like most of us, I'm busy at work all day, every day, and love to come home and exhale. I live an indoor-outdoor type of life at home, with good food, music, and fresh flowers being some of my favorite things. I love natural light and try to maximize it wherever possible by enlarging windows when I can and painting with soft whites that reflect the light beautifully for a light and airy feel. I love an easy-breezy

previous
A vintage painting hangs atop a wallpaper mural in my client's office.

opposite
A newly added massive window in our clients' kitchen allows the light to come in and reflect off of all the materials. I wanted to create something for our clients that was sophisticated and slightly austere. Handmade tiles and textured drywall that feels like plaster create an envelope of texture for the space.

vibe where a home seamlessly connects with the outdoors, so I pull in lots of natural materials and objects, but there is much more that goes into atmosphere. To really create a meaningful atmosphere in our homes, we need to utilize elements that affect all five of the senses: sight, hearing, smell, touch, and taste. The senses exist, so even if we are ignoring a few of them—such as hearing or smell—we are still experiencing them. Maybe we hear or smell "nothing," but we are hearing and smelling

nonetheless. Doing nothing about any of the senses is a missed opportunity. When we have finished "designing" a home and have selected all of our fabrics, furniture, and finishes, we are only halfway there in creating an atmosphere that feels like home.

Think of the sounds that have an effect on you. Music is a powerful force on our emotions. When I feel like I need to calm my kids down, they'll get a good dose of Enya, and when I want them to have fun and party, my dance mix goes

above
Shadows and light play on the natural materials in this kitchen. The dark floors and stained cabinetry create a deep and moody backdrop for all the sunlight running in.

on. I even have "Saturday" mixes that I play to celebrate that it's Saturday, and it instantly makes everyone happy. (Creating playlists is a hobby of mine, and many of my favorites can be found on my app, Lauren Liess & Co., and are available for free download.) These sounds and songs come to mean something to us and become intertwined with home. Silence can be just as powerful. Open windows and the sounds of birds (or cars!) also have an effect on our moods. We live on a main road near our town, where every Saturday morning there is a "cars and coffee" event at the local coffee house owned by a friend where car aficionados meet up to talk shop and display their vintage cars. When we sleep with the windows open, I'm often awoken on a Saturday morning by some dude downshifting and then punching it as he rounds the bend of the road. When we first moved in, I was *not* happy about this, but as time went by, the sound of the cars waking me up on Saturdays when the windows are open has become a happy sound. Sometimes Dave and I will be out and about and hear a car switch gears randomly and we smile because we associate it with Saturday mornings, and it puts us in a good mood. During the COVID-19 quarantine, we don't hear the cars anymore, and I never thought I would, but I miss those downshifts dearly.

Now think about the sense of smell. It is the sense most closely tied with our memories. It not only has the power to shape what we think about when entering a space, but it also affects our future memories and associations with that space and those of all who live and visit there. Scent is another of those "decisions" I mentioned in which we should have a reason for. (Your "reason" can simply be because you like it; your answer doesn't need to be anything mind-blowing.) Though not quite as permanent,

consider selecting the scents for each room of your home in the way you would a paint color—with thought and care. Think about what you want your home to smell like. I love woodsy green scents and developed a signature one that's a mix of cedar, cucumber, and moss called "White Cypress," and use it throughout my house. When coming home after being away for a bit, I'm greeted with a scent that makes me exhale and relax. Though I have "White Cypress" generally throughout our place, I use a sent called "Potager"—which I developed to remind me of my kitchen garden—in my kitchen because it blends beautifully with food, and one called "Heirloom"—which is soft and romantic—in the bedroom. In each of the four seasons, for different moods, I pull in others. Though they're all so different, almost every single one of my scents has a slight undertone of cedar so that they play well with each other. Natural cedar planking is one of my favorite materials to bring into interiors on ceilings or walls because it has that beautiful soft, clean, woody scent.

The scent of food cooking is another one that can drastically affect the atmosphere and, by effect, our moods. Cookies in the oven, onions sautéing, and homemade chicken broth on the stove all make me feel warm and fuzzy. I remember coming down the stairs as a kid when my Beautiful Grandmother was cooking dinner and the sound and the smell of the onions sizzling just felt like home, while the scent of celery takes me back to my Grandma Maestranzi's Chicago kitchen.

There is nothing that makes or breaks my day like food. When I have an amazing meal, I am on cloud nine. Even the knowledge that an amazing meal is coming puts me in a good mood.

It's easy to feel as if life is a series of trashing the kitchen and then cleaning it, only to wait forty minutes (I've timed it) and trash it all over again. The more creative and thoughtful we are with our food, the happier we are. A few houses ago, I realized—because we need to cook for such a sizable crowd—that I needed to embrace food, so food and the experience of cooking and dining have become a form of entertainment in our house. The number of hours each day devoted to meals is astonishing, so the more we can learn to enjoy it, the more fulfilled we will be. Like smell, taste brings on the memories and the feelings. Think about how your favorite meals to cook—your signature dishes—make you and those around you feel. There is excitement in the air, and people feel loved because you are taking the time to feed them and there is an instant association with delicious meals of the past and knowing how good it's going to be. It's literally comfort food.

When I design kitchens, I like to understand how my clients eat and cook. Do they dine casually or formally? Who is cooking the majority of the meals? Are the meals simple, complicated, rustic, or fancy? I envision how the main chef (or chefs) and the food will feel most at home and authentic. Think about cupcakes and desserts and how bakeries are often light and white, with pastel colors. Materials and colors that make the food look its best and showcase it are selected. Think about the general style of cooking and entertaining that will be happening within a kitchen or dining room and design around it. We eat fairly simply and casually, with lots of fresh homegrown ingredients and herbs, charcuterie boards, soups and salads, and a bit of a rustic Northern Italian edge, so my kitchen and dining room are simple, rustic, and strong, with a little bit of a primitive European vibe. We serve a lot of our food on wooden boards or on casual handmade pottery. Nothing is precious, and I have lots of helpers, so I like to keep things easy

to grab and put away, so we have a variety of open shelving in the kitchen , and we store many of our daily use items low, at kid-height.

Texture, pattern, color, and light are some of the most powerful tools for creating atmosphere. Texture can be both seen and touched. I use natural textures like it's my job (I guess technically, it *is* my job!) all over homes to add warmth, interest, and to make them feel more natural and relaxed. Solid materials and textures calm a space, while patterns with lots of movement and/or contrast wake it up. Sheen and light reflection also play a role. Polished stone and glossier materials make a place more formal and sophisticated, whereas honed, rougher surfaces feel more relaxed and natural. I personally gravitate toward the latter for a more down-to-earth vibe, which is generally what's being shown throughout this book. Patterns create "movement" and energy in a space, whereas solids or soft tonal variations feel calm and quiet. Figuring out your pattern-to-solid ratio is key in creating atmosphere.*

When I fall for a home, it's often because of the type of natural light it gets. It doesn't always have to be light and bright for me to love it. Think about places or photos of various places . . . the warm, sunny light of Los Angeles vs. the cool, moody light of Amsterdam. The lighting in some places is just special. Walls can be made to feel more interesting with the addition of texture that will catch the light. Plaster and stucco are some of my favorite surface textures to use in a home because they have more texture than drywall and the light catches on their movement and reflects off of it, giving the surface the appearance of depth. Stone, tile, brick, woodwork, and virtually any material that provides texture can make walls feel more interesting. That's not to say that drywall can't be interesting too, however. I have

opposite
A built-in china cabinet with wavy glass made to look antique is layered in with our clients' beautiful collection of dishware. We continued the handmade tile from the backsplash to the inside of the china cabinet for added texture and layering.

*I write about determining your pattern-to-solid ratio in Habitat.

it all over my house, and it's in the majority of my clients' homes, and the key is selecting a paint that looks right with the light in the house. Some of my favorite white paints are used throughout this book, and they can be found in the resources sections at the end of the book.

One of the first things I think about when designing a room is if it will be a dark space or a light space. As you may have noticed in this book, I often do lighter main spaces, such as kitchens and living rooms, with darker, cozier ancillary rooms such as libraries or offices. Darker colors and materials feel moodier and/ or edgier, whereas lighter ones feel fresh and clean. Painting woodwork darker or having raw, waxed, oiled, or stained woodwork gives a room a little age and mood. To make a space even moodier, consider painting the walls dark, too. Taking the woodwork to a much darker color than the walls creates a high-contrast, edgier vibe and adds a bit of energy, whereas woodwork that matches walls feels more relaxed and subdued. For cozy moodier spaces, I often do a lot of dark on dark, meaning walls, trim, and other elements throughout, such as upholstery or rugs, all go dark with only slight variation so there's a sort of "cocooning" feeling going on that adds to a sense of privacy and warmth. Richer fabrics and materials such as velvet, leather, and thick hemps and linens add heft and depth to a space. Alternately, to lighten up a room, lighter paint and upholstery do the trick, along with lighter materials such as unlined linen or cotton and raw woods. Wherever possible, have all hardwired lighting put on dimmers so that atmosphere can be played with and changed throughout the day as needed.

Just as appealing to all five senses enriches a home and fills it with meaning and emotion, the seasons also change atmosphere and affect our moods. We decorate for the holidays to tweak the atmosphere of our home, making it feel joyful, festive, wintry, or freshened up for spring, etc. Bringing that Christmas tree into the house—smelling the pine and seeing the twinkling lights—results in a physiological reaction in much the same way "coming home" does for us. It's that bit of nostalgia created by seeing and smelling the tree and going through the process you've been through so many times before that brings on the feelings. I see lots of people change out throw pillows to deeper hues in the colder months and lighter ones in the spring and summer, and swap bedding, rugs, etc. I like to make some of the easier or more subtle changes, like adding fuzzy throw pillows and extra blankets around in colder months.

Using the elements—water, fire, air, and earth— at home is another way to wake up the senses and bring us to the present moment. Think about how being near water relaxes and puts us at ease—nothing is quite like hanging by the ocean, or a river or lake—but even a simple bath or a shower can have that calming, healing, relaxing effect on us. Candlelight and cozy fires create ambiance and a play of light that is primal and mysterious. Captivating, it has the power to both excite and soothe us. Breezes and open windows bring about a feeling of freedom and help us exhale. Pulling in natural objects like stones, shells, driftwood, and plants can ground a home and make us feel more secure, more connected to the earth. We have been deeply conditioned to notice and respond to the elements, and employing them intensifies the atmosphere around us and fills it with emotion and meaning. We cannot be oblivious to it, even if we are responding to it on a subconscious level. I've noticed that even my kids always seem to gravitate toward the natural elements in any space, and we can't keep them away. The elements have a pull that piques their curiosity.

above
A black island and slate floors contrast with plaster walls and handmade-tile.

There is an art in taking someone through various feelings and moods as they move through and experience a home whose rooms have subtly different atmospheres. In these sorts of houses, if you pay attention, you can feel the mood evolve as you move from room to room.

To do this in your home, think about how you will enter your house and what you will want to feel as you move from room to room. Then, design around these desired states of mind. In a

kitchen, for example, many people are after light and bright so they can cook and feel energized and productive, whereas in a library, many of us are drawn to darker, cozier spaces where curling up with a book feels like the best thing to do. To some extent, the mood of each room in a house is different, but others of us keep a more consistent atmosphere through an entire home. There is no wrong or right here . . . it's whatever you feel will most fulfill you. ✦

ROMANTIC CURIOSITY

THE HOUSE IN THIS chapter is one of those houses in which the atmosphere shifts slightly from room to room, subtly playing with materials, forms, and fabrics to create various moods. When we first met our clients, we could see that the process of building a house for them wasn't just about building a haven for their family, it was also a creative and personal journey of sorts that they would continue on long after the house was "finished," even sharing the house's progress and their feelings, thoughts, and art finds on social media. Thoughtful, intuitive people, they understood the power of atmosphere and the emotions it causes and wanted to create a home that made them feel safe and free to be themselves. We worked with Barnes Vanze Architects and CarrMichael Construction. My goal was to take the beautiful envelope the architects had created and to try to fill it in with color and emotion, to create an atmosphere that would make our clients feel both free and safe, joyful and thoughtful, and comfortable yet inspired.

An avid art collector, my client wanted the perfect backdrop for her ever-growing collection. A connection with nature was also important to our clients, and because the project was a new build, we also wanted to introduce a sense of age and depth. We brought in lots of blended colors, tone-on-tone patterns, and washed and tea stain–like finishes and fabrics that would create a soft, romantic backdrop and allow some edgier pieces of furniture and art and hits of black throughout the house to stand out. As the house is entered through the more public spaces—the foyer, living room, main hall, and kitchen—I wanted the materials and palette to feel open and airy like the architecture, but as the house meanders, I wanted there to be a feeling of discovery and a bit of an escape where someone could just be alone, reading, writing, playing music, or thinking, such as the library, office, and cabin. Walking through from one end of the house to the other is like a journey in which you experience different feelings and emotions along the way. ✦

opposite
An oversize mural creates a large impact in the little guest bedroom.

The foyer links so many different areas of the home—the living room, dining room, basement, library, and of course, the outside—that it needed to blend and connect all of these spaces. Earth-toned, timeworn vintage rugs and "Fern Star" curtains soften the hardworking space. An antique door from the house's original cabin hangs in the stairway and is in and of itself a work of art. Immediately upon entering, there is a mix of materials and elements—wood, iron, linen, artwork, and sunwashed rugs—that are an introduction to what's to come in the rest of the house.

Each piece of art my client brings home carries intense meaning for her. She wanted to be surrounded by what inspires and is meaningful to her, stirring up powerful emotion and thoughts. When the house was finally finished being built and our team took over to install. We had so much fun placing that final layer of art and accessories she had collected around the house, because we knew it was the layer that would mean the most to our client, the layer that would make the place feel like home. for her.

The foyer includes work by Susanna Bauer, Jennifer Dailey, Kerry Harding, Charlie Leal, William McClure, Ryn Miller, Amy Berlin Opsal, Lindsey J. Porter, and Rebekka Seale.

Warmth, texture, and light are
at play in the great room, which
is one large space along the back
of the house that we broke into
separate spaces for more intimate
conversation areas. Tonal variations
with lots of what I call "blended"
color, where one color sort of leaks
into the next to create a sort of
soulful vibe. As I was designing the
house, I was also in the process of
designing many of the pieces for
my upcoming furniture collections,
and even designed pieces with
the house in mind, so our clients
approved much of the furniture for
the house from sketches, drawings,
and concepts rather than photos
of actual pieces. I remember just
wanting to make sure they loved
every last little thing we brought
into the house, and I will be forever
grateful to my clients for this leap of
faith they took.

A maidenhair fern is potted in a
pewter compote layered on top
of books, with an antique Chinese
calligraphy brush.

There is a balance of texture and color throughout the space and a variety of heights so that there is depth and interest from every view of the long great room. The breakfast room is right off of the kitchen and features a white resin table with cheeky faux bois detailing mixed with a pair of antique Ming chairs and six leather and chrome "revival" chairs from my collection.

Long, clean tables like this one offer an opportunity for combining chair styles, one of my favorite things to do because I'm a bit chair-obsessed and love mixing unexpected styles.

A close-up view of the main living space shows the blended fabrics at play. There are soft wheats in the vegetable-dyed rug and damask mid-century-style sofa mixing with watery blues, tea stains, grays and browns in the pillow, and curtain fabrics juxtaposed with hits of black creating a romantic-yet-cool vibe. The main living space is centered around the fireplace, where two large sofas anchor the room. We wanted something interesting and textural and quiet, yet bold enough to make a statement over the fireplace, and selected a piece by Mary Little, an artist I had been dying to work with for years. A golden-toned, vegetable-dyed rug is layered over a soft jute rug.

I hoped to create beautiful, sculptural, soulful spaces within this house that held a bit of quiet drama. A pair of Chelsea Fly watercolor landscapes on raw canvas hangs above a pair of demilunes in the breakfast room (one side is shown at left). Throughout the house are paintings of these types of mysterious trees, which are very dear to my client.

A four-chair seating arrangement might just be my very favorite furniture arrangement. It's almost impossible not to have focused, true conversation in one. There's something about the fact that it's contained around a central table and each chair is facing the others that keeps people engaged.

A massive central island in oiled white oak is set against slate floors and pale greige cabinets. The iron pendant is spare and restrained in the large space.

The sink overlooks the incredible backyard views. I love foraging in the yard for branches to bring inside.

The bigger and wilder they are, the better. I love displaying them in a big vase on the kitchen island.

Handmade tile throughout the kitchen adds depth and character to the clean kitchen. A simple plaster range hood with reclaimed wood is graceful and understated.

Chicken wire and glass cabinet doors
allow for views of our clients' humble
yet beautiful handmade dinnerware,
by local ceramicist Lindsey Augustine
for my shop.

An unstyled moment, right, snapped on my iPhone at the end of the photo shoot. I love moments like this where a kitchen is really used and messed up in the best of ways—over fresh bread, wine, cheese, fruit, and good conversation.

A large mural, far right, creates a deep and moody backdrop in the dining room, right. Spare open-back dining chairs with brown leather seats are shown here with removable linen slipcovers for seasonal changes and surround a long, rustic harvest table.

The slipcovered chairs sit atop a wheat-toned, hand-spun Aubusson rug, which adds a bit of history and romance to the space.

The library is filled not only with books but also with interesting and thoughtful objects, such as natural curiosities, pieces collected during travels, and sculpture, which creates a feeling of wonderment and learning.

Glass pull-down doors with locks, left, display our client's coin collection and other treasures.

Found natural objects sit in front of *Natural Curiosities*, a favorite display book with beautiful animal studies on every page.

A black velvet sofa makes a cozy reading or napping spot.

My client's office is a tiny jewel box near the kitchen. We wrapped the walls in a mural and used a built-in desk to maximize space.

The powder room, right, is planked in painted pine. A simple-yet-sculptural vessel sink sits atop a rustic washstand.

I was blown away the first time I saw the original log cabin on the property that was built in the 1860s. The new house was connected to it, and it now serves as a family room and entertaining space. Flagstone flooring complements all of the wood and chinking beautifully. Two large, rustic tables are pushed together and mixed with a variety of mismatched chairs for a casual feel. Cedar cabinets, left, contrast with flagstone floors.

Also a piano-playing and TV-watching space, we wanted the cabin to feel cozy and comfortable. Pieces I designed (seen on the next page) mix with antique and vintage furnishings for a collected feel. I often pair new upholstery with antique or vintage rugs to add patina and age.

We installed this piece, above, in the evening as the sun was coming in through the doorway, and we couldn't believe how beautifully the light hit it. Our client loves it and says it holds a secret meaning for her.

Throughout the house, we created little gallery spaces with wall lights where our client could display her ever-growing art collection. Pieces by artists William McLure, Martin Campos, and Elissa Barber are hung in the hallway vestibule leading to our clients' bedroom.

The main bedroom is light and airy, with gorgeous backyard views.

We swathed the walls in hand-block-printed curtains for pattern and warmth in our clients' bedroom. The spare wrought-iron bed is upholstered in a glowy brown linen floral. Seagrass brings natural texture to the space, and a beautiful antique Kars rug is layered on top. The layers create a soft, romantic vibe.

A vintage gold floral fabric with hints of pale blue mixes with a pheasant needlepoint and pale blue pillows on the bed. Curtains in a hand-block-printed fabric by Les Indiennes line the walls, and the iron bed is upholstered in a tonal brown block print. These layers of blended and tone-on-tone fabrics feel refined, soft, and peaceful.

An old tapestry my client found for a song just fit in the main bedroom and adds so much depth and patina to this neutral area of the room. It's set off almost like a piece at a museum.

A collection of vintage Tamegroute Moroccan glazed green pottery candlesticks, above, sits on the dresser.

Glazed terra-cotta tile floors are paired with oiled white oak vanities in the bathroom. On "her" side of the room, we selected more feminine details . . . the vanity sconces are golden wheat stalks and the mirror is classical feminine, with an acanthus leaves and shell design. On "his" side—seen in the reflection of her mirror—we selected simple and straight brass sconces and a plain, traditional mirror.

A gleaming copper tub sits in front of the lace-clad windows. Ogeed corners in the bath nook add interest and make the bath nook feel more special, setting it apart from the rest of the bathroom.

A cozy little family room upstairs is a nesting spot for the family.

Recessed bookshelves line the hallway to the kids' bedrooms, where an antique bench sits.

Our clients' son requested a palette of blue, black, silver, and "golden" for his bedroom, and we were happy to oblige. He's got an edgy little vibe we just loved putting together.

The bathroom is a continuation of the bedroom's palette, with black marble floors and glazed blue terra-cotta tile walls and shower.

Flower power rules in this sweet little girl's room.

A cheerful Lulie Wallace paper lines the walls and ceiling. A wrought-iron bed, Victorian moss mohair child's chase, and antique Chinese pictorial rug add sophistication and depth, and keep the room from feeling too sweet or one-note.

The antique Chinese rug depicts colorful animals and dragons. It's the type of piece I like to imagine she will have forever and pass down to her children.

A window seat overlooking the back-yard is tucked between bookshelves.

Lauren Liess Textile pillows in shades of gold and sepia layer over the patterned paper.

WORDS TO LIVE BY

Ask yourself how "home" *feels* to you?

Determine the feeling you want your home to have.

Create an **atmosphere** that appeals to all of the five **senses**.

Think about how you can incorporate the **elements**—earth, air, water, and fire—into your home.

Experience the **seasons**.

opposite
I fell for a pair of crazy black velvet and gilt daisy chairs (a pair flanks the entrance) the moment I saw them and wasn't quite sure what my clients would think when presented with them, but they too immediately "got it"! I love including quirky, fun, or "off" pieces in rooms.

ARCHITECT BARNES VANZ
BUILDER CARRMICHAEL CONSTRUCTION
LANDSCAPE DESIGNER JENNIFER HORN

CHAPTER 6

EMBRACE IMPERFECTION

"There is no perfection,
only beautiful versions of brokenness."
—SHANNON L. ALDER

WHEN DAVE AND I WERE newlyweds in our first house, I put a lot of pressure on myself to have the "perfect" house. This was before I knew what a blog was and way before social media and Pinterest were big (Thank God, because I can't imagine how much more time I would have spent!), but I was so excited about having a place and so full of ideas for how I wanted home to feel, that I would not rest until I had finished decorating our place. The two of us would sit down to hang out after a day of fixing up the house, and I'd notice all of the things that still needed to be done . . . I'd see the holes in our hand-me-down sofa (our dog chewed her way through the side of it—long story!) and the blank walls we had yet to fill, and my house felt like one giant to-do list. It was like I couldn't turn off my brain and relax. But then a year or so later we had our son Christian—and after that the kids just kept coming—and I realized that trying to make everything "perfect" or "finished" was futile. I had so much less time on my hands, and having kids relaxed me (or broke me in a good way, possibly?) and refocused my attention away from the house to my life. I realized that a relaxed attitude toward perfection and things

not being "finished" brought me joy. It helped me exhale and be OK with whatever point I was at, no matter how imperfect or unfinished it felt to me. I wanted my house to look and feel good, but it was no longer something I obsessed over.

The perfectly styled and neatened-up houses you see in the photos of these pages are here to inspire and excite you, but please know that they are the "glamour" shots of these houses, with fresh flowers and perfectly made beds. I'll admit, some of these homes look like this most every time I see them, but others—mine in particular!—do not. They all are lived in and they get messed up and trashed like every other house out there. They are full of kids and pets and *life*.

I've realized that I'm not happy when I'm trying to achieve "perfection," because it's not a truly attainable goal and I will inevitably fall short. I've lost before I've started if perfection is what I'm after. I'm able to do so much more and take action when I give something "my best," knowing it might not be perfect, but that I can always go back and refine it later if needed. It's a more relaxing and forgiving way to go through

previous
Paintings by my son Christian—inspired by the work of Malene Birger—hang over a mid-century-style sideboard layered with interesting objects, including concrete forms by my friend Amy Meier.

opposite
A messy bouquet of wildflowers awaits arranging.

life, and it keeps me happier. When I first started blogging, I used to spend hours editing my blog posts and making them perfect, getting interrupted by the baby crying or needing me and I would have to go back to it multiple times before posting. After a while, I started hitting "publish" when I got interrupted before I had a chance to proofread just to get the post out. I'd tell myself I would go back, but by the time I sat down again, I ended up writing new posts about something else I was excited about and rarely ever went back to correct my typos. I knew it would lose me readers and that it wouldn't be "perfect," but I realized that in general, people could see what I was trying to say and that the number of hours that proper editing took would stymie me, not allowing me to get out as many posts or getting posts out in real time, which, in turn, would keep the blog from being real and relevant. This breaking free from the confines of perfection allowed me to relax and enjoy what I was doing and forgive myself for not doing it all the "right" way. Life is the same way. The saying "Do your best and forget the rest" started out as a joke around our place, but it's become our mantra in almost every aspect of life. My business isn't perfect, my house isn't perfect, my family isn't perfect, my life isn't perfect, and I'm nowhere near perfect, but I am simply doing my best.

I like for design to feel the same way . . . relaxed and living and imperfect. My advice is to just have fun with your house. I find that most people aren't that serious, yet they decorate seriously. It's like we feel we have to create these "correct" grown-up houses. I did it in my first house, for sure. The more personality and fun you can bring into your home, the less "stuffy" it feels. A painting by a child, for example, can be both beautiful and surprising in a formal living room, and make it feel more relaxed and livable.

Rooms that feel like they've evolved over time and have "something off" in them feel more interesting to me than perfectly done spaces. Quirky, meaningful pieces that technically shouldn't work excite me over typical, pretty ones any day. Designing for real living, where there isn't a place for "perfect," enables us to relax and enjoy the process. Never once have I heard someone equate the feeling of home with perfection. Home is real and raw and messy and beautiful.

Forget about the notion of perfection and instead, set actionable, attainable goals. Understand the big picture of your entire project, but don't feel pressured to do it any faster than is comfortable. Ideas of perfection can be very limiting and can keep us from seeing the good things right in front of us. ✦

opposite
In the foyer, vintage art hangs over an antique Chinese bench where there was once a door to the powder room.

THE HOUSE IN THE WOODS

WHEN PURCHASING OUR FIRST homes, I began to notice that there was a type of house that seemed undervalued all throughout our area. This type of home was, on average, much cheaper per square foot, with big windows and workable floor plans. It was the 1970s "cedar contemporary." I'd heard people talking about them as if they were "less than" other more traditional "ideal" homes, and, in fact, they were actually worth less because of people's perceptions. Needless to say, we have lived in multiple cedar contemporaries because they are such a great value due to people's perceptions that they're innately flawed. Most of them can easily be turned into something cool and fresh. They typically have good, clean bones and pretty views, so not surprisingly, I fell for this one the instant I saw the photos of it sent to me by my real estate brokerage cofounder, Maura. It was quirky and on the small side, with a tricky floor plan, and far from perfect, but I loved it all the same. The ceilings were soaring, and the forest views were magical. The house sits on over four acres of beautiful forest in our town, and it reminded me so much of our black cedar contemporary—one of my favorite houses I've

ever lived in—so I felt an immediate affinity toward it. When we bought it, I spent hours trying to figure out how to fix the original floor plan, which consisted of a series of smallish rooms, to make it more open and livable without spending an arm and a leg. We ended up moving a powder room in the center of the house to another area so that we could expand the tiny kitchen, which I knew would be getting the most use out of all of the rooms on the first floor.

I was inspired by some of the sculpture left on the property by the sellers and decided to go for a sort of groovy artsy vibe for the interiors. When staging a house to sell, we have to use what we already have, and there's a lot of beg, borrow, and stealing going on, and it is a total exercise in *not* being a perfectionist. You have to put yourself out there and do the best you can with what you have and be OK with it.

In staging to sell a home, the general rule is to design generically, in a way that has mass appeal, but after having designed and sold so many of my own homes and seeing how buyers react to more personally designed homes, I beg to differ. I think people seem to respond

most favorably to a house with a strong point of view, a house with a story. The house may not appeal to as many people, but the appeal is much stronger for those who do get it, and it only takes one buyer. It's for this reason that, even when designing and staging a house we're going to sell, I design it in much the same way I would for a client. I don't necessarily have an imaginary client in mind, but I come up with an overall vibe and palette. I envision how people will best live in the home and function, and I picture myself living there and do everything I can to design in a way that makes living there easy and exhilarating. I try to create what I think of as a beautiful life for someone to step into.

Every house I do has a little place in my heart, but this one in particular really got me. The house went under construction right when the COVID-19 pandemic started. It was heartbreaking for everyone and the first time we'd ever gone through that sort of isolation. Suddenly so much of what used to matter felt trivial, and "perfect" truly was out the window. I remember just feeling raw and kind of numb in the very beginning, but one day when going to check out the house with the kids in tow, I saw that the camellias and the daffodils had bloomed all around the house and throughout the woods, and it was crazy beautiful. I have never seen so many daffodils in my life. We walked the property with the kids and let them play for hours in the woods, and it took us out of the scariness that was life at that point. We went back often, checking on progress and tweaking the designs, keeping our heads busy, always taking home armfuls of flowers, and soaking in the beauty of the forest. Life slowed down when we were exploring there. We left feeling a little renewed each time; the place and the land had a healing quality about it.

When we finally sold the house—after briefly considering moving there ourselves!—all the leaves were on the trees and the daffodils were a memory, but I felt so thankful for having that house when I needed it . . . for it needing all that work from me in a time when best thing I could do to take my mind of off the uncertainty and sadness was stay busy and dream about what that place could be. For me, this little place was an exercise in surrendering to real life and all of its imperfections. ✦

The original dining room, shown here, stumped me. It wasn't large enough for a very big table, and when I imagined myself living here, I realized we would need a big table to accommodate the family and saw that there wasn't room. I decided to turn the family room next to the kitchen into the dining room, and turn the dining room into a cozy "four-chair" room, a favorite floor plan of mine I mentioned earlier.

I started with a simple palette of black, white, and wood, and then pulled in burnt orange and earthy browns throughout the house for a warm, "groovy seventies" vibe. We didn't have the budget to buy anything to decorate with other than curtains and curtain hardware, so we used some of the mid-century pieces we had in storage, along with some simpler pieces from our personal houses, for a collected feel. It was a total hodgepodge, but keeping to a fairly tight palette and having pieces with clean lines helped pull the space together. A tapestry painted by my friend Lauren Rose Jackson depicts a forest scene similar to what's right outside the windows.

About halfway through the construction on this house, Dave and I thought about what life would be like there, and we considered moving in—an exercise it seems we take part in with almost every single investment property we work on. (I guess we like to dream?) It was the windows, the views, and the property, that got us. You could sit on that sofa and just see the trees swaying, feeling totally at peace.

A view of the four-chair room toward the two-sided fireplace. This area is my favorite spot in the house.

Fresh-picked stems of wildflowers sit in a large glass vase on the coffee table layered with books and objects in the living room. A casual arrangement like this one has that relaxed, "imperfect" vibe I love so much. I'll take weeds and wildflowers over florist flowers any day.

An arrangement of chive blossoms from my garden feels modern and unexpected. It's that little bit of "something off" in a room that I love.

Once a family room, we opened the kitchen into this space and turned it into a dining room large enough to accommodate a long table and more seating than the original dining room could.

Tree stump stamps by Linton art, right, have a graphic impact on the focal wall.

We enlarged the kitchen, stealing space from a powder room we moved, and opened up both sides of it so that it would be central to the living and dining spaces and to open up the views and allow for two sides of counter-height seating. We had the cabinet frames painted white, and the doors and drawers are an ebonized maple from my collection with Unique Kitchens and Baths. Vintage art in lieu of upper cabinets softens and warms up the modern, high-contrast space.

The range is flanked by the
refrigerator on one side and a
cabineted pantry on the other.

WORDS TO LIVE BY

Let go of *perfection*.

Do your *best* and *forget* the rest.

Stay *busy* with real life and
you won't have time to
obsess about your project.

Don't sweat the *small* stuff.

opposite
Soft stone shower
walls and floors in
the main bathroom
feel organic and
earthy. A floating
limewashed vanity is
rustic yet modern.

BUILDER KELLEY HOME IMPROVEMENT

CHAPTER 7

HABITUAL JOY

"Habits are not a finish line to be crossed but a lifestyle to be lived."

—JAMES CLEAR

THERE ARE DAYS when I wake up and go about my entire day on autopilot, without thinking about why I'm doing what I'm doing. I'll check my emails and mindlessly scroll through social media posts on my phone past the point of enjoyment, wasting time. I'll eat a quick breakfast with Dave and the kids and head off to work. I'll dig right in, get stuck in my email without making much progress on design work, and order lunch at lunchtime, eating food that's not great for me and that I don't fully enjoy, working late and then racing home, where I'll scarf down a lukewarm dinner and head upstairs to get everyone ready for bed before getting in bed myself, scrolling again on my phone, catching up on emails, and watching Netflix with Dave. This happens on more days than I'd care to admit.

I'm aware that I do this but am not always aware when I'm doing it. And I'm aware that it's not the way I want to live. I know that picking up my phone and checking emails and responding to DMs is not a relaxing or healthy way to wake up in the morning, yet I do it all too often anyway. I know how plugged-in the life I'm living is—my business hinges on being plugged

in, even though it's at such odds with my general philosophy of living, and I do it even more than I should or need to because it's become such a habit. I may have designed my home in a way that makes living there potentially wonderful, but if I'm not consciously experiencing my life and living it the way I want to live it, I have the tendency to let it pass me by; to work and scroll it away.

On the days when I don't do this, the days that are good and real, I go about what I have to do with intention. I wake up and put on my workout clothes and go for a quick run, listening to favorite songs. I leave my emails and DMs for when I'm at work and cook eggs with the kids. I give the girls a bath and spend time getting ready with them, doing their hair and chatting. I bring my lunch to work and all day long I know what I'm cooking for dinner and already have the ingredients for it, being sure to leave on time so I have the time to cook it. When I pull into the driveway, I'm able to stop and see the chickens and the geese before heading inside to start dinner. The music goes on, and sometimes a bottle of wine gets opened, and Dave and I prep food together, catching up on our day while the

opposite
We have been working with our clients for years, going room by room through the house before finally doing the kitchen and main living space (shown on pages 80–85) and the office (shown on pages 114–115).

kids run in and out, talking so loudly we often can't hear each other, which still feels OK. The kids set the table, and we remember to light the candles at dinner. We all talk and everyone's pretty nice because dinner was on time and no one's gotten hangry yet. We sometimes have time for a walk outside or a visit with the birds before getting ready for bed. We read books and snuggle . . . and then I read or watch a movie with Dave.

There are times in my life when these good days filled with joy-inducing actions come all in a row for long periods of time and they become a habit, and then there are times when they're few and far between because I'm not thinking—because I forget what my intentions for life are. The good times come when I make a conscious choice to be fully present and intentional—often writing down all that I need to do to get done at home, such as meal planning, and scheduled quality time with the family—in order to get it done. It allows me to be more efficient with my time so that there is more room to do the things I love to do and be with the people I love.

When we design and plan our homes, we are setting ourselves up for an intentional, meaningful life. We think about all that we physically need to go about our days efficiently—maybe cabinets with interior hooks in a mudroom, or a desk in the corner of the living room—and all that we need that brings about happiness—maybe a cozy throw blanket on the sofa or a painting we love—but we often stop short of continuing on to designing our lives and schedules. Deciding what sorts of rituals and habits we want in our lives is the follow-up that we need once we've completed our homes. Having a schedule or setting goals builds anticipation for the good parts that come with each day, week, month, or season, depending

upon what the "habit" or ritual is. It makes each day feel more special.

Nothing helps us enjoy being home more than appreciating the little things each day. Things like meal planning, grocery shopping on regular days so that the fridge and pantry are well stocked, having a workout schedule, a cleaning schedule, having a chore chart for the kids, making time for passions like sports, gardening, art, music, reading, etc., and penciling in family and social time, aids in the organization of life and makes our experiences at home more focused and meaningful. There is a simple joy in regularity and making good habits and in knowing what to expect and having something to look forward to. Create a rhythm, a cadence, a pace of life that you intentionally choose and take part in—rituals that make life flow and function better. If you want to live life more slowly, do it. Develop habits and routines that allow you to be fully present in your life, creating a sense of stability and joy. It's just as important as how everything looks and feels in creating a home and a life with meaning.

Living in harmony with our values and beliefs creates an authentic life full of purpose, a life in which we feel completely free to be ourselves, and a life full of contentment. We need to research, dream, and soul search to create our vision for an ideal life. Knowing what things I value in my life has allowed me to think about how I can get more of it in my life through design. I want gardens to tend, pets to cuddle, good ingredients for food, music, candlelight, good company and lots of dancing, good books, and I feel better when I'm in shape . . . and as much family time as is humanly possible. I've realized I need regular doses of nature in my life. The more I have of it, the more grounded and ready to face the world I feel. Even just looking out my window in the morning makes me feel good. Large windows (or the potential for them) and views are the things I look for in a home and that I take into account when designing them. Natural materials, palettes, and objects that bring the outside in connect a home with nature, and I use them abundantly. I want to have the time to help people and have a house that's easy to live in without a lot of stuff making messes, wasting precious time. Living intentionally requires us to take an honest look at our goals and values, so we can prioritize them and work them into our lives. List the priorities and activities you value and want in your life on a daily basis, and figure out how to insert them into the design of your home, effectively inserting them into your life. We have planted gardens and gotten pet chickens when we felt like we had no time and the last thing we needed was another chore in our life, because we wanted to spend more time outside. We knew that if we could just have a place with a bit of responsibility attached to it—feeding, watering, planting, weeding, and harvesting— we would be forced to spend more time outside, thereby inserting more nature into our lives. The other evening, as I was watering plants in the garden with a sinkful of dirty dishes inside, I was able to just exhale. The kids and I picked vegetables together and had a little alone time, and it reminded me again why we do it all.

More than a decades ago, I wrote about "simple pleasures" on my blog and asked readers to comment on some of their favorites, and it was so interesting to see that many of us shared the same universal simple pleasures. They're listed on the following page, which I want to be able to open to when I need it, as a reminder that every day we have the opportunity for happiness. It's in our control, and we can almost always decide

to take the time to enjoy something, even if only for a few minutes. These simple joy-inducing moments help us appreciate our lives.

Create a general schedule and leave time for simple pleasures wherever you can. I'm working on trying to see the chores in my life more positively, knowing that they make my life better. See what habits can be added to your life—even if they are chores like weeding the garden or doing laundry—that allow you to enjoy your passions. Design the life you want to live. ✤

above
Time spent in my garden is never a waste. I always come away feeling more grounded and energized.

time with **loved ones**, a cup of coffee or tea & taking the time to really **enjoy** it, fresh breezes blowing through the house and sleeping with the windows open, time spent **talking** with your partner, **reading** a good book, laughing, **listening** to the rain, fresh flowers on the nightstand, **time** with the people you love, an **unexpected note** on nice paper, space, **al fresco** dining, a place for everything, reading **leisurely**, an exceptionally comfortable sofa, a mudroom, a fire in the fireplace, a simple yet **beautiful** meal, candlelight, an organized closet, time, time & more time, relaxing weekend mornings, a good meal, walks, walking through your garden and **appreciating** the little **changes**, cooking with someone you love and taking the time to make a great meal, going out to eat, a hot bath, **enjoying** the sunshine, a nap, watching the **sun rise** . . . and watching it set, **cuddling** with little ones, birds chirping, **watching** the kids in your life play and **playing** with them, watching them sleep, and let's not forget our fur babies, watching our **pets** play & playing with them, exercising, biking, running, hiking, yoga, picking flowers, carryout, a new book, **sitting** on the patio/porch/deck alone or with someone you love **talking** over the day, getting into a bed with **crisp**, clean, fresh sheets, the water: the ocean, a lake, a pond, hearing your family **laugh** from another room, swings & **hammocks**, a great movie, wine, being **barefoot**, outdoor showers, creating something, whether it's a craft, a drawing, a **vignette**, sitting by the fire, watching ducks and birds (it cracked me up that multiple people had some form of this in the comments, but I so agree!!) . . . candles, being the only one **awake** at dawn and spending a **quiet** moment **alone**, lying in bed with our **kids** . . . reading, chatting, snuggling, walking to get **ice cream** on a warm evening, a hot bath, farmer's market **trips**

EARTHY SIMPLICITY

OUR CLIENTS LOVED their home before it was even theirs. They had walked by it for years, dreaming about living in the charming 1920s Spanish Colonial bungalow in their neighborhood. When it finally went on the market and they snapped it up. They lived there for a while with their three young children, getting to know the house and their habits there before deciding to renovate. There had been some renovations and additions done in the past—a closing in of an original porch along with stylistic "updates" that were now outdated, and there were lots of areas in the house that they wanted to change, so we met to walk through the house and discuss which parts of the house it made the most sense to start with and would have the most impact on their daily lives.

The original home itself had so much charm and soul, so our goal was to take it back to its roots and remove the outdated and inauthentic styling that had been added throughout the years, including out of place crown moldings, stair railings, and other architectural elements, so we enlisted CarrMichael Construction for the renovation. The floor plan was also a challenge, and my clients didn't feel like they were using the rooms in the house as best they could, so I focused on rearranging and reassigning room functions throughout, creating a sense of order. The family is close and does a lot of cooking together. This ritual of cooking as a family and spending that quality time together stood out to me as being important to the family, so we expanded the narrow galley kitchen into the dining room, making it much larger so that they could more easily cook together. The dining room was moved to another room in the house that hadn't been getting much use. From there, we focused on the foyer and main living and dining areas of the first floor, where the family does most of their living. Our clients were drawn to clean, earthy elements, and we brought in some authentic and Spanish Colonial–inspired pieces to harken back to the house's architectural style. I focused on bringing a sense of timelessness back to the house, a sort of celebration of what was originally there mixed with fresh upholstery, some newer pieces, and lots of antiques sprinkled in. Each choice was conscious and meaningful, and now that the home has been designed to fit their life, it allows for patterns of habitual joy that work for them and make each day easier and more fulfilling. ✦

opposite
The kitchen, as viewed from the foyer, where a massive potted ficus greets guests.

The living room, having been enclosed in a series of additions at both front and back, felt dark and closed in, so we were able to open the walls to expose hidden original steel windows, which let the light in. Using a palette of whites, glowy browns, and black keeps the vibe simple and textural.

The new antique iron chandelier feels as if it's always been there.

We stripped down inauthentic crown molding and whitewashed everything so the strong Spanish colonial–inspired pieces like the coffee table and iron light fixtures would stand out.

A pair of my comfy "thinking chairs" in machine-washable linen is kid and pet friendly. The tapestry is from our team member designer Lauren Reynolds's home—we put it up to test it out, and once we saw it there we knew it had found its home!

The dining room (shown here and on the previous pages) was once an empty addition. We filled the long, narrow space with a long table, chairs, and a backless slipcovered bench to keep the room feeling open to the living room.

Vintage and antique pieces are casually layered on and above the sideboard for a relaxed feel.

Our client uses her grandmother's china (following spread, right) as everyday dishware.

Hand-painted "Sol de Folium" terra-cotta tile from my tile collection with Architessa brings energy and a graphic punch to the kitchen. We layered oak cabinets from my collection with Unique Kitchens and Baths and honed marble countertops in front to soften it a bit. Playful vintage rattan island pendants lighten up the mood of the space.

We created a pantry (following spread, right) out of a lonely niche in the kitchen and used glass oak doors to let the sunshine from the windows into the kitchen.

The breakfast room is a simple white shell that allows the furnishings—antique Spanish leather chairs, a refinished family table, and an oversize capiz globe pendant—to take center stage.

WORDS TO LIVE BY

Get off *autopilot*.

Live with intention.

Design your home and life around *how* you want to live.

Create *habits* of joy.

Live in *harmony* with your values and beliefs.

Appreciate the *little things* every single day of your life.

opposite
An all-white backdrop allows each piece to be appreciated for its shape, color, and texture.

BUILDER CARRMICHAEL CONSTRUCTION

THE PRACTICE OF GRATITUDE

"I would maintain that thanks are the highest form of thought; and that gratitude is happiness doubled by wonder."

—G. K. CHESTERTON

THE HOUSE THAT FRANCOIS BUILT

GROWING UP, I REMEMBER both of my grandparents' houses having the "home" feeling for me. My maternal grandfather, my "Geedaddy," a disciplined coal miner's son, was a major general in the Marine Corps, and my maternal grandmother, "My Beautiful Grandmother" (she told me this was her name and it stuck; note to self!), a poised and creative Missouri farmer's daughter, stayed at home with the kids, managing the house and regularly hosting dinner parties for officers and visiting dignitaries. My dad's parents were immigrants from Italy. My quiet and calm "Nonoo" had a knife-sharpening route in Chicago, and my "Grandma Maestranzi" was an energetic boss-lady who raised the kids and ran the house. The families couldn't have been more different, but both sets of grandparents started with practically nothing and had to build a life for themselves and their families through serious scrappiness, industriousness, and penny-pinching. Not a single thing was wasted. They were so careful about everything they did or purchased. My grandma Maestranzi used to have my Nonoo pull the car over to fields on the side of the road to pick dandelions and wild radicchio for salads so they didn't have to buy produce. My Beautiful Grandmother used to make many of her own clothes. Though neither set of grandparents had a lot and they rarely shopped, they treasured what little they did have and did their very best to make their homes feel loved. Their houses—though not large or perfect—were always cared for, orderly, and well kept, with neatly made beds and fresh flowers or greens from the yard set about, and planned-out meals with set dinner times and candlelight. I have found so much inspiration from both of my grandmothers in the simple way they lived and in their talents for making their homes and lives beautiful using just what was around them. There was an art to their way of life.

I'm sure my grandparents lived in much the same way many in their generation did . . . they planned carefully, took care of what they had, and life was simple. They had everything they needed and they were content not because what they had was perfect, but because they were grateful they had *enough*.

But somewhere along the way, as technology has advanced, the general speed of life has increased, shopping is at our fingertips, and

right
I often think of
spaces in "views" or
elevations. The foyer
in my house leads
to the living room,
which is separated
from the dining
room by a double-
sided fireplace.

people are doing and communicating more than ever before, our society seems to have lost sight of appreciating what we have. We're exposed to others who have much more than we do and we see photoshopping and airbrushing on a daily basis (even the photos in this very book were perfectly styled for each shot!), and we have so much that it's almost as if we've been left with an insatiable appetite for more. Comparison of the glossy "perfect" homes we constantly see photos of with our own real, often messy or unfinished houses can seep in. "Success" today is often defined by money or fame rather than contentment in the realization that we have so much to be grateful for.

I used to subconsciously believe that there would be some sort of moment of "arrival" when everything would fall into place and suddenly be easy—my house and businesses would be "finished," my life would be perfectly organized and "balanced," and I would be completely satisfied with the results—but I now see that contentment is not an end point I can reach in life, but rather, a mindset I can choose to adopt for the journey. Seeing potential in a home, keeping only what we love and need, surrounding ourselves with meaningful things and thoughtful design and nurturing atmosphere—effectively, taking all of the steps in this book to create a meaningful environment for ourselves—are all integral parts of finding happiness at home, but having peace within is the lynchpin. This book is called *Feels Like Home: Relaxed Interiors for a Meaningful Life*, but the truth is, a relaxed interior—and as a result a more meaningful life—requires a relaxed "you."

Just as my grandparents' generation overcame adversity through perseverance and gratitude, the challenges we currently face are an opportunity for reflection and change. On any

given day we can choose to let what we have be enough. We're not going to find "enough" in a house alone, because no matter how badly we want it, all the pretty houses in the world can't give us contentment. We have to look within ourselves. It begins with choosing to be grateful for what we have. To be OK with our homes and all their flaws and to appreciate what we have. To exhale and relax. A mindset of gratitude brings meaning to life, and as a result, the home, not the other way around.

I've moved my family of seven half a dozen times in my fifteen years of marriage, initially looking to find "the one" (house, that is, I'm good with the hubby). I'm house-obsessed. But somewhere in the middle of those moves, I found a peace in knowing that no matter where life takes us—be it in the same house for fifty years or twenty houses in fifteen—we'll be OK.

• • •

DAVE AND I FOUND our house on a whim, in much the same way we found the others. We'd seen it on the market for years and had always been intrigued by the pond and the white geese on the property we'd get glimpses of as we drove by on our way to work, but never thought seriously about it as it was so far out of our price range. We'd had a whirlwind of a year with a new baby (our fourth), a new house close to the city—the Cape Cod with the white floors and smaller yard I shared in Chapter 1—more client work than we could handle, a couple of out-of-state design showhouses, and my first book coming out and subsequent book tour with said new baby, and I remember feeling completely depleted and exhausted by our pace of life. I was literally dreaming about retirement at the ripe old age of thirty-four.

One day, as Dave and I were getting ready in the morning—it's when we make a lot of our

life decisions—we were talking about how we planned to move "out" to Great Falls when we retired and he looked at me and said, "Why are we waiting until we retire to live where we want to live? Why don't we just do it now?" I had no answer for him, and we decided to look at real estate listings. I saw that "the house" I had been keeping an eye on for years had just had a drastic price reduction and was nearer to our price range. We drove by it on the way to work a few days later and Dave pulled up into the tree-lined drive.

I got chills all over as we ducked under the wisteria to take a peek at the house that was hidden behind all the vines and trees and saw a home that reminded me of the chalets in Giustino, the village in Northern Italy that my family is from. I'd never seen anything like it here. We immediately called our real estate agent and got a showing. We opened the front door to a dark and mysterious space that felt as if it were centuries old. We turned right into an empty living room. It was moody with beams, and the views of the forest outside the windows were incredible. We opened the massive floor-to-ceiling windows—which had authentic antique brass cremone bolts—and it felt like the entire wall was opening up to the outside. I was in love.

But it was still out of our price range, and we still had a house to sell, so it was a long shot. I remember walking the property that day thinking, *Will this really help me exhale . . . or will this just be the place we live that I never get to enjoy because I'm way too busy to get the chance to enjoy it?* I was so hopeful as I took my flip-flops off to wade through the creek, wondering if the place could actually help us slow down, but also sad, because I knew that even moving there wouldn't give me more hours in a day. I was drained, and the thought that there wasn't an

end in sight scared me, and deep down, I knew we had to make a change.

We submitted an offer and, miraculously, it was accepted. I was literally gaga. We hadn't even finished the house we'd moved into less than a year before and now had to renovate the bathrooms and finish it in order to put it on the market, sell it, and hopefully close in time to be able to buy the new house. There were times when I didn't think we were going to be able to do it, but Dave pushed the renovation through in record time with sheer willpower and not very much sleep. It was then that we began filming a sizzle reel for our future HGTV show, *Best House on the Block*.

When we moved to the house and entered into the biggest renovation we've ever lived through, I felt like the house and the land started to heal me. To say we arrived there depleted was an understatement, but I found myself just heading outside randomly for five to ten minutes to take in the land, the trees, and all the wild animals on our property . . . and it's like it gave me a little boost of needed energy and kind of filled me back up. It made sense . . . I've always loved nature, and it inspires so much of my work, so I shouldn't have been so surprised at what an effect being able to enjoy it so frequently was having on me, but I was. I guess I didn't realize that my little walks outside (whether alone or with Dave and/or the kids) would give me an instantaneous little jolt of inner calm and strength.

I got so many new textile and product ideas, and thoughts on our business and how I wanted to shift and grow it. It was then that I realized that nature is a kind of "creative fuel" for me. I wrote my last book, *Down to Earth*, in this house after gaining more of an understanding of nature's effects on me.

But just as more frequent exposure to nature started to make me feel better, the reality is that we had also begun to live more intentionally. We were living the life that felt right for us and making the physical changes needed so that we could slow down and set ourselves up for habitual joy. We'd made a conscious choice to make a life change . . . to choose to be around nature and live the type of life that made us feel and function our best; to try to make a place where we could truly exhale. We chose contentment.

We bought our house from the Haeringer sons, who own and operate one of the most well-known and loved French restaurants around, Jacque's Brasserie at L'Auberge Chez François. The house was built in 1979 by their parents, Francois and Marie-Antoinette Haeringer, and designed by Thomas Williams and Bart Post to feel like an authentic country house that could have been in Francois and Marie-Antoinette's native Alsatian countryside. We feel so much of them in the house. It has a history and a soul. The family left us some things that we treasure—crucifixes from France, the embossed brass spoon rest we keep next to the stove, and a silver candelabra in our dining room we affectionately call Lumière, after Disney's *Beauty and the Beast* character. But much more life-changing than the things, we were also left with a pair of twenty-year-old white fairy-tale-esque geese who, as it turns out, conveyed with the house. Francois had once hand-fed a flock of homestead geese on the property and loved taking care of them, but now there was only a single pair left, and they stole my heart. We feel almost like we have inherited something and sort of stepped into a way of life. We had no intentions of ever owning geese, but now we're geese people. In other houses, we just sort of moved in and lived there . . . in this house, we feel like we're sort of stewards of something

bigger than us. We feel so grateful to be a part of the house's story. We've gotten to know Chef Jacques and his incredible fiáncee, Carol, over the years we've lived here, and love spending time with them, hearing bits about the family's history, and about the house. Visiting Jacque's Brasserie at L'Auberge Chez Francois with the kids and walking the vegetable gardens there has become a family treat and is always memorable. It always gets me excited all over again about where we live.

It took about a year or so to do much of the heavy lifting with the house renovation—reworking the floor plan, redoing the kitchen and some of the bathrooms, and the not-so-fun things like fixing the roof, boiler, and other mechanical systems—but it will be a while before we actually finish it. I have yet to decorate all the kids' bedrooms, finish the flooring in several areas of the house, and I have an empty family room on the first floor without much furniture in it other than a toy kitchen, but I'm OK with all of that. When we can get to these things, we will, and for now, I'm just grateful for what we have gotten done. Outside, we've added gardens and pens and coops for our geese and chickens. I don't think we'll ever be done with the yard, but again, I'm finally at a place where I feel OK that it can't all happen right now. There is no arrival point, just the journey. I care about our house, but I've got a life, kids, and businesses to focus on as well, and sometimes "home" has to take a back seat. I love the life we've made at this place and will be forever grateful for the series of events and people that led us here. I've learned that I'll never know what the future holds for us, but for now, I've found my peace here and am completely content to call this house our home. ✦

I loved our house from the moment I saw it. The style and materials were beautiful, but I wanted to lighten up the house a bit to suit us better. I say this carefully because I am a big believer in design being personal and needing to fit those who live in a home. Much of what we did in our home was to simply make it our own. We swapped out the heavy wooden front door for a steel-and-glass door to let light into the once-dark space.

Sometimes I feel like I'm in another world at this place. It transports me out of reality a bit.

We've had so many good nights on the hill overlooking our property, having fires in the fire pit or wine and cheese at the bistro table.

I replaced deep red terra-cotta hexagonal floor tiles in the foyer with slightly larger terra-cotta tile in an ivory glaze that would remind us of what was once there, but feel lighter and airier. We sanded down the dark-stained woodwork throughout the entire house to reveal much lighter, raw wood, which has made the house feel more primitive and casual. Original bullseye stained glass windows with leaded glass run throughout the house and in the foyer; one is fitted into the wall between the foyer and the coat closet. The kids love turning the coat closet light on at night so the colors glow. An old church pew sits under the window, and a crucifix left for us by the family we bought the house from hangs above. A pair of massive lanterns feel as if they could have been original to the house, and the painted cowhide rug is easy to clean and care for.

I stow my picking basket under a sculptural and heavy-duty concrete console in the foyer so I can easily grab it whenever I need to harvest vegetables from the garden or pick flowers. It's always there at the ready, and because of that, I'm constantly reminded and inspired to go outside and forage. The flowers pictured here and in most of the photos of the house are from a wildflower hill I planted in front of our house.

Our living room is the essence of "home" to me. I love being in here with the family, talking, sitting by the fire, and reading together. You might recognize a lot of the furniture from our past houses shown at the beginning of the book. My dogs decided the legs of the leather sofa were delicious to chew on when they were puppies, and much of it has taken a beating but it's still standing!.

The moment I first opened the original windows with brass cremone bolts made me giddy. I fling them open (there are screens) on any remotely temperate weather day, and I'm guaranteed an "instant exhale." The cypress tree root my dad gave me hangs above our sofa once again.

I wanted my kitchen (shown here and on the following pages) to actually feel like it could have been in an old Alsatian country house, so I chose simple, rustic details. Our kids do the dishes, so I had an extra-large and deep sink made, which makes it easier for them to wash without splashing everywhere. I opted not to do a cabinet under the sink and instead hung a sink skirt made from an old Ikea curtain to hide the kids' step stool, which gets pulled in and out multiple times a day. A wall-mounted, articulating unlacquered brass faucet ensures that we can wash the entire sink yet not lose any depth in the sink for a typical faucet platform.

Oversize globe lights and Cesca-style chairs contrast with the mostly old-world elements throughout. We added beams in the kitchen to connect it with the beamed living room that it's open to. The frames of our kitchen cabinets are made of drywall textured to match our walls, and the cabinets themselves are white oak that I and the guys working on our house from CarrMichael Construction hand-stained with a combination of oils, coffee, tea, stain, and sandpaper.

Our countertops are fumed granite. I frequently hang herbs and flowers, seen on previous pages, to dry in the kitchen for use in arrangements, meals, and teas.

We opened up the wall between the kitchen and the living room so we could feel connected with the people in the living room—often the kids—during meal prepping. I used the same arc shape from the openings on our fireplaces for the doorway, which I thought had a sort of Hobbitesque, fairy-tale quality to it befitting the house.

The dining room walls are covered in framed black-and-white paintings by my kids, mixed with a few vintage pieces. I'm always on the lookout for cool antique or vintage frames, and I hang them up on the wall to get filled whenever someone feels the urge to paint. There is a close-up of the gallery wall on page 9. A simple Parsons table with wooden and leather mid-century Cesca-style chairs mixes with slipcovered host chairs and granny floral curtains. A painted cowhide is easy to clean when my kids spill—which is quite frequently.

The "Four-Chair Room," as we call it, is a cozy little family room that leads from the foyer to our porch and vegetable garden terrace. We practically live in this room in the fall and winter, having at least a few fires in it each week. When working from home, I can be found on the chair to the left of the fireplace, and it's where I wrote most of this book. It's open to a barely furnished room where the play kitchen and hodgepodge of rotating furnishings live, affectionately called "the room of requirement," à la Harry Potter.

In our bedroom, a vintage gold rococo headboard—we finally got a king-size!—upholstered in soft brown velvet is flanked by an antique marble-topped writing desk on one side and an old black dresser on the other. I keep my own bed very simple—there are too many kids and pets filling it up—with a classic Martha Washington coverlet and white sheets and pillowcases. A tiny Rembrandt reproduction I found at one of my favorite antique shops, German Favorite Antiques, is the only thing hanging over the bed. I keep my bedroom purposefully spare, because the plainness relaxes me. An empty old pine chest at the foot of the bed is often pulled out and used for the main event during the kids' "magic shows." A catchall basket under the writing desk corrals books and toys the kids leave around the room, which I hide with a throw blanket. Though I wish I could say we are no-TV-in-the-bedroom people, we have a big one that sits on the opposite side of the room, and I love cuddling up with the whole family in here for movie marathons.

When we bought our house, approximately a third of the second floor was unfinished storage space. The main bedroom was originally on the first floor, but we wanted to be up with the kids on the second floor, so we took one of the upstairs bedrooms that was near the unfinished storage space and used the storage space for a bathroom and closet, and also to add a bedroom for our oldest son. The window by the tub was the only thing that we kept in the room, and we coated the walls in waterproof stucco and added beams. We installed heating elements under the tile floors, and the dogs love it in there.

A spare space that gives me room to breathe, the bathroom—though often graced with kids and pets roaming in and out—is also my respite.

My favorite thing to do on a cold Friday after work is take a hot bath with the windows open and some good tunes on. The copper tub, shown on the previous pages, retains heat for a long time, and it's the best spot in the house when it's snowing outside. With five kids, we don't travel much, and so this place is where I go to get away.

The bathroom and shower walls are made from waterproof stucco. I love the undulating, irregular finish. It has so much depth and adds a sense of age that you can't get from drywall.

The mirror over our vanity was one of the very first purchases Dave and I made when we first got married, and I remember thinking we'd keep it forever. It's moved from house to house with us and still reminds me of being newlyweds. It's pictured hanging in our old bedroom in Chapter 1.

Our girls' bedroom is papered in Gisele's Web, a pattern I drew just after my first daughter, Gisele, was born. I could see how much she loved yellow from a young age (It was uncanny—she always picked yellow anything when she had a choice!), and I had it made into a wallpaper with a yellow colorway. A pair of mid-century accordion wall lamps flank her rattan bed, and a vintage oil painting hangs above it. I don't have any photos of my boys' bedrooms because I haven't yet "finished" them and they look more like sad dorm rooms.

A vintage pastoral scene with sheep hangs above my second daughter, Aurora's brass crib. One of our three dogs, Fawn, strikes a pose with the dog statue. (I don't know what it is, but whenever we are having a photo shoot, Fawn likes to jump in the pictures, which is why she's generally seen more than my other two pups.)

Our back porch, left, was enclosed when we bought the house, but when Jacques and Carol gave us the original architects' drawings and photos of the house when it was first built, we saw that the space was open, and we loved it, so we opened it back up. We now use it as a potting station and kids' table when we have parties with friends in the garden.

For my thirty-fifth birthday, Dave surprised me by lighting up the pond with floating candles, top right. Hansel and Gretel, our geese, went for a swim in the candlelight while we sat on the bench by the white azaeleas, and it was one of the sweetest things I think I've ever seen. They were more than twenty years old and died the next winter.

I drew a tile, above, for my hand-painted tile collection with Architessa and called the pattern "Love Story" after our sweet geese.

I'd never call myself a gardener, but it's something I love doing. Being outside relaxes and grounds me.

After knowing how much we loved our vegetable gardens in the past, we decided to make a kitchen garden terrace off of the back of our house, with a dining table in it so we could eat out there. It's truly my happy place, and we love being out there with the kids and dogs, planting, weeding, and harvesting. It's a lot of work, and it doesn't always look this good, but we got it in tip-top shape when *Southern Living* magazine asked to come shoot it for their garden issue. (Photo by Hector Sanchez.) I love making salads and soups (above) from fresh garden ingredients.

CHAPTER 8 / THE PRACTICE OF GRATITUDE

WORDS TO LIVE BY

*Don't wait to live
the **life** you want to live.*

*The only way to be **truly
happy** with your home is to be
content within yourself.*

*Choose **gratitude**.*

***Embrace** the idea of "enough."*

*There's **something** to
love in **every** day.*

ORIGINAL OWNERS FRANCOIS AND MARIE-ANTOINETTE HAERINGER

ORIGINAL 1979 ARCHITECTS THOMAS WILLIAMS AND BART POST

RENOVATED BY CARRMICHAEL CONSTRUCTION

RESOURCES

CHAPTER 1
EQUESTRIAN SPIRIT

RENOVATION KELLEY HOME IMPROVEMENT

WHITE PAINT THROUGHOUT SHERWIN WILLIAMS "HIGH REFLECTIVE WHITE"

DEEP GRAY PAINT BENJAMIN MOORE "RIVER ROCK"

BLACK DOORS SHERWIN WILLIAMS IRON ORE

BRICK FLOOR TILE LOWE'S

KITCHEN CABINETRY LAUREN LIESS "VINEYARD" & "HEIRLOOM" COLLECTIONS FOR UNIQUE KITCHENS AND BATHS

TILE THROUGHOUT LAUREN LIESS "POTTERS" FOR ARCHITESSA

KITCHEN SINK LAUREN LIESS FOR ATMOSPHYRE

FURNISHINGS VINTAGE, ANTIQUE, AND FROM LAUREN LIESS & CO. AND RESTORATION HARDWARE

CHAPTER 2
YOUR OWN KIND OF MINIMALISM

RENOVATION CARRMICHAEL CONSTRUCTION

WHITE PAINT THROUGHOUT BENJAMIN MOORE "SIMPLY WHITE"

CURTAIN FABRIC LAUREN LIESS "THISTLE" IN NAVY

PAIR OF CHAIRS LAUREN LIESS "ARCHITECT CHAIR" FOR TAYLOR KING

LEATHER WING CHAIR LAUREN LIESS & CO.

RUG LOLOI

KITCHEN CABINETRY DESIGNED BY LAUREN LIESS AND CO. AND BUILT BY CARRMICHAEL CONSTRUCTION

KITCHEN BACKSPLASH TILE LAUREN LIESS "POTTERS" FOR ARCHITESSA

LIGHTING AND FURNISHINGS VINTAGE, ANTIQUE, AND FROM LAUREN LIESS & CO.

NATURAL CHARM

RENOVATION CARRMICHAEL CONSTRUCTION

WHITE PAINT THROUGHOUT SHERWIN WILLIAMS "PURE WHITE"

KITCHEN CABINETRY DESIGNED BY LAUREN LIESS AND CO. AND BUILT BY CARRMICHAEL CONSTRUCTION

MARBLE KITCHEN SINK SIGNATURE HARDWARE

KITCHEN BACKSPLASH TILE LAUREN LIESS "POTTERS" FOR ARCHITESSA

COUNTERTOPS CAESARSTONE AIRY CONCRETE

ENTRY WALLPAPER SCHUMACHER

LIVING ROOM SLIPCOVERED SOFAS LAUREN LIESS "LIBRIS" SOFAS FOR TAYLOR KING

FURNISHINGS, LIGHTING, AND RUGS THROUGHOUT VINTAGE AND NEW THROUGH LAUREN LIESS & CO.

CHAPTER 3
LIVING HISTORY

BLACK PAINT BENJAMIN MOORE "BLACK"

CURTAIN FABRIC LAUREN LIESS TEXTILES "BOHO STRIPE" IN DUSTY BLUE

FURNISHINGS, LIGHTING, AND RUGS THROUGHOUT VINTAGE AND NEW THROUGH LAUREN LIESS & CO.

URBAN SANCTUARY

FURNISHINGS, LIGHTING, AND RUGS THROUGHOUT VINTAGE AND NEW THROUGH LAUREN LIESS & CO.

UPHOLSTERY THROUGHOUT VERELLEN

VINTAGE CHAIR FABRIC PATTERN VIRGINIA KRAFT TEXTILES "BLOCKTOWN" IN WHEAT

BOTANICALS IN BEDROOM BLACKWELL BOTANICALS

CHAPTER 4
VINTAGE GRACE

ARCHITECT CUNNINGHAM QUILL

RENOVATION CARRMICHAEL CONSTRUCTION

LANDSCAPE DESIGNER JENNIFER HORN

LIVING ROOM WALLPAPER ANNA FRENCH "PALAMPORE" IN NAVY ON CREAM

LIVING ROOM CURTAIN FABRIC LES INDIENNES "LA REINE" IN OLIVE

LIVING ROOM SOFAS LAUREN LIESS "LIBRIS" SOFA AND "GENTLEMAN" SOFA FOR TAYLOR KING

FOYER WALLPAPER LES INDIENNES

DINING ROOM CURTAIN FABRIC LEE JOFA OSCAR DE LA RENTA "JESSUP" IN SEPIA/INDIGO

FAMILY ROOM/DINING AREA CURTAIN FABRIC RAOUL TEXTILES "LAUREL" IN RAISIN

FAMILY ROOM SLIPCOVERED SOFA LAUREN LIESS "CAVALIER" SOFA FOR TAYLOR KING

FAMILY ROOM SLIPCOVERED CHAIRS LAUREN LIESS "THINKING" CHAIR WITH MINISLIP FOR TAYLOR KING AND PILLOWS IN LAUREN LIESS TEXTILES "FERN STAR" IN SEPIA

FAMILY ROOM SLIPCOVERED OTTOMAN LAUREN LIESS "TOWN" OTTOMAN FOR TAYLOR KING

FABRIC ON ANTIQUE CHAISE SCHUMACHER "LES FOUGERES" IN ANTIQUE

FURNISHINGS, LIGHTING, AND RUGS THROUGHOUT VINTAGE AND NEW THROUGH LAUREN LIESS & CO.

CHAPTER 5
COMPOSING ATMOSPHERE

CABINETRY DESIGN BY LAUREN LIESS & CO., AND BUILT BY CARRMICHAEL CONSTRUCTION

BACKSPLASH TILE CLE "RICE PAPER" 4×4

SLATE FLOORING ARCHITESSA

PERIMETER COUNTERTOP SOAPSTONE/ ISLAND COUNTERTOP: MARBLE

LIGHTING VINTAGE AND NEW AVAILABLE THROUGH LAUREN LIESS & CO.

ROMANTIC CURIOSITY

ARCHITECT BARNES VANZ ARCHITECTS

BUILDER CARRMICHAEL CONSTRUCTION

WHITE PAINT THROUGHOUT SHERWIN WILLIAMS "GREEK VILLA"

TRIM PAINT THROUGHOUT SHERWIN WILLIAMS "JOGGING PATH"

GUEST BEDROOM MURAL ANTHROPOLOGIE

FOYER CURTAIN FABRIC LAUREN LIESS TEXTILES "FERN STAR" IN SEPIA

FOYER WALL-MOUNT CONSOLES LAUREN LIESS "STABLE CONSOLE" FOR WOODBRIDGE

GREAT ROOM SOFAS LAUREN LIESS "EVOLUTION WATERFALL SOFA" AND "ARCHITECT SOFA" FOR TAYLOR KING

GREAT ROOM CONSOLE VINTAGE

GREAT ROOM LEATHER WING CHAIR LAUREN LIESS "PHILOSOPHER'S CHAIR" FOR TAYLOR KING

GREAT ROOM COFFEE TABLE LAUREN LIESS "DAIS TABLE" FOR WOODBRIDGE

GREAT ROOM CURTAIN FABRIC ROSE TARLOW "OTELLO" IN MONARCH

GREAT ROOM FOUR SLIPCOVERED CHAIRS LAUREN LIESS "THINKING CHAIR" FOR TAYLOR KING

KITCHEN BACKSPLASH TILE CLE "RICE PAPER" 4×4

KITCHEN ISLAND WHITE OAK IN CUSTOM STAIN

SLATE FLOORING ARCHITESSA

DINING ROOM MURAL FRENCH MARKET COLLECTION

DINING ROOM TABLE LAUREN LIESS "FOREVER TABLE" FOR WOODBRIDGE

DINING ROOM CHAIRS LAUREN LIESS "SILHOUETTE CHAIRS" FOR WOODBRIDGE

DINING ROOM SIDEBOARD LAUREN LIESS "BAKER'S SIDEBOARD" FOR WOODBRIDGE

LIBRARY BLACK VELVET SOFA RESTORATION HARDWARE

OFFICE WALLPAPER ANTHROPOLOGIE

CABIN SLIPCOVERED SOFA LAUREN LIESS "CAVALIER SOFA" FOR TAYLOR KING

CABIN LEATHER CHAIRS LAUREN LIESS "EVOLUTION CHAIR" FOR TAYLOR KING

OWNER'S BED TARA SHAW WITH CUSTOM SUZANNE TUCKER "CRICKET" IN UMBER UPHOLSTERY

OWNER'S BEDROOM CURTAINS LES INDIENNES "RAYURE" IN CHOCOLATE

OWNER'S BATHTUB SIGNATURE HARDWARE

OWNER'S BATHROOM TILE SENECA TILE

FAMILY HANGOUT ROOM SOFA LAUREN LIESS "SHELTER SOFA" FOR TAYLOR KING

FAMILY HANGOUT OTTOMAN LAUREN LIESS "VILLAGE OTTOMAN" FOR TAYLOR KING

LITTLE BOY BLUE BATHROOM TILE SENECA TILE

LITTLE GIRL BEDROOM WALLPAPER LULIE WALLACE "MARY" IN SUNBURST

FURNISHINGS, LIGHTING, AND RUGS THROUGHOUT VINTAGE AND NEW THROUGH LAUREN LIESS & CO.

CHAPTER 6
THE HOUSE IN THE WOODS

RENOVATION KELLEY HOME IMPROVEMENT

KITCHEN CABINETRY LAUREN LIESS "RESOLUTION" COLLECTION IN EBONY WITH WHITE FRAME FOR UNIQUE KITCHENS AND BATHS

KITCHEN TILE LAUREN LIESS FOR ARCHITESSA

OWNER'S BATH TILE ARCHITESSA

FURNISHINGS, LIGHTING, AND RUGS THROUGHOUT VINTAGE AND NEW AVAILABLE THROUGH LAUREN LIESS & CO.

CHAPTER 7
EARTHY SIMPLICITY

RENOVATION CARRMICHAEL CONSTRUCTION

KITCHEN CABINETRY LAUREN LIESS "BOHEMIAN" COLLECTION FOR UNIQUE KITCHENS AND BATHS

TILE THROUGHOUT LAUREN LIESS "SOL DE FOLIUM" FOR ARCHITESSA

COUNTER STOOLS LAUREN LIESS "REVIVAL STOOL" FOR WOODBRIDGE

LEATHER SOFA LAUREN LIESS "ARCHITECT" FOR TAYLOR KING

SLIPCOVERED CHAIRS LAUREN LIESS "THINKING CHAIR" SLIPCOVERED TO FLOOR FOR TAYLOR KING

LIVING ROOM RUG ANNIE SELKE

DINING ROOM CURTAINS LES INDIENNES "SERAPHINE" IN FRENCH GRAY

SLIPCOVERED DINING BENCH LAUREN LIESS "THANK YOU BENCH" FOR TAYLOR KING

SLIPCOVERED DINING CHAIRS LAUREN LIESS "LINGER CHAIR" FOR TAYLOR KING

IRON AND LEATHER DINING CHAIRS LAUREN LIESS "CARPE DIEM CHAIR" FOR WOODBRIDGE

DINING TABLE LAUREN LIESS "FOREVER TABLE" FOR WOODBRIDGE

PLASTER AND OAK BOOKCASES LAUREN LIESS "SCULPTOR'S BOOKCASE" FOR WOODBRIDGE

BREAKFAST ROOM PENDANT RESTORATION HARDWARE

FURNISHINGS, LIGHTING, AND RUGS THROUGHOUT VINTAGE AND NEW AVAILABLE THROUGH LAUREN LIESS & CO.

CHAPTER 8
THE HOUSE THAT FRANCOIS BUILT

ORIGINAL OWNER FRANCOIS AND MARIE-ANTOINETTE HAERINGER

ORIGINAL 1979 ARCHITECTS THOMAS WILLIAMS AND BART POST

RENOVATION CARRMICHAEL CONSTRUCTION

DINING ROOM CURTAIN FABRIC CREATIONS METAPHORES

DINING TABLE RESTORATION HARDWARE

DINING HOST CHAIRS VERELLEN

DINING SIDE CHAIRS VINTAGE WITH REPRODUCTION LL "REVIVAL" CHAIRS FOR WOODBRIDGE

FAMILY ROOM FOUR CHAIRS VERELLEN

LITTLE GIRL BEDROOM WALLPAPER LAUREN LIESS TEXTILES "GISELE'S WEB" IN MARIGOLD

BATHROOM TILE SENECA TILE

FURNISHINGS, LIGHTING, AND RUGS THROUGHOUT VINTAGE AND NEW AVAILABLE THROUGH LAUREN LIESS & CO.

LAUREN LIESS & CO.

EDITOR: Rebecca Kaplan
DESIGNER: Sarah Gifford
DESIGN MANAGER: Danielle Youngsmith
MANAGING EDITOR: Lisa Silverman
PRODUCTION MANAGER: Denise LaCongo

Library of Congress Control Number: 2021932492

ISBN: 978-1-4197-5119-6
eISBN: 978-1-64700-142-1
B&N Exclusive Edition ISBN: 978-1-4197-6073-0

Printed and bound in the United States
10 9 8 7 6 5 4 3 2 1

Abrams books are available at special discounts when
purchased in quantity for premiums and promotions
as well as fundraising or educational use. Special editions
can also be created to specification. For details, contact
specialsales@abramsbooks.com or the address below.

Abrams® is a registered trademark of Harry N. Abrams, Inc.

195 Broadway
New York, NY 10007
abramsbooks.com

THANK-YOUs

I'M BEYOND GRATEFUL to all the many
people who helped make this book a reality by
believing in it and me: Abrams and my editor,
Rebecca Kaplan; my book designer, Sarah
Gifford; my agent, Berta Treitl; photographer
Helen Norman; contractor Mike Carr and all
the architects we work alongside; my product
partners; our Property Collective co-founders,
Maura and Daan DeRaedt, and our team; our
amazing clients; my social media buddies;
our vendors and installers; my left-and-right-
hand-ladies at Lauren Liess Interiors, Lauren
Reynolds and Tara Trainer; and my friends
and family. To Dave and our kids—Christian,
Justin, Louie, Gisele, and Aurora—thank you for
teaching me home is anywhere we're together.